Philosophical Perspectives on Infinity

This book is an exploration of philosophical questions about infinity. Graham Oppy examines how the infinite lurks everywhere, both in science and in our ordinary thoughts about the world. He also analyzes the many puzzles and paradoxes that follow in the train of the infinite. Even simple notions, such as counting, adding, and maximizing, present serious difficulties. Other topics examined include the nature of space and time, infinities in physical science, infinities in theories of probability and decision, the nature of part/whole relations, mathematical theories of the infinite, and infinite regression and principles of sufficient reason.

Graham Oppy is Associate Dean of Research in the Faculty of Arts at Monash University in Australia. He is the author of *Ontological Arguments and Belief in God* and the forthcoming *Arguments about Gods*, and he has received fellowships from the Australian Research Council. He is an associate editor of the *Australasian Journal of Philosophy* and sits on the editorial boards of *Philo, Religious Studies*, and *Sophia.*

Philosophical Perspectives on Infinity

GRAHAM OPPY
Monash University

CAMBRIDGE UNIVERSITY PRESS
Cambridge, New York, Melbourne, Madrid, Cape Town, Singapore, São Paulo, Delhi

Cambridge University Press
32 Avenue of the Americas, New York, NY 10013-2473, USA

www.cambridge.org
Information on this title: www.cambridge.org/9780521108096

First published 2006
This digitally printed version 2009

A catalog record for this publication is available from the British Library

Library of Congress Cataloging in Publication data

Oppy, Graham Robert.
Philosophical perspectives on infinity / Graham Oppy.
p. cm.
Includes bibliographical references (p.) and index.
ISBN 0-521-86067-9 (hardback)
1. Infinite. I. Title.
BD411.O67 2006
111′.6 – dc22 2005021715

ISBN 978-0-521-86067-3 hardback
ISBN 978-0-521-10809-6 paperback

Contents

Preface

This book began life as the intended first part of a larger work with the provisional title *God and Infinity.* While it will still be used by me as a starting point for further work in the philosophy of religion, the book has grown into a final product that is more or less entirely independent of that starting point. What it does is to explore various issues about the infinite that emerge in many different areas of philosophy and whose resolution ought not to be tied to the details of those particular areas of philosophy in which particular versions of those issues arise. For those who are not interested in philosophy of religion, this is all that you need to know by way of introduction; you can now happily proceed to the book proper. However, those who are interested in philosophy of religion may like to know a little bit more about the reasons that I had for starting to work on this book. The remainder of this Preface is for you.

When I completed my book on ontological arguments (Oppy 1995c) I immediately commenced work on the next stage of the larger project announced in the preface of that earlier book: an examination of cosmological arguments for and against the existence of various deities. My plan was to follow the structure of the discussion that I provided of ontological arguments in Oppy (1995c), namely, to obtain an exhaustive taxonomy of cosmological arguments discussed in the philosophical literature and to use a thorough discussion of all of the key concepts that are used in those arguments as a basis for criticism of those arguments. Since a thorough discussion of cosmological arguments would require a thorough discussion of *time, causation, necessity and contingency, infinity, sufficient reason,* and *contemporary cosmology* – and maybe other topics as well – it is perhaps predictable that I eventually came to realise that a comprehensive discussion of this kind is not something that I could ever carry out. While I am convinced that it is a mistake to try to discuss arguments about the existence of God without paying attention to wider philosophical debates about the concepts that are employed in those arguments, I now suspect that a frontal assault on cosmological arguments – of the magnitude that I initially envisaged – may be beyond the reach of any individual researcher.

In view of these difficulties, I decided to try a different approach. Rather than divide up discussion in philosophy of religion according to the received topics, I decided to choose one of the key concepts that figures in cosmological arguments, and then to see how that concept is treated both in wider philosophical debates and in other areas of philosophy of religion. If this approach is fruitful, then it can be repeated using some of the other key concepts that figure in cosmological arguments – and, perhaps, over the long term, something like the project that I initially conceived might eventually be completed. Of course, if we approach the subject matter in this way, then the results of discussion of particular topics are provisional: What we say about cosmological arguments from the standpoint of considerations about the infinite will not exhaust what there is to say about cosmological arguments when other considerations are taken into account (and likewise for the other topics to which we give attention). On the other hand, there are advantages to approaching the subject matter in this way: In particular, questions about the consistency of the application of the concept of infinity across a range of different subjects in philosophy of religion come clearly into view in a way that is not possible if we stick to more orthodox ways of dividing up our subject matter. Moreover, a suitably extensive examination of the use of the concept of infinity in a range of wider philosophical contexts helps to concentrate attention on the costs and benefits of particular choices that one might make in particular domains in the philosophy of religion.

According to the plan suggested by the remarks that I have just made, I decided to write a book divided into two parts. The first part – *A Primer on Infinity* – would be an attempt to discuss wider philosophical views about infinity that, in one way or another, bear on discussions of the infinite in the context of philosophy of religion. The second part – *The Infinite in Philosophy of Religion* – would then apply the discussion of the first part to a range of topics in philosophy of religion. In particular, the second part of the book would focus on the role that the concept of infinity plays in traditional monotheistic conceptions of God and the attributes of God, and on the role that the concept of infinity plays in traditional monotheistic arguments for the existence of God.

While I would like to be able to say that this work is part of a larger project, I think that the most that I can reasonably claim is that it is clearly part of a *possible* larger project. Moreover, it is also worth noting that work on a similar plan might be conducted using the concepts of time, causation, sufficient reason, design, person, goodness, cosmology, and so forth as their foci. I see no reason to suppose that such work would not turn up interesting results concerning the consistency and broader philosophical adequacy of treatments of these topics in orthodox philosophy of religion.

Part of my interest in philosophy of religion stems from the conviction that it must be possible to convince reasonable religious believers that traditional monotheistic *arguments* for the existence of God are worthless. Hence, not surprisingly, one of the subsidiary goals for the projected larger work is to make some contribution to the case for supposing that reasonable religious believers ought to recognise that the arguments for the existence of God provide no reason at all for reasonable nonbelievers to change their minds. However, another part of my interest in philosophy of religion stems from the conviction that it must be possible for reasonable nonbelievers to hold that there are reasonable believers, that is, from the conviction that it is not the case that all religious believers are, *ipso facto*, the subjects of certain kinds of failings of rationality. Hence, not surprisingly, another of the subsidiary goals for this projected larger work is to make a plausible case for the claim that there are conceptions of the infinite that can be integrated successfully into relatively orthodox monotheistic conceptions of the world.

Perhaps it is worth noting here that there are *prima facie* plausible arguments that support the contention that there is no conception of the infinite that can be successfully integrated into relatively orthodox monotheistic conceptions of the world.

If we are strict finitists – and thus reject all actual and potential infinities – then we are obliged to say that God is finite, and that the magnitudes of the divine attributes are finite. But what reason could there be for God to possess a given magnitude to degree N rather than to degree $N+1$? More generally, how could a finite God be the kind of endpoint for explanation that cosmological arguments typically take God to be?

If we are potential infinitists – that is, if we reject all actual infinities but allow that some entities and magnitudes are potentially infinite – then it seems that we will be obliged to say that God is potentially infinite and that the magnitudes of the divine attributes are potentially infinite. But what kind of conception of God can sustain the claim that God is susceptible of improvement in various respects? If God possesses a magnitude to degree N even though God could possess that magnitude to degree $N+1$, surely God just isn't the kind of endpoint for explanation that cosmological arguments typically take God to be.

If we are neither strict finitists nor potential infinitists, then it seems that we must be actual infinitists, that is, we must suppose that God is actually infinite and that the magnitudes of the divine attributes are actually infinite. But is there a conception of the infinite that can sustain the claim that God is actually infinite, and the claim that the magnitudes of the divine attributes are actually infinite without undermining the kinds of considerations to which orthodox cosmological arguments appeal in attempting to establish that God exists? Indeed, more generally, are there conceptions of the infinite that can sustain the claim that God is actually infinite, and the claim that the magnitudes of the divine attributes are actually infinite *tout court*? Moreover, if there is a conception of the infinite that can sustain the claim that God is actually infinite, can this conception of the infinite also sustain the idea of an incarnate God, and the idea that there is an afterlife in which people share the same abode as God?

Perhaps some theists will claim that we are not forced to choose among the three options outlined above. Even if these options are unattractive, why not say instead that we can say nothing positive about God – so that, while we can say that God is neither finite nor potentially infinite, we cannot say that God is actually infinite; or that we can speak only analogically about God – so that we cannot say, literally, that God is either finite, or potentially infinite, or actually infinite; or that God so exceeds our limited comprehension that we should not expect to be able to talk sensibly about whether God is finite, or potentially infinite, or actually infinite; or . . . ?

I think that there are several reasons why one should not take any of these options. On the one hand, if we are interested in the standing of arguments for the existence of God, then we need to be able to give literal content to the claim that God exists. If there is no literal content to give to the claim that God exists, then there is no contest: Nontheists win by default. An argument for the conclusion that "well, there's something but I can't make any literally true claims about what it is like and, indeed, I haven't the least understanding what it is literally like" is hopelessly crippled before it begins. And, on the other hand, if we are interested in the doxastic credentials of theism – can there be reasonable belief that God exists? – then, again, we need to be able to give literal content to the claim that God exists. Perhaps one can believe that "well, there's something but I can't make any literally true claims about what it is like and, indeed, I haven't the least understanding what it is literally like," but it is very hard to see how one could have *reasons* for holding such a belief. Moreover, of course, if one is going to take any line of this type, then one has to take the line consistently: It is not good taking this line here – in order to avoid a confronting objection – while elsewhere supposing that there are positive, literal claims about God that one is perfectly well placed to make. Any theology based on these kinds of assumptions should be very *brief*.

Since all that this brief introduction aims to do is to make it seem plausible that there is a *prima facie* interesting question to address, I shall leave further discussion of this argument to the future. When I return to consider it further, I shall be able to draw on the following examination of the role of the concept of infinity in a wide range of philosophical discussions that have no obvious connections at all to the philosophy of religion. While I do not insist that the role of the concept of infinity in these other areas determines the role that the concept can play in philosophy of religion, I do insist that one cannot ignore these other discussions when one turns to the philosophy of religion: There is a single concept of the infinite that is required to have application outside the philosophy of religion, and no concept that is inadequate to those external applications can be deemed adequate for the purposes of philosophy of religion.

Acknowledgments

Monash University supported the writing of this book in various ways. In 1997, the structure of the Honours Program at Monash allowed me to present a series of seminars on infinity to a group of senior students; much of the material in this book was assembled during the teaching of that course. In 2002 and again in 2003, I received generous Monash Research Fund grants that allowed me to make time to work on my manuscript. Then, in the first half of 2004, I was granted a sabbatical during which I was able to devote myself full-time to the completion of this work. I am very grateful for the support that I have received from my colleagues at Monash, from within the School of Philosophy and Bioethics, from within the Faculty of Arts more widely, and from within the university community as a whole.

Some of the material in this book was developed during the time between the completion of my book on ontological arguments and my appointment to Monash, while I was still a Research Fellow in the Philosophy Program, in the Research School for the Social Sciences (RSSS), at the Australian National University. Here, I would just like to underscore the appreciative remarks that I made in my acknowledgments in my book on ontological arguments: The Philosophy Program at RSSS is a national treasure, and it is a great privilege to have spent time working there.

There are many people with whom I have discussed material that appears in this book. While I am sure that I won't be able to recall everyone who ought to be mentioned at this point, I can make the beginnings of a list.

I was introduced to Cantor's paradise in John Groves's first-year lectures on algebra and geometry in 1980, and to many of the topics that are discussed in the first half of this book by Allen Hazen in lectures and conversation during the period 1982–7. I am indebted to Allen, in particular, for his guidance and encouragement during those formative years (though, somehow, his enthusiasm for constructivism and intuitionism seems not to have rubbed off in quite the way that he might have hoped).

David Dowe went through the undergraduate mathematics program at Melbourne University at the same time as I did; our conversations on topics that appear in this book – as well as on a great range of other topics – have continued ever since.

I had many conversations with John Broome, Frank Jackson, Doug MacLean, Peter Menzies, and others about the two-envelope paradox and the St. Petersburg game during 1993, and some very enlightening correspondence with David Chalmers on this and related topics. More recently – towards the end of 2003 – I also had extensive correspondence with Bruce Langtry on the two-envelope paradox.

Jeremy Aarons, Steve Gardner, and Brian Weatherson attended the 1997 lectures and subjected the presented material to very careful critical scrutiny; and Alan Hájek gave a guest performance on Pascal's wager that was *the* highlight of the course. I have had many conversations with Brian and Alan on the topics discussed herein and have been greatly influenced by them in many different ways.

Some of the material discussed in this book is examined far more carefully and deeply in Daniel Nolan's doctoral dissertation. I have learned a great deal from discussions with Daniel – and Greg Restall – about most of the more technical matters that are mentioned in this book.

While I am indebted to all of my colleagues at Monash, I am particularly grateful to Dirk Baltzly, John Bigelow, Lloyd Humberstone, and Aubrey Townsend for discussion of material that is included in this volume.

There are a couple of places where I have drawn on my own previously published work. In particular, part of section 7.3 is taken from Graham Oppy, "Countable Fusion Not Yet Proven Guilty: It Could Be the Whiteheadian Account of Space Whatdunnit," *Analysis* 57, no. 4 (1997): 249–53, reprinted with kind permission of Blackwell Publishing. Part of section 7.8 is taken from Graham Oppy, "Humean Supervenience?" *Philosophical Studies* 101, no. 1 (2000): 75–105 (© 2000 Kluwer Academic Publishers), with kind permission of Springer Science and Business Media. Parts of Graham Oppy, "Arguing about the *Kalām* Cosmological Argument," *Philo* 5, no. 1 (2002): 34–61, are reprinted with kind permission of *Philo.*

There are also places where I draw heavily on the work of other philosophers and mathematicians. My exposition of set theory in section 2.1 owes a lot to Drake (1974); and the exposition of material on nonstandard numbers in section 2.5 relies on Conway (1976), Nelson (1977; 1987), Boolos and Jeffrey (1980), and Lavine (1994). Section 4.2 makes much use of Grünbaum (1953), while section 4.3 is indebted to Skyrms (1983). Section 4.6 follows Earman and Norton (1993), and section 4.7 depends extensively on Earman (1995). Sections 5.1 and 5.2 are indebted to Ehrlich (1982), while section 5.4 draws on Teller (1989) and section 5.5 follows Harrison (1987). Section 6.1 largely follows Ross (1988), while section 6.3 is reliant on Rapaport (1998), and section 6.5 owes quite a bit to Dreier (2003). Section 7.2 has a considerable debt to Lewis (1991), and section 7.5 draws on Lavine (1991). Finally, sections 8.2 to 8.6 make considerable use of Lavine (1994).

I am grateful to the readers at Cambridge University Press for extensive and helpful comments and suggestions; I am also grateful for the various kinds of editorial support provided by Beatrice Rehl and Stephanie Sakson.

Last but not least, I must acknowledge the support of friends and family, without whom this book would never have been completed. In particular, Camille, Gilbert, Calvin, and Alfie have had to put up with me during the seemingly endless hours in which I have been thinking obsessively about the material that is presented in this book. While they may be ambivalent about the trade-off that has been effected, this book is for them.

Introduction

Controversy about the infinite is more or less ubiquitous in philosophy. There are very few areas of philosophy where questions about the infinite do not arise; and there are very few areas of philosophy where questions about the infinite do arise, and where there is no serious dispute about how those questions should be answered. Furthermore, questions about the infinite are foundational in many areas of philosophy: There are many quite fundamental parts of philosophy in which the most basic questions that arise are concerned with the role of the infinite in those parts of philosophy.

Obviously enough, questions about the infinite arise in the most fundamental parts of logic and philosophy of mathematics. One of the most fundamental observations that one can make about the natural numbers – the numbers that are generated when one starts counting from one, adding one unit each time – is that there is no last or greatest natural number: for any number to which one counts, one can go further by adding more units. This observation is one of the fundamental sources of theorising about the infinite, and its consequences extend far beyond the domain of the philosophy of mathematics.

While there are serious questions about the development of concepts of the infinite in logic and mathematics, there are far more immediate problems about the development and application of concepts of the infinite in other realms. Indeed, there are many puzzles and arguments across a wide range of different subject matters that are intended to make difficulties for the suggestion that concepts of the infinite can find application outside the domains of logic and mathematics.

In chapter 1, we begin with a survey of some puzzle cases that are intended to make trouble for the suggestion that concepts of infinity can find application outside the realm of logic and mathematics. After noting a few elementary distinctions among different kinds of concepts of the infinite, we provide a catalogue of seventeen arguments – and puzzle cases – that have been proposed in order to try to establish the conclusion that it is absurd to suppose that certain concepts of the infinite do find legitimate application outside the realm of logic and mathematics. We shall suppose that these arguments and puzzle cases do present a *prima facie* challenge to those who defend the claim that the relevant concepts of the infinite could find legitimate application outside the realm of logic and mathematics, and we shall go on to consider how this challenge might be met.

However, before we undertake this task, we turn – in chapter 2 – to a brief survey of mathematical treatments of the infinite that are needed for serious philosophical discussions of the infinite. Some of the topics of discussion in chapter 2 – for example, standard theories of number and standard theories of analysis – are required in order to provide an adequate discussion of some of the puzzles mentioned in chapter 1; other topics discussed in chapter 2 – such as set theory, Cantor's paradise, and various kinds of nonstandard number systems – are required only for later chapters in the book. Since the presentation is quite compressed, and the material under consideration is not all straightforward, some readers may prefer to skip over this chapter and to come back to those sections that they find are essential for understanding of later parts of the book. While there is nothing in this chapter that is gratuitous, some readers may decide that they can understand the subsequent material well enough without wrestling with all of the mathematical details.

In chapter 3, we turn to a discussion of the arguments and puzzles that were set out in chapter 1. The aim of this discussion is to consider how someone who wants to maintain that concepts of the infinite could find application outside the realm of logic and mathematics could respond to these arguments and puzzles. While the general view that is defended is that these arguments and puzzles cause no serious difficulties for those who maintain that concepts of the infinite could find application outside the realm of logic and mathematics, the details of the discussion vary considerably from one case to the next. Sometimes, it turns out that an allegedly impossible scenario really is impossible for reasons that are relevant to the question of the application of concepts of infinity outside the realms of logic and mathematics: No one should think that concepts of infinity could have *that* kind of application to the extramathematical realm. Other times, it turns out that an allegedly impossible scenario is impossible for reasons that have nothing to do with the question of the application of concepts of infinity outside the realms of logic and mathematics: There are many different ways in which a scenario that involves infinities can be problematic without in any way impugning the possibility that concepts of the infinite can find application outside the realm of logic and mathematics. And, yet other times, an allegedly impossible scenario turns out not to be impossible at all: If concepts of infinity could have certain kinds of application outside the realm of logic and mathematics, then the world would be a strange and different place – but there is a vast difference between *strange* and *impossible.*

Having completed an initial tilt at questions about the application of concepts of infinity outside the realm of logic and mathematics, we then turn our attention to particular subject matters in which questions about the infinite have particular importance. We begin, in chapter 4, with an examination of the role of concepts of infinity in theories of space and time. Our initial point of departure is Zeno's paradoxes of motion, and some sophisticated questions about measures and metrics that are prompted by consideration of Zeno's paradoxes. The remainder of chapter 4 is taken up with considerations about the role of the concept of infinity in more contemporary theorising about the nature of space, time, and spacetime. We consider the arguments from Kant's first antinomy of pure reason concerning the finitude or infinitude of space and time; the range of views that one might take about the mereological structure of space and time, focusing in particular on the question of whether there are spatial and temporal atoms (points and instants, respectively); the suggestion that the obtaining of results from the carrying out of infinitely many distinct operations in a finite amount of time might be finessed in general relativistic spacetimes; and some questions about the classification of singularities in general relativistic spacetimes.

In chapter 5, we turn our attention to questions about infinities that arise in the physical sciences. The first part of the chapter is devoted to a discussion of three case studies: one concerning the existence of hotter than infinite temperatures in physically realised systems; a second concerning the role of renormalisation in quantum field theory; and a third that considers the way in which considerations about infinity have borne on attempts to explain why the sky is dark at night. The remainder of the chapter is then taken up with some more general considerations about the ways in which infinities can enter into physical science, including some fundamental considerations that are relevant to attempts to address the question of whether it is possible for there to be physically instantiated infinities of one kind or another.

The next subject taken up – in chapter 6 – is the role of the concept of infinity in theories of probability and decision. The chapter begins with an elementary exposition of orthodox theories of probability and an examination of the different kinds of additivity principles that one might include in a theory of probability. Attention then turns to decision theory and, in particular, to an examination of the various different ways in which considerations about infinity might be introduced into decision theory. After providing some general reasons for supposing that the construction of infinite decision theory is fraught with difficulties, we conclude the chapter with a discussion of three cases – the two-envelope paradox, the St. Petersburg game, and the puzzle of Heaven and Hell – that can be taken to support the contention that there is no acceptable account of reasoning with unbounded utility functions.

Chapter 7 takes up mereology, the general theory of part/whole relations. Our main interest in this chapter is twofold: On the one hand, we consider principles of composition and arguments that are intended to show that we should be wary of unrestricted claims about the existence of infinite fusions; on the other hand, we consider some claims about infinite divisibility and the existence of mereological atoms. Other topics addressed in this chapter include the arguments in the second Kantian antinomy of pure reason, the question of the bearing of considerations about vagueness on arguments for the existence of infinite collections, some reasons for supposing that indistinguishable quantum mechanical particles are not mereological atoms, an argument for the conclusion that there is no such thing as 'the universe', and some further considerations about the connections between the concept of *continuity* and the concept of a *mereological atom.*

Having completed our tour of individual extramathematical subject matters in which questions about infinity are of particular importance, we turn – in chapter 8 – to a consideration of some more fundamental philosophical questions about our understanding of the infinite. We begin with some general philosophical considerations – concerning, for example, distinctions between actual and merely potential infinities – and then move on to a brief survey of philosophies of pure mathematics and, in particular, of attempts to explain how it is that we are able to understand the classical mathematical concept of infinity. After endorsing Lavine's proposal that we arrive at the classical conception of infinity by a process of *extrapolation* from finite mathematics, we move on to a discussion of philosophies of applied mathematics. The chapter concludes with some remarks about Skolem's paradox and the concept of an infinitesimal quantity.

The last chapter of this part of the book takes up some questions about infinite regresses and the uses and abuses of principles of sufficient reason. Part of the aim of this chapter is to exhibit a circle of concepts – *partial sufficient reason, completed infinity, infinite regress* – whose application to particular cases is a point of serious contention. More generally, this chapter attacks the suggestion that there are acceptable strong principles of sufficient reason and defends the claim that defensible principles of sufficient reason are so weak that it is implausible to suppose that they possess serious metaphysical bite.

While there are some places where the book is polemical – in particular, this is true of chapters 3 and 9 – it should be emphasised that the primary purpose is to gain a clear view of the ways in which the concept of the infinite is used and of the challenges that confront any attempt to gain an adequate understanding of the employment of this concept. Rather than argue for a particular philosophical account of the infinite, I have taken as a primary goal the exhibition of the costs and benefits of adopting any of the rival accounts of the infinite that have been endorsed by contemporary philosophers. When, in subsequent work, I come to consider the role of the concept of infinity in philosophy of religion, I shall be interested in considering how matters stand on *each* of the accounts of the infinite that finds serious support, and not merely in the question of how things stand on the account of the infinite that I am myself most inclined to accept.

1

Beginnings and Puzzles

There are many different ways of organising discussions of the infinite. We begin by distinguishing among different kinds of problems of the infinite:

(1) There are problems of **large** infinities – collections with at least denumerably many members – and there are problems of **small** infinities (or infinitesimals) – quantities that are nonzero and yet smaller in absolute magnitude than any finite quantity.

(2) There are problems of **denumerable** infinities – collections that are, in some sense, equinumerous with the natural numbers – and there are problems of **nondenumerable** infinities – typically, though not always, collections that are, in some sense, equinumerous with the real numbers. Many of the problems about nondenumerable infinities are related to problems about infinitesimals and connect to questions about the understanding of **continuous** quantities.

(3) There are problems about **theoretical** (or abstract) infinities – infinite collections of numbers, sets, propositions, properties, merely possible worlds, or the like – and there are problems about **physical** (or actual, or instantiated) infinities – infinite collections of physical objects, infinite values of physical quantities, and the like. Of course, there are some entities whose classification is problematic, given this distinction: For instance, should we say that spacetime points are physical objects, or should

we classify them as merely theoretical entities? Indeed, more generally, there are serious questions about whether we should suppose that there *are* numbers, sets, propositions, properties, merely possible worlds, spacetime points, and so on.

Many of the best-known problem cases concern **large, denumerable, physical** infinities. The following are some examples.

1. **Al-Ghazali's Problem**: Suppose that past time is infinite, and that the solar system has persisted unchanged throughout that infinite time. Then both Jupiter and the earth have made infinitely many rotations about the sun – that is, they have made the same number of rotations about the sun. And yet, for every rotation that Jupiter makes, the earth makes thirteen rotations – that is, the earth must have made thirteen times as many rotations as Jupiter. But surely, this is a contradiction. And so, surely, we can conclude that it is incoherent to suppose that past time is infinite – and, moreover, surely we can conclude that there cannot be large, denumerable, physical infinities.[1]
2. **Hilbert's Hotel**: Suppose that there is a hotel – Hilbert's Hotel – with an infinite number of rooms, each of which is occupied by one or more guests. Suppose further that a new guest turns up at reception. Then the proprietors of Hilbert's Hotel can easily accommodate the new guest: They just move the guests in room 1 to room 2; the guests in room 2 to room 3; . . . ; the guests in room N to room $N + 1$; . . . ; and house the new guest in room 1. But this is absurd! Given that the hotel was already full, there is no way in which any further guests could be accommodated unless already accommodated guests doubled up. Even worse, if infinitely many new guests arrived, it would be possible to accommodate them in the full hotel; just move the guests in room N to room $2N$, for each N, and then accommodate the newly arrived guests in the odd-numbered rooms. And worse again, if the infinitely many people in the odd-numbered rooms check out, then there are still just as many – because infinitely many – people left in the hotel; but if the infinitely many people

[1] Al-Ghazali's problem is mentioned in Craig (1979a: 98) and Mackie (1982: 93). Brown (1965) attributes a very similar argument to Bonaventure.

in rooms 4, 5, 6, . . . , N, $N+1$, . . . , check out, then the hotel is all but emptied, even though no more people have left than under the previously described circumstances. The absurdities that surface in this story provide compelling reason to suppose that there cannot be large, denumerable, physical infinities.[2]

3. **Craig's Library**: Suppose that there is a library that contains an infinite collection of books, with a distinct natural number printed on the spine of each book. (We shall consider later the question of how this printing task might be realised.) Then the total number of books in the library is equal to (and not greater than) the number of books that have even numbers on their spines and to the number that have prime numbers on their spines (since the total collection of books, the collection of books that have even numbers on their spines, and the collection of books that have prime numbers on their spines is each a denumerably infinite collection). Moreover, it seems that it is impossible to add an extra book to the collection, since there is no distinct number that could be placed on the spine of the extra book. And what happens if all of the odd-numbered books are taken out on loan? Surely, the missing books would occupy an infinite volume of space on the shelves – and yet, when we push the remaining books together, the shelves will remain full! Once again, the absurdities that arise in this story provide good reason for supposing that there cannot be large, denumerable, physical infinities.[3]
4. **Tristram Shandy**: Suppose that Tristram Shandy writes his autobiography at the rate of one day per year – that is, that it takes him one year of writing to cover one day of his life. If it is possible for Tristram Shandy to have been writing from infinity past, then it is possible for Tristram Shandy to have finished his autobiography by now. But there is no way that Tristram Shandy could have completed his autobiography by now. For suppose that there was a day on which he stopped writing. Since it takes

[2] Hilbert's Hotel is introduced in Gamow (1946: 17); Craig (1979a: 84–6) has initiated considerable recent discussion of this case.

[3] Craig's Library is first discussed in Craig (1979a: 82–6). Subsequent discussions include Smith (1987).

him about 365 days to write about one day, the last day that he could have written about was not the day on which he stopped writing. But in order to complete his autobiography, he must write about the day on which he stops writing. So it seems that it could not have been the case that Tristram Shandy has been writing since infinity past; and so it seems that there cannot be large, denumerable, physical infinities.[4]

5. **Counting from Infinity**: A man counts: "10, 9, 8, 7, 6, 5, 4, 3, 2, 1, 0, done! I've counted all of the natural numbers backwards; I've been counting from infinity past, and I'm finally done. Thank goodness that's over!" Before we can consider the question of whether we have – or could have – reason to believe that what the man says is true, we need to consider the question of whether we so much as understand what the man is saying. Many people have followed Wittgenstein in supposing that what the man says is not so much as intelligible: We cannot give any content to the suggestion that someone might have "counted backwards from infinity". But if that's right, then we have the strongest possible reason for denying that there can be large, denumerable, physical infinities.[5]

Other well-known problem cases involve both **large, denumerable, physical** infinities and **small, denumerable, physical** infinities. The following are some examples.

6. **Infinite Paralysis**: Suppose that Achilles wants to run straight from A to B but that there are infinitely many gods who, unbeknownst to one another (and to Achilles), each have a reason to prevent him from so doing. The first god forms the following intention: If and when Achilles gets halfway, to paralyse him (instantaneously). The second god forms the following intention: If and when Achilles gets one-quarter of the

[4] The first Tristram Shandy puzzle occurs in Russell (1903: 358–60). It is discussed by Diamond (1964), among others. The very different puzzle presented in the main text is due to Craig (1979a: 98). There has been extensive recent discussion of this case. See, e.g., Sorabji (1983), Conway (1984), Small (1986), Smith (1987), Eells (1988), Craig (1991a), Oderberg (2002a; 2002b), and Oppy (2002c; 2003).

[5] I suspect that this puzzle has an ancient origin. Wittgenstein considered various versions of it. There are more recent discussions in: Dretske (1965), Bennett (1971), Craig (1979a), Moore (1990), and Oderberg (2002a).

way, to paralyse him (instantaneously). The Nth god forms the following intention: If and when Achilles gets $1/2^N$th of the way, to paralyse him (instantaneously). All the gods have the ability to carry out their intentions. Achilles cannot make any progress without violating the intention of at least one of them – indeed, without violating the intention of infinitely many of them. Yet if he is unable to move, it is unclear why: Until he makes some progress, none of the gods will have actually paralysed him! (Remember, the intentions of the gods are all *conditional* in form.) On the assumption that we can make sense of the idea that there are gods with the ability to paralyse people (instantaneously), it seems that the apparently absurd conclusion of this story – that someone can be rendered immobile by a nested sequence of (conditional) intentions on which no one has acted – provides compelling reason for rejecting the suggestion that there can be both small, denumerable, physical infinities and large, denumerable, physical infinities. (Note that the number of gods in this example involves a large, denumerable, physical infinity, while the lengths that Achilles would traverse before being paralysed involve both a large, denumerable, physical infinity – the number of lengths – and a small, denumerable, physical infinity – the successively decreasing magnitudes of the lengths.)[6]

7. **Stick**: Suppose that an infinitely divisible stick is cut in half at some point in time; and that each half is in turn cut in half, half a minute later; and that each quarter is cut in half, a quarter of a minute after that; . . . ; and each $1/2^n$th part is cut in half one $1/2^n$th of a minute after that; . . . . At the end of the minute, what will be left? No answer to this question seems appealing. First, we might say that we are left with infinitely many infinitesimally thin pieces. But it seems very doubtful that we can even make sense of this idea. In particular, when we ask about the identification of the particular infinitesimal that "measures" the thickness of the pieces, there seems to be no sensible answer that can be given. Second, we might say that we are left with infinitely many pieces

[6] This case was introduced by Benardette (1964: 259–60). It is discussed by Moore (1990), Priest (1999), Yablo (2000), and Perez-Laraudogoitia (2003).

of zero thickness. But that violates the very strong intuition that you can't decompose something of finite thickness entirely into elements of zero thickness, even if there are infinitely many such elements. Third, we might say that we are left with infinitely many finitely thin pieces of equal thickness. But that clearly won't do: Infinitely many finitely thin pieces lumped together should make a whole with infinite thickness. No other answer to the question suggests itself. So it seems that we have here compelling reason to reject the suggestion that there can be small, denumerable, physical infinities. (This time, the number of cuts – and presumably the number of cutters – involves a large, denumerable, physical infinity. Moreover, the time intervals in which the cuts are made involves both a large, denumerable, physical infinity – the number of time intervals – and a small, denumerable, physical infinity – the successively decreasing magnitudes of these time intervals.)[7]

8. **Spaceship**: Suppose that there is a spaceship that, after travelling in a straight line for half a minute, doubles in speed; and, after a further quarter of a minute, doubles its speed again; . . . ; and after a further $1/n$th of a minute doubles its speed again; . . . . Where will the spaceship be at the end of the minute? Since no answer to this question seems appealing – since, for instance, we can't so much as make sense of the idea that the spaceship will be infinitely far away, and travelling at infinite speed – it seems that we have here compelling reason to reject the suggestion that there can be both small, denumerable, physical infinities and large, denumerable, physical infinities. (This time, the speed in this example is a large, denumerable, physical infinity, while the time interval involves both a large, denumerable, physical infinity – the number of time intervals – and a small, denumerable, physical infinity – the successively decreasing magnitudes of these time intervals.)[8]
9. **Thomson's Lamp**: There are reading lamps equipped with buttons that, if pressed, switch the lamp on if it is off, and switch the lamp off if it is on. Suppose that one of these lamps is

[7] Benardete (1964: 252) and Moore (1990: 5, 26, 138, 214) discuss this case. I do not know where it originates, but it is surely very old.

[8] Moore (1990: 70–1) discusses this case.

initially on. Suppose, further, that the switch is pressed once during the first minute, once during the next half minute, once during the next quarter minute, . . . , one during the next $1/2^n$th minute, . . . , and so on. After two minutes, the switch ceases to be pressed. Plainly, at the end of two minutes, the lamp is either on or off but not both. Yet it seems that the lamp can be neither on nor off: For, at the very least, it seems entirely arbitrary to suppose that the lamp is on, and it seems entirely arbitrary to suppose that the lamp is off. Supposing that there can be both large and small denumerable, physical infinities leads us into direct conflict with modest and plausible principles of sufficient reason: The lamp can be on at the end of the minute only if there is a sufficient reason for it to be on; and the lamp can be off at the end of the minute only if there is sufficient reason for it to be off. But there is no sufficient reason for the lamp to be on at the end of the minute; and there is no sufficient reason for the lamp to be off at the end of the minute. So we have good reason to reject the contention that there can be both large and small denumerable, physical infinities.[9]

10. **Black's Marble Shifter**: Suppose that, between two trays of infinite length, there is a machine with a mechanical scoop. Initially, the left tray is lined with marbles, regularly spaced at a distance of one metre; the right tray is empty. The left tray incorporates a conveyor belt that brings distant marbles towards the scoop; the right tray is lined with a sticky substance whose stickiness increases with distance from the machine. When the machine is started, it uses the first minute to pick up a marble from the left tray and throw it a distance of one metre into the tray on the right; it uses the next half-minute to pick up the second marble from the left tray and throw it a distance of two metres into the tray on the right; it uses the next quarter-minute to pick up the third marble from the left tray and throw it a distance of three metres into the right tray; . . . ; it uses the next $1/2^{N-1}$

[9] There are many different versions of this problem: Instead of turning a switch on and off, one might step forwards and backwards, or pick up and set down an object, or open and close one's mouth, etc. The initial case was introduced in Thomson (1954). It is discussed in Benacerraf (1962), Chihara (1965), Grünbaum (1968); (1973a), Thomson (1970), Craig (1979a), Berresford (1981), Moore (1990), Earman and Norton (1996), and McLaughlin (1998).

minutes to pick up the *N*th marble from the left tray and throw it a distance of *N* metres into the right tray; . . . After two minutes, the machine comes to a halt. The left tray is empty, and the right tray is lined with marbles, regularly spaced at a distance of one metre. Given that there can be large and small denumerable, physical infinities, it seems that the described scenario ought to be possible, and yet surely it is absurd to suppose that what has been described here is possible. So we have been given good reason to suppose that there cannot be large and small denumerable, physical infinities.[10]

11. **Pi Machine**: If there can be large and small denumerable, physical infinities, then, at least in principle, we can construct a machine to print all of the digits of the decimal expansion of pi. Here is how it works: The machine prints the first digit of the decimal expansion of pi in the first minute; the second digit of the decimal expansion of pi in the next half-minute; the third digit of the decimal expansion of pi in the next quarter-minute; . . . ; the *n*th digit of the decimal expansion of pi in the next $1/2^n$th minute; . . . . After two minutes, the machine halts – and every digit in the decimal expansion of pi has been printed. To avoid certain kinematical inconsistencies, we can suppose: (i) that the heights from which the press descends to the paper to print the successive digits forms a geometrically deceasing series that converges to zero; and (ii) that the widths of the successive numerals to be printed converge to zero in such a way that all of the digits can be printed in a single horizontal line on a finite strip of paper. However, even if we can avoid all kinematical inconsistencies in this story, it surely remains the case that it is absurd to suppose that there could be a machine that can print out all of the digits of the decimal expansion of pi in finite time – and so this story provides yet more reason to suppose that there cannot be both large and small denumerable, physical infinities.[11]

[10] This example is due to Black (1951). It is discussed in Taylor (1951), Watling (1952), Grünbaum (1970), Craig (1979a), and Earman and Norton (1996).

[11] This puzzle is introduced in Grünbaum (1968) and discussed further in Grünbaum (1973a).

12. **Goldbach Machine**: If there can be large and small denumerable, physical infinities then, at least in principle, we can construct a machine that will check unresolved conjectures in number theory. Here, for example, is how our machine could be used to check the Goldbach conjecture – that is, the conjecture that every even number may be represented as the sum of two prime numbers. In the first minute, the machine checks (by exhaustion) whether 2 is the sum of two primes; in the next half-minute, the machine checks (by exhaustion) whether 4 is the sum of two primes; in the next quarter-minute, the machine checks (by exhaustion) whether 6 is the sum of two primes; ...; in the next $1/n$th minute, the machine checks (by exhaustion) whether $2(n+1)$ is the sum of two primes; .... If, at any time, the machine finds an even number that is not the sum of two primes, then it prints an 'X' and stops. After two minutes, the machine will definitely have stopped: If the print-out is blank, then Goldbach's conjecture is true; otherwise, the conjecture is false. But surely it is obvious that there cannot be a machine that can resolve Goldbach's conjecture in this way; indeed, aren't there fundamental theorems in logic that prove that there can be no such machine? Whence we may conclude that there cannot be both large and small denumerable, physical infinities.[12]
13. **Ross Urn**: Suppose that we have a machine, an infinitely large urn, and an infinite collection of numbered balls. In each period of operation, the machine puts some balls into the urn, and takes others out. We describe three different cases:

(a) At one minute to twelve, balls numbered 1 through 10 are placed in the urn, and ball 1 is withdrawn. At half a minute to twelve, balls numbered 11 through 20 are placed in the urn, and ball 2 is withdrawn. At a quarter minute to twelve, balls numbered 21 through 30 are placed in the urn, and ball three is withdrawn.... At $1/2^n$th minutes to twelve, balls numbered $10n + 1$ through $10(n + 1)$ are placed in the urn, and ball $n + 1$ is withdrawn....

(b) At one minute to twelve, balls numbered 1 through 9 are placed in the urn, and a zero is added to the label of ball 1, so that it becomes

[12] This puzzle is also introduced in Grünbaum (1968), and discussed further in Grünbaum (1973a).

ball 10. At half a minute to twelve, balls 11 through 19 are added to the urn, and a zero is added to the label of ball 2, so that it becomes ball 20. At a quarter minute to twelve, balls 21 through 29 are added to the urn, and a zero is added to ball 3, so that it becomes ball 30.... At $1/2^n$th minutes to twelve, balls $10n + 1$ through $10n + 9$ are added to the urn, and a zero is added to the label of ball $n + 1$, so that it becomes ball $10(n + 1)$.... (Thus, in general, this procedure differs from the previously described procedure in that, instead of withdrawing the ball with the smallest number, we add a zero to the label of that ball instead.)

(c) We suppose that there are labelled places inside the urn, each big enough to accommodate just one ball. We repeat the procedure described in (b), but with the requirement that the label on a ball must correspond to the label of the place that it occupies. Hence, for example, as soon as the ball labelled '1' becomes the ball labelled '10', it is moved from the place labelled '1' to the place labelled '10'.

What should we say about these three cases? In particular, how should we answer the following question: How many balls are there in the urn at twelve o'clock, and what are the labels on these balls? A little thought might well suggest that there is no coherent answer to be given to this set of questions – and this in turn might well be taken to be further compelling reason to deny that there can be both large and small denumerable physical infinities.[13]

14. **Deafening Peals**: Suppose that a sequence of instantaneous deafening peals – that is, instantaneous peals that render one instantaneously deaf – are issued at one minute past twelve, half a minute past twelve, a quarter of a minute past twelve, ..., $1/2^n$ minutes past twelve, ... Suppose that, before any of the peals is issued, that is, at twelve, one has perfect hearing. At any time after twelve, it seems that one must be deaf. But what could be the cause of one's deafness? For any peal, there are earlier peals; consequently, there can be no particular peal that makes one deaf. But if there is no particular peal that makes one deaf, then surely one is not deaf. This case surely makes it very plausible

[13] This puzzle was introduced in Ross (1988). There are discussions of this puzzle in Allis and Koetsier (1991; 1995), Holgate (1994), Van Bendegem (1994), and Earman and Norton (1996).

to suppose that there cannot be both large and small denumerable, physical infinities.[14]

15. **Invisibility**: Suppose that a man is encased, on all sides, from head to toe, in a sequence of opaque capsules. The innermost capsule is 1 cm thick; the next innermost capsule is 0.5 cm thick; the third innermost capsule is 0.25 cm thick; . . . ; the *n*th innermost capsule is $1/2^{n-1}$ cm thick; . . . . When you look at the man, what do you see? If you were looking at a man encased in a 2-cm thick opaque capsule, then there is no problem about what you would see. Light would be reflected from the outermost capsule to your eye, and, in consequence, you would be able to see the outermost surface of the opaque capsule. But, in the problem case, there is no outermost surface from which light will be reflected. For each capsule, no matter how thin, there are even thinner capsules that lie around it, and from which light will be reflected. Yet it must be the case that there is something that you see: After all, you can certainly see behind the man everywhere up to and including the surface that is everywhere 2 cm from his body. Given that it is hard to see how there can be any coherent answer to the question of what you see when you look at the encased man, we have here further reason to suppose that there cannot be both large and small denumerable physical infinities.[15]
16. **Infinity Mob**: The Infinity Mob has decided to rub out a victim, but no member of the Mob wants to have the death on his conscience. So the members of the Mob decide on the following method of execution: At one minute past twelve, mobster 1 will fire a bullet into the victim's heart; at half a minute past twelve, mobster 2 will fire a bullet into the victim's heart; . . . ; at $1/2^n$ minutes past twelve, mobster *n* will fire a bullet into the victim's heart; . . . . Plainly enough, the victim is alive at twelve o'clock, but dead at any time thereafter. Moreover, there is no particular

[14] This puzzle is introduced in Benardete (1964: 259ff.).

[15] There are many different versions of this problem: Instead of looking at a nested series of sheaths or capsules, one might look at a nested stack of boards (with the thicker boards stacked below the thinner ones), or a nested stack of pages of a book (with the thinner pages stacked above the thicker pages), etc. All of these versions – including the one in the main text – are considered in Benardete (1964: 234–84).

bullet that is responsible for the victim's death: For each bullet that might have been the cause of death, there is an earlier bullet that ensures that the later bullet enters the heart of a man who is already dead. So it seems that the mobsters can plausibly claim that not one of them is responsible for the death of the victim – even though the victim dies in a hail of bullets, and in circumstances in which there is no other plausible cause of death. But this is surely absurd, whence it follows that we have yet more reason to deny that there can be both large and small denumerable, physical infinities.[16]

17. **String**: Suppose that we have a piece of string. At one minute to twelve, the string is formed into an equilateral triangle. At half a minute to twelve, the string is formed into a square. At a quarter minute to twelve, the string is formed into a regular pentagon.... At $1/2^n$ minutes to twelve, the string is formed into a regular $(n+3)$-gon.... What shape does the string form at twelve? Given the construction described, there is some temptation to say that the string must be shaped into a circle: But is there really any good justification for this claim? After all, a circle is not any kind of *n*-gon: There is surely a categorical difference between the shapes that the string takes on at the specified moments and the shape that it has at twelve if it is a circle at twelve. But no other suggestion about the shape of the string at twelve has any appeal. So, yet again, we have here reason to deny that there can be both large and small denumerable physical infinities.

The kinds of problems about infinity that we have mentioned so far are all problems that are designed to get us to suppose that there are good reasons to deny that there can be large and small denumerable, physical infinities – that is, denumerable collections of physical objects (such as hotel rooms, library books, intervals of time, marbles, or bullets; denumerable collections of physical actions (such as shootings, divisions, relocations, switchings, or rearrangements; physical objects, physical actions, and spatial and temporal intervals, with no nonzero lower bound on their measure; and so forth. While we shall begin

[16] This case is discussed in Benardete (1964: 259).

by considering how a friend of large and small denumerable, physical infinities might respond to the challenges raised by these kinds of examples, it is important to note that there are many other kinds of puzzles about infinity that also need to be addressed.[17] We shall get to these other kinds of puzzles in the later chapters of this book.

Before we can turn to a discussion of these various puzzles, we need some mathematical equipment. The aim of the next chapter is to introduce standard mathematical tools that can be used to make discussion of infinities precise. We do not assume that these mathematical tools will, of themselves, afford a solution to even one of the problems that have just been presented. However, we do suppose that a proper grasp of these tools is necessary in order to reach an understanding of the options that are available to friends of large and small denumerable, physical infinities.

[17] There are, of course, many other puzzles like the ones set out in this chapter. However, there is an architectonic reason for exhibiting just seventeen of these puzzles: We thereby acknowledge the key role played by Paul Benacerraf in the development of the analysis of these kinds of puzzles. See, in particular, Benacerraf (1962).

2

Mathematical Preliminaries

In this chapter, I provide a very quick tour though some of the parts of mathematics that are relevant to the discussion of infinities of the large and small. The tour begins with set theory, which – according to many – provides foundations for the rest of mathematics. It then takes in the natural numbers – ordinal and cardinal – and Cantor's theory of the infinite ordinals and cardinals. Next, we look at the theory of the real numbers, and the standard analysis of limits and continuity. Finally, we have a brief look at some alternatives to the standard account of limits and continuity, based on the notion of infinitesimals, and a very quick glance at the area of finite mathematics. The aim throughout is merely to introduce some of the mathematical tools and results that might be considered in a serious discussion of the infinite and the infinitesimal.

2.1 SET THEORY

As noted above, there are many people who suppose that set theory can provide secure foundations for all of mathematics. During the 1980s, some people touted Category theory as a competitor; but enthusiasm for this proposal seems to be on the wane.

There are different versions of set theory. We shall look at what is probably the best-known, and best-loved, version of set theory, Zermelo-Frankel set theory (ZF for short). We shall note some alternatives to, and some extensions of, ZF.

Following closely the presentation of Drake (1974), I shall give both a formal version of the axioms of ZF and an informal gloss. The language of the formal version is the predicate calculus. We use the variables $x, y, z, \ldots$ to range over sets, and we use a, b, c as constants that denote sets. (We also use our variables to range over individuals, and our constants to denote individuals. But in the development of the pure theory, we shall not suppose that there are any individuals.) There are two distinguished relation symbols: $=$ (which represents the identity relation) and $\in$ (which represents the set-membership relation). $\{x\colon \Phi(x)\}$ is the set of things that satisfy the condition Φ. Abstraction terms can be eliminated; that is, they are a useful but not essential part of the development of the theory. The background logic in which the axioms are located is classical.

Axiom 1: (Extensionality) $\forall z(z \in x \leftrightarrow z \in y) \rightarrow x = y$. If two sets have the same members, then they are identical.

Axiom 2: (Foundation) $\exists y(y \in x) \rightarrow \exists y(y \in x \mathbin{\&} \forall z{\sim}(z \in x \mathbin{\&} z \in y))$. If x has any members, then it has members that are disjoint from x.

Axiom 3: (Axiom of Subsets) $\exists y \forall x(x \in y \leftrightarrow x \in a \mathbin{\&} \Phi(x))$. For any set a, there is a subset of a consisting of just those members of a that satisfy the condition Φ.

Axiom 4: (Empty Set Axiom) $\exists y \forall x x \notin y$. There is a set with no members. We shall call this set 'φ'.

Axiom 5: (Pair Set Axiom) $\exists y \forall x(x \in y \leftrightarrow x = a \vee x = b)$. There is a set whose only members are a and b.

Axiom 6: (Power Set Axiom) $\exists y \forall x(x \in y \leftrightarrow \exists z(z \in x \rightarrow z \in a))$. There is a set whose members are all of the subsets of a.

Axiom 7: (Sum Set Axiom) $\exists y \forall x(x \in y \leftrightarrow \exists z(x \in z \mathbin{\&} x \in a))$. To each set a there corresponds a set whose members are exactly the members of the members of a.

Axiom 8: (Axiom of Infinity) $\exists w(\varphi \in w \mathbin{\&} \forall x(x \in w \rightarrow \exists z(z \in w \mathbin{\&} \forall u(u \in z \leftrightarrow u \in x \vee u = x)))$. There is a set that has φ – the empty set – as a member, and is such that if x is a member, then so is $x \cup \{x\}$. This axiom entails that there are infinitely many sets.

Axiom 9: (Axiom of Replacement) If $\Psi(x, y)$ is a formula with x and y free, not involving b, then $\forall x \forall y \forall z(\Psi(x,y) \mathbin{\&} \Psi(x,z) \rightarrow y = z) \rightarrow \exists b \forall y(y \in b \leftrightarrow \exists x(x \in a \mathbin{\&} \Psi(x,y)))$. Given a set a, we can form a new set by replacing the members of *a* with other sets, provided that no member of *a* is replaced by more than one set.

There is a further axiom that is added to ZF to give ZFC. The further axiom can be shown to be independent of the other axioms. It can be given in various forms. I shall mention some of these equivalent forms, but make no attempt to show that they are equivalent.

Axiom 10: (Axiom of Choice) $\forall x(x \in z \rightarrow x \neq \varphi \ \& \ \forall y(y \in z \rightarrow x \cap y = \varphi \vee x = y)) \rightarrow \exists u \, \forall x \, \exists w(x \in z \rightarrow u \cap x = \{w\})$. If z is a set of nonempty sets that are pairwise disjoint, then there exists a 'choice set' u which has exactly one member in common with each member of z.

Alternative formulations of the Axiom of Choice include:

Zorn's Lemma: If $[P,<]$ is a partially ordered set with the property that all chains in P under the partial ordering $<$ are bounded above, then P has a maximal element.

Zermelo's Well-Ordering Theorem: Every set has a well-ordering. (A set is well ordered if there is a relation on the set that is transitive and irreflexive, that compares all of the members of the set, and under which every nonempty subset of the set has a first member under the relation.)

Hausdorff Maximal Principle: Any chain in a partially ordered set is included in a maximal chain.

Tukey-Teichmuller Lemma: Every set of finite character has a maximal element. (A set a is of finite character iff: $x \in a \leftrightarrow \forall y \subset x(\mathrm{Fin}(y) \rightarrow y \in a)$, where $\mathrm{Fin}(y)$ iff there is no one-one map of y with a proper subset of itself.)

There are various changes that we could make to our axioms. For instance, we could weaken Axiom 1 to allow individuals (ur-elements) other than the empty set, by requiring that Axiom 1 applies only to sets with members: $\exists z(z \in x) \ \& \ \forall z((z \in x \leftrightarrow z \in y) \rightarrow x = y)$.

We can also omit Axiom 2, thereby obtaining set theories without foundation. In set theory without foundation, there can be cycles of membership – $x \in x$, $x \in y \in x$, and so on. – and there can be infinite descents – $\cdots x_3 \in x_2 \in x_1 \in x_0$. Most of mathematics can be developed without Axiom 2, but many people find the resulting theory rather unintuitive.

There are various questions that are not answered by the axioms of ZFC. However, we need to say something about the definition of the ordinal and cardinal numbers in ZFC before we can describe (some of) these questions.

2.2 NUMBERS

There are various distinctions to be drawn among different kinds of numbers and different kinds of number systems. Perhaps the most fundamental distinction, at the level of kinds of numbers, is the distinction between ordinal numbers and cardinal numbers. *Ordinal* numbers are used to order sequences of things; *cardinal* numbers are used to quantify, to say how many things of a given kind there are. While we can identify ordinal numbers and cardinal numbers when we restrict our attention to finite arithmetic, we need to distinguish carefully between ordinal numbers and cardinal numbers when we turn our attention to transfinite arithmetic.[1]

At the level of systems of finite numbers, we should at least distinguish the *integers* (positive and negative), the *rational* numbers, the *real* numbers, and – though we shall not consider them at all – the *complex* numbers. When we turn our attention to transfinite numbers, we shall begin by considering the extension of the positive integers into the infinite (thereby obtaining the *Cantorian* theories of the transfinite ordinals and the transfinite cardinals). Later, we shall consider nonstandard theories that can be thought of as something like extensions of the rational numbers and the real numbers into the domain of the transfinite (nonstandard models of the real numbers, internal set theory, surreal numbers, and so forth). Moreover, we shall also give some brief attention to the different kinds of mathematical theories that can be erected on the basis of the various different kinds of number systems.

(a) Ordinals

There are different ways of defining the ordinals in set theory. We follow Zermelo and von Neumann. We need a preliminary definition. A set x is *transitive* if every member of x is a subset of x, that is, every

[1] Perhaps it might be more natural to speak of 'infinite arithmetic', but 'transfinite arithmetic' is the standard term.

member of a member of x is a member of x. Then a set x is an *ordinal* iff x is transitive and the $\in$–relation well-orders x. The ordinals are: φ, $\{\varphi\}$, $\{\varphi,\{\varphi\}\}$,....We represent them by their standard names: '0', '1', '2',....We can prove that the ordinals as thus defined do behave appropriately. We note that the least infinite ordinal – ω – is the set of all the finite ordinals.

(b) Cardinals

Given this definition of the ordinals, there is a natural way to define the cardinals. a is a cardinal number if a is an ordinal number that is not equinumerous to any smaller ordinal number, that is, if a is an initial ordinal. (Remember: Two set are equinumerous iff they can be put into one-one correspondence.) The smallest infinite cardinal – which also happens to be the smallest infinite ordinal, ω – is customarily called $\aleph_0$. The reason for having a distinct system of names will become apparent in a moment.

You might well be sceptical about the identification of numbers with certain sets. No matter how you do it – and you can do it in infinitely many different ways! – the identification has odd consequences, for example, that numbers are members of other numbers. This scepticism is the main theme of Benacerraf (1965). We shall not attempt to take up this issue here. The important point for our purposes is that there are collections of sets that are isomorphic in structure to the collections of ordinal and cardinal numbers. So the sets serve all of the purposes of mathematicians, whether or not the mooted identification is plausible.

2.3 CANTOR'S PARADISE

Given the standard axioms of set theory and the definitions of the ordinals and cardinals, a vast domain of transfinite or infinite numbers opens up to us. We shall give but the briefest indication of the contours of this domain, beginning with an exhibition of some of the lower reaches of the transfinite ordinals. After reviewing the Cantorian proof that the power set of a set – that is, the set of subsets of a set – always has greater cardinality than the set itself, we go on to look at the definition of arithmetical operations on the transfinite ordinals and cardinals, and then consider additional axioms that might be added to ZFC in order to resolve certain questions and in order to generate higher orders of transfinite ordinals and cardinals.

(a) Infinite Ordinals and Infinite Cardinals

Cantor was the first person systematically to explore the infinite ordinals and cardinals. I shall make some brief and unsystematic remarks about his accounts of the infinite ordinals and cardinals. Much of this discussion presupposes acceptance of the axiom of choice. (As an awful reminder, we shall recall what cardinal arithmetic looks like in the absence of this axiom. But this will be an exception to our usual practice.)

The ordinals begin as follows: $0, 1, 2, 3, \ldots, \omega, \omega + 1, \omega + 2, \ldots, \omega + \omega$ $(= \omega.2)$, $\omega.2 + 1, \omega.2 + 2, \ldots, \omega.3, \omega.4, \ldots\ldots \omega.\omega$ $(= \omega^2), \ldots\ldots \omega^3, \ldots\ldots \omega^4, \ldots\ldots \omega^\omega, \ldots\ldots {\omega^{\omega^\omega}}, \ldots\ldots \varepsilon_0$ (= limit of the sequence $\omega, \omega^\omega, \omega^{\omega^\omega}, \ldots$), ...

The cardinals are "the same" up to ω $(=\aleph_0)$. But what is the next cardinal? How far along the list of ordinals that we have already developed do we need to go in order to find new cardinals? Perhaps surprisingly, the answer is that you have to go very far indeed: All of the ordinals from ω to ε_0 are equinumerous. In fact, no arithmetic operations on ordinals can take us to higher initial ordinals – we need to involve the power set operation in some way or other.

Cantor showed that the power set of a set – that is, the set of all subsets of a set – has a higher cardinality than does the set itself. (The assumption that the members of a set can be put into one-one correspondence with the subsets of that set leads to a contradiction.) So, for example, the set of sets of integers has higher cardinality than the set of integers $(=\aleph_0)$. Since the set of sets of integers can be put into one-one correspondence with the real numbers, it turns out that the set of real numbers has a higher cardinality than the set of integers. The standard is to represent the cardinality of the real numbers by *c*.

(b) Cantorian Arguments

It will turn out to be useful to have examined the details of a couple of Cantor's proofs.

First, we review his method for showing that the cardinality of the rational numbers is the same as the cardinality of the natural numbers. Consider the Table 1 (in which $r = \sum_{i=1}^{N} i$ and $s = (\sum_{i=1}^{N-1} i) + 1$).

	1	2	3	4	5	6	7	8	...	N	...
1	1	2	4	7	11	16	22	29	...	s	...
2	3	5	8	12	17	23	30	38	...	$s+N+1$	...
3	6	9	13	18	24	31	39	48	...	$s+2N+3$	...
4	10	14	19	25	32	40	49	59	...	$s+3N+6$	...
5	15	20	26	33	41	50	60	71	...	$s+4N+10$	...
6	21	27	34	42	51	61	72	84	...	$s+5N+15$	...
7	28	35	43	52	62	73	85	98	...	$s+6N+21$	...
8	36	44	53	63	74	86	99	113	...	$s+7N+28$	...
...	...	...	...	...	...	...	...	...	...	...	...
N	r	$r+N$	$r+2N+1$	$r+3N+3$	$r+4N+6$	$r+5N+10$	$r+6N+15$	$r+7N+21$	...	$r+NN+s$	...
...	...	...	...	...	...	...	...	...	...	...	...

This table shows how to establish a mapping between the natural numbers that has the following properties: First, each natural number is mapped to a rational number; second, each rational number is mapped onto by at least one natural number. (For definiteness, let's suppose that the row number establishes the numerator of the target rational number and that the column number establishes the denominator of the target rational number. So, for example, under the defined mapping, 9 maps to 3/2.) This mapping establishes that the cardinality of the natural numbers is at least as great as the cardinality of the rational numbers. But it is easy to establish that the cardinality of the rational numbers is at least as great as the cardinality of the natural numbers. Whence it follows that the cardinality of the rational numbers is equal to the cardinality of the natural numbers: There are just as many natural numbers as there are rational numbers.

Second, we review Cantor's method for showing that the cardinality of the real numbers is strictly greater than the cardinality of the natural numbers. For purposes of *reductio*, suppose that the cardinality of the reals is the same as the cardinality of the natural numbers. If this is so, then we can make a list that pairs off the real numbers between 0 and 1 with the natural numbers, as follows (where d_{ij} is the *j*th digit in the decimal representation of the *i*th real number on our list):

1. $0.d_{11}d_{12}d_{13}d_{14}d_{15}\ldots d_{1n}\cdot\ldots$
2. $0.d_{21}d_{22}d_{23}d_{24}d_{25}\ldots d_{2n}\cdot\ldots.$
3. $0.d_{31}d_{32}d_{33}d_{34}d_{35}\ldots d_{3n}\cdot\ldots.$

.. ..

r $0.d_{r1}d_{r2}d_{r3}d_{r4}d_{r5}\ldots d_{rn}\cdot\ldots..$

.. ..

By hypothesis, every real number between 0 and 1 is on our list. But we can construct a real number $R = 0.d_1 d_2 d_3 d_4 d_5 \ldots d_n \ldots$ that is not on our list, as follows: For each digit d_n, let $d_n = d_{nn} + 1$ if $d_{nn} \in \{0, 1, 2, 3, 4, 5, 6, 7\}$ and let $d_n = d_{nn} - 1$ otherwise. Since R differs from r in the nth digit – and since R does not end with an infinite sequence of 9s or 0s – R is clearly a real number that is not on our list. So we cannot make a list that pairs off the natural numbers with the real numbers, contrary to the assumption that the cardinality of the real numbers is equal to the cardinality of the natural numbers. Since it is clear that the cardinality of the natural numbers cannot be greater than the cardinality of the reals (because the natural numbers are properly included amongst the real numbers), it follows that the cardinality of the real numbers is strictly greater than the cardinality of the natural numbers.

Third, we review Cantor's method for showing that the cardinality of the power set of a set is strictly greater than the cardinality of the set itself. For purposes of reductio, suppose that there is a set N that is such that the cardinality of the power set of N – that is, the cardinality of the set of subsets of members of N – is the same as the cardinality of the set N itself. If this is so, then we can pair off the members of the power set of N with the members of N: For each $s_i \in$ the power set of N, there is a unique member r_i $(= I(s_i)) \in N$, under our pairing function I from the power set of N to N; and for each $r_i \in N$, there is a unique member s_i $(= I^*(r_i))$ the power set of N under the inverse I^* of our pairing function I from the power set of N to N. (This inverse function is guaranteed to exist because, *ex hypothesi*, our mapping is one-one.) By hypothesis, then, each s_i in the power set of N is uniquely paired off with an $r_i \in N$ under the mappings I and I^*. But we can construct a member M of the power set of N that is not paired off with any member of N under I and I^*, as follows: For each $r_i \in N$, $r_i \in M$ iff $r_i \notin s_i$ $(= I^*(r_i))$. Plainly, by construction, M is a member of the power set of N that was not paired off with any of the members of N under our mapping; and this contradicts our initial assumption that there is such a pairing. Since it is clear that the cardinality of a set cannot be greater than the cardinality of the power set of that set – just consider any mapping that takes the unit set of each element of the set to itself – we can conclude that the cardinality of the power set of any set is strictly greater than the cardinality of that set itself.

(c) Arithmetic for Infinite Ordinals and Infinite Cardinals

We define Hartog's aleph function: $\aleph(x) = \{\alpha : \alpha \preceq x\}$, where '$\preceq$' denotes the 'has lower cardinality than' relation, and where x is infinite. We can then define the transfinite sequence of infinite initial ordinals by the following inductive definition: $\aleph_0 = \omega$; $\aleph_{\alpha+1} = \aleph(\aleph_\alpha)$; $\aleph_\lambda = \cup_{\beta<\lambda} \aleph_\beta$ if λ is a limit ordinal. This gives us all of the infinite cardinals, by our earlier definition.

Arithmetic for ordinals is based on the following rules:

$\alpha + 0 = \alpha$
$\alpha + (\beta + 1) = (\alpha + \beta) + 1$
$\alpha + \lambda = \cup_{\delta<\lambda} (\alpha + \delta)$, if λ is a limit ordinal
$\alpha.0 = 0$
$\alpha.(\beta + 1) = (\alpha + \beta) + \alpha$
$\alpha.\lambda = \cup_{\delta<\lambda} (\alpha.\delta)$, if λ is a limit ordinal
$\alpha^0 = 1$
$\alpha^{\beta+1} = \alpha\beta.\alpha$
$\alpha^\lambda = \cup_{\delta<\lambda}\alpha^\delta$, if λ is a limit ordinal

Notice that under these definitions, + and . are neither commutative nor distributive. We have, for example, $1 + \omega = \omega$; $2.\omega = \omega$; $2^\omega = \omega$. So we have some, but not all, of the usual features of addition, multiplication, and exponentiation reproduced in the case of transfinite ordinal arithmetic. Of course, we do not have inverse operations such as subtraction, division, extracting roots, or taking logarithms.

Arithmetic for cardinals can also be defined. (Here, again, we follow Drake (1974).) If we do not help ourselves to the axiom of choice, then, following Scott, we define card $(x) = \{y\colon y \sim x \,\&\, \forall z\colon z \sim x \rightarrow \rho(z) \geq \rho(y)\}$, where $\rho(x)$ is the rank of x (i.e., $\cup\{\rho(y) + 1\colon y \varepsilon x\}$), and give the following definitions:

1. Cardinal Addition: $\sum_{i\varepsilon S} m_i = \pi$ iff, for disjoint sets $(x_i)_{i\varepsilon S}$, card $(x_i) = m_i$ for each $i \varepsilon S$ and card $(\cup_{i\varepsilon S} x_i) = \pi$. (Here, $\cup_{i\varepsilon S} x_i$ is the set-theoretic union of the $(x_i)_{i\varepsilon S}$.)
2. Cardinal Multiplication: $\prod_{i\varepsilon S} m_i = \pi$ iff, for disjoint sets $(x_i)_{i\varepsilon S}$, card $(x_i) = m_i$ for each $i \varepsilon S$ and card $(X_{i\varepsilon S} x_i) = \pi$. (Here, $X_{i\varepsilon S} x_i$ is the Cartesian product of the $(x_i)_{i\varepsilon S}$.)
3. Cardinal Exponentiation: If σ, π, and ρ are cardinals, then $\sigma^{\pi} = \rho$ iff for sets x, y, z with card $x = \sigma$, card $y = \pi$, we have card $({}^{y}x) = z$. (Here, ${}^{y}x$ is the set of all functions from y into x.)

Since the defined sets are complex and lacking in nice properties, it is much more satisfactory to assume the axiom of choice and to define the cardinals in terms of the initial ordinals. For all ordinals $\geq \omega$, the cardinal operations $+$ and $\times$ are given by: card (α) + card (β) = card (α) $\times$ card (β) = card (max (α, β)). Given this definition, it is easy to show that each of addition and multiplication for cardinals is commutative, associative, and distributive and that exponentiation is well defined. We have, for example: $\aleph_0 + \aleph_0 = \aleph_0$; $\aleph_0 \times \aleph_0 = \aleph_0$; $\aleph_0 + \aleph_1 = \aleph_1$; $\aleph_0 \times \aleph_1 = \aleph_1$; and so forth.

(d) Additional Axioms?

As mentioned earlier, there are various questions that are not answered by the axioms of ZF(C). We are now in a position to identify some of these questions.

1. *The Generalised Continuum Hypothesis*: Is $2^{\aleph_\alpha} = \aleph_{\alpha+1}$ for every ordinal α? Cantor's Continuum Hypothesis gives a positive answer in the special case in which $\alpha = 0$ (i.e., it affirms that $2^{\aleph_0} = c = \aleph_1$); the Generalised Continuum Hypothesis gives an affirmative answer in all cases. Gödel showed that the Generalised Continuum Hypothesis cannot be refuted in ZFC. Cohen showed that the Generalised Continuum Hypothesis is

independent of ZFC. Many mathematicians now accept the Generalised Continuum Hypothesis, there is no interesting alternative, and there are many interesting results that can be proved if one assumes it.

2. *The Axiom of Constructibility*: Gödel called sets generated by a certain process (that he defined) "constructible". The axiom of constructibility claims that all sets are constructible (in Gödel's idiosyncratic sense). In the context of ZF, this axiom entails the axiom of choice, the axiom of foundation, and the generalised continuum hypothesis. There are interesting competitors to this axiom, for example, the axiom that claims that there are measurable cardinals.
3. *Axioms of Strong Infinity*: Following Fraenkel and others, we review the means available in ZFC for obtaining sets of larger and larger cardinality. The axiom of infinity guarantees the existence of denumerable sets (of cardinality $\aleph_0$). Using the power set axiom, we obtain sets of cardinalities: $2^{\aleph_0}$, $2^{2^{\aleph_0}}$, ... Now, consider the set $A = \{\omega, P\omega, PP\omega, \ldots\}$ where ω is the least infinite ordinal. The cardinality a of its union set $\cup A$ is greater than the cardinality of each of its members, that is, $> \aleph_0, > 2^{\aleph_0}, > 2^{2^{\aleph_0}}, \ldots$. By means of the power set operation, we now get the sets $P \cup A$, $PP \cup A, \ldots$, of cardinalities 2^a, 2^{2^a}, ... Then we consider the set $B = \{\cup A$, $P \cup A$, $PP \cup A, \ldots\}$: The cardinality b of this set is greater than all the cardinals considered thus far. And so on. We note (i) that the power set of a set of cardinality c has cardinality 2^c; and (ii) that the cardinality of the union set of a set D such that each $t \in d$ has the cardinality d_t is at most $\sum_{t\in D} d_t$. So a set of cardinality e cannot be obtained from sets of smaller cardinality by means of the operations of power set and union if (i) for every cardinal c such that $c < e$, we have $c < 2^e$; and (ii) for every indexed sum $\sum_{t\in D} d_t$ of cardinal numbers d_t such that for every $t \in d$, $d_t < e$ and $|D| < e$, we have $\sum_{t\in D} d_t < e$. We say that a cardinal is regular if it is infinite and not the sum of $< e$ cardinal numbers each of which is $< e$. We say that e is *inaccessible* if (i) $e > \aleph_0$; (ii) e is regular; (iii) for every $c < e$, $2^c < e$. If there are inaccessible cardinals, they are very big indeed. If ZFC is consistent, then one cannot prove in ZFC the existence of any inaccessible

cardinals. However, there is (at least so far) no proof in ZFC that there are no inaccessible cardinals. There are lots of axioms that assert the existence of inaccessible cardinals that have been studied.

4. *Axioms of Restriction*: An axiom of restriction, added to the formulation of a set theory, would say: There are no sets other than those whose existence follows directly from the axioms written down so far. Added to ZFC, this axiom would entail that there are no non-well-founded sets – that is, no sets in which there are cycles of membership or infinite descents of membership – and that there are no inaccessible cardinals. Friends of big infinities are unlikely to look fondly on axioms of restriction.

2.4 STANDARD ANALYSIS

What I am here calling 'standard analysis' is the theory of functions on the real numbers that was developed during the nineteenth century by Weierstrass and others. We shall briefly review the definition of the real numbers, the simplest analyses of the notions of continuity and convergence, and some elementary definitions of differentiation and integration. We shall apply these definitions infrequently in the course of our subsequent discussion, but we shall frequently need to be able to suppose that they are understood.

(a) Rational Numbers and Real Numbers

It is easy to get the rational numbers from the integers: The rationals are all numbers of the form m/n, where m and n are integers, $n \neq 0$. So, in the above formulation, we can just use ordered pairs of the sets that 'are' the integers in order to define the rationals. (Given this change, we then need to redefine the arithmetic operations so that they apply to the new 'numbers' that have been introduced. But this is a straightforward matter.) Note that, unlike the integers, the rational numbers are *dense*: Between any two distinct rational numbers, there is a third rational number, distinct from each. If $a/b < c/d$, where a, b, c, and d are all positive integers, then $a/b < (ad + cb)/2bd < c/d$.

There are two standard means of constructing the reals. Following Dedekind, we can take the real numbers to be nonempty proper initial segments of rationals that have no largest element, that is, sets of rational numbers $\{x_i\}_{i\in N}$ that have the following three properties: (i) there exists $k \in Q$ such that $x < k$ for all $x \in \{x_i\}_{i\in N}$; (ii) for each $x \in \{x_i\}_{i\in N}$, there exists $y \in \{x_i\}_{i\in N}$ such that $y > x$; and (iii) for each $x \in Q$, if $x \in \{x_i\}_{i\in N}$, then for all $y \in Q$ such that $y < x$, $y \in \{x_i\}_{i\in N}$. Or, following Cantor, we can take the reals to be equivalence classes of Cauchy sequences of rationals, that is, equivalence classes of sets of rational numbers of the form $\{x_i\}_{i\in N}$ for which, for any k, there is an m such that for all $n \geq m$, $|x_n - x_m| < 1/k$. It is tedious but straightforward to show that both of these constructions provide a complete field – that is, an ordered field in which every nonempty subset that is bounded above has a least upper bound – that is unique up to isomorphism.

(b) Continuity and Convergence

Given the reals, we can now define a mathematical notion of continuity: A function $f: \Re \rightarrow \Re$ is *continuous* at a point c provided that $\lim_{x\rightarrow c} f(x) = f(c)$, that is, provided that, for any $\varepsilon > 0$, there is a δ such that if $0 < |x - c| < \delta$, then $|f(x) - f(c)| < \varepsilon$. (This definition can be extended in a straightforward way to functions of more than one variable.)

The definition of continuity makes use of the mathematical concept of a *limit*. We can use this concept to make sense of the limits of infinite sequences and the sums of infinite sequences. An infinite sequence $s_1, s_2, \ldots, s_R, \ldots$ has the *limit L* provided that, for any $\varepsilon > 0$, there is an N such that $|s_R - L| < \varepsilon$, for all $R > N$. An infinite sequence $s_1, s_2, \ldots, s_R, \ldots$ has the *sum S* provided that, for any $\varepsilon > 0$, there is an N such that $|(\sum_{R=1}^{N} s_R) - S| < \varepsilon$ for all $R > N$.

Infinite sequences that have a limit under the above definition are said to be *convergent*. All other infinite sequences are *divergent*. There are different kinds of divergent sequences. Consider the differences among $1, 2, 3, \ldots$; $1, -1, 1, -1, \ldots$; $1, -2, 3, -4, \ldots$. (Do the second and third sequences have sums? If so, what are they?) The series of partial sums of the first sequence simply increases without limit as the number of terms increases. The series of partial sums of the second sequence oscillates between 1 and 0. And the series of partial sums of the third sequence oscillates between positive values that increase without limit, and negative values that increase without limit.[2]

(c) Differentiation

A function f: $\Re \to \Re$ has the first derivative $f'(a)$ at a just in case $\lim_{\delta x \to 0}$ $(f(a + \delta x) - f(a))/\delta x = f'(a)$. In general, $f'(x) = \lim_{\delta x \to 0}$ $(f(x + \delta x) - f(x))/\delta x$. Intuitively, one can think of the derivative function as the tangent function to a given function. Plainly enough, the derivative function can be defined only where a function is continuous; but the mere continuity of a function is not enough to guarantee that it is differentiable. The definition of differentiation admits of ready generalisation to functions of more than one variable and to higher orders (since the derivative function, in turn, may be differentiable). A function is *smooth* at a given point iff all of its derivatives – first-order, second-order, third-order, and so forth – are defined at that point. While it is sometimes very hard to calculate the derivative of a given function, and no less difficult to demonstrate from first principles that one function is the derivative of a second, there are, I think, few further conceptual difficulties involved in understanding differentiation.

(d) Integration

Integration is the inverse operation to differentiation. Intuitively, at least in the simplest case, an integral is an area under a graph. If we begin with a differentiable function $f(x)$, then it is a fundamental constraint on integration that $\int_a^b f'(x) \cdot dx = f(b) - f(a)$. However, there are several different – nonequivalent – definitions of integration.

The simplest integral is the Riemann integral. Again, we consider just the simplest case of a function f: $\Re \to \Re$. The integral of the function f between the points a and b, if it exists, is defined in the following way. Suppose that we divide the interval $[a, b]$ into n equal-sized subintervals x_i. Suppose further that $f(x_i)$ is the maximum value

[2] It is worth noting that our account of divergence for sequences can be extended to physical magnitudes in the following way. A physical magnitude M diverges with respect to a variable x at a value x_0 just in case that is a sequence of values of x – $x_1, \ldots, x_n, \ldots$ – that converges to x_0, for which the series of values of M – $M(x_1), \ldots, M(x_n), \ldots$ – diverges.

that f takes in the interval x_i, and the $g(x_i)$ is the minimum value that f takes in the interval x_i. Let $F_n = \sum_{i=1}^{n}((b-a)/n)\cdot f(x_i)$ and $G_n = \sum_{i=1}^{n}((b-a)/n)\cdot g(x_i)$. If $\lim_{n\to\infty}F_n$ and $\lim_{n\to\infty}G_n$ are both defined and $\lim_{n\to\infty}F_n = \lim_{n\to\infty}G_n = A$, then $\int_a^b f(x)\cdot dx = A$. This definition can, of course, be extended to functions of more than one variable. Moreover, this definition of definite integrals (on specified intervals) also can be extended readily to the case of indefinite integrals (in which an integral function is defined up to a constant of integration, or, in other words, a family of integral functions is defined).

2.5 NONSTANDARD NUMBERS

The theory of analysis presented in the previous section was developed in the nineteenth century. Unlike its precursors, it does without the notion of an infinitesimal, that is, a nonzero number that is smaller than any standard real number. The notion of an infinitesimal had been relied on during the early development of the differential calculus and was much criticised. In very recent times, however, the notion of an infinitesimal has made something of a comeback. We shall briefly review three recent developments of this idea: (1) nonstandard models for standard theories of real numbers, (2) internal set theory, and (3) the theory of surreal, or Conway, numbers. After that, we shall conclude with a brief presentation of some recent work in the area of finite mathematics, and, in particular, with the replication of classical mathematics in finite domains using finitary methods.

(a) Model Theory

The revival of serious interest in infinitesimals, and in the prospects for nonstandard analysis, begins with Robinson (1961; 1966). Robinson's work draws on some of the standard results in model theory that had been discovered during the preceding forty or so years. So we need to begin by reviewing these results. (Here, we follow closely the presentation in Boolos and Jeffrey (1980: 96–195).)

A *first-order language* contains the following vocabulary: the logical symbols – &, $\vee$, $\sim$, $\rightarrow$, $\leftrightarrow$, =, $\exists$, $\forall$, (,) – and denumerable stocks of variables, names, function symbols, predicate letters, and sentence letters.

There are standard rules for constructing the sentences of first-order languages from this primitive vocabulary.

An *interpretation* for a first-order language specifies five things: (i) a nonempty set – the *domain, universe,* or *universe of discourse* – that is the range of any variables that occur in sentences; (ii) for each name, an object in the domain (the designation, bearer, denotation, or reference of the name); (iii) for each function symbol, a function that, for some value of n, assigns a value in the domain to each n-tuple of arguments in the domain; (iv) for each predicate letter, a characteristic function, that, for some value of n, assigns a value in the set $\{T, F\}$ to each n-tuple of arguments in the domain; (v) for each sentence letter, a value in the set $\{T, F\}$.

An interpretation for a first-order language recursively determines a value from $\{T, F\}$ for every sentence in the language, according to the following rules:

1. $V(\sim S) = T$ iff $V(S) = F$.
2. $V(S \,\&\, R) = T$ iff $V(S) = V(R) = T$.
3. $V(S \vee R) = F$ iff $V(S) = V(R) = F$.
4. $V(S \rightarrow R) = F$ iff $V(S) = T$ and $V(R) = F$.
5. $V(S \leftrightarrow R) = T$ iff $V(S) = V(R)$.
6. $V(\forall xGx) = T$ iff $V_0^a\,(G_v a) = T$ for every o in the domain, where V_0^a is an interpretation that differs from V at most in that it assigns 0 to a.
7. $V(\exists xGx) = F$ iff $V_0^a(G_v a) = F$ for every o in the domain, where V_0^a is an interpretation that differs from V at most in that it assigns 0 to a.
8. $V(s = t) = T$ iff $V(s) = V(t)$.
9. $V(Rt_1 \ldots t_n) = T$ iff $\Phi(V(t_1) \ldots V(t_n)) = T$, where Φ is the characteristic function of the n-place predicate letter R in interpretation V, and the t_i are terms whose denotations are $V(t_i)$ in V.

A *model* of a sentence is an interpretation of that sentence under which that sentence is assigned the value T. A *model* of a set of sentences is an interpretation under which every sentence in that set is assigned the value T. A sentence S is *implied* by a set of sentences Δ (i.e., $\Delta \models S$) iff $V(S) = T$ for any V that is both a model of Δ and an interpretation of S. A set of sentences is *satisfiable* iff it has at least one model. (Note that Δ implies S iff $\Delta \cup \{\sim S\}$ is unsatisfiable.) Two sentences S and R are *logically equivalent* iff, for any V that interprets both S and R, $V(S) = V(R)$.

There are many different ways of constructing a *proof theory* – a system of *derivation* – that has the property that a given sentence S is derivable from a given set of sentences Δ ($\Delta \vdash S$) iff $\Delta \models S$, that is, iff Δ implies S. For present purposes, we need only suppose that we have selected a particular proof theory that is, indeed, sound and complete with respect to the class of all interpretations described above. Given our adequate proof theory, we will have the means for showing that a set of sentences is *inconsistent*, that is, allows the derivation of an explicit contradiction iff that set of sentences is unsatisfiable.

We define a *theory* to be a set of sentences that is closed under derivation: There is no sentence that can be derived from members of the set that is not a member of the set. The members of a theory are *theorems*. Note that we do not presuppose that some of the members of a theory are distinguished as the axioms of a theory, even though some theories can be given axiomatic presentations.

We say that two interpretations, V and W, are *isomorphic* just in case: (1) V and W are interpretations of the same language, (2) $V(S) = W(S)$ for any sentence letter S, and (3) there is a one-one mapping H from the domain of V to the domain of W that satisfies the following conditions: (i) if $V(N) = d$, for some name d, then $W(N) = H(d)$; if $V(F) = f$, for some n-place function symbol F, then $W(F) =$ the function g that is such that, for any $d_1, \ldots, d_n$, d in the domain of V, $f(d_1, \ldots, d_n) = d$ iff $g(H(d_1), \ldots, H(d_n)) = H(d)$; and (iii) if $V(P) = \Phi$, for some n-place predicate letter P, then $W(P)$ is the characteristic function Ψ that is such that, for any $d_1, \ldots, d_n$ in the domain of V, $\Phi(d_1, \ldots, d_n) = \Psi(H(d_1), \ldots, H(d_n))$. If any two models of a theory T are isomorphic, then the theory is *categorical*. If any two denumerable models of a theory T are isomorphic, then the theory is *aleph-null categorical*.

Key results in first-order predicate calculus that we are now in a position to state include the following.

1. *Compactness Theorem*: If a set of sentences is unsatisfiable, then some finite subset of those sentences is unsatisfiable.

2. *Downward Lowenheim-Skolem Theorem*: If a set of sentences has a model with a domain of any infinite cardinality, then it has a model with a denumerable domain.
3. *Upward Lowenheim-Skolem Theorem*: If a sentence has a model with a denumerable domain, then it has a model with a domain of any infinite cardinality.
4. *Arithmetic is not aleph-null categorical.*

For present purposes, the crucial result is the last: What this result says is that there are *nonstandard models of arithmetic* that have denumerable domains. These models contain only countably many members, but they are not isomorphic to the standard model of arithmetic. What do these models look like? Well, the elements of these models are linearly ordered by the "less than" relation. Under this ordering, there is an initial segment that is isomorphic to the natural numbers. Then, above this (according to the ordering), there is a dense collection of segments, each of which is isomorphic to the series of all of the integers (i.e., negative integers, zero, positive integers). That is, there is a sequence of segments, each isomorphic to the integers, where this sequence is of the same order type as the rational numbers. (Since a countable union of countable sets is countable, and since the rational numbers are countable, there are only countably many members in any nonstandard model for arithmetic.)

So far, we have achieved some understanding of the fact that there are nonstandard models that satisfy all of the standard claims of arithmetic, and of the way in which this fact can be demonstrated. Using more complex techniques – from set theory (as in Robinson (1966)) or model theory (as in Robinson (1961)) – it can be shown that there are also nonstandard models that satisfy all of the standard claims of the theory of real numbers. Since one of the standard claims of the theory of real numbers is that every nonzero element has a multiplicative inverse, it should come as no surprise that these nonstandard models of the theory of the real numbers contain both infinite elements and infinitesimal elements (related to each other as multiplicative inverses). Before we turn to an attempt to say something about what these nonstandard models of the real numbers are like, we shall consider an alternative formulation of Robinson's approach to nonstandard analysis that was developed in the 1970s by Nelson (1977; 1987) and others.

(b) Internal Set Theory

We start with ZFC and introduce a new, undefined one-place predicate Σ. We shall say that a formula in our extension of ZFC is *internal* iff it contains no occurrences of Σ (i.e., iff it is a formula of unextended ZFC); else, we shall say that a formula is *external*. Further, we introduce a new, defined one-place predicate **Fin**: x is Fin iff there is no bijection – one-one map – of x with a proper subset of itself. Finally, we introduce three new axioms and a rule that govern the behaviour of our new, undefined predicate, Σ, in the new system IST. (The simplest formula that contains the new predicate Σ, Σx, is to be read "x is standard" or "x is a standard set".)

First, the rule:

Set formation in IST: No external formulae may be used in the definition of subsets in IST.

Given this rule, it follows that, in IST, the axiom of subsets requires restatement: For any set a, there is a subset of a consisting of just those members of a that satisfy the condition Φ, *provided that* Φ *is internal*. We achieve this result by replacing the axiom of subsets with what we will call the new axiom of standardisation.

Second, then, the new axioms:

Transfer: Let $A(x, t_1, \ldots, t_k)$ be an internal formula with free variables $x, t_1, \ldots, t_k$, and no other free variables. Then $(\forall t_1\colon \Sigma t_1) \ldots (\forall t_k\colon \Sigma t_k)\ \{(\forall x\colon \Sigma x) A(x, t_1, \ldots, t_k) \rightarrow (\forall x) A(x, t_1, \ldots, t_k)\}$. (If we have constants – names – in IST, these must be sorted into those that are standard and those that are nonstandard, and we must insist, further, that $A(x, t_1, \ldots, t_k)$ contains no nonstandard constants.)

Idealisation: Let $B(x, y)$ be an internal formula with free variables x, y, and possibly others as well. Then $(\forall z\colon \Sigma z \text{ and Fin } z)\ [(\exists x)(\forall y \in z) B(x, y) \leftrightarrow (\exists x)(\forall y\colon \Sigma y) B(x, y)]$.

Standardisation: Let $C(z)$ be a formula – internal or external – with free variable z, and possibly other free variables as well. Then $(\forall x\colon \Sigma x)\ (\exists y\colon \Sigma y)\ (\forall z\colon \Sigma z)\ (z \in y \leftrightarrow (z \in x \mathbin{\&} C(z)))$.

Suppose that A is an internal sentence – that is, an internal formula in which there are no free variables – and let A_Σ be the sentence obtained by replacing each occurrence of a Σ-unrestricted quantifier (Qv) with an occurrence of a Σ-restricted quantifier $(Qv\colon \Sigma v)$. We call A_Σ the *relativisation of A to the standard sets.* It is easy to see that successive applications of Transfer establishes that $A \leftrightarrow A_\Sigma$. So, all of the theorems of ZFC continue to hold when they are relativised to the standard sets; and, in order to prove an internal theorem, it suffices to prove the relativisation of that theorem to the standard sets. One consequence of these results is that, whenever there is a unique x that satisfies an internal formula $A(v)$ whose only free variable is v, then x is a standard set. Hence, it follows that all of the uniquely specified objects of conventional mathematics are – or, at least, can be interpreted to be – standard sets. The set of all of the natural numbers, N, is standard, as is the set R of all of the real numbers. In IST, there is only one real number system, the system R that is described in conventional mathematics.

Using the new axioms of IST, it is relatively easy to show that

1. For any set x, all of the elements of x are standard iff x is a standard finite set.
2. There is a finite set f such that, for all standard x, $x \in f$.
3. Let $A(x, y)$ be a formula, either internal or external, with free variables x, y, and possibly others. If x and y are standard sets such that, for each standard element $z \in x$, there is a standard element $w \in y$ satisfying $A(z, w)$, then there is a standard function $f\colon x \rightarrow y$, such that, for all standard $z \in x$, $A(z, f(z))$.

From the first of these results, we see that every infinite set has a nonstandard element; so, for example, the set N of all the natural numbers contains nonstandard elements. Moreover, in understanding the second of these results, we recognise that any set f that contains all of the standard sets x cannot itself be standard.

Using the above results, it is easy to see that all of the following claims are true of N in IST:

1. 0 is standard
2. For all $n \in N$, if n is standard, then $n + 1$ is standard
3. There exists a nonstandard $n \in N$

4. Let $A(x)$ be a formula, either internal or external, that contains the free variable x. If $A(0)$, and if for all standard $n \in N$, $A(n) \rightarrow A(n+1)$, then for all standard $n \in N$, $A(n)$.

So, on this approach, it turns out that we are to suppose that N has the structure of the "nonstandard" models that we described in our earlier discussion of Robinson's work. While it is somewhat counterintuitive to suppose that the nonstandard elements were *always* part of the conventionally described numbers, there is a large pay-off for this supposition when we turn our attention to the real numbers.

We begin by introducing some useful external notions for the field R of the real numbers. A real number r is *infinitesimal* iff $|r| \leq \varepsilon$ for all $\varepsilon > 0$ (i.e., iff $|r| \leq 1/v$ for some nonstandard natural number v). (So 0 is the only standard infinitesimal.) A real number r is *limited* iff $|r| \leq v$ for some standard real number v; else, it is *unlimited*. It follows directly from Idealisation that there are nonzero infinitesimals and that there are unlimited real numbers.

If x and y are real numbers, then (1) x and y are *infinitely close* (or *nearly equal*) – $x \approx y$ – iff $x - y$ is infinitesimal; (2) x is *weakly less* than y – $x \leqq y$ – iff $x \leq y + a$ for some infinitesimal a; (3) x is *weakly greater* than y – $x \geqq y$ – iff $y \leqq x$; (4) x is *strongly less* than y – $x \ll y$ – iff $x < y$ and not $x \approx y$; (5) x is *strongly greater* than y – $x \gg y$ – iff $y \ll x$. As Nelson (1987: 17) says, it helps to visualise the relations $\approx$, $\leqq$, and $\ll$ on the real number line. To "the naked eye", $\approx$ looks like $=$, $\leqq$ looks like $\leq$, and $\ll$ looks like $<$.

The extended real line **Я** consists of R together with two other points, $-\infty$ and ∞. We write $-\infty < x < \infty$ for all x in R. For all x in R, $x \approx \infty$ iff x is positive and unlimited, $x \ll \infty$ iff not $x \approx \infty$, and $x \gg \infty$ iff not $x \approx -\infty$. So $|x| \ll \infty$ iff x is limited, and $|x| \approx \infty$ iff x is unlimited. (Note that $-\infty$ and ∞ are *not* elements of R. We introduce **Я** only to ease description of R. The extended reals conform to the following axioms: (i) $-\infty < x < \infty$; (ii) $x + \infty = \infty$, $x + (-\infty) = -\infty$; (iii) $x.\infty = \infty$, for $x > 0$; $x.(-\infty) = -\infty$, for $x < 0$; $0.\infty = \infty$; (iv) $\infty + \infty = \infty$; $-\infty + (-\infty) = -\infty$; (v) $\infty.(\pm\infty) = \pm\infty$; $-\infty.(\pm\infty) = \mp\infty$.)

Given the above definitions, it is easy to show, for example, that (1) $x \approx 0$ iff x is infinitesimal; (2) $x \approx 0$ iff for all $\varepsilon > 0$ $|x| \leq \varepsilon$; (3) infinitesimals are limited; (4) if $x \neq 0$, then $x \approx 0$ iff $1/x$ is unlimited;

(5) $|x| \approx \infty$ iff $1/x \approx 0$; (6) if x and y are limited, then so are $x + y$ and xy; (7) if x and y are infinitesimal, then so are $x + y$ and xy; (8) if $x \approx 0$ and $|y| \ll \infty$, then $xy \approx 0$; (9) $x \lesseqq y$ and $y \lesseqq x$ iff $x \approx y$; (10) if $x \approx y$ and $y \approx z$ then $x \approx z$.

A more demanding result that can be proved, given the earlier definitions, is that every limited real number is infinitely close to a unique standard real number. Given this result, for any limited real number r, we define the *standard part* of r – $\mathrm{st}(r)$ – to be the unique standard real number that is infinitely close to r. If a and b are standard real numbers and x is the closed interval $[a, b]$, then x is a limited real number and $\mathrm{st}(x) \in [a, b]$. Indeed, in general, if E is a standard closed and bounded subset of R and $x \in E$, then x is limited and $\mathrm{st}(x) \in E$.

One of the features of IST is that it often turns out that a complicated internal notion is equivalent, on standard sets, to a simple external notion. Consider, for example, continuity. We shall say that a function $f: R \rightarrow R$ is *continuous* at a point x iff for standard f and standard x, for all y, if $y \approx x$ then $f(y) \approx f(x)$. This definition is much easier to grasp than the standard ε-δ definition that we gave above.

Another of the features of IST is that it often turns out that a complex proof in ZFC corresponds to a much simpler proof in IST. Given the theorem (proven by Powell) that every internal theorem of IST is a theorem of ZFC, it follows that IST can be used freely in the proof of conventional theorems. It is this result that explains both the interest in and the utility of IST. The bulk of Nelson (1977) is taken up with the production of examples of results that are easily proven in IST but whose proof is far more elaborate in conventional mathematics. (Similarly, the aim of Nelson (1987) is to show how easy it is to lay the foundations for reasonably advanced theory of probability using a little bit of nonstandard analysis.) Of course, as Nelson points out, Powell's theorem also establishes that, for the purposes of conventional mathematics, one *can* avoid the methods of IST.

The discussion to this point still leaves incomplete the task of describing a nonstandard model of the real numbers. Rather than attacking this task directly, let's change tack again and describe a quite different approach to the construction of a field of numbers that contains both infinitesimal and infinite elements.

(c) Conway Numbers

Conway (1976) provides an extraordinarily elegant construction of a nonstandard field of numbers. I shall first give Conway's account of the construction, and then describe some of the features of the resulting field. There are various other ways in which Conway numbers (or, as they are sometimes known, *surreal numbers*) can be represented – as, for example, in the work of Knuth (1974) and Gonshor (1986). The field *No* that Conway describes is very large; its domain is a proper class. As Conway notes, it is possible to see this construction as a marriage of Dedekind's construction of the real numbers from the rational numbers and Cantor's construction of the infinite ordinals, as discussed in sections 2.2, 2.3, and 2.4 above.

The **construction** of the numbers is summarised in a single principle: If L, R are any two sets of numbers, and no member of L is $\geq$ any member of R, then there is a number $\{L|R\}$. All of the numbers in *No* are constructed according to this principle. The first number that is constructed is, of course $\{|\}$, where $L = R = \varphi$. This number we call 0; it turns out to have all of the properties that we would expect 0 to have.

To facilitate description, we follow Conway in introducing the convention that, if $x = \{L|R\}$, then $x = \{x^L|x^R\}$, where x^L and x^R are representative elements from L and R. Similarly, we allow ourselves to write $x = \{a, b, c, \ldots | d, e, f, \ldots\}$, where $a, b, c, \ldots$ are representative elements from L, and $d, e, f, \ldots$ are representative elements from R. We then make the following **definitions**:

1. $x \geq y$ iff no $x^R \leq y$ and $x \leq$ no y^L.
2. $x \leq y$ iff $y \geq x$.
3. $x = y$ iff $x \geq y$ and $y \geq x$.
4. $x > y$ iff $x \geq y$ and not $y \geq x$.
5. $x + y = \{x^L + y, x + y^L | x^R + y, x + y^R\}$
6. $-x = \{-x^R | -x^L\}$
7. $x.y = \{x^Ly + xy^L - x^Ly^L, x^Ry + xy^R - x^Ry^R | x^Ly + xy^R - x^Ly^R, x^Ry + xy^L - x^Ry^L\}$

The real-closed field that satisfies these definitions has a very rich – and, indeed, remarkable – structure. There are various features of this system that make it difficult, at least at first sight, to appreciate just how rich this structure is. One point that must be noted is that, in this system, equality is a defined relation: There are many apparently different definitions that produce the very same number. Consequently, we distinguish between the form $\{L \mid R\}$ and the number that it "represents". Despite this fact, it turns out that the field that has been defined is a proper class.

Following Conway, we shall think of the construction of the numbers as a process that happens in stages. At the first stage, as already noted, we get the number $0 = \{|\}$. At the second stage, we get the numbers $1 = \{0|\}$ and $-1 = \{|0\}$. At the third stage, we get the numbers $2 = \{0, 1\ |\} = \{1|\}$, $\frac{1}{2} = \{0|1\}$, $-\frac{1}{2} = \{-1|0\}$, and $-2 = \{|-1\}$. At the fourth stage, we get the numbers $3 = \{2|\}$, $\frac{3}{2} = \{1|2\}$, $\frac{3}{4} = \{\frac{1}{2}|1\}$, $\frac{1}{4} = \{0|\frac{1}{2}\}$, $-\frac{1}{4} = \{-\frac{1}{2}|0\}$, $-\frac{3}{4} = \{-1|-\frac{1}{2}\}$, $-\frac{3}{2} = \{-2|-1\}$, $-3 = \{|-2\}$. And so on. At the ωth stage, we get such numbers as $-\omega = \{|0, -1, -2, -3, \ldots\}$, $\frac{1}{\omega} = \{0|1, \frac{1}{2}, \frac{1}{4}, \frac{1}{8}, \ldots\}$, $\frac{1}{3} = \{\frac{1}{4}, \frac{5}{16}, \frac{21}{64}, \ldots | \frac{1}{2}, \frac{3}{8}, \frac{11}{32}, \ldots\}$, $1 - \frac{1}{\omega} = \{\frac{1}{2}, \frac{3}{4}, \frac{7}{8}, \ldots |1\}$, $\omega = \{0, 1, 2, 3, \ldots |\}$. At the $\omega + 1$th stage, we get such numbers as $-(\omega + 1) = \{|0, -1, -2, -3, \ldots, -\omega\}$, $\frac{1}{2\omega} = \{0| \frac{1}{\omega}\}$, $\frac{2}{\omega} = \{\frac{1}{\omega}|1, \frac{1}{2}, \frac{1}{4}, \ldots\}$, $2 - \frac{1}{\omega} = \{\frac{3}{2}, \frac{7}{4}, \frac{15}{8}, \ldots |2\}$, $2 + \frac{1}{\omega} = \{2| \frac{5}{2}, \frac{9}{4}, \frac{17}{8}, \ldots\}$, $\omega - 1 = \{0, 1, 2, 3, \ldots |\omega\}$, $\omega + 1 = \{0, 1, 2, 3, \ldots, \omega|\}$. At the $\omega.2$th stage, we get such numbers as $\omega.2 = \{|-\omega, -(\omega + 1), -(\omega + 2), |(\omega + 3), \ldots\}$, $\frac{1}{\omega^2} = \{0| \frac{1}{\omega,} \frac{1}{2\omega,} \frac{1}{4\omega,} \ldots\}$, $\frac{\omega}{2} = \{0, 1, 2, 3, \ldots | \omega, \omega - 1, \omega - 2, \omega - 3, \ldots\}$, $\omega.2 = \{\omega, \omega + 1, \omega + 2, \omega + 3, \ldots |\}$. And so forth. Since all of the real numbers defined by Dedekind can be defined as Dedekind sections of the dyadic rational numbers – that is, numbers of the form $\frac{m}{2n}$, where m and n are integers – all of the standard real numbers, including such numbers as $\sqrt{2}$, e, and π, are defined by the ωth stage. One of the square roots of ω is $\{0, 1, 2, 3, \ldots |\omega, \frac{\omega}{2}, \frac{\omega}{4}, \frac{\omega}{8}, \ldots\}$. Numbers such as ${}^3\sqrt{(\omega + 1)} - \pi/\omega$ are eventually constructed.

Proving that *No* forms a totally ordered field requires some work. Conway shows that the definitions of order, equality, addition, negation, and multiplication yield all of the standard properties and that order, equality, addition, negation, and multiplication interact as they ought. Conway notes that we can define $y = \{0, [1 + (x^R - x)y^L]/x^R, [1 + (x^L - x)y^R]/x^L | [1 + (x^L - x)y^L]/x^L, [1 + (x^R - x)y^R]/x^R\}$, and show that y is a number such that $xy = 1$. Thus, division can also be defined for *No*. With more work, it can be shown that there is a good sense in which *No* contains both the real numbers and the standard infinite ordinals. It can also be shown that every number has a unique 'normal form' expression of the form $\Sigma_{\beta<\alpha}\, \omega^{y\beta}.r_\beta$, where α is an ordinal, the $r_\beta (\beta < \alpha)$ are nonzero reals, and the numbers y_β form a descending sequence of numbers (and that every expression of this form denotes a number).

Following the construction of *No*, Conway proposes that we can consider Dedekind sections of *No* itself. Following Conway out onto "the ice", we consider $\Xi = [L|R]$, where L and R are disjoint, and *No* is the union of L and R. If Ξ is a *gap* and x is a number, then $x + \Xi$ is the gap $[x + L|\ x + R]$, $-\Xi$ is the gap $[-R \mid -L]$ and ω^{Ξ} is the gap $[L'|\ R']$, where L' contains all numbers $\omega^{l}.s$ and R' all numbers $\omega^{r}.s$ for $l \in L$, $r \in R$ and s any positive real number.

On is the gap $[No\,|]$ at the end of the number line; $1/On$ is the gap between 0 and all positive numbers; ∞ is the gap between the reals and the positive infinite numbers; $\frac{1}{\infty}$ is the gap between the infinitesimals and the positive reals. (All gaps have one of the following two forms: $\sum_{\beta \in On} \omega^{x}\beta.r_\beta$ and $\sum_{\beta < \alpha} \omega^{x_\beta} r_\beta \pm \omega^{\Xi}$, where in each case x_β is a decreasing sequence and each r_β is a nonzero real number, and in the second case Ξ is a gap $[L'|\ R']$ for which R' contains all the $x_\beta (\beta < \alpha)$.)

There is much more to be said about the algebra and analysis of Conway numbers. However, we close here with the observation – again taken from Conway – that, while it would be possible to use small subfields of *No* as a vehicle for the techniques of nonstandard analysis developed by Robinson and Nelson, there is not much point in doing so: It is much easier to use the models that Robinson's work produces than it is to try to carve such models out of *No*. On the other hand, it should also be noted that the normal form expressions for Conway numbers do suggest a way of thinking about nonstandard models for the real numbers: Each number should have an expression of the form $\sum_{\beta \in R} \omega^{\beta}.r_\beta$ where the r_β are standard real numbers, and the numbers in the model should collectively form a field.

(d) Finite Mathematics

I learnt about the work of Mycielski (1981; 1986) from Lavine (1994); I shall follow Lavine's presentation of these ideas fairly closely. The basic result that Mycielski derives is that, for any set T of sentences, there is another set of sentences Fin(T) that has certain important finitary properties: In particular, if T is a consistent theory, then Fin (T) is a theory in which every finite set of sentences has a finite model. Moreover, when we turn our attention to ZFC, we can show – using only finitistically acceptable methods – that ZFC is consistent iff every finite subset of Fin (ZFC) has a finite *natural* model. (We explain later exactly how this claim is to be interpreted.)

Suppose we begin with a theory T that is couched in the language of first-order predicate calculus. Then the vocabulary of Fin (T) will be the vocabulary of T together with monadic predicate symbols Ω_q, $q \in Q$. (Roughly, $\Omega_q x$ will be true if x belongs to a suitable *indefinitely large* – but nonetheless finite – domain of objects.)

We shall say that a formula φ of the language of Fin (T) is *regular* iff (1) it is bounded, that is, it contains no quantifiers that are not restricted by the Ω_q; and (2) if Ω_q occurs with the scope of a quantifier that is restricted by Ω_p in φ, then $p < q$. We shall also say that a formula φ of the language of Fin (T) is a *relativisation* of a formula ψ of the language of T iff ψ can be obtained from φ by deleting all of the bounds or restrictions, that is, by changing $(\exists x\colon \Omega_p x)$ to $(\exists x)$ and $(\forall x\colon \Omega_p x)$ to $(\forall x)$, for all variable x and all subscripts p, wherever they occur in φ.

Roughly, each instance of each of the following schemas is an axiom of Fin (T); more exactly, the predicate Fin (T) holds of any instance of each of the following schemas:

1. $\Omega_p c$, for each constant symbol c in the vocabulary of T.
2. $(\forall x_1 \colon \Omega_p x_1) \ldots (\forall x_n \colon \Omega_p x_n) \Omega_q f(x_1 \ldots x_n)$, for each function symbol f in the vocabulary of T, and $p < q$.
3. $(\forall x\colon \Omega_p x) \Omega_q x$, for $p < q$.
4. $(\forall x_1 \colon \Omega_p x_1) \ldots (\forall x_n \colon \Omega_p x_n)\ ((\forall x\colon \Omega_q x)\varphi \leftrightarrow (\forall x\colon \Omega_r x)\varphi)$ for $p < q$, $p < r$, $r < s$ for all s such that Ω_s appears in φ, φ regular, and the free variable of φ among $x, x_1, \ldots, x_n$.

Intuitively, these axioms give necessary and sufficient conditions for the Ω_q to be indefinitely large, and for Ω_q to be indefinitely large with respect to Ω_p whenever $p < q$.

We shall say that an occurrence of a quantifier in a formula is *general* iff either the quantifier that occurs is universal and it occurs in the formula positively or the quantifier that occurs is existential and it occurs in the formula negatively. (For formulae that contain no occurrences of $\rightarrow$ and $\leftrightarrow$, an occurrence of a quantifier is *negative* iff it lies in the scope of an odd number of negation signs, and *positive* iff it is not negative. The extension of this definition to the excluded cases is straightforward but tedious.) We shall say that an occurrence of a quantifier in a formula is *restricted* iff either the quantifier that occurs is existential and it occurs in the formula positively or the quantifier that occurs is universal and it occurs in the formula negatively. Finally, we shall say that a formula φ in the language of Fin(T) is *semi-regular* iff (1) every quantifier in φ is bounded by a Ω_q; (2) for all q, if Ω_q occurs in the scope of a quantifier bounded by Ω_p, then $p \leq q$; and (3) for all q, if Ω_q occurs in the scope of a quantifier bounded by Ω_p, and Ω_q is the bound of a quantifier, and the occurrences of the quantifiers bounded by Ω_p and Ω_q are of distinct types – that is, one is general and the other is restricted – then $p < q$.

Fin(T) consists of Axioms (1) to (4), together with semi-regular relativisations of the sentences of T. The key results about Fin(T) are the following two theorems, each of which can be proven in a primitive recursive system that is widely agreed to be free of any non-finitary commitments.

Theorem 1: If φ is a sentence in the language of T and φ' is a regular relativisation of φ, then φ is a theorem of T iff φ' is a theorem of Fin(T).

Theorem 2: T is consistent iff every finite subset of Fin(T) has a finite model.

There two results do not guarantee that, in general, a theory T is consistent iff every finite subset of Fin(T) has a finite and intuitively reasonable – that is, natural – model. Moreover, as Lavine (1994: 277) argues, it seems that one cannot get this stronger general result using finitistically acceptable methods. However, when we turn out attention to Fin(ZFC), we find that we can get this stronger result for a plausible definition of natural models of Fin(ZFC).

Before we describe Fin(ZFC), we need some definitions. A set is *pure* iff it, and its members, and their members, and so on, are free of ur-elements. A set is *hereditarily finite* iff it, and its members, and their members, and so on, are finite. A set is an *hfpset* iff it is both hereditarily finite and pure.

The vocabulary of Fin(ZFC) consists of a binary relation symbol = for identity; a binary relation symbol ∈ for membership; a constant symbol φ for the empty set; a binary function symbol ; for the "union with singleton" function – $x; y$ is thus equivalent to $x \cup \{y\}$ – and the unary predicate symbols Ω_q, $p \in Q$ for indefinitely large hfpsets.

The axioms of Fin(ZFC) consists of Axioms (1) to (4) above – the axioms of indefinitely large size – together with some appropriate axioms for identity, and semi-regular relativisations of the axioms of ZFC, including the definitions of φ and ;. The most interesting axiom of Fin (ZFC) is the *Axiom of a Zillion* – the semi-regular relativisation of the Axiom of Infinity in ZFC – which says that $(\exists x{:}\ \Omega_0 x)(\varphi \in x \,\&\, (\forall y{:}\ \Omega_1 y)(y \in x \rightarrow y;\, y \in x)$. Intuitively, this axiom says that the Ωs are not transitive: There are numbers that are 'available to us', but that are not 'available to us from below'.

Let us say that a model of a set of sentences in Fin(ZFC) is a *finite natural model* iff the elements of the model are hfpsets, and φ, ∈, and ; are given their intended interpretations in the model. The key result that can be proven, using finitistically acceptable methods, is this:

Theorem 3: ZFC is consistent iff every finite subset of Fin(ZFC) has a finite natural model.

One might have hoped to be able to show that Fin(ZFC) has a finite natural model. While this cannot be done, it seems right to follow Lavine (1994: 306n55) in observing that it is hardly in the spirit of finite mathematics to ask for such a model (even though it is very much in the spirit of ordinary set-theoretic mathematics to ask for a standard model of ZFC).

One of the most interesting general points that arises is that the Mycielskian theory of indefinitely small quantities turns out to have numerous points of contact with the ideas that Leibniz used in developing the theory of calculus. Finite mathematics is yet another nonstandard way of doing analysis that delivers back the very same range of mathematical results and mathematical tools, though often in a form that is intuitively easier to grasp.

3

Some Cases Discussed

There are various different strategies that friends of large and small denumerable, physical infinities can pursue in the face of the problem cases presented in the first chapter of this book. Perhaps the single most important strategy that friends of large and small denumerable, physical infinities can pursue is simply to *outsmart*[1] those who present these problem cases for consideration: In many cases, these allegedly absurd situations are just what one ought to expect if there were large and small denumerable, physical infinities. Another important strategy that crops up repeatedly is consideration of the effects of altering the order of quantifiers in an apparently problematic claim. However, it is important to recognise that there are other strategies that need to be pursued as well: Some of the details of the stories embody genuine confusions that need to be cleared up. No one – whether friend or foe of large and small denumerable, physical infinities – wants to deny that it is possible to tell *inconsistent* stories about large and small denumerable, physical infinities. It is, after all, possible to tell inconsistent stories about anything you please. The question at issue is whether it is possible to tell consistent stories involving large and small denumerable, physical infinities – and so the allegedly problematic cases

[1] *Outsmart,* v. To embrace the conclusion of one's opponent's *reductio ad absurdum* argument. "They thought they had me, but I outsmarted them. I agreed that it is sometimes just to hang an innocent man." Also *smart,* v. To argue against someone until what is going on in him is like what would be going on in him had he sat on a tack. "That smarts!" (Daniel Dennett, *The Philosophers' Lexicon.*)

before us may need to be amended in order to remove merely extraneous inconsistencies.

3.1 AL-GHAZALI'S PROBLEM

To discuss Al-Ghazali's objection to large, denumerable, physical infinities, we need to begin with the distinction between ordinal and cardinal numbers. Remember that ordinal numbers are used to order sequences of things, whereas cardinal numbers are used to quantify, to say how many things of a given kind there are. In finite cases, ordinal numbering and cardinal numbering 'coincide': No matter how you order the things that you count, the final ordinal at which you arrive gives you the cardinal number of the collection. So, for example, if I have six apples, I can count 'first apple', 'second apple', . . . , 'sixth apple' in any order, and arrive at the conclusion that there are six apples in the collection. Moreover, in finite cases, any proper subset of a set must have fewer members than the set. If I take some – but not all – of the apples, then I must take somewhere between one and five apples. However, as we learned in our discussion of Cantor's paradise, infinite collections are different: In infinite collections, ordinal numbering gives different results depending on the order in which the members of the collection are taken; consequently, it is not possible to read off the cardinal number directly from any ordinal numbering (there can be no 'coincidence' between ordinal and cardinal numbers). Moreover, according to Cantor, the principle that any proper subset of a set must have strictly smaller cardinality than the set should be given up.

Now, consider the case that is described. There is a natural way of assigning ordinal numbers to the revolutions of the earth and Jupiter – based on the natural way of assigning ordinal numbers to succeeding years – according to which, in finite cases, the earth makes thirteen times as many revolutions as Jupiter does (i.e., according to which the cardinal number of revolutions of the earth is thirteen times the cardinal number of revolutions of Jupiter). Perhaps there are other (less natural) ways of assigning ordinal numbers to the revolutions of the earth and Jupiter according to which there can be any relation one pleases between the cardinal numbers of revolutions of the earth and Jupiter in finite cases – that is, perhaps we can gerrymander the notion of 'same time interval' in any manner we please – but nonetheless it does seem straightforwardly true that the earth makes thirteen times as many revolutions as Jupiter (on average).

Once we move to the infinite case, however, things are quite different. Since there is no 'coincidence' between ordinal and cardinal numbers, the fact that the natural ordering entails that the cardinal number of revolutions of the earth is thirteen times the cardinal number of revolutions of Jupiter in finite cases (on average) has no bearing at all on the question of the relation between the cardinal number of rotations of the earth and Jupiter in the infinite case. To answer the question 'How many rotations does planet x make in infinite time?', we need a notion of cardinal numbers that is appropriate in the infinite case. Cantor's suggestion is that collections that can be put into one-one correspondence are the same size (i.e., have the same cardinality). Since the rotations of Jupiter and the rotations of the earth can be put into one-one correspondence with the integers (and, indeed, with one another), it turns out that – under Cantor's criterion – the cardinal number of rotations of the earth and Jupiter in infinite time is the same, viz $\aleph_0$. So, on Cantor's account, it turns out that the earth and Jupiter make the same number of rotations in infinite time.

I suppose that one might be tempted to object that, on the Cantorian theory, it must be true that the earth makes thirteen times as many rotations as Jupiter, since $13.\aleph_0 = \aleph_0$. But, of course, if we take this line, then we have just as much reason to say that the earth makes n times as many rotations as Jupiter (for any $n \in N$), and just as much reason to say that the earth makes $1/n$ times as many rotations as Jupiter (for any $n \in N$). Consequently, if we take this line, then there is nothing left of Al-Ghazali's objection to large, denumerable, physical infinities. Since the cardinality of each of the sets of rotations is $\aleph_0$, there is one strict sense in which the two planets make the same number of rotations in infinite time. But since for finite N, $N.\aleph_0 = \aleph_0$, there is another (less strict) sense in which no sentence of the form 'in infinite time, the earth makes N times as many rotations as Jupiter makes' is false – and yet there is nothing contradictory or objectionable about this fact.

Perhaps it will be objected that there must be something more to the idea that the earth makes thirteen times as many rotations as Jupiter even in infinite time. For consider the limit as t tends to infinity of the cardinal number of rotations made by the earth in period t divided by the cardinal number of rotations made by Jupiter in period *t*, that is, $\lim_{t\to\infty}$ (rotations of earth in time *t* / rotations of Jupiter in time *t*). Plainly, that limit is 13; and surely this shows that the earth makes thirteen times as many rotations as Jupiter, even in infinite time.

There is no disputing that this limit is, indeed, thirteen. Moreover, it seems reasonable to allow that this argument can be taken to establish that there is *a* good sense in which the earth makes thirteen times as many rotations as Jupiter even in infinite time. But, even if so, there is no way that this resurrects Al-Ghazali's objection to large, denumerable, physical infinities – for, at best, we now have *one* sense in which the earth makes thirteen times as many rotations as Jupiter does in infinite time, and *another* sense in which either the earth makes the same number of rotations as Jupiter does in infinite time or there is no nonarbitrary answer to the question of how many more times the earth rotates than Jupiter does in infinite time. Understood in this way, Al-Ghazali's objection simply involves an *equivocation* on the notion of 'making the same number of rotations as' – an equivocation that is harmless in finite cases, but not in infinite cases. (If you reject Cantor's account of the infinite cardinals, then you actually have no justification at all for claiming that the earth and Jupiter make the *same* number of rotations in infinite time, until you provide an alternative – clear and consistent! – account of the cardinal arithmetic that is obeyed by infinite collections.)

3.2 HILBERT'S HOTEL

If we suppose that signals can travel only at finite speeds, and if we suppose that people and hotel rooms have a constant, finite size, then we shall not find it difficult to respond to the allegedly problematic scenarios that are described in the case of Hilbert's Hotel.

Suppose that the hotel is, indeed, full – there are people in every room – and that one new guest arrives. There is surely no problem involved in placing the new guest in room 1, moving the guest in room 1 to room 2, moving the guest in room 2 to room 3, and so on. But, plainly enough, other guests will die (or move out) long before they are asked to change rooms. Once this is seen, we can note that – for this particular problem, namely, accommodating a new guest in a hotel that has no empty rooms – the very same strategy could be used if the hotel were finite but extremely large. Of course, those guests who are asked to change rooms in the middle of the night will not be happy – but this doesn't count at all against the feasibility of making accommodation time for the new guest by subtracting a small amount of accommodation time for each of a large number of already accommodated guests.

The general point to be made here is that mere acceptance of the possibility of a hotel with infinitely many rooms does not commit one to acceptance of the possibility of manipulating all of the infinitely many rooms in a finite amount of time. For all that has been argued so far, it might be that one can accept that there can be a hotel with infinitely many rooms while also denying that one can accommodate a new guest by moving the occupants of room N to room $N+1$ (for all N).

Suppose, for example, that we live on a plain that extends to infinity in all directions. Suppose, further, that there is a building, with rectangular cross-section, which has a façade at a given location, and then extends to infinity from that façade. The rooms in the hotel may be supposed to be assembled into groups of one hundred, each governed by its own sub-reception. The sub-receptions, in turn, may be supposed to belong to groups of one hundred, each governed by an administrative office (the first of which will thus be about 10,000 rooms from the façade). These administrative offices, in turn, may be supposed to belong to groups of one hundred, and so on.[2] If a guest turns up to the sub-reception nearest to the façade at a time at which there are no unoccupied rooms in the hotel, then it may well be possible to accommodate this guest by slightly inconveniencing many other guests – but there is nothing at all in this story that forces us to allow that the guest can be accommodated by moving the occupants in room N to room $N+1$ (for all N).

Suppose we grant that the hotel might be constructed in such a way as to prohibit the various manoeuvres that are taken to be problematic by some foes of large, denumerable, physical infinities. Plainly, it does

[2] As we ascend to higher levels of administration, the amount of control that they exert will plainly diminish – since it will take longer and longer for signals to pass between the units that are joined together) – except, perhaps, over very long periods of time. This does not seem to me to amount to a reason for denying that we have a single hotel.

not follow that the hotel cannot be constructed in such a way as to permit these various manoeuvres. For instance, we might suppose that the hotel is constructed according to the following plan. The hotel is a skyscraper, in which each floor is half the size of the previous floor. Moreover, inside the hotel, things halve in size as they move up from one floor to the next; and the elevator – from the standpoint of those inside the hotel – doubles its average speed as it passes from one floor to the next, as do all other things that are in motion. Given these amendments – or, at any rate, given these *kinds* of amendments – such things as the checking out of infinitely many guests can be accomplished in finite time. Of course, there are various ways in which this kind of story contradicts known physics – for example, it supposes that there is no smallest quantum of energy or matter, that there is no upper limit to particle velocities, that matter is stable under arbitrarily large accelerations and decelerations, and so forth – but it should not be supposed that this is a reason for denying that the envisaged scenario is metaphysically possible.

I have not tried very hard to give a detailed account of a hotel that will permit the checking out of infinitely many guests in a finite amount of time. While I am fairly confident that this could be done, it is not necessary for present purposes. For the foes of large, denumerable, physical infinities clearly face a dilemma at this point. On the one hand, if there is a way of carrying out such a detailed account, then the friend of large, denumerable, physical infinities wins by outsmarting his foes: There can, after all, be a hotel in which infinitely many new guests are accommodated, even though all rooms are full, via the simple expedient of moving the guests in room N to room $2N$ (for all N). On the other hand, if there is no way of carrying out such a detailed account, then the friend of large, denumerable, physical infinities wins by claiming that, despite the fact that there can be a hotel with infinitely many rooms, the various manoeuvres that the foe of large, denumerable, physical infinities takes to be impossible are, indeed, impossible.

3.3 CRAIG'S LIBRARY

The case of the infinite library is due to Craig (1979a). According to Craig, the kinds of questions that he raises about the infinite library are sufficient to establish that there could not be a large, denumerable, physical infinity. While the details of the case do not raise any issues that do not also arise in the case of Hilbert's Hotel, there will be some value in looking more closely at the details of Craig's arguments.

The *first* point that Craig makes is that we would not believe someone who told us that there is a library that contains a large, denumerable infinity of books. Suppose, for example, that all of the books in the library are either red or black, and that the books alternate in colour so that it is never the case that there are two red books that are adjacent on a shelf, and it is never the case that there are two black books that are adjacent on a shelf. Craig asks: 'Would we believe someone who told us that the number of red books in the library is the same as the number of red books plus the number of black books?' If we believe that the library contains a denumerable infinity of red books and a denumerable infinity of black books – which is easy enough to believe if we believe that there can be a library that contains a large, denumerable infinity of books – then there is no difficulty at all in believing that the number of red books in the library is the same as the number of red books plus the number of black books; after all, this is just what consistency requires! So the question that Craig raises here is merely whether we could believe that there is a library that contains a large, denumerable infinity of books. If we take this to be a question about what it could be reasonable for us to believe, then it is not clear that it should be given an affirmative answer; it clearly requires work to describe circumstances in which one has good reason to believe that a library contains a denumerable infinity – as opposed to a very large finite number – of books. However, our primary question is about whether there could *be* a library that contains a denumerable infinity of books – and the answer to that question does not turn at all on whether it is possible for us to have good reason to believe that there is a library that contains a denumerable infinity of books. If someone were to say to me that there is a library that contains a denumerable infinity of books, I would reject their testimony, but that does not in any way commit me to the claim that there could not be a library that contains a denumerable infinity of books.

The *second* point that Craig makes is that there are certain kinds of denumerable collections to which no addition is possible. Suppose, for example, that each book in the library has a unique natural number printed on its spine. Then, plainly enough, it is impossible to add a new book to the library, subject to the condition that this new book also have a natural number printed on its spine, since all of the natural numbers have already been used in the numbering of the books. However, it should not be supposed that this point somehow entails that it is impossible to add new books to the library, for we could simply use a different system of identification for the newly added books. (For example, we might label the new books: 'A1', 'A2', 'A3',....) Furthermore, it should not be supposed that the correct point somehow entails that it is impossible to add new books to the library subject to the constraint that each book in the library is labelled with a distinct natural number, *unless* we have some reason to suppose that it is not possible to remove all of the existing labels, and then to apply new labels to all of the books in the collection. If, for example, we suppose that the books in the library are arranged on a single shelf that stretches out to infinity, then, on plausible assumptions, there will be no way of relabeling all of the books in the library in finite time. But there is nothing in this consideration to support the conclusion that there cannot be large, denumerable, physical infinities.

The *third* point that Craig makes is that, if it is possible to make additions to infinite collections, then surely the library holdings increase when more books are placed on the shelf (or shelves). ('We can see ourselves add and remove the book – are we really to believe that when we add the book there are no more books in the collection and when we remove it there are no less books in the collection?') Here, we need to guard against a tempting equivocation. Given that the collection of books is denumerably infinite, adding a further book results in a new collection that is also denumerably infinite. So, the *cardinality* of the library collection does not change on the addition of a new book. But it does not follow from this that there was no addition to the library holding when the new book was added to the collection. After all, when we map the new holding to the old under a mapping that takes each book present in both collections to itself, we find that there is one book in the new collection that was not present in the old (and no book present in the old collection that is not present in the new) – and so, exactly as we supposed, it turns out that there has been an addition to the library holding! In the finite case, change in cardinality of holding is a sufficient (but not necessary) condition for change in holding;

but this is not so in the infinite case. However, in both the finite and infinite case, there is change in holding exactly if either there is some book initially present but subsequently absent or there is some book initially absent but subsequently present.

The *fourth* point that Craig makes is that, if we suppose that we can remove all of the odd-numbered books from the collection, then surely we shall need to suppose that our shelf will remain full after we 'push the books together to close the gaps' once the infinitely many odd-numbered books are removed. This is plainly not so. If we suppose that we can remove and reshelve all of the books in the collection, then we can reshelve our initial collection with any finite amount of initial shelf space free. (For example, we can put book '1' where book '*N*' is, for any '*N*', and then shelve the rest of the books in order, going off to infinity.) What happens after we 'push the even numbered books together' depends on the precise details of our 'pushing': We can, if we wish, fill the shelf; or we can, if we wish, leave any finite initial part of the shelf empty. Of course, as we noted previously, it might be that it is impossible to remove all of the odd-numbered books from our shelf – and it might be that it is impossible to 'push' all of the even numbered books together when the odd numbered books are removed – even though it is possible for there to be a library with infinite holdings. (It is uncontroversial that we can expand the case to make these things impossible; it is much more controversial whether we can expand the case to make these things possible. While I shall go on to insist that there is no good argument for the claim that these further things *are* impossible, I don't need to rely on that further insistence here.) So our outsmarting response to Craig is carefully tempered: The mere existence of a library with a countable infinity of books does not entail the further consequences that Craig here finds absurd.

3.4 TRISTRAM SHANDY

There is already a very large literature about the 'Tristram Shandy case'. The puzzle, in the form in which I presented it above, is due to Craig (1979a). Russell (1903) gave the title 'Tristram Shandy paradox' to the observation that, if Tristram Shandy were to commence writing now and to take one year to account for one day of his life, no part of his biography need remain forever unwritten, provided that he lives forever and does not weary of his task. While one might think that limitations of memory, and so forth, would eventually defeat Tristram Shandy – since, as time goes by, the number of days lived but not yet written about continues to increase without limit – it is clear that this kind of consideration does not provide a reason for claiming that there cannot be *any* large, denumerable, physical infinities. In particular, it should be noted that this objection depends on the assumption that human memory is *essentially* finite. At least for all that has been argued here, we have been given no reason to suppose that it could not be the case that time is infinite in extension even though no human being lives for more than a fixed finite number of years.

Craig's own puzzle confronts a very different kind of difficulty. It is true that, if Tristram Shandy has always been writing his autobiography at the rate of one day per year, then he cannot now put down his pen, with his autobiography completed. Moreover, the reason for this is the one that Craig gives: Given that it takes Tristram Shandy 365 days to write about one day, it is impossible for him to have completed his account of the day on which he puts down his pen. However, given the assumptions in play, it is simply a mistake to suppose that, if Tristram Shandy has been writing from infinity past, then it is possible for him to have finished writing his autobiography. No matter how long we suppose Tristram Shandy to have been writing, there is no way that he can put down his pen with his autobiography completed. Since no sensible friend of large, denumerable, physical infinities would suppose otherwise, there is no genuine challenge here to be met.[3]

[3] There is a sense in which Craig (1991: 396) concedes the point that is argued here. However, he goes on to insist that it is no less problematic to suppose that Tristram Shandy is still writing his autobiography, having been writing in the usual way from eternity past – and that this new 'paradox' really does show that an infinite series of past events is absurd. ("At any point in the past or present.... Tristram Shandy has recorded a beginningless, infinite series of consecutive days. But now the question inevitably arises: which days are these? Where in the temporal series of events are the days recorded by Tristram Shandy at any given point? The answer can only be that they are days infinitely distant from the present.... What seems to follow from the Tristram Shandy story is that an infinte series of past events is absurd.") Once again, the difficulties here *cannot* be sheeted back to the assumption that there is an infinite series of past events. If we suppose that Shandy spends each year writing about Christmas Day of the preceding year, then we are not prompted to consider any of the questions that Craig raises. On the other hand, as Craig in effect notes, it is simply inconsistent to suppose that Shandy is now writing about a particular past day, having

(To rule out one possible line of objection to this last claim, let's suppose that we have stipulated that Tristram Shandy is not a time traveller and that he is not able to record the days of his life before those days happen.)

There are related scenarios that might be taken to pose more of a challenge to friends of large, denumerable, physical infinities. Suppose, for example, that Tristram Shandy takes one year to plan one day of his life. If he has been writing 'from infinity past', then it seems that he can put down his pen, having planned every moment of his life to the instant at which he puts down his pen. As in Russell's case – for which the present scenario is a kind of temporal inverse – one might worry that the scenario requires that there be no bounds on the amount of information that can be stored in Tristram Shandy's brain – since, at earlier times, the days that Tristram Shandy plans are more distantly future. However, if this is a legitimate objection, it casts no doubt at all on the possibility of an infinite past; that is, it is not an objection to large, denumerable, physical infinities *per se*.

There is another kind of worry that one might have about the related scenario, that seems not to arise in Russell's original case, and that is urged by various commentators, including Craig himself. Suppose that, under the related scenario, Tristram Shandy puts down his pen at time *T*. Why does he put down his pen at time *T*, rather than at some other time? Indeed, given that he has had an infinite amount of past time, surely we are entitled to the assumption that he ought to have been in a position to put down his pen at any earlier time (since, at any earlier time, it would still be true that an infinite amount of time had elapsed). Don't these questions point to a genuine difficulty in the suggestion that it is possible that past time is infinite?

If we suppose that Tristram Shandy won't put down his pen until his planning catches up with his life, then we have an explanation of

been writing since infinity past – 'at the rate of one day per year' – treating the days of his life in the precise order in which they occur. Adding further assumptions, we can generate an inconsistency from the claim that there is an infinite series of past events – but, of course, this is true of *any* other claim that you care to consider, and in itself does nothing towards showing that it is impossible for the series of past events to be infinite. What follows from (this part of) Craig's discussion of the Tristram Shandy story is that, if the series of past events is infinite, then there isn't anyone who has *always* been writing his autobiography at the rate of one day a year, treating the days in the order in which they occurred.

why he puts down his pen at time *T*: It is because his writing has always been converging on *T* that he puts down his pen at *T*. (That is, at all times, it has been true that, if Tristram Shandy sticks to his writing schedule, then he will put down his pen at *T*, having planned every moment of his life up until *T*.) In order for him to put down his pen at some other time T', his writing would need to have been converging on that other time. Given that his writing has always been converging on *T*, the fact that he has been writing 'from infinity past' gives us no reason at all to think that he ought to have been able to lay down his pen at some earlier time T'.

Perhaps it might be objected that the explanation just given is unsatisfactory, because no reason has been given – and, moreover, no reason can be given – why Shandy's writing has always been converging on *T* rather than on some other time T'. Even if we were to accept the implausible suggestion that there is no way to consistently extend the Tristram Shandy scenario currently under examination so as to include an explanation of why Shandy's writing has always been converging on *T* rather than on some other time T', it is not clear that this would be a serious difficulty for friends of large, denumerable, physical infinities. Why not suppose that this is a brute feature of the scenario, that is, a feature that has no explanation? True enough, if we make this supposition, then we are rejecting certain kinds of principles of sufficient reason – but, at the very least, it is highly contentious whether any of those principles of sufficient reason is acceptable. If there can be brute contingent truths, why shouldn't it be a brute contingent truth that Shandy's writing has always been converging on *T* rather than on some other time T'?

3.5 COUNTING FROM INFINITY

Suppose you came across an elderly person saying "..., 5, 4, 3, 2, 1, 0, finished", and, upon inquiry, you were told that this person had just finished counting backwards from *one billion* (without skipping any of the natural numbers between one billion and one). Would you believe them? I hope not! There are 28,800 seconds in eight hours. Consequently, even a very assiduous counter could not be expected to get through more than about 25,000 numbers a day. Hence, an assiduous counter would need 40,000 days – that is, about 109 years – to count backwards from a billion. Since the maximum age to which people have lived is about 120 years, we do not even need to appeal to considerations about plausible desires and plausible lives in order to rule out the suggestion that someone has actually counted backwards from a billion. (Even if – most implausibly – someone had the strongly resilient, overwhelming desire to count backwards from a billion, there is very little chance that he or she would succeed in this venture.) Moreover, if you are sceptical about the details of this calculation, consider instead the claim that someone has counted backwards from *one trillion* (or from some much larger number, such as *one googol*): You won't need to search very hard to find a number *N* such that you will reject out of hand the claim that someone has successfully counted backwards from that number.[4]

In view of the above considerations, we can certainly agree with the judgment – often attributed to Wittgenstein – that if we came across a person saying "..., 5, 4, 3, 2, 1, 0, finished", we would immediately dismiss the suggestion that this person had succeeded in counting backwards from infinity. After all, if we reject out of hand the claim that someone had successfully counted backwards from some number *N*, then consistency alone requires that we reject out of hand the claim that someone has successfully counted backwards from infinity. However, these considerations also show that we cannot conclude, from our disposition to reject out of hand the claim that someone has counted backwards from infinity, that it is *impossible* that a being should succeed in counting backwards from infinity. While we reject out of hand the claim that someone has successfully counted backwards from *N*, we are in no doubt about the possibility that a being should successfully count backwards from *N*; we can describe the kinds of circumstances that would be required to make such an outcome possible. Consequently, the mere fact that we reject out of hand the claim

[4] Lavine (1994: 166) notes that the artist Jonathon Borossky counted to 3,265,772, and documented the entire process carefully. (Why did he stop at this number? Lavine doesn't say.) Lavine also notes that Roman Opalka began painting consecutive details of "1–∞" in 1965, at that, by 1994, the last detail that he had completed was a canvas that included the numbers from 4,776,969 to 4,795,472. Finally, Lavine notes that, on July 7, 1992, McDonald's served its 90,000,000,000th burger, having commenced operations on April 15, 1955. In this last case, of course, there is no one person who counted all of the burgers.

that someone has successfully counted backwards from infinity does not give us good reason to hold that it is impossible for there to be someone who counts backwards from infinity.

Of course, even given the above considerations, it may yet be true that it *is* impossible for there to be someone who counts backwards from infinity. We can divide the considerations into two kinds: those that would count equally as reasons for saying that it is impossible for there to be someone who counts forwards to infinity and those that turn particularly on the fact that the counting involves subtraction rather than addition.

Dretske (1965) claims to prove that there are no logical or conceptual difficulties in the suggestion that someone counts forwards to infinity. The key assumptions that are made in the proof are (1) that if someone does not stop counting, then he or she does count to infinity and (2) that if someone stops counting, then this is because some 'purely contingent' circumstance intervenes. (Examples of 'purely contingent circumstances' provided by Dretske are mental or physical breakdown, e.g., loss of consciousness or paralysis of the vocal chords; loss of motivation, e.g., tiredness or loss of interest; or death.)

The first assumption seems to me to be unproblematic. One counts to infinity just in case, for each finite number *N*, one counts past *N*. But unless one stops counting, one will eventually reach any given finite *N*. Consequently, the key question concerning Dretske's premises is whether it is true that, if someone stops counting, then this is because some 'purely contingent' circumstance has intervened. If this premise is deemed acceptable, then the only remaining question will be whether Dretske's two premises do indeed entail the conclusion that there are no logical or conceptual difficulties in the suggestion that someone counts forwards to infinity.

As we have already noted, it is not clear that it is true that there are only 'purely contingent' limitations on the ability of agents to keep on counting. Suppose, for example, that there cannot be an agent with unlimited information storage and information processing capacities. Then, plausibly, while it may be true that, for each *N*, there is an agent who can count up to *N*, it will also be true that there can be no agent of whom it is true that, for each *N*, the agent can count up to *N*. If we consider a particular agent, *G*, it may well be true that it is merely a contingent fact about *G* that it has the particular limitations on information storage and information processing that it in fact has. Consequently, it may well be true that there is a good sense in which it is a 'purely contingent' matter that this agent is unable to continue to count beyond the point that is sanctioned by the particular limitations on information storage and information processing to which the agent is subject. Nonetheless, it is *not* a 'purely contingent' matter that it is not true that, for all N, this agent is able to continue to count past N: The agent must have some limit, even though there is no particular limit that the agent must have.

The upshot of this discussion is that Dretske's argument fails. Depending on how we interpret the claim that *if someone stops counting, then this is because some 'purely contingent' circumstance intervenes*, we shall say either that the second premise of the argument is false or that the conclusion of the argument fails to follow from the premises. Of course, if we are prepared to defend the claim that there can be agents with unlimited information storage and information processing capacities, then we shall have reason to revisit Dretske's argument.[5] (Alternatively, we might contest the claim that counting (forwards) makes ever-increasing demands on information storage and information processing. If our person is merely reading digits as they appear on a screen: "one, two, three, four, five, six, seven, eight, nine, one, zero, one, one, one, two, one, three, one, four, . . .", then this kind of objection to the claim that there can be an agent who counts forwards to infinity will lapse.)

Even though Dretske's argument fails, there might be some other way of establishing that there are no logical or conceptual difficulties in the suggestion that someone counts forwards to infinity. Moreover, even if there is no other way of establishing that there are no logical or conceptual difficulties in the suggestion that someone counts forwards to infinity, it may be that there are no logical or conceptual difficulties in the suggestion that someone do something very much like counting forwards to infinity. (Compare the suggestion at the end of the previous

[5] If, for example, we are prepared to allow that an agent can be constituted by an infinite series of subagents, then the kind of construction that we consider in our discussion of the pi machine suggests ways in which we might rehabilitate a variant of Dretske's position. Grünbaum (1968: 402–3) provides an interesting discussion of the construction of a machine – the Peano machine– that recites all of the natural numbers in a finite period of time.

paragraph.) However – as noted above – even if something very much like counting forwards to infinity turns out to be unproblematic, it remains highly doubtful whether anything like counting backwards from infinity is similarly unproblematic. All of the kinds of objections that were raised in connection with the Tristram Shandy case will arise here as well; we shall need a detailed examination of principles of sufficient reason in order to determine whether we should allow that it is possible that there be a creature that does something much like count backwards from infinity.

3.6 INFINITE PARALYSIS

There has been considerable recent interest in Benardete's "paradox of the gods" and variants thereof. (See, e.g., Priest (1999), Perez-Laraudogoitia (2000; 2003), Yablo (2000).) At first sight – and perhaps not only at first sight! – these cases do seem to lend strong support to the claim that there cannot be large and small denumerable, physical infinities.

In the case of the initial scenario that we presented, one good question to ask concerns the mechanism by which the intentions of the gods will be carried out. Suppose it works like this: Each god erects a 'force field' at the appropriate radius from the point (or volume) at which Achilles begins. The effect of this force field is to instantaneously paralyse anyone who comes into contact with it. Then we have a continuous volume of force field around Achilles, not including the closed volume that ends with his outer surfaces. And the effect of this volume of force field is to paralyse Achilles just as effectively as the corresponding force field that contains no 'internal hole' would. ('Paralysis' here just means 'state of being rendered incapable of motion'.) Once we allow that force fields, and so on, can be located precisely down to the level of open and closed regions – so that a force field can extend throughout an open region without extending through the closure of that region – it seems that we are bound to allow the possibility of the kinds of effects that are described in Benardete's example. So this seems to be a good case in which the defender of the possibility of large and small denumerable, physical infinities should just outsmart opponents: What else would you expect? (Of course, there might be some other mechanism by means of which the intentions of the gods will be carried out.

For instance, we might postulate that there is instantaneous action at a distance or that there is no bound on the speed with which the gods can act: The gods are all seeing, all-knowing, and *very* quick indeed. But, to the extent that there is anything more mysterious about other ways of filling out the case, it seems to me that that must be a product of the details of the filling out of the case – action at a distance is pretty mysterious! – that raises no particular difficulties for the claim that it is possible that there are large and small denumerable, physical infinities. Plainly, you can tell mysterious stories involving infinities if those stories involve independently mysterious objects and properties, but *those* stories give you no special reason to think that *infinities* are mysterious.)

Priest (1999) introduces a variant of Benardete's case in which – as Perez-Laraudogoitia (2003) observes – the field of force is independent of position and acts only on particles at certain instants of time (whereas, in Benardete's original case, the field of force is independent of time and acts only on particles in certain positions). Suppose that a particle is moving with constant velocity v when $t < 0$. The first god decides to stop the particle at $t = 1/2$, wherever the particle is, if it is not already at rest. The second god decides to stop the particle at $t = 1/4$, wherever the particle is, if it is not already at rest.... The nth god decides to stop the particle at $t = 1/2^n$, wherever the particle is, if it is not already at rest. In this case, the particle is halted at $t = 0$ at the place – wherever it is – that it has reached while moving at constant velocity when $t < 0$, even though there is no particular god that is responsible for the halting of the particle. If we assume – as Priest in effect does – that the particle can be halted only if there is a particular god who is responsible for bringing the particle to rest, then this version of the story is simply inconsistent. However, as Perez-Laraudogoitia (2003) points out, one need not make this assumption; one might suppose, instead, that the particle is halted by the collective activity of the gods without being halted by the individual activity of any one of the gods. Moreover, one can apply this analysis to Benardete's original case as well: We can suppose that the collected intentions of the gods bring about the paralysis of Achilles even though there is no individual intention of any one of the gods that brings about the paralysis.

Perez-Laraudogoitia (2003) describes an interesting variant of Priest's case that is alleged to avoid the consequence that there is a discontinuous change of state. Suppose that our particle is moving, with constant velocity, for some $t < 0$. The first god decides to bring the particle smoothly to rest, if it is not at rest already, in the interval $[1/2, 1]$, no matter where the particle is at $t = 1/2$ and the god decides that if the particle is already at rest at $t = 1/2$, then the god will keep the particle at rest throughout the interval $[1/2, 1]$. The second god decides to bring the particle smoothly to rest, if it is not at rest already, in the interval $[1/4, 1/2]$, no matter where the particle is at $t = 1/4$ and the god decides that if the particle is already at rest at $t = 1/4$, then the god will keep the particle at rest throughout the interval $[1/4, 1/2]$. The third god decides to bring the particle smoothly to rest, if it is not at rest already, in the interval $[1/8, 1/4]$, no matter where the particle is at $t = 1/8$ and the god decides that if the particle is already at rest at $t = 1/8$, then the god will keep the particle at rest throughout the interval $[1/8, 1/4]$.... The nth god decides to bring the particle smoothly to rest, if it is not at rest already, in the interval $[1/2^n, 1/2^{n-1}]$ no matter where the particle is at $t = 1/2^n$; and the god decides that if the particle is already at rest at $t = 1/2^n$, then the god will keep the particle at rest throughout the interval $[1/2^n, 1/2^{n-1}]$.... Given that the gods succeed in carrying out their intentions, the particle will be at rest for all $t > 0$. Since the particle has a constant velocity for some $t < 0$, the assumption that there can be no discontinuous changes of state in physical systems will require us to suppose that there is an $\varepsilon > 0$ such that, in the interval $(-\varepsilon, 0)$, the particle comes smoothly to rest at $t = 0$. If we suppose that the nth god establishes a force field where the particle would be if the particle continued to move with constant velocity until $t = 1/2^n$, then the result is that the combined activity of the gods is to establish a force field whose sphere of activity extends to where the particle would be at $t = -\varepsilon$, even though the activity of each god alone would establish a force field whose sphere of activity is restricted to where the particle would be for some $t > 0$.

There are various responses that friends of large and small denumerable infinities might make to Perez-Laraudogoitia's new puzzle. If we are serious in our determination to avoid discontinuities in physical quantities, then I think that we shall insist that the magnitude of the force field cannot be unbounded at any point. Consequently, it seems that we shall insist that it cannot be that there is an infinite sequence of feasible actions that, for each n, see the particle brought to rest in the interval $[1/2^n, 1/2^{n-1}]$. If there is to be an infinite sequence of feasible actions, then these actions will see the particle brought to rest in intervals $[-\varepsilon + 1/2^n, 1/2^{n-1}]$. for sufficiently large n; and so there is no surprise that the force field has a sphere of activity that extends to where the particle would be at $t = -\varepsilon$. However, while taking this course does appear to restore consistency, it also removes much of the charm involved in the postulation of large and small denumerable infinities: It is precisely because we can have an infinite sequence of functions, each continuous at a given point, which has as its limit a function that is discontinuous at that point, that large and small denumerable infinities have many of the charms that they in fact possess.

If we were to suppose both that there can be large and small denumerable infinities and that there can be no discontinuous changes, then it seems (as Perez-Laraudogoitia suggests) that either we shall be committed to 'mysterious retrocausal influence' or we shall need to suppose that the collective action of the gods is impossible even though there is no problem with the individual action of any one of the gods, nor with the collective action of any finite number of the gods. Since neither of these alternatives is particularly attractive – and in view of the considerations mentioned in the previous paragraph – it seems to me that there is no good reason for friends of infinities to be opposed to *all* kinds of physical discontinuities. Rather, at worst, friends of infinities should be prepared to discriminate, and to countenance *supervenient* discontinuities of the kind that appear in Perez-Laraudogoitia's puzzle. Whether friends of infinities might reject nonsupervenient (or categorical) discontinuities is a matter that we shall not inquire into further at this point.[6]

3.7 STICK

Suppose that the stick is made from gunk, that is, from nonatomic matter. Then there is no problem with the suggestion that the stick is composed from uncountably many nonoverlapping parts. Moreover,

[6] Perhaps it might be more accurate to speak of 'constituted discontinuities'. The intuitive idea is that, while As are wholly constituted by – or logically supervene on – Bs, there are discontinuities at the level of the As, but no discontinuities at the level of the Bs.

we might suppose, there is no obvious problem with the suggestion that the stick might actually be divided into countably many pieces, by the application of countably many acts of division. Given that the stick is of finite measure – let it be the standard metre, for the sake of an example – then all but finitely many of the parts will be of measure zero. Perhaps we might go further, and suppose that all of the parts of the stick are of infinitesimal measure. However, it is not clear that we can go on to suppose that all of the parts of the stick have identical infinitesimal measure (and so it is not clear that we can make sense of the idea that the parts of the stick are 'halved' infinitely many times, if this is understood in a very strict sense).

If we consider the example from a standard Cantorian point of view, then we are supposing that the stick is cut into χ_0 pieces. If the pieces were to be all exactly the same size, then each would need to have measure $1/\chi_0$. But, of course, from the standard Cantorian point of view – and even from Conway's unorthodox point of view – there is no such thing as the number $1/\chi_0$. Perhaps we might try saying that, from a nonstandard point of view, the stick could be cut into I pieces of measure $\frac{1}{I}$, where I is one of the infinities in Conway's field of numbers, and $\frac{1}{I}$ is one of the infinitesimals. (Perhaps even better, we might try saying that the stick is cut into J pieces, each of measure $\frac{1}{J}$, where J is one of the infinities in Conway's field of numbers.) However, given the 'gap' between the finite numbers and the infinite numbers, it is quite unclear how there could be a fact of the matter that the stick had been cut into I pieces rather than I' pieces, for some other infinity I' in the Conway field of numbers; and it is also unclear how it could be true that the stick is cut into J pieces, each of measure $\frac{1}{J}$, where J is one of the infinities in Conway's field of numbers, unless there is a fact of the matter about which infinity I' from the Conway field of numbers orders the pieces into which the stick is cut. Moreover – and more importantly – this proposal would trade on a confusion between ordinals and cardinals: If we have a collection that can be ordered by the number I from the Conway field of numbers, then the collection can be reorganised and ordered by many distinct I' in the Conway field of numbers. So we cannot suppose that numbers of the form $\frac{1}{J}$ assign a nonarbitrary measure to the pieces of the stick, if J is merely one of the ordinals from the Conway field of numbers.

If we suppose that we can divide our metre stick into countably many parts of measure zero, there is a question that arises about what happens if we put the parts back together under a different arrangement from that with which we began. Should we suppose that, no matter how we organise the parts, we shall always end up with a stick that is one metre in length, or should we suppose that we can make a stick of any length we choose by appropriate choice of construction? After all, if we had started with a stick that was two metres in length, we could also have divided it into countably many parts of measure zero. But, then, what would be the difference between the countably many parts of measure zero that we obtained from the one metre stick, and the countably many parts of measure zero that we obtained from the two metre stick (particularly if we suppose that there is no non-arbitrary way of assigning any infinitesimal measures to the pieces of the sticks)?

If we suppose that there is no distinction between infinitesimal measures, then it seems plausible to think that order matters: We can rebuild our one metre stick to any length we please, simply by cutting it into infinitely many parts, reordering, and reassembling. If we suppose that there is a distinction to be drawn among different infinitesimal measures, then we seem led into the difficulties raised in the preceding paragraphs. Perhaps, then, we should deny that a stick can be divided into countably many infinitesimal pieces, even if the stick is composed of atomless gunk, and even if we allow that it is possible for some kinds of infinite processes to be carried out in finite time. Of course, there is no obvious difficulty with the suggestion that the stick be divided into countably many pieces: Suppose that the stick has a diameter of 1 cm at one end (which we shall say is one metre from our origin) and goes smoothly to diameter 0 cm at our origin. We begin with a cut at 0.5 cm from our origin at 0.5 seconds to midday, followed by a cut at 0.25 cm from our origin at 0.25 seconds to midday, and so forth. Since the stick is thinner closer to our origin, we require progressively less force to cut it, and hence need less displacement of the knife to cut the stick. This process can end, at midday, with the knife at our origin, and the stick cut into infinitely many pieces. But, in this case, there is no question of reordering the pieces to produce a different length; it is only the suggestion that the stick is cut into countably many infinitesimal pieces that makes the original case difficult.

3.8 SPACESHIP

Suppose that space is both Euclidean and infinite: From any point, there is no finite limit to the distance that one can travel in any given direction, even though any given pair of points are only finitely far apart. Can it be that a spaceship, beginning from a given point, and travelling in a single straight line, covers one kilometre in the first half minute, one kilometre in the next quarter minute, . . . , one kilometre in the next 1(2^{n}th minute, . . . ? It would seem not, for there is no point, only finitely far from the starting point, which can be a limit for the (divergent) process that has been described. If this is right, then – before we turn our attention to other divergent quantities (e.g., speed, acceleration, force) – we already have sufficient reason to reject the claim that the case initially described is a logical possibility.

Of course, this is not to say that we cannot coherently discuss scenarios in which there is travel over an infinite distance. If someone travels at one kilometre an hour along an infinite straight line, then, given enough time, they will reach any given point that lies on the line (in the direction in which they are moving), and – as Russell noted in connection with the Tristram Shandy case – it will be true that, if the traveller does not deviate, then there is no point on the line (in the direction in which they are moving) that remains forever unvisited by the traveller. Moreover, if someone has always been travelling at one kilometre an hour in a straight line, then, given that they have always been travelling in that fashion, it can be true that there is no point behind them on the line along which they are travelling that they have not already visited. Perhaps less controversially, if someone travels back and forth over the same one-kilometre line forever, then he or she will travel an infinite distance; and if someone has always been travelling back and forth over the same one kilometre line (since 'infinity past'), then he or she will already have travelled an infinite distance.

If we assume a non-Euclidean structure to space in which straight lines can form closed curves (if projected sufficiently far), then there is no obvious problem with the suggestion that one might travel infinitely far in a straight line without ever changing direction. (We can think of this case as a variant of the 'less controversial' version discussed at the end of the previous paragraph: Someone could go on following the same closed curve forever, or someone could always have been following the same closed curve 'since eternity past'.) However – as intimated above – even if we make these assumptions, we are still unable to accept the possibility of the scenario that we set out to discuss. True enough, we can make sense of the idea that the speed of the spaceship doubles in an interval of the form $[1/2^n, 1/2^{n+1}]$, for any $n \in N$. That is, roughly speaking, for each $n \in N$, there is a possible world in which the speed of the spaceship doubles in the interval $[1/2^n, 1/2^{n+1}]$. But it does not follow from this – and is, I think, not true – that there is a possible world in which, for each $n\varepsilon N$, the speed of the spaceship doubles in the interval $[1/2^n, 1/2^{n+1}]$. While there is no upper bound on the speed that it is possible for the spaceship to attain, there is no possible world in which the speed of the spaceship is infinite (i.e., not equal to some particular finite value).

Apart from the difficulties involved with infinite speed, there are also problems raised by the suggestion that there can be infinite acceleration. In the example with which we began, the speed doubles in each interval of the form $[1/2^n, 1/2^{n+1}]$. Consequently, as we approach the end of the minute, the acceleration also diverges. Go back to the example of an object that shuttles back and forth on a single line. Suppose that it is initially at rest. Suppose, further, that in the first half-minute, it moves one metre to the right, and comes to rest again; in the next quarter-minute, it moves one-half metre to the left, and comes to rest again; in the next eighth-minute, it moves one-quarter metre to the right, and comes to rest again. And so on. There is a clear limit for the location of the object as the end of the minute approaches. Moreover, the *average* (mean) speed of the object throughout each interval of the form $[1/2^n, 1/2^{n+1}]$ is only 0.5 metres per minute. Nonetheless, the acceleration diverges – and so, I think, even this version of the story does not describe a possible scenario.

This is not to say that no possible scenario of this generic kind can be described. Consider, for example, the discussion of staccato runs in Grünbaum (1968; 1973b). Following the suggestion of Friedberg – as reported by Grünbaum (1973b: 640n2) – we can consider the case of someone who runs the successive distances $\frac{1}{K}e^{-n^2}$ (for $n = 1$, 2, 3,...) at speeds $(\frac{1}{IK})\sum_{n=0}^{n=\infty} 2^{n+2} g(2^{n+2}[t-1+2^{-n}])e^{-n^2}$, where $K = \sum_{n=0}^{n=\infty} e^{-n^2}$, $I = \int_{t=0}^{t=1} g(t)\,dt$ and $g(x) = e^{-\csc^{2\pi x}}$ for $0 < x < 1$, and 0 otherwise. There are no divergences in the speed, acceleration, or higher order derivatives of the motion of this runner, even though there are infinitely many pauses in that motion in a finite amount of time during which a finite distance is travelled.

In light of Friedberg's construction, we can be quite confident that the mere requirement that there should be infinitely many distinguishable accelerations does not present an insuperable difficulty for the spaceship example with which we began. Nonetheless, as we have already indicated, there are several independent considerations that support the conclusion that it is impossible for there to be a spaceship that conforms to the description presented in that example.

3.9 THOMSON'S LAMP

Following Grünbaum (1968: 403–5), suppose that we have a button equipped with an electrically conducting base that can close a circuit when fitted into the space between the exposed circuit elements E1 and E2. Suppose, further, that there are consecutive downward and upward pushes of this switching button – alternatively closing and breaking the circuit – that produce displacements of the button. If we suppose that these pushes – and displacements – form an infinite series that converges appropriately to zero, then there is no obvious *logical* difficulty with the claim that a lamp connected to this circuit does have a determinate state at the end of the infinite series, since the circuit will be closed at this time. Of course, we need to make various contrary-to-fact physical assumptions – for example, that there is no electrical arcing or sparking across any space, however small, between the conducting button base and the exposed circuit elements E1 and E2 – in filling out the story in this way, but there is no reason to suppose that, for example, contraventions of quantum-mechanical restrictions are anything other than broadly logical possibilities. By adding a further stipulation about whether the lamp is on or off when the circuit in question is closed, we can obtain a determinate answer to the question about the status of the lamp at the end of the infinite series of button pushes.

There is a general moral to be extracted from the above response to the alleged difficulty that is posed by the Thomson lamp case. It is clear that there are ways of filling out the story in which there are divergent physical quantities. For instance, if we suppose that the switch must move at least a certain fixed minimum distance in order to change the state of the circuit – or if we suppose that the pushes must possess a certain fixed minimum force in order to change the state of the circuit – then there will be divergent kinematic and dynamic quantities: For example, the speed and the acceleration of the switch will both become infinite as the limit time is approached. Plausibly, those ways of filling out the story lead to incoherence. But there are other ways of filling out the story in which there are no divergent physical quantities – or, at least, in which it is not obvious that there are any divergent physical quantities – and, for all that has been said so far, it remains an open question of whether those ways of filling out the story are coherent. Moreover – and interestingly – there is no violation of even allegedly modest and plausible principles of sufficient reason in those versions of the story in which there are no (evident) divergent physical quantities: Grünbaum's filling out of the story both removes any suggestion that there are (evident) divergent physical quantities and provides a sufficient reason for the terminal state of the switch and lamp. Consequently, the mere telling of the original version of this story provides no reason at all to suppose that there cannot be both large and small denumerable, physical infinities.

3.10 BLACK'S MARBLE SHIFTER

In the original version of the marble shifter case, there are various divergent quantities: for example, the speed of the moving tray, the speed of the projected marbles, the deceleration of the marbles as they land on the sticky tray, and the acceleration and deceleration of the scoop. Perhaps some of these divergent quantities could be eliminated without serious damage to the story, for example, by allowing that both trays house conveyor belts; however, it seems that it would require a vastly different story about marbles to end up with a case in which there are no divergent quantities.

Black (1951) argues for the logical impossibility of the marble shifting machine by appealing to what he claims is a related example: namely, a case in which a machine transfers a single marble from the (otherwise stationary and empty) left tray to the right, whereupon it is transferred back to the left tray by an identical machine. Clearly, Black's thought is that the originally described marble shifting machine is possible iff the newly described machine is possible;

whence, since the newly described machine is not possible, the originally described machine is not possible either. However, it seems much easier to describe a logically possible version of the new machine than it is to describe a logically possible version of the original machine. Suppose, for instance, that the distance that each machine moves the marble decreases according to a geometric proportion and that the weight (and size) of the marble decreases according to appropriately determined geometrical proportions (because, say, each contact between a machine arm and the marble removes an appropriately sized chip from the marble). In this case, there is no evident reason why the two machines cannot move the marble back and forth along a line in such a way that the back-and-forth motion of the marble converges on a particular point at the end of an infinite series of shifts (where the two machine arms will come to rest, with nothing at all to separate them).

The closest that I can get to a coherent version of the original story is this: Suppose that we have an infinite line of marbles, each all but touching the next, and each all but touching a straight line that runs parallel to the straight line formed by the marbles. The first marble weighs 1 gram, the second marble weighs 0.5 grams, the third marble weighs 0.25 grams, and so on; the centre (of mass) of the first marble is 1 cm from the straight line; the centre (of mass) of the second marble is 0.5 cm from the straight line; the centre (of mass) of the third marble is 0.25 cm from the straight line; and so forth. A machine, consisting of an arm mounted on a frictionless rod, pushes each marble in turn, with just sufficient force to bring the marbles to rest on the other side of the straight line, at the same distance from the line as they began. Each time that the hand on the arm pushes a marble, a suitable proportion of the underneath side of the arm detaches, and begins to fall to the ground, so that the surface area of the arm that comes into contact with the marbles decreases in appropriate geometric proportion as time advances. Clearly, the controls for the movement of the arm will need to admit of 'infinite precision'; but there are various ways in which the story could be elaborated to achieve this degree of control of the movement of the arm. Given that we can coherently describe the motions of the arm in a way that removes all divergent quantities (speed, acceleration, kinetic energy, and so forth), it seems that we will have succeeded in describing a scenario in which an infinite number of marbles are shifted across a line in a finite amount of time.

It is interesting to note that Black (1951: 99) writes: "Every machine that performed an infinite series of acts in a finite time would have to include a part that oscillated 'infinitely fast', as it were, in an impossible fashion." If this were so, then I think that we should agree with Black that such machines are, indeed, impossible. Moreover, if this were so, then we shouldn't worry about the obvious questions that are raised by the initial version of the story that we considered, in which – as we noted above – there are obvious difficulties raised by divergent quantities. (How does the machine get to throw more and more marbles greater and greater distances in less and less time? How could a kinematically consistent catapult be designed to carry out this task? First, there is the problem of getting the shots off. Second, there is the problem of 'winding' the mechanism that generates the propulsive force. Third, there is the problem of applying the propulsive force to the marbles. There seems to be no hope of obtaining satisfactory answers to questions like these.) However, I see no reason to suppose that Black is right in thinking that 'infinity machines' must involve divergent quantities: Wherever we turn in stories such as the one with which we began, we can replace divergent quantities with convergent quantities, without introducing further divergent quantities in their wake.

3.11 PI MACHINE

Following Grünbaum (1973: 643) we shall suppose that a machine that is capable of printing an omega-sequence of digits in a finite amount of time conforms to the following requirements: First, the height from which the press descends to the paper to print the successive digits form a sequence that converges *suitably* to zero, and, second, the size – height and width – of the successive numerals to be printed also converges *suitably* to zero in such a way that all of the digits can be printed in a horizontal line on a single, finite strip of paper.[7] Doubtless, these requirements cannot be met given the laws of physics that actually obtain: The atomic constitution of matter, the requirements of

[7] We require that the distance travelled by the press and the quantity of paper used for printing are finite. So, sequences that converge to zero but sum to infinity – such as $\frac{1}{2}, \frac{1}{3}, \frac{1}{4}, \frac{1}{5}, \ldots$ – won't cut the mustard.

thermodynamics, and the requirements of quantum mechanics would all conspire to defeat the 'infinite' precision that this kind of construction requires. However, it is at the very least an open question whether there is a possible world in which suitably altered laws of physics permit the kind of construction that Grünbaum describes.

If we suppose that the press operates in the manner of an old-fashioned typewriter, then we might imagine, for example, that it consists of an omega-sequence of collections of inked keys, with each of the digits '0' through '9' in each of the collections. In turn – according to the requirements of the omega-sequence to be printed – one from each of these collections of inked keys is pressed to the paper, to produce the printing of a single digit. If the collections have a suitable initial arrangement, then it can be the case that the distance that the successive keys must travel in order to leave an imprint on the page forms a sequence that converges suitably to zero.

Even if there is no problem with the part of the machine that is supposed to print all of the digits in the decimal representation of pi, one might worry (1) that it will not be possible to *program* the machine to compute all of the digits in a finite amount of time and (2) that, even if it were possible to program the machine to compute all of the digits in a finite amount of time, it would not be possible to arrange for the computations to *trigger* the printing of all of the digits in a finite amount of time. It is not clear that either of these worries is well founded.

Suppose that the machine consists of infinitely many submachines, the *n*th of which is designed to compute the *n*th digit in the decimal expansion of pi. Suppose, further, that the *n*th submachine is attached directly to the collection of inked keys that will be responsible for the printing of the *n*th digit in the output. If we suppose that the connections between the submachines and the collections of inked keys are properly characterised by sequences that converge suitably to zero, then it seems that we can set aside worries about the triggering of the printing in finite time if we can meet worries about the completion of the computations in finite time. So, the one remaining question is whether we can describe a sequence of machines of which it is true that the *n*th member of the sequence computes the *n*th digit in the decimal expansion of pi in, say, $1 - 1/2^n$ seconds, without introducing any divergent physical quantities.

At least at first sight, it might seem that there is no way that this can be done, since the number of computations that must be performed in order to compute the *n*th digit in the decimal expansion of pi is certainly not itself convergent to zero as *n* increases. However, even if the number of computations that must be performed in order to compute the *n*th digit in the decimal expansion of pi is divergent as *n* increases, it might be possible to 'compensate' for this fact by allowing the size of the submachines to be even more rapidly convergent to zero. Moreover, if we suppose that the submachines are electronic, then we can also allow that the speed at which the electrons travel increases as they get smaller: For each *n*, there is a finite limit to the speed at which the electrons travel in submachine *n*, but there is no upper limit to the speed at which electrons can travel. This kind of 'divergence' is harmless, since there is no physical quantity that takes on an infinite value: for each size of electron, there is a finite maximum speed at which that kind of electron can travel. Given the kinds of considerations just introduced, it is surely an open question whether we must be pessimistic about the prospects for an infinite series of submachines, each of which calculates more rapidly than the one before, but in which there are no objectionable divergences in physical quantities.

Even if one were to accept that there can be a machine that computes and prints all of the digits in the decimal representation of pi in a finite amount of time, one might think that one could not *build* the various parts of the machine (in finite time) and that one could not *program* the machine to perform the calculation (in finite time). However, given what has already been said in this section, the line of response is predictable: There is no reason why we can't invoke other kinds of 'infinity machines' to perform the building and the programming that is required, if indeed it is required. No doubt it is true that, if you have only finite initial resources, you can't get from them to 'infinity machines' in finite time; but there is no evident vicious circularity in the thought that 'infinity machines' will inevitably depend on other 'infinity machines' – isn't that just what you would expect? – and nor is there any evident vicious circularity in the suggestion that, if there are to be 'infinity machines', then there will always have been 'infinity machines' – again, isn't that just what you would expect?

Wittgenstein (1975: 166) considers the case of someone's having (purportedly) written down the last digit of pi, after an eternity of writing, and takes this to be 'utter nonsense, and a *reductio ad absurdum* of the concept of an infinite totality'. However, friends of 'infinite totalities' can agree with Wittgenstein that it is absurd to suppose that someone might write down the last digit in the decimal expansion of pi, since there is no such digit. Moreover, friends of 'infinite totalities' can agree with Wittgenstein that it is absurd to suppose that someone might succeed in completing the writing down of the decimal expansion of pi in infinite time, writing at a uniform rate, if what this requires is that the person set down his or her pen with no digits in the decimal expansion unwritten (since, again, there is no last digit in the decimal expansion of pi). But, despite these points of agreement, friends of 'infinite totalities' can insist that it may well nonetheless be possible for someone to write down the entire decimal expansion of pi in finite time, and they can also insist that the points that Wittgenstein makes in no way constitute a *reductio ad absurdum* of the concept of an 'infinite totality'. (Wittgenstein is also reported to have claimed that, if we came across a man who said '. . . five, one, four, one, point, three – finished' and were told that he had just completed a backwards recitation of the digits of pi that he had been carrying out 'since eternity past', we would immediately dismiss this suggestion as absurd. Bearing in mind the various qualifications introduced in our discussion of Counting to Infinity, it seems to me that there is plenty of room for friends of 'infinite totalities' to dispute this claim: It is by no means obviously impossible for there to be a machine – composed of infinitely many submachines – that has concluded a backwards recitation of the digits of pi, computing each digit before reciting that digit.)

3.12 GOLDBACH MACHINE

If we can make a machine that can resolve the Goldbach conjecture in the way described, then, plausibly, for any unresolved conjecture in number theory, we can make a machine to resolve that conjecture. Even if we have a conjecture about *n*-tuples of natural numbers, for any *n*, we can use Cantorian methods to describe an 'infinity machine' (with infinitely many submachines) that will determine, in finite time, whether or not the conjecture is true. But, if that's right, then it seems that, in order to allow the Goldbach machine, we must be allowing a machine that can decide any arithmetical statement. Yet it is a fundamental result in modern logic that arithmetic is not decidable: Unless Church's thesis is false, there just is no effective method for deciding whether an arbitrary sentence in the language of arithmetic is true or false of the standard natural numbers. (Roughly speaking, Church's thesis says that any mechanical routine for symbol manipulation can be carried out by some Turing machine or other. There are a number of different ways of making the notion of a mechanical routine for symbol manipulation precise – of which the notion of Turing-machine computability is but one – but all of the ways that have hitherto been countenanced have turned out to be provably equivalent.)

There is no genuine difficulty here. What the result from modern logic says is that there is no finite-state machine that, for any given arithmetical conjecture, can answer that conjecture in finite time (i.e., taking only finitely many computational steps). This result is silent on the possible accomplishments of infinite-state machines that can carry out infinitely many computational steps in a finite amount of time. So, even before we make any careful scrutiny of the above argument, we can be sure that there is nothing here that can threaten the secure results of modern logic.

Moreover – and perhaps more importantly – there is a mistake in the argument that we used to suggest that the possibility of the Goldbach machine is a threat to the fundamental results in modern logic. Suppose it is true – as seems plausible – that, for each arithmetic conjecture, there is an 'infinity machine' that is able to decide that conjecture. It does not follow from the truth of this claim that there is an 'infinity machine' that is able to decide every arithmetic conjecture. If we suppose that there are uncountably many arithmetic conjectures (of which only countably many can be stated in the language of arithmetic in sentences of finite length), then the mere possibility of 'infinity machines' of the kind here countenanced is not sufficient to entail the possibility of a machine that can decide all arithmetic conjectures. (And, I would add, there are uncountably many arithmetic conjectures: For every nonempty subset of the natural numbers, there is an arithmetic conjecture about that subset.)

Clearly, there is room for a much more careful discussion of the matters raised in the preceding paragraphs; however, I shall not attempt to undertake that kind of discussion here. I do not think that it is very controversial to claim that a more careful discussion will bear out the claims that I have just been making.

3.13 ROSS URN

According to Allis and Koetsier (1991), the correct answer to the of question of 'How many balls are there in the urn, and what are the labels on these balls?' seem to be (i) in the first case, *none*, even though, for each n, at 2^{1-n} minutes to twelve, there are $9n$ balls in the urn; (ii) in the second case, *infinitely many*, each ball with a label that ends with an omega-sequence of zeroes, even though, for each n, the contents of the urn in this case cannot be distinguished from the contents of the urn in the previous case; and (iii) in the third case, *infinitely many*, each ball with a label that end in an omega-sequence of zeroes, even though no numbered place in the urn is occupied.

If we suppose that any consistent story involving large and small denumerable, physical infinities is required to avoid divergent quantities, then we are constrained to interpret each of the three cases so as to conform to this requirement. Among the difficulties that we face, one of the most pressing is how to describe the internal organisation of the urn in the third case. In the first two cases, the urn could be an infinite row of similarly sized boxes, each more than large enough to accommodate one of the similarly sized balls. (We can then imagine that each box has two guardians, one of whom puts in balls and the other of whom takes out balls (case 1), or one of whom puts in balls, and the other of whom paints zeroes on balls (case 2). The details of the putting in and taking out, and of the painting of zeroes on the balls, can be filled in along the lines followed in our discussion of the marble shifter and the printing machines, without raising any obvious difficulties involving divergent quantities. We can also suppose that we begin with an infinite sequence of perfectly synchronised and perfectly accurate clocks, one attached to each of the boxes.) However, in the third case, if we suppose that the urn conforms to this kind of arrangement, then we shall find that the speed with which the balls are moved around diverges.

Here is one way that the internal organisation of the urn might be configured in the third case. There is an infinite sequence of sub-urns. Each sub-urn consists of an infinite sequence of boxes, each of which is only half the size of the one before. The boxes in the first sub-urn are labelled, in turn, '1', '10', '100',...; the boxes in the second sub-urn are labelled, in turn, '2', '20', 200',...; the boxes in the third sub-urn are labelled, in turn, '3', '30', '300',...; and so on. Initially, there is a ball and a guardian outside each box, and a guardian inside each box. The balls and guardians are initially so arranged that the first pair of guardians and ball in each sub-urn are twice the size of the second pair of guardians and ball, which in turn are twice the size of the third pair of guardians and ball, and so forth. Once a ball is placed in the urn, it halves in size every 2^{1-n} minutes. Given – as seems plausible – that this scenario can be consistently extended to fill in missing details, it seems that we have ended up describing a case in which there are *no* balls inside the urn at the end of the minute: Each ball has shrunk away to nothing after being placed in the urn. (I assume that the guardians inside the urn travel with their assigned balls, and that they too halve in size every 2^{1-n} minutes. This allows for the printing of zeroes to be carried out in a consistent manner.)

Is there is a consistent telling of the third case according to which one ends up with infinitely many balls inside the urn? Perhaps we might try the following: Let the location of a ball be identified simply by its centre of mass, and suppose that the locations n, $10n$, $100n$, $1000n$, and so on form an appropriate geometric sequence, so that a ball can be shifted from one location to the next by a corresponding geometrically decreasing force. Thus, we may think of the urn as consisting of a collection of sub-urns, where each sub-urn is a single box of finite volume that can accommodate a ball whose centre of mass is at any of the locations n, $10n$, $100n$, $1000n$, and so on. If we suppose that the series of locations n, $10n$, $100n$, $1000n, \ldots$, converges to a location (which, for convenience, we shall call $n\omega$), then it seems that we can have it turn out that the urn ends up containing infinitely many balls, each with a label that ends with an omega-sequence of zeroes. While this case can clearly be adapted to serve the purposes of the second story – by maintaining the addition of zeroes, but removing the requirement that the balls are moved – it seems that no urn of this kind can fit the requirements of the first story: For there is no upper limit to the number of balls that would need to be accommodated in a single sub-urn at some point during the procedure that is outlined in the first story.

In view of the above considerations, I am at least tempted by the suggestion that the overall story of the Ross Urn is incoherent: There cannot be a single urn that accommodates all three of the stories told, even though, for each of the stories, there could be an urn that accommodates that story. If we are to have labelled places so arranged that there are convergent subsequences of these labelled places, then – it is tempting to say – we cannot also have labelled places such that there is no upper limit to the number of these places that are simultaneously occupied, if the occupants of the places are all of the same size and shape. Of course, whether or not one ought to give into this temptation, it is clear that there is nothing in the Ross Urn example to support the suggestion that there cannot be both large and small denumerable, physical infinities.

3.14 DEAFENING PEALS

According to Benardete (1964: 261): 'If it is the case that none of the peals is heard by us, then how gratuitous to suppose that we have been struck deaf. But if we have retained our hearing unimpaired, then we must have heard all of the peals. But if we have heard all of the peals, then we must have been struck deaf by each in turn, and hence we should not have heard any of them. Not having heard any of the peals, our hearing must have been retained unimpaired, in which case we should have heard all of the peals.'

Perhaps we could quibble about the first of Benardete's claims. I think that one can be struck deaf by a noise that one does not hear: Perhaps, for example, a vibration could damage the ear in such a way that no input to the audio-processing part of the brain is carried forward from that vibration. However, there is nothing essential to the example that is lost if there is point to this quibble: For what is puzzling about the case is that it seems that the ear is permanently damaged before *any* of the vibrations from the deafening peals actually reaches the ear. If there can be an infinite sequence of vibrations, each sufficiently large to instantaneously and permanently destroy hearing, arranged with the structure that Benardete proposes, then it seems that one would be struck deaf before any of the vibrations actually reaches one's ears.

Perhaps one might wonder whether it is possible to arrange for the production of infinitely many deafening peals in the manner specified. If we suppose that sound intensity drops off rapidly with distance – as it does in the actual world – then there is some reason for suspicion that one will need problematic divergent physical quantities. (Either the sources of the peals will need to get stronger (without limit) as we move away from the location of the person who is to be deafened or else we shall need to be able to produce vibrations of the required deafening magnitude from mechanisms that are arbitrarily small, which suggests that quantities such as kinetic energy and velocity will be divergent.) However, it is not clear that this suspicion is well founded. Even if the sources of the peals do need to get stronger (without limit) as we move away from the location of the person who is to be deafened, it remains the case that the source of each peal is finite: There is no single mechanism that possesses a physical property that becomes infinite in a temporal limit. Even if we are required to be able to produce vibrations of deafening magnitude from mechanisms that become arbitrarily small, it remains the case that each of the mechanisms is finite: There is no single mechanism that possesses a physical property that becomes infinite in a temporal limit.

Following a similar line of thought, one might also wonder whether it is possible to arrange the peals so as to avoid a divergence in the sum of the magnitudes of the peals at some location. Each peal alone is required to be deafening, that is, (at least) to be greater than a certain fixed finite magnitude. If – as seems plausible – a peal cannot be instantaneous, then the number of overlapping peals diverges as midday is approached 'from above'. On the assumption that the peals are additive (or cumulative), it seems that there is an objectionable divergence in a physical quantity here. However, it will be recalled that we avoided a similar conclusion in Benardette's related case of the paralysing gods – Infinite Paralysis – by assuming that each god establishes a force field in the interval $[1/2^n, 1/2^{n-1}]$. Plausibly, we can avoid the repugnant conclusion by supposing that the peals are 'pulses' – with ever-diminishing magnitude – that add together to produce a deafening peal of constant magnitude throughout the interval $(0, 1]$.

If we suppose that there is a consistent description of the case of the deafening pulses, then the considerations that arise are much the same as those that arose in the case of Infinite Paralysis. If there can be large and small denumerable physical infinities, then it is predictable that an infinite series of deafening peals throughout an open interval will produce deafness that obtains from the initial closure of that interval. While there is no particular peal that is responsible for the deafness, the collective effect of the infinitely many peals is to bring about deafness. While this is odd, it doesn't seem to be so intolerably odd that one cannot reasonably believe that it is broadly logically possible.

3.15 INVISIBILITY

Hazen (1993) provides an excellent discussion of ways to answer the question of what it would be like to look into an 'open serrated continuum'. Since his article is a response to Arsenijevic (1989), let's begin with the latter.

Arsenijevic asks whether it is possible for a finite brick to be composed of infinitely many, successively thinner, layers of two distinguishable sorts of homogeneous matter, alternate layers being of r-stuff and g-stuff, say. If it is possible for there to be such a brick, then there must be a good answer to the question of what the brick would look like if it were observed 'from above'. Arsenijevic reasons that the brick can't look like r-stuff (because every layer of r-stuff is masked by a layer of g-stuff), and the brick can't look like g-stuff (because every layer of g-stuff is masked by a layer of r-stuff). But no other answer to the question of what the brick would look like has any plausible motivation. Whence, it seems that we can conclude that there could not be a brick of this kind.

Hazen (1993: 191) suggests the following response. Hypothesise a light-analogue composed of tophons, that is, of photon-like particles with energy directly proportional to wavelength. Suppose that it is feasible to produce observable amounts of this light-analogue with any desired wavelength. Finally, hypothesise some laws to govern the interactions of tophons with r-stuff and g-stuff: (1) Tophons are spherical with diameter equal to wavelength. (2) Tophons pass unaffected through layers of r-stuff and g-stuff thinner than their own diameter. (3) When a tophon is entirely contained in homogeneous r-stuff or homogeneous g-stuff, it is immediately reflected. (4) Tophons have a detectable property of polarisation in addition to wavelength, and tophons reflected by r-stuff are v-polarised, whereas tophons reflected by g-stuff are h-polarised.

Under these assumptions, each of the infinitely many layers in our brick is a physically distinguishable object, since shining appropriate wavelengths of light-analogue on the brick and observing the polarisation of reflected tophons will enable us to discriminate any layer from any other layer. Moreover, when the brick is illuminated with homogeneous light-analogue – that is, light-analogue that is composed of tophons all of which have the same wavelength – there is no mystery at all about what our observer will see: On the one hand, if the wavelength is too small for the observer to detect (and if there is no other source of illumination), then the observer won't see anything at all; and, on the other hand, if the observer is able to detect light-analogue with this wavelength, then the brick will appear to be made from the kind of stuff from which the light-analogue of the given wavelength is reflecting.

Hazen's suggestion can be extended in various ways. As things stand, we have no answer to the question of what an observer would see if the brick were illuminated from above by nonhomogeneous light-analogue that contains tophons of different wavelengths. Suppose, in particular, that we illuminate the brick with light-analogue that contains tophons of all wavelengths. (We suppose that the wavelengths are quantised, so that there are only countably many distinct kinds of tophons. We can also suppose, if we wish, that there is a largest tophon.) How should we now answer the question concerning the observations that will be made by one who looks down on the brick 'from above'?

Plainly, we can suppose, if we want, that the tophon-receptors in the eye-analogues in observers also have a Russian doll structure, as do the neuron-analogues from which the brain-analogue is composed. If we are prepared to go this way, then I don't see why it would be wrong to allow that there is a *sui generis* 'look' that the brick has for such observers; after all, some of us have no end of difficulty imagining what it would be like to have the experiences of a mere bat! (At the very least, it is hard to see why an inability to answer questions about the experiences of such an observer should count seriously against the suggestion that there could be a world in which this scenario is realised.) On the other hand, if we don't want to allow that the tophon receptors in the eye-analogues can have a Russian doll structure, then we shall say that, for each observer, there is a minimum photon that that observer can detect – and then there will be no hard mystery involved in the description of what any given observers sees when he or she looks down on the brick 'from above'. Either way, it is hard to see why we should think that there are insuperable difficulties involved in the supposition that there might be observers who looked down on an 'open serrated continuum'.

Given our discussion of the case introduced by Arsenijevic, it is straightforward to transfer our conclusions to the Invisibility case introduced by Benardete. There is no straight answer to the question of what would be seen by an observer who looked at a man encased in an 'open serrated continuum' of opaque capsules. Rather, there are various ways in which the details of the case can be extended, and there are different answers to the question of what is seen in different extensions of the case.

3.16 INFINITY MOB

It isn't easy to construct a really satisfying detailed realisation of the story of the Infinity Mob. If we suppose that the members of the Mob are all about the same size, that their weapons are also all about the same size, and that the bullets all travel at about the same speed, then any possible spatial distribution of the Mob that will allow them to fire bullets whose trajectories conform to the requirements of the story (whether or not we allow the members of the Mob to fire bullets that pass through other members of the Mob) will have no upper bound on the distance between members of the Mob and the victim, and hence no upper bound on how long ago members of the Mob fired their weapons. Given plausible assumptions about what is required for the story as it is actually told – familiar Mobsters, familiar weapons, familiar ammunition, actual physics, prior agreement between the Mobsters on the method of executing the victim, and so on – the right thing to say is that this story does not describe a possible scenario. But, of course, in giving this response, we give no weight to the claim that there cannot be large and small denumerable, physical infinities; the impossibility here derives from a combination of assumptions, most of which have nothing to do with the existence of large and small denumerable, physical infinities.

There are various ways in which the story might be retold in order to restore consistency. Suppose, for example, the mobsters – and guns and bullets – can be as thin as you like and that we have an infinite sequence of mobsters, each twice as thin (or thick) as the next. Suppose that the mobsters are stacked up in a line against the victim (with thinner mobsters closer to the victim and thicker mobsters further away from the victim). Suppose that the heart of the victim is composed of layers, each twice as thin as the next, with thinner layers closer to the surface. Suppose, further, that the victim is wearing his or her heart on his or her sleeve and that the heart is made of a special material that interacts with the mobsters' bullets, even though these bullets pass straight through skin, other bodily materials, guns, and so forth. Suppose, next, that the rupturing of any one of the layers of the victim's heart is sufficient to cause death. Suppose, finally, that the mobsters all fire their guns simultaneously and that each mobster shoots through all of the mobsters who stand in front of him.

It might be more satisfying to suppose that the mobsters – and guns and bullets – can be as *small* as you like and that we have an infinite sequence of mobsters each twice as short (or tall) as the next. In this case, each mobster will be able to shoot over all of those standing in front. Nonetheless, we shall still need to have the mobsters forming a series that converges on the topological closure of the victim's heart – and hence we won't be able to do without the supposition that the victim is wearing his or her heart on his or her sleeve, and so on.

3.17 STRING

If we suppose that it is possible that, for each n, a piece of string is formed into a regular n-gon at $1/2^n$ minutes to twelve, then it seems to me that a piece of string that, for each n, is formed into a regular n-gon at $1/2^n$ minutes to twelve will be formed into a circle at twelve. After all, a circle is the limit of various series of regular n-gons as the number of sides of those regular n-gons increases 'to infinity' (and there is no other shape that can be the limit of such series of regular n-gons). Hence, the difficulties that arise here principally concern the question of whether we can describe a mechanism that forms the piece of string into a regular n-gon at $1/2^n$ minutes to twelve.

Suppose that we have a disk mounted on a central spindle that is fixed to the ground (in the position that will be the centre of all of the figures into which the string is formed). Around the perimeter of the disk, there are n equally spaced spindles of diameter $D/2^n$ for each length of the form $L/2^n$, for all $n > 2$, $n \in N$. Initially, there are three spindles in contact with the string, and they exert enough pressure to form the string into the shape of an equilateral triangle. In an interval $[1/2^n, 1/2^{n+1}]$ the spindles currently in contact with the string are retracted (and, indeed, move to protrude an equal distance through the other side of the disk), and the disk drops down just far enough to bring the next set of spindles into contact with the string. We shall suppose that the disk contracts slightly, and then expands slightly (with the amount of contraction and expansion diminishing according to a geometric ratio) over the course of each interval, so that there is no danger that any of the spindles lies outside the string, and so that tension is restored to the string. Moreover, we suppose that the string is elastic, since the length of the string will need to increase steadily as the number of spindles in contact with the string increases. On the assumption that there is a possible realisation of the initial configuration of the spindles as described, it seems that we have managed to describe a scenario in which, at the end of the minute, the string will be formed into a circle that is just touching the outer edge of the disk.

Even if there are no problems with the account of the mechanism that is to form the series of regular n-gons, one might worry about the physics that would be required to permit a piece of string to be deformable according to the specifications of the above account. Clearly, we can't be supposing that the string is composed of finite atoms. However, if we suppose that the string consists of atomless gunk, then we shall need an account of what happens between two points on the string to which tension is applied, in cases in which the string is not already a uniform straight line. What exactly is involved in the straightening out of what was previously one of the corners of a regular n-gon? Indeed, if the string has some finite thickness, then won't the thickness of the string limit the precision with which the corners of the regular n-gon can be formed? (If we allow the thickness of the string to decrease over time in geometric fashion, then the limit will not be a circular piece of string, but rather an empty space where the disappearing string had once been.) Perhaps we can circumvent these worries by making further assumptions about what happens at the points where the spindles are in contact with the string; or perhaps we can circumvent these worries in some other way, for example, by considering, instead, what might be possible with a series of 2^n-gons. I shall not attempt to pursue these suggestions here. (As in previous cases, it is clear that there is nothing in the string example to concern friends of large and small denumerable, physical infinities. If it is impossible to form a series of n-gons in the described way, then that has no consequences for the possibility of other, very different kinds of large and small denumerable, physical infinities.)

3.18 SOME CONCLUDING REMARKS

There are a number of general conclusions that have been arrived at in the course of the preceding discussion. It may well be useful to collect these conclusions here.

Perhaps the most important general point is that it is very easy to make the mistake of supposing that, when one is presented with a description of a situation, involving large and small denumerable, physical infinities, which really is impossible, the impossibility must arise because of the presence of the large and small denumerable, physical infinities. It is very easy to tell a story about *any* subject matter that is inconsistent. It is very easy to tell a story about *any* subject matter in which there are events for the occurrence of which no sufficient reason is provided within the story. So one cannot argue from the *mere* fact that one has described an inconsistent scenario involving the occurrence of large and small denumerable, physical infinities to the conclusion that it is impossible for there to be large and small denumerable, physical infinities. At the very least, one has to be able to show that the inconsistency arises *only* because of the presence of large and small denumerable, physical infinities (and, hence, cannot be removed by varying other features of the story while holding constant the fact that the story involves large and small denumerable, physical infinities).

Furthermore, it is very easy to make the mistake of supposing that, because *certain* kinds of large and small denumerable, physical infinities really are impossible, it follows that *all* kinds of large and small denumerable, physical infinities are impossible. There are certain kinds of divergences – or singularities – that it seems to me even friends of large and small denumerable, physical infinities ought to reject: For example, it cannot be that there is any extensive physical quantity whose value diverges as a particular instant of time is approached (from either the past or the future). However, even if we agree that the possibility of *these* divergences – and singularities – ought to be rejected, there are many other kinds of large and small denumerable, physical quantities whose possibility is much less obviously problematic. To take but one example, it may be possible that there are physical quantities whose value diverges as one approaches an initial temporal singularity from the future. More generally, it may be possible that there are physical quantities whose value diverges as any kind of spatiotemporal singularity is approached along any appropriate trajectory within the spatiotemporal manifold. We shall return to these suggestions in the next chapter.

A final point to note is that it should not be supposed that the discussion in this chapter really proves very much. For all that has been argued here, it might be that each of the scenarios that has been discussed really is impossible; and, for all that has been argued here, it might be that there cannot be either large or small physically instantiated infinities. However, I think that the kinds of arguments deployed in this chapter make it plausible to suppose that there is no prospect of defending the claim that there cannot be either large or small physically instantiated infinities merely by describing one or other of these scenarios and commenting on the strange properties that are exhibited in it. To argue successfully that there cannot be either large or small physically instantiated infinities, one needs to take a more analytical approach.[8]

[8] Earman and Norton (1996) make a very plausible case for the stronger claim that there is no inherent incoherence in the notion of a supertask. While I am sympathetic to their conclusion, I do not think that it is easy to point to considerations that would suffice to persuade a convinced finitist or a convinced intuitionist.

4

Space, Time, and Spacetime

Many of the most interesting problems involving the infinite concern the structure of space and time. Some of these problems involve large infinities: Could there have been a countably infinite number of past days? Could there be a countably infinite number of future days? Could there be no upper bound to the length of straight lines through space? Other problems involve both large and small infinities: Can we make sense of the suggestion that space is composed of points? Can we make sense of the suggestion that there is no lower limit to the size of spatial volumes and spatial intervals? Can we make sense of the suggestion that time is composed of instants? Can we make sense of the suggestion that there is no lower limit to the size of temporal intervals?

Questions such as these have bothered philosophers since the dawn of philosophy. We shall begin our discussion with some puzzles that are due to Zeno of Elea, the pupil and principal defender of Parmenides of Elea. (Note that Zeno of Elea should not be confused with Zeno of Citium, the founder of Stoic philosophy. Zeno of Elea was born around 490 B.C. Parmenides was born around 515 B.C.) While the puzzles that have come down to us from Zeno seem to admit of satisfactory answers, they raise – or, at any rate, suggest – quite deep questions about geometry and topology that are not at all easy to settle. After considering questions about the theory of dimensions and the theory of measure, we shall move on to a range of other issues that unite questions about space and time with questions about infinity, including a discussion of theories of space and time that avoid points, a discussion of Kant's views about conceptions of the global structure of space and time, a discussion of the possibility that there are general relativistic spacetimes in which infinity machines can be finessed, and a discussion of singularities in general relativistic spacetimes.

4.1 ZENO'S PARADOXES

While we possess only fragments of Zeno's defence of Parmenides, it seems plausible to suppose that Zeno constructed lots of arguments for the unreality of the pluralistic world that we ordinarily take ourselves to inhabit. Many of the arguments that have come down to us – by way of Aristotle and other commentators – seem to be intended to make difficulties for the idea that there can be motion by making difficulties for all of the available conceptions of the nature of space and time. It seems right to think that, if there is really motion, then there must really be space and time – for, whatever else is required for the analysis of motion, it seems clearly true that, when something moves, it changes its spatial position over time. Moreover, if there really is space and time, then, at least initially, it seems plausible to think that space and time must really be assemblages of points and that these assemblages of points must either be discrete (and hence of the order type of the natural numbers) or else dense (and hence of no lower order type than the rational numbers). What Zeno's paradoxes might be taken to show, and what I shall suppose that they are intended to establish, is that space and time cannot be assemblages of points, since either assumption – that the points are discrete or that the points are dense – leads to contradiction.

Of course, if my account of Zeno's paradoxes is correct, then, even if Zeno's arguments were cogent, one could respond by giving up the claim that space and time are assemblages of points, while nonetheless holding onto the claim that there really is space and time. Perhaps this means that I haven't got Zeno right; or perhaps the truth is that Zeno had other arguments against conceptions of space and time that reject the claim that space and time are assemblages of points; or perhaps there is some more fundamental error in my interpretation of Zeno. However, from here on, I shall stop worrying about the correct interpretation of Zeno. Whatever Zeno's intentions, the puzzles have taken on a life of their own. I think that it is fairly clear that the puzzles *can* be interpreted as constituents of an argument for the conclusion that space and time are not assemblages of points and that there is merit in discussing the puzzles under this interpretation.

(1) **Achilles and the Tortoise**: Suppose that space and time are dense assemblages of points. Suppose, further, that Achilles runs ten times as fast as the Tortoise, and that he gives the Tortoise 100 metres start in a race over 120 metres. To win the race, Achilles must first make up his initial handicap, by running 100 metres; but, while he does this, the Tortoise will advance 10 metres. To win the race, Achilles must now make up the ground between them by covering the 10 metres; but, while he does this, the Tortoise will advance 1 metre. To win the race, Achilles must now make up the ground between them by covering 1 metre; but, while he does this, the Tortoise will advance one-tenth of a metre. And so on. So, contrary to what we all know, it follows that Achilles will never catch the Tortoise, and so will not win the race. Of course – as many commentators fail to point out – the same reasoning establishes that the Tortoise won't get to the finish line, either, since the Tortoise won't even get to $111\frac{1}{9}$ metres from the start. So, at least Achilles can console himself with the thought that he is not defeated in the race! In general, the argument seems to be intended to show that no interval can be traversed since, in order to traverse the interval, one must first traverse $x\%$ of that interval, and then $x\%$ of the remaining $(1-x)\%$ of the interval, and then $x\%$ of the remaining $((1-x)\%)^2$ of the interval, and then $x\%$ of the remaining $((1-x)\%)^3$, and so on. Since one will never reach the endpoint of the initial interval, one cannot traverse that interval. But this conclusion is absurd; and so we are invited to draw the conclusion that space and time cannot be dense assemblages of points.[1]

[1] Among the many discussions of this puzzle, there are the following: Cajori (1915), Blake (1926), Russell (1929), Wisdom (1941; 1952), Jones (1946), Ushenko (1946), King (1949), Black (1951), Grünbaum (1952b;1955; 1967; 1973b), Watling (1953), Hinton and Martin (1953/4), Owen (1958), Brook (1965), Lee (1965), White (1965), Gruender (1966), Vlastos (1966b), Salmon (1970), Bostock (1972/3), Craig (1979a), qFiasco (1980), Corbett (1988), Moore (1990), McLaughlin and Miller (1992), Zangari (1994), Faris (1996), and Alper and Bridger (1997).

(2) **Dichotomy**: Suppose that space and time are dense assemblages of points. Suppose, further, that Achilles wishes to run to a point 120 metres away. To do this, he must first run to a point 60 metres away. But to do that, he must first run to a point 30 metres away. But to do that, he must first run to a point 15 metres away. And so on. So, contrary to what we all know, it is impossible for Achilles even to start moving towards a point 120 metres away; for, in order to move to a point distinct from the one that he occupies initially, Achilles must first move to a point that is midway between his starting point and the distinct (terminal) point. Again, this is absurd; and, again, we are invited to draw the conclusion that space and time cannot be dense assemblages of points.[2]

(3) **The Arrow**: Suppose that space and time are assemblages of points, either dense or discrete. Consider an arrow in flight. Suppose that it is true that, at each point in time, the tip of the arrow occupies a definite point in space. Then it follows that, at each instant of time, the tip of the arrow is at rest at a particular point in space – for this is what it means to say that the tip of the arrow occupies a particular point. But if the tip of the arrow is at rest at each moment of time, then the arrow is always at rest – and this contradicts the stipulation that we are considering an arrow in flight. So it cannot be true that, at each point in time, the tip of the arrow occupies a definite point in space – and this because it cannot be true that space and time are assemblages of points.[3]

(4) **The Stadium**: Suppose that space and time are discrete assemblages of points. Hence, suppose that, for bodies in motion, an instant of time corresponds to the passage of the body from a point to an adjacent point. Suppose further that A, B, and C are three equiform rigid bodies, that B is fixed, that A approaches B from the left, that C approaches B from the right, and that there is a moment of time at which A, B, and C form a straight

[2] For discussion of this puzzle, see Cajori (1915), Craig (1979a), Earman and Norton (1996), and Faris (1996).

[3] For discussion of this puzzle, see Cajori (1915), Jourdain (1910), Grünbaum (1967), Salmon (1970), Lear (1981), Sorabji (1983), White (1987), Faris (1996), Harrison (1996), Alper and Bridger (1997), Zuckero (2001), and Angel (2002).

> line perpendicular to the motion of A and C. The speed of A relative to C will be twice the speed of A relative to B – that is, any point in A will be passing twice as many points in C as it passes points in B. So, at the instant after the one as which A, B, and C form a straight line perpendicular to the motion of A and C, each point of A will have shifted one point with respect to B, and two points with respect to C – that is, there will be no moment of time at which each point of A has shifted only one point with respect to C. But this is absurd. So it cannot be the case that, for bodies in motion, an instant of time corresponds to the passage of a body from a point to an adjacent point – and hence it cannot be the case that space and time are discrete assemblages of points.[4]

These puzzles have been much discussed throughout the history of philosophy, and there are many different points to be made about each. The following discussion is brief and quite selective in its focus.

Suppose, first, that we do hold that space and time are composed of dense assemblages of points. Indeed, for greater precision, suppose that we do hold that time has the structure of the real number line, that space has the structure of a three-dimensional real-valued Euclidean manifold, and that any object whose position in space changes with time is quite properly said to be in motion.

In making the assumptions listed in the previous paragraph, we are supposing that a temporal instant separates time into three distinct regions: the punctual present, and two open intervals that would be closed by the addition of the point that is the punctual present. If we consider an object that is at rest and then subsequently in motion, then either there is no last instant at which the object is at rest or there is no first instant at which the object is in motion. (This much follows simply from the fact that the assemblage of points is dense.) If we suppose that there is a last instant, t, at which the object is at rest, and consider matters from the standpoint of this instant, then we are committed to the claim that there is some $\varepsilon > 0$ for which it is true that the object is in motion in all intervals of the form $(t, t + \delta)$, $\delta < \varepsilon$, even though there is no instant t' at which the object is first in motion. If we suppose that

[4] For discussion of this puzzle, see Faris (1996).

there is a first instant, t, at which the object is in motion, and consider matters from the standpoint of this instant, then we are committed to the claim that there is some $\varepsilon > 0$ for which it is true that the object is at rest in all intervals of the form $(t - \delta, t)$, $\delta < \varepsilon$, even though there is no last instant t' at which the object is last at rest.

In making the assumptions listed two paragraphs back, we are also supposing that objects with perfectly precise spatial boundaries are such that (i) these objects are topologically closed, and hence such that there are no nearest points to the boundary of the object that lie outside the object; or (ii) these objects are topologically open, and hence such that there are no nearest points to the boundary of the object that lie inside the object, or (iii) these objects are neither topologically closed nor topologically open. For definiteness, in our discussion of the Zeno cases, let's suppose that all objects are topologically closed and that, where appropriate, we can treat objects as point masses, located at the centres of mass of the objects proper.

To further simplify our discussion of Achilles and the Tortoise, let's suppose that the race has a rolling start, that is, that Achilles and the Tortoise are already travelling at constant speed when the race begins. Suppose that Achilles travels at 10 metres per second and that the Tortoise travels at 1 metre per second. Then, it will take Achilles 12 seconds to reach the finish line, and it will take the Tortoise 20 seconds to reach the finish line. Moreover, it will take Achilles $111\frac{1}{9}$ seconds to catch the Tortoise, at which point he will have travelled $111\frac{1}{9}$ metres and the Tortoise will have travelled $11\frac{1}{9}$ metres. (Let D metres be the distance that Achilles has travelled when he catches the Tortoise, and T seconds be the time that both have been travelling. Then $D = 10T = 100 + T$.)

In Zeno's reasoning, we have an infinite series of distances that Achilles travels: 100 metres + 10 metres + 1 metre + 0.1 metres + . . . ; and an infinite series of times in which Achilles travels: 10 seconds + 1 second + 0.1 seconds + ... Furthermore, we have an infinite series of distances that the Tortoise travels: 10 metres + 1 metre + 0.1 metres + . . . ; and an infinite series of times in which the Tortoise travels: 10 seconds + 1 second + 0.1 seconds + ... If we sum the series, we find that the limit of the series of distances that Achilles travels is $111\frac{1}{9}$ metres, the limit of the series of times that Achilles travels is $11\frac{1}{9}$ seconds; the limit of the series of distances that the Tortoise travels is

$11\frac{1}{9}$ metres; and the limit of the series of times that the Tortoise travels is $11\frac{1}{9}$ seconds. So, there is no mathematical difficulty here: Zeno's description of the motions of Achilles and the Tortoise yields the same result as the more straightforward descriptions that one would ordinarily give. But what other kind of difficulty could there be?

In our reconstruction of Zeno's argument, we attributed to Zeno the claim that the identified infinite series establishes that Achilles will never catch the Tortoise. This attributed claim is plainly mistaken: Consideration of those infinite series establishes no such thing. If we allow that space and time are correctly modelled with real numbers, then we can analyse motion into all kinds of convergent series in which limit points are attained. There is nothing even *prima facie* puzzling about this. While the assumption that space and time are correctly modelled with real numbers entails that there are continuum-many spatial points in any finite spatial region and continuum-many temporal instants in any finite temporal interval, this assumption also entails that there are infinite sequences of temporal instants that *converge* to attained limits in finite time and that there are infinite sequences of spatial points that converge to attained limits in finite distance. If one is worried that dense space and time require objects in constant motion to do infinitely many things in finite time, then one should note that this is a kind of "Cambridge" performance of infinitely many tasks in finite time. Grünbaum's "staccato" version of Achilles and the Tortoise is far more controversial precisely because it involves a far more substantial performance of infinitely many tasks in finite time.

Given the above considerations, there is not much left to say about Dichotomy. To simplify our discussion of this case, let us suppose that Achilles is standing still at the instant T, at the point D, and that he accelerates smoothly to a speed of 10 metres per second in the first second of motion (with constant acceleration of 10 metres per second per second), and thereafter continues in rectilinear motion at constant speed. There is an infinite series of points D + 120, D + 60, D + 30, D + 15, . . . that *converges* to D; and there is a corresponding infinite series of instants $T + 12.5$, $T + 6.5$, $T + 3.5$, $T + 2, \ldots$, that *converges* to T. For each point in the series, there will be infinitely many points in the series that Achilles passes through before he reaches the given point; for each instant in the series, there will be infinitely many earlier instants at which Achilles is in motion before he is in motion at the given instant. Moreover, given that Achilles is standing still at the instant *T* at the point D, there is (of course) no first instant at which Achilles is in motion, and no first point that he moves to when he moves from the point at which he is at rest. But it would be a mistake to suppose that these considerations show that there cannot be motion – or change in state from being at rest to being in motion – if space and time have the structure of the real numbers. There is, after all, nothing incoherent in the supposition that space and time have the kind of structure that has just been described. (Of course, we could suppose that there is a first instant at which Achilles is in motion and a first point at which he is moving. But, in that case, we would find that there is no last instant at which he is at rest and no last point at which he is not in motion. As we noted earlier, if space and time are dense assemblages of points, then there is no avoiding the properties that are possessed by all dense assemblages of points.) The case of Dichotomy is no more successful than the case of Achilles and the Tortoise in establishing that it is incoherent to suppose that space and time are dense assemblages of points.

The case of the Arrow seems not to be so much as a *prima facie* plausible objection to the hypothesis that space and time are assemblages of points. Even if we deny that it is correct to *define* motion in terms of change of position with time, it can hardly be denied that stereotypical cases of motion do involve change of position with time and that stereotypical cases of absence of motion involve the absence of change in position with time. If an arrow is lying on the ground, undisturbed, then – at least relative to the surface of the earth – it is not changing in position with time, and it is not in motion. If an arrow is flying through the air, then – again relative to the surface of the earth – it is changing in position with time, and it is in motion. Moreover, if, in the latter case, we consider the state of the arrow at a particular instant of time *T* – when it occupies a particular spatial region R – it would simply be a mistake to say that the arrow is at rest in region R at time *T*. That an object *occupies* a given spatial region at a given temporal instant is not to say that the object is at *rest* in that region at that instant (contrary to the key claim in our reconstruction of the Arrow). Whether the object is at rest in the region can depend on where the object is at nearby times, whereas whether the object occupies the region merely depends on how things are at the instant in question. Since the key distinction here is available to all proponents of the view that space and time are assemblages of points, there is nothing in the Arrow to trouble those who hold that space and time are discrete assemblages of points, and neither is there anything in the Arrow to trouble those who hold that space and time are at least dense assemblages of points. (Perhaps it is worth noting here that those who hold that space and time are discrete assemblages of points will not find even *prima facie* difficulty in either Dichotomy or Achilles and the Tortoise, since it is impossible to construct the relevant infinite series of instants and points in the discrete cases. While there are difficulties that arise in thinking about the discrete version of Achilles and the Tortoise, these difficulties are all brought out in the case of the Stadium, to which we now turn.)

If we suppose that space and time are discrete assemblages of points, then there are interesting questions that arise about the conception of motion. Let's focus on the case of rectilinear motion and, for simplicity, suppose that we have a point mass. If we insist that our object can travel along a line only by passing through every point on the line, then there will be a maximum speed for our point mass: It can move no further than from one point on the line to the next as we move from one instant to the next. Moreover, if an object is to travel with genuinely uniform speed, then it seems that it can travel only at this maximum speed; an object that travels more slowly must be spending some instants at rest, before moving on to the next point on the line. Perhaps, in view of these consequences, we should hold instead that an object that travels along a straight line does not need to pass through every point on the line; rather, all that is required is that, at each instant, the object occupies a point on the line. In this case, there will be a minimum for travel with genuinely uniform speed: An object that is moving more slowly than from one point to the next as we move from one instant to the next will not be moving with uniform speed.

The case of the Stadium is a case involving relative motion. Suppose that we have three parallel straight lines, A′, B′, and C′, and that A, B, and C are point masses on these lines. A is travelling to the right on A′, B is stationary on B′, and C is travelling to the left on C′. At time *T*, A, B, and C form a straight line L, perpendicular to the lines A′, B′ and C′. At time $T - 1$, A is one point to the left of the intersection of L with A′, and C is one point to the right of the intersection of L with C′. At time $T + 1$, A is one point to the right of the intersection of L with A′, and C is one point to the left of the intersection of l with C′. If we consider the change of position of A and C between T and $T+1$, we see that there is a sense in which they have moved 'two points' apart, even though only one instant of time has lapsed.

But why should we suppose that this is problematic? On the one hand, if we insist that no object can move along a line without passing through all of the points on that line, then we can say that there has been no violation of this requirement in the case of the Stadium. Each of A and C has moved to the next point at the next instant, and there is no distinct object that has 'skipped a point' at that instant. The 'relative' change of position of A and C does not involve any violation of the constraint that there is a maximum speed that objects can travel relative to the points of space and time. (If we suppose that the points of space and time form a Cartesian grid, and if we suppose that 'diagonal' motion is prohibited, then we can infer that there is a maximum speed that objects can travel relative to one another, which is double the maximum speed that objects can travel relative to the points of space and time.) On the other hand, if we allow that objects can move along a line without passing through all of the points on the line, then the case of the Stadium doesn't even raise a *prima facie* difficulty for the view that space and time are discrete assemblages of points.

While – as I noted earlier – there is much more to be said about Zeno's paradoxes, I think that the above discussion bears out the conclusion that modern mathematics – standard analysis and measure theory – is the *most* that friends of infinities need in order to construct satisfactory responses to the paradoxes presented above. However, even if this is right, it should not be denied that there are quite deep problems associated with the conception of a continuum of points and that some of our discussion of the paradoxes presented above has already touched on these problems. We shall continue to pursue these problems in the next sections of this chapter.

4.2 GRÜNBAUM'S METRICAL PUZZLE

There are results in geometry and topology that are apt to seem paradoxical. For example, it seems that geometry tells us that a line segment of finite length is composed of points, each of which has length zero. But how can one get something that has a measure other than zero by aggregating zeroes? Similarly, in topology, we have it that a one-dimensional line can be composed of nothing but zero-dimensional points. Yet how can one put together things that are all zero-dimensional and end up with something that is one-dimensional? (Of course, these questions can be repeated over and over for spaces of higher dimensions.) These kinds of questions crop up all over the place: How can a temporal interval be composed of instants? How can a finite temporal interval be composed of infinitely many instants, all of which have the same magnitude? How can a finite length be composed of infinitely many nonoverlapping parts, all of which have the same magnitude? And so on.

Grünbaum (1953) identifies an assumption that he supposes Zeno to have made and that he takes to be pivotal to the intuition that the results of geometry and topology are paradoxical, namely, that *the sum of any finite or infinite number of 'dimensionless' magnitudes is necessarily zero.* Since Grünbaum's discussion of this claim is exemplary, we shall profit by following it closely. (Grünbaum also claims that Zeno assumed – correctly – that the sum of an infinite number of equal positive magnitudes of arbitrary smallness must necessarily be infinite, but insists that this is irrelevant to the question of the possibility of a consistent conception of the extended linear continuum as an aggregate of unextended elements. However, it requires more argument to establish that the second part of this is right: For someone might think to object that it may be possible to form consistent conceptions of infinitesimal lengths, and hence possible to form consistent conceptions of finite line segments as mereological sums of infinitely many line segments of equal, nonzero length. I shall not attempt to address this argument here.)

(a) Dimension

Consider a set E of elements. A set S of subsets of E is a *topology* on E – and $<E, S>$ is a *topological space* – iff (1) φ and E both belong to S; (2) for any subset of S, the union of the members of that subset is itself a member of S; and (3) for any finite subset of S, the intersection of the members of that subset is itself a member of S. (In other words: Given any set, the subsets of that set that are closed under union and finite intersection are topologies for the given set.) The subsets of E

belonging to S are the *open sets* of the topology defined by S, and the elements of S are the *points* of the space.

In a topological space, a *neighbourhood* of a subset A is any set that contains an open set that contains A. The neighbourhoods of a subset $\{x\}$ that contains only one point of E are the *neighbourhoods* of the point x.

A topological transformation – *homeomorphism* – of one (point set) space into another is a map between the points p of the space and the points p′ of the image space that is biunique and bicontinuous, that is, such that (1) for any arbitrary point p of the space and any neighbourhood n' of its image point p', there exists a neighbourhood n of the point p such that the images of the points of this neighbourhood lie inside the chosen neighbourhood n' of p', and (2) for any arbitrary point p' of the space and any neighbourhood n of its image point p, there exists a neighbourhood n' of the point p' such that the images of the points of this neighbourhood lie inside the chosen neighbourhood n of p. Two sets satisfying these conditions are topologically equivalent, or *homeomorphic*. For example, the sphere, the cube, and the pyramid (but not the torus) are all homeomorphic.

A point p is a *boundary point* of a set S if every neighbourhood N of p contains at least one point in S and at least one point not in S. (A boundary point may, but need not, belong to the set of which it is a boundary point.) The set of all the boundary points of a set S is the *boundary* of S, bdry(S).

A collection of subsets $\{G_i: i \in I\}$ of E is an *open covering* of a subset K of E iff each of the G_i is an open set and $K \subseteq \cup_{i \in I} G_i$.

Following the approach that was pioneered by Bolzano, Poincare, Brouwer, and Menger, we give the following recursive definition of the *dimension* of a topological space (in terms of the separation of the space by subspaces of smaller dimension):

(1) $\dim(S) = -1$ iff $S = \varphi$ (i.e., the null set is stipulated to be –1-dimensional).
(2) $\dim(S) \leq n$ iff for each point $x \in S$ and each open set G such that $x \in G$, there exists an open set U such that $x \in U \subset G$ and $\dim(\text{boundary } U) \leq n - 1$
(3) $\dim(S) = n$ iff $\dim(S) \leq n$ and not $\dim(X) \leq n - 1$
(4) $\dim(S) < \infty$ iff $\dim(S) \leq n$ for some $n \in N \cup \{-1\}$

There is a more fundamental recursive definition – *the* currently accepted mathematical definition – that agrees with the above definition for topological spaces that are metrisable (i.e., upon which a metric function can be defined):

(1) $\dim(S) = -1$ iff $S = \varphi$
(2) $\dim(S) \leq n$ iff in any finite open covering of S one can inscribe a finite open covering of S of multiplicity $\leq n + 1$
(3) $\dim(S) < \infty$ iff $\dim(S) \leq n$ for some $n \in N \cup \{-1\}$
(4) $\dim(S) = \min\{n: \dim(S) \leq n\}$

On either of these definitions, a space has *dimension 0* at a point p iff p has an arbitrarily small neighbourhood with empty boundaries, that is, iff for each neighbourhood U of p there exists a neighbourhood V of p such that $V \subset U$ and $\text{bdry}(V) = 0$. A nonempty space has *dimension 0* iff it has dimension 0 at each of its points. (The 0-dimensionality of points and spaces is a topological invariant.)

It is easy to see that every nonempty finite or countably infinite point set on the real number line is 0-dimensional. In particular, then, the set Q of rational points on the real number line is 0-dimensional. Moreover, it is also easy to see that the set of irrational points on the real number line is 0-dimensional. Yet the union of these two 0-dimensional sets – the set of rational points and the set of irrational points – is 1-dimensional. Hence, as Grünbaum argues, if we interpret the claim that *a sum of any finite or infinite number of 'dimensionless' magnitudes must necessarily be zero* to be the claim that *a finite union of spaces of 0-dimensional spaces must itself be 0-dimensional*, then this claim is falsified by the well-established analysis of dimensionality. According to the modern theory of dimensionality, you can put together 'zeroes' and end up with something 'nonzero'. But there is no inconsistency in the modern theory of dimensionality. So the assumption that Grünbaum attributes to Zeno should be discarded (at least in *this* kind of case).

Perhaps it might be objected that the concept of dimensionality that is elaborated in modern mathematical theory is not applicable to physical space: The best understanding of the claim that physical space is four-dimensional is one that depends on some quite different account of dimensionality. While it seems wrong to me to think that the mathematical theory does not yield an account of dimensionality that applies to physical space, perhaps all that needs to be noted here is that there is a burden of proof on those who would reject the modern mathematical account of dimensionality as an account of the dimensionality of physical space. What other account of dimensionality is applicable to physical space? And why do working physicists simply take over their account of dimensionality from the mathematicians when they have need of an account of dimensionality?

(b) Measure

Consider an n-dimensional Euclidean space (point set) that satisfies the following two conditions: (1) there is a one-one correspondence between the points of the space and a real coordinate system $(x_1, \ldots, x_n)$; and (2) if the points x and y have coordinates x_i and y_i, then there is a real-valued function $d(x, y) = \{(x_i - y_i)^2\}^{1/2}$ that gives the Euclidean distance between these points. (Of course, this is not the most general case. But we needn't here concern ourselves with irrelevant complexities introduced by, for example, the special and general theories of relativity.)

A finite interval on a straight line is the (ordered) set of all real points between – and perhaps including one or both – of the endpoints of the interval. For the open interval (a, b), the distance between a and b – the length of the open interval (a, b) – is the nonnegative quantity $b - a$. (In fact, this quantity is the length of all of the intervals $[a, b]$, $[a, b)$, $(a, b]$ and (a, b), regardless of whether or not the endpoints are included in the interval.) In the limiting case in which $a = b$, the interval is *degenerate*, and its length is zero.

If an interval I is the union of a finite number of intervals, no two of which have a common point, then the length of the total interval is the arithmetic sum of the individual lengths of the subintervals. In other words, the Euclidean measure that we have described has the property of *finite additivity*.

Define the arithmetic sum of a progression of finite cardinal numbers to be the limit of any sequence of partial arithmetic sums of members of the sequence (provided that there is such a limit). Then the length of an interval that is subdivided into a denumerable number of subintervals without common points is equal to the arithmetic sum of the lengths of these subintervals. In other words, the Euclidean measure that we have described has the property of *countable additivity*.

The Euclidean measure does not possess the property of *uncountable additivity* . We can divide the interval $[a, b]$ into uncountably many degenerate intervals, each of measure zero (one for each of the points on the real number line between a and b). Nonetheless, the length of the interval $[a, b]$ is the nonnegative quantity $b - a$.

Hence, as Grünbaum argues, if we interpret the claim, that *a sum of any finite or infinite number of 'dimensionless' magnitudes must necessarily be zero* to be the claim that *an uncountable union of degenerate intervals of measure zero must itself be of measure zero*, then this claim is falsified by the well-established analysis of measure. According to the modern theory of measure, you can put together 'zeroes' and end up with something 'non-zero'. But there is no inconsistency in the modern theory of measure. So the assumption that Grünbaum attributes to Zeno should be discarded (at least in *this* kind of case).

It should be noted that it would be a mistake to object that the modern theory of measure on which Grünbaum relies merely *assumes* that lengths are not uncountably additive. On the contrary, the various highly plausible assumptions of the modern theory of measure entail that length is not uncountably additive. If we assume that space and time are composed of points – uncountably many points – then (setting aside the possibilities that are afforded by nonstandard analysis and the like) we are *required* to reject the principle of uncountable additivity, on pain of contradiction.

(c) A Zeno-Style Argument

As Grünbaum says, one can construct 'paradoxes' if one is prepared to make each of the following four assumptions:

(i) Infinite divisibility guarantees the possibility of a complete process of infinite division, that is, of a complete yet infinite set of division operations.

(ii) Completion of a process of 'infinite division' is achieved by the last operation in the series and terminates in the attainment of a final product of division, namely, a mathematical point with measure zero.

(iii) The product of a complete process of infinite division is an infinite collection of distinct elements.

(iv) A complete process of infinite division (1) begins with a first operation, (2) is such that each operation has an immediate successor, and (3) is such that each operation but the first has an immediate predecessor.

In particular, it seems that any conception of space and time as aggregates of infinitely many points must collapse under the weight of these assumptions.

More or less following Grünbaum, we respond to the challenge laid down in this set of assumption by rejecting both parts of (ii). (There are also questions to be raised about (i). However, we postpone discussion of these questions until later.) On the one hand, completion of a process of 'infinite division' can be achieved only by carrying out *all* of the operations in the series, and not by carrying out the *last* operation in the series, since, necessarily, there is no last operation in the series. On the other hand, if we begin with a finite interval of the real line and divide it according to the specifications of Stick (so that, at each stage, all of the subintervals from the preceding stage are divided), then we *cannot* end up with a countable collection of points (though we will end up with a countable collection of entities, not all of measure zero, some of which may be points).

While the result is, perhaps, counterintuitive, it turns out that we *can* consistently claim both (i) that the line and its intervals are infinitely divisible and (ii) that the line and its nondegenerate intervals are uncountable unions of indivisible degenerate intervals. The crucial point is that, in the theories that we are here countenancing, there is no meaning to the words 'form the arithmetic sum' in cases in which we have uncountably many elements. It is this fact that allows us to consistently make all four of the following claims: (i) the finite interval (a, b) is the union of continuum many degenerate subintervals, (ii) the length of each degenerate subinterval is zero, (iii) the length of the interval (a, b) is given by the number $b - a$, and (iv) the length of an interval is not a function of the cardinality of the degenerate subintervals from which it is constituted.

One option that deserves consideration here is to reject the assumption of countable additivity. Grünbaum's consistent conception of the extended linear continuum as an aggregate of unextended elements relies on the fact that additivity is denied for sufficiently large collections. The standard theory rejects uncountable additivity and, in this way, acquires consistency. But perhaps we should go further, and reject countable additivity as well. In that case, it seems, we could consistently suppose that the result of countably many acts of division is to divide a line into countably many points of measure zero.

While there are various points to be made in connection with this suggestion, it seems to me that the most significant consideration is that this proposal is not acceptable if we lose too many of the results that can be obtained in real analysis and those other parts of mathematics that are based on the theory of real numbers. Without countable additivity, it seems – for example – that we must lose the result that an arithmetic sum of an infinite series is the limit of the partial sums. At the very least, there is a burden of proof here: If there is a consistent conception of the extended linear continuum as an aggregate of countably many unextended elements, then that conception remains to be exhibited. (We shall return to these considerations when we discuss a parallel suggestion in connection with the theory of probability.)

4.3 SKYRMS'S MEASURE PUZZLE

Skyrms (1983) provides a very elegant presentation of what he calls "Zeno's paradox of measure". We begin by supposing that a finite line segment is divided into equal parts ω times, according to the specifications of Stick. We then argue as follows:

(1) Either the parts all have zero magnitude or they all have positive magnitude.
(2) If the parts all have zero magnitude, then the line segment has zero magnitude, since the magnitude of the whole is the sum of the magnitudes of the parts.
(3) If the parts all have positive magnitude, then the line segment has infinite magnitude, since the magnitude of the whole is the sum of the magnitudes of the parts.

Skyrms identifies five assumptions that he supposes are required by this argument.

(1) **Partition**: The line segment can be partitioned into an infinite number of parts.

(2) **Measurability**: The line segment can be partitioned into an infinite number of parts such that the concept of magnitude applies to its parts.
(3) **Invariance**: The line segment can be partitioned into an infinite number of parts such that either the parts all have equal positive magnitude or the parts all have zero magnitude.
(4) **Archimedean Axiom**: The line segment can be partitioned into an infinite number of parts such that there are no infinitesimal magnitudes.
(5) **Ultra-Additivity**: The line segment can be partitioned into an infinite number of parts such that the magnitude of the whole is the sum of the magnitudes of the parts, in the following sense: Let S be an infinite set of magnitudes, and let S^* be the set of finite sums of magnitudes in S. A real number is an upper bound for S^* iff it is greater than or equal to every member of S^*. Let the sum of S be the least upper bound of S^* if a real least upper bound exists, and infinity otherwise.

As Skyrms notes – and as we have seen exemplified in the case of Grünbaum – modern discussions have tended to focus on Invariance and Ultra-Additivity (= Uncountable Additivity), whereas ancient discussions tended to focus primarily on Partition and Measurability (though some attention was paid to Invariance and to the Archimedean Axiom). However, even if we are satisfied that the puzzle can be resolved through rejection of Invariance (if we suppose division into countably many parts), and Ultra-Additivity (if we suppose division into uncountably many parts), it will be worth looking to see whether modern theories of measure support the assumption of Measurability. Following Skyrms, we present three different conceptions of measure that have been developed in modern mathematics.

(1) **Peano-Jordan Measure**: On the line, intervals (a, b) are assigned measure $b - a$. These measures are fundamental, and the concept of measure is extended to other point sets as follows. Consider finite sets of intervals that cover the set of points in question. Associate with each such covering the sum of the lengths of the intervals in it. The greatest lower bound of these numbers is the outer content of the set. Working from the other side, consider finite sets of nonoverlapping – pairwise disjoint – intervals

whose union is contained in the set in question. The least upper bound of these numbers is the inner content of the set. If the outer and inner content of a point set are equal, then the set is measurable in the sense of Peano and Jordan, and that number is its measure; if not, the set is not measurable, and the concept of (Peano-Jordan) measure simply does not apply.

(2) **Borel Measure**: A collection of subsets of a nonempty universal set U is a *sigma-algebra* if it is closed under countable union, countable intersection, and complementation with respect to U. The Borel measurable sets on the line segment are the smallest sigma-algebra of point sets containing the open intervals. The rationals in [0, 1] have Borel measure 0; hence the irrationals in [0, 1] have Borel measure 1. Borel measure differs from Peano-Jordan measure in that it is countably additive, and not merely finitely additive. (Note that there are uncountable sets that have Borel measure 0, for example, the Cantor ternary set that is constructed by starting with [0, 1] and, at each stage, removing the middle third open interval from each of the closed intervals of the preceding stage.)

(3) **Lebesgue Measure**: On the line, intervals $[a, b]$ are assigned measure $b - a$. These measures are fundamental, and the concept of measure is extended to other point sets as follows. Consider countable sets of intervals that cover the sets of points in question. Associate with each such covering set the sum of the lengths of the intervals in it. The greatest lower bound of these numbers is the outer measure of the set. For the inner measure of a bounded set S, consider the closed intervals $[a, b]$ that contain it. For each, take its length, $b - a$, and subtract the outer measure of the set of points not in S. The inner measure is the least upper bound of these numbers. If the outer measure and the inner measure of a set are equal, then the set is measurable in the sense of Lebesgue, and that number is its measure; if not, the set is not measurable, and the concept of (Lebesgue) measure simply does not apply. The Lebesgue measurable sets include the Peano-Jordan measurable sets and the Borel measurable sets. Moreover, Lebesgue measure has the property of translation invariance: $m(S) = m(S + a)$ for any real number a. Finally, it can be proved that Lebesgue measure is countably additive.

Given the discussion to this point, one might think that Lebesgue measure is just what we need for our consistent conception of the continuum. However, as Skyrms notes, Lebesgue measure does have some rather unusual properties.

First, as Vitali initially proved, there are sets that are not Lebesgue measurable. Consider the interval [0, 1), and the equivalence relation $x - y$ is rational. This partitions [0, 1) into equivalence classes. Choose one member from each of these classes – which we can do if we assume the axiom of choice! – to form a choice set C. For each rational r in [0, 1) let C_r be the set obtained by adding r (mod 1) to each member of C. The C_rs form a denumerable partition of [0, 1). If they are Lebesgue measurable, they all have the same measure. Hence, the measure of [0, 1) would be either 0 or infinity. But it is neither, being instead 1. So the C_rs are not Lebesgue measurable. (And, of course, this construction makes it clear that nonmeasurable sets are ubiquitous.)

Second, there are desirable properties of the Lebesgue measure that hold only for spaces of one or two dimensions, but not for spaces of three dimensions. Banach and Tarski showed that there is a finitely additive, real-valued, translation-invariant measure defined on all subsets of [0, 1] and that agrees with Lebesgue measure on all Lebesgue-measurable sets. Moreover, there is a measure defined for all subsets of the unit interval that takes its values in a nonstandard interval of the reals that is finitely additive, translation invariant up to an infinitesimal, infinitesimally close to Lebesgue measure on the Lebesgue-measurable sets, and regular (so that only the empty set gets measure zero). But, alas, the Banach and Tarski construction cannot be extended to three dimensions: In spaces of three dimensions or more, one cannot construct a finitely additive measure that assigns the unit cube the measure 1, assigns congruent point sets equal measure, and assigns a measure to all subsets of the unit cube. (Say that two sets of points in a metric space are *equivalent by finite decomposition* iff there exists a finite partition $[p_1, \ldots, p_n]$ $[q_1, \ldots, q_n]$ whose respective members – p_i, q_i – are congruent. Then, in a Euclidean space of dimension $n \geq 3$, two arbitrary bounded sets with interior points – for example two spheres of differing radii – are equivalent through finite decomposition. Moreover, in the case of Euclidean spaces of dimension 1 and higher, two arbitrary sets containing interior points are equivalent by denumerable decomposition.)

Third, as Banach and Kuratowski and Ulam showed, given the continuum hypothesis, there is no nontrivial countably additive measure defined on the entire power set of [0, 1] that gives all the unit point sets measure zero.

Given the above results, it is clear that the concept of Lebesgue measure is not without counterintuitive consequences if we suppose that it has direct application to physical space. However, it is not clear that there are any insuperable difficulties here for the view that Lebesgue measure is the measure theory of physical space (as Grünbaum implicitly supposed). Nobody supposes that there are physical processes that can effect the finite decompositions that are described in the results of Banach and Tarski. Moreover, this would remain so even if physical objects were composed of atomless gunk. The existence of sets that are not Lebesgue measurable is, perhaps, a mildly surprising consequence of the theory, but it hardly seems sufficient to undermine the claim that space is a real continuum of points.

Moreover, returning to the puzzle with which we began, it seems that there is nothing in these considerations to shake our confidence in Partition and Measurability. Even if it is true – as the Banach-Tarski result suggests – that the line segment *can* be partitioned into an infinite number of parts such that the concept of magnitude fails to apply to some of those parts, it is still true that the line segment *can* be partitioned into an infinite number of parts such that the concept of magnitude applies to its parts. Perhaps we can't have everything that we would like to have in our measure theory, but we certainly have more than enough to get by.

4.4 POINTS, REGIONS, AND FINITE LATTICES

So far, we have considered ways in which friends of infinity might defend the claim that space and time are infinite assemblages of points against various kinds of objections. I have argued that there is nothing in Zeno's paradoxes, nor anything in the more sophisticated paradoxes of measure, that ought to deter those who believe that space and time are infinite assemblages of points. However, there are various other kinds of reasons why one might wish not to believe that space and time are infinite assemblages of points; we shall begin to examine some of these further reasons here.

(a) Regions as Primitives

It is sometimes suggested that, since points are evidently ideal entities, one should begin with the assumption that regions are the fundamental spatial entities, and then show how points can be 'constructed' as limits of sequences of regions. (It is less popular to make the same suggestion in the case of time, but there is no obvious reason why one shouldn't take temporal intervals to be fundamental, and then show how instants can be 'constructed' as limits of sequences of intervals.) On this suggestion, there aren't really any points: Points are 'ideal' entities – convenient fictions – that ease description of the world but that play no (ontologically committing) role in a canonical account of what the world is like.

There is no doubt that one can take regions to be fundamental. However, if our aim is to allow the 'ideal' reconstruction of a Euclidean space that is composed of points, then we shall need to suppose that there are uncountably many regions, with no nonzero lower limit on the size of regions. Consequently, in point of commitment to infinite collections, there is actually no advantage to be gained in the move from points to regions: There may be *other* reasons to prefer regions to points, but mere scruples about infinite collections can hardly figure among them. Moreover, this same point carries over even if our aim is to construct a nonclassical space, say, of the kind that would be suitable for quantum mechanics, in which we take regions or localisations to be primitive. (See, e. g., the constructions in Jozsa (1986).) Even if it is true that points are unlovely, there is nothing in mere considerations of cardinality that give one reason to suppose that regions are more lovely.

(b) Relations as Primitive

It is sometimes suggested that, since points and regions (and, indeed, space and time themselves) are evidently ideal entities, one should begin with the assumption that objects or entities are fundamental, and then (re)construe talk about points, regions, space, time, and so forth, as talk about certain kinds of *relations* that obtain between these objects or entities. On any of the many variants of this suggestion, there aren't any points or regions: Points and regions (and space and time) are 'ideal' entities – convenient fictions – that ease description of the world but that play no (ontologically committing) role in a canonical account of what the world is like.

There are questions to be asked about whether it is possible to construct an adequate relational account of space and time;[5]and there are questions to be asked about the further ontological commitments that are required of such an account in order for it to have the same explanatory power as accounts that avail themselves of points and regions. For instance, it might be that such accounts require quantification over merely possible objects, in order to make sense of talk about "unoccupied spatial locations" and "empty spaces". If points and regions are traded in for countably or uncountably many merely possible objects – or uncountably many tropes, or countably or uncountably many property instances, or the like – then it is not clear that there is any advance in point of commitment to displeasing infinities. At the very least, then, we can see that whether a relational account of space and time gives opponents of infinities all that they want will depend on the details of the relational account: We cannot simply assume, in advance, that there is an adequate relational account in which there is no commitment to countable or uncountable infinities.

(c) Fictionalism

It is sometimes suggested that we should be fictionalists concerning talk about space, time, points, regions, and so forth, in the following strong sense: We should suppose that this talk is all misconceived and serves no useful purpose. I think that this kind of scepticism is not worth taking seriously: There is no doubt that there are useful purposes served by our spatial and temporal discourse; consequently, there is no doubt that, if we don't take this talk at face value, then we need to be able to give an account of how it is that this talk is able to further the purposes that it does in fact further.

It is also sometimes suggested that we should be fictionalists concerning talk about space, time, points, regions, and so forth, in the following weaker sense: We should suppose that this talk is all, strictly speaking, false but that it serves various useful purposes for us to act as if this were not so, that is, to act as if there are true claims that commit

[5] The *locus classicus* for discussion here is the Leibniz-Clarke correspondence.

us to the existence of space, time, points, regions, and so forth. On this proposal, it isn't that this talk can be (re)construed in terms of talk about relations, or tropes, or possibilia, or the like, and that, under this reconstrual, the talk is literally true; rather, the claim is that there is no literal interpretation of talk about space, time, points, regions, and so forth, on which that talk turns out to be true. While this proposal is not so manifestly objectionable as the stronger fictionalism that we considered initially, it is worth noting that it may not give those who wish to avoid countable and uncountable infinities all that they want: For, on this view, too, there will need to be an account of how it is that talk about space, time, points, regions, and so forth serves the purposes that it does; and that account will have ontological commitments to objects and properties of various kinds. Until we have the details of that account, we cannot be sure that we don't get back commitment to some other kind of countable or uncountable infinity.

(d) Supervenience

Since we're canvassing options, we shouldn't neglect the view that claims that space, time, points, regions, and so forth are supervenient entities: They bear, to some other subvenient entities, the same kind of relation that clubs have to their members. While it is hard to find live cases of theorists who have endorsed supervenience theses for space, time, points, regions, and so forth, it is not clear that there is any insuperable barrier to adopting such views. However, as in the cases discussed above, there are reasons for suspecting that adopting a view of this kind might not help those who don't like countable and uncountable infinities to avoid commitment to them. Of course, there is a sense in which this kind of view obviously doesn't help: Supervenient entities are still entities, after all. Uncountably many supervenient points are still uncountably many points. But one could take the view that a supervenient infinity is an infinity that can be explained away: Provided that there are only finitely many entities at the subvenient level, there is a sense in which the world is fundamentally finite.

The difficulty is that it is hard to see how there could be infinitely many entities at the supervenient level, and only finitely many entities at the subvenient level. Supervenience is a relation of modal dependence: no variation at the supervenient level without variation at the subvenient level. Consequently, one expects that there will no less complexity at the subvenient level than there is at the supervenient level; and, as a special case of this general point, one expects that there will be no fewer entities at the subvenient level than there are at the supervenient level. Of course, this argument is hardly a proof: There is always the possibility, for example, that one might be able to trade off infinite ontological commitment to entities at the supervenient level for infinite ideological commitments at the subvenient level. However, at the very least, we can say again that whether this kind of view can help those who wish to eschew countable or uncountable collections of entities depends on the hitherto undeveloped details of the view. (Examples from physics that seem, at least on first appearance, to fit this model – perhaps, for example, twistor theory – are all examples in which there are no fewer entities at the subvenient level. So perhaps there is some reason to make a pessimistic induction.)

(e) Lattices and Graphs

Perhaps the most direct response that foes of infinity can make to those who insist that space and time are infinite assemblages of points is to maintain, to the contrary, that space and time are *finite* assemblages of points. At any time, there are only finitely many distinct points in space; and there are only finitely many distinct instants of time in the history of the universe. Moreover – we might as well add – there are only finitely many properties instantiated at each point, and finitely many relational properties that are instantiated in tuples of points. The world is finite through and through.

There are considerable difficulties that face a view of this kind. However, I do not think that the possibility that a view of this kind is true should be ruled out *a priori*. It is undeniable that much of our most successful science models the world using the resources of real analysis; but it seems *possible*, for example, that the world is truly described using difference equations that can be approximated as closely as you like using differential equations. It is also, I believe, true that, to date, we have been unable to produce a theory of this kind that comes close to empirical adequacy and yet that does not involve unrenormalisable infinities. Since the 1920s, there have been quantum theorists who have supposed that quantum mechanics really requires recasting in a framework in which there are spatial and temporal atoms; but none of these theorists has been able to produce a theory that is not bedevilled by unrenormalisable infinities. While there is some irony in the fact that the ambition of finitists has, to date, been thwarted in this way, it is at least conceivable that there is a finite theory that does not suffer from these kinds of deficiencies.

Perhaps there are other ways of avoiding the claim that space and time are infinite assemblages of points, apart from those that I have considered here. However, even if this is so, the discussion to this point will suffice for the purposes of the present work. Rather than pursue further questions about the small-scale structure of space and time, we turn now to worries about their large-scale magnitude. Even if we allow that space and time have the structure of the continuum, we might still deny that space and time can be infinite in extent or measure. We discuss the possibility of this kind of denial in the context of the work of Immanuel Kant.

4.5 FIRST KANTIAN ANTINOMY

In the First Antinomy of Pure Reason (in the *Critique of Pure Reason*, A426–A434, B454–B462), Kant offers what he calls "proofs" of conflicting theses – "thesis" and "antithesis" – about the finitude and infinitude of space and time. Kant's ambition in setting forward these "proofs" is, perhaps, something like this: to show that there are apparently well-formed claims that dogmatic philosophers are wont to champion and yet that reason is powerless to decide, since we can make equally compelling "cases" for these claims and for their negations. While Kant is at pains to deny that his "proofs" are sophistical, I think that careful examination shows that he is mistaken: There is not one of his "proofs" in the first antinomy that is anything other than a tissue of errors. Consequently, whatever Kant hoped to achieve in setting out the "proofs" contained in the first antinomy, his hopes meet only with disappointment.[6]

[6] For other discussions of these Kantian arguments – some of which provide a higher estimation of the virtues of the arguments – see Russell (1929), Swinburne (1966), Huby (1971; 1973), Whitrow (1978), Bell (1979), Craig (1979a; 1979b), Weingard (1979), Smith (1985), Krausser (1988), Moore (1990), Loperic (1990), and Moore (1992).

(a) The world has a beginning in time

The first part of the thesis is that the world has a beginning in time. The "proof" runs as follows. If we suppose that the world has no beginning in time, then up to every given moment an eternity has elapsed, and there has passed away in the world an infinite series of successive states of things. But the infinity of a series consists in the fact that it can never be completed through successive synthesis. Hence, it is impossible for an infinite world series to have passed away: a beginning of the world is necessary condition of the world's existence.

I think that we can grant to Kant that, if the world has no beginning in time, then *each* moment is preceded by an infinite past: at any time, there has been an infinite series of prior (and successive) states of things. Moreover, we can grant to Kant that there cannot be a complete infinite series that is completed through successive synthesis *if*, by this, we mean that there cannot be an infinite series with a first member and a last member, in which each member but the first is the unique successor of some other member, and in which each member but the last is the unique predecessor of some other member. But if the world has no beginning, then there is no first member in our infinite series that terminates in the present, and so there is no ensuing contradiction.

Perhaps it will be objected that Kant's key assumption is surely that there cannot be an infinite series with a last member in which each member is the unique successor of some other member. While it must be said that this assumption does lead to contradiction when added to the claim that the world has no beginning in time, it should also be said that there is nothing in the notion of *infinity* that justifies this further assumption. The infinity of a series merely *consists* in the fact that there is a one-one correspondence between the members of the series and the natural numbers. The infinite series 1, 2, 3, . . . , *n*, . . . cannot be completed by successive synthesis, if what is required is that there should be a last member of the series that is reached by adding units. But, if we consider the very same series of elements in reverse order, . . . , *n*, . . . , 3, 2, 1, then we do have an infinite series that is completed by successive synthesis: Each member of the series is the successor of the immediately preceding element – reached by subtracting a unit – and there is a last element. If we understand the proposal that the world has no beginning in time to be the proposal that the series of states of the world is in one-one correspondence with the series ..., *n*, ..., 3, 2, 1, then Kant's key assumption seems to be a very crude begging of the main point at issue.

It might be worth adding here that it would be a very bad objection to the above reasoning to insist that successive synthesis requires addition rather than subtraction and to claim on this basis that Kant's argument is vindicated after all. "Successive synthesis" requires no more than that each member of a series is derived in a law-governed fashion from the preceding member of the series. So our chosen example does refute the claim that there cannot be an infinite series with a last member in which each member is the unique successor of some other member. Perhaps, though, one might suggest that what Kant needs is the amended claim that there cannot be an infinite series with a last member in which each member is obtained from the immediately preceding member by the addition of a unit. While it must be conceded that our chosen example is no counterexample to this claim, we don't need to look much further to find a counterexample: Consider, instead, the series ..., $-n$, ..., -3, -2, -1. In this series, each member is obtained from the preceding member by the addition of a unit: Successive synthesis if ever there were such a thing!

For all that has been argued here, it might still be true that it is necessary that the world have a beginning in time. The only point that I have been trying to make is that the "proof" of the first half of the thesis of Kant's first antinomy establishes no such claim. To make a case for the claim that it is necessary that the world have a beginning in time, one would need to appeal to very different, substantive considerations than those considerations to which Kant appeals in his "proof" – for example, perhaps, to one or another version of the principle of sufficient reason.

(b) The World is Spatially Finite

The second part of the thesis is that the world is "limited as regards space", that is, has a strictly finite volume. The "proof" runs (at least roughly) as follows. Suppose that the world is infinite (in volume, in extent, in the number of objects that it contains). Since an infinite world cannot be seen to be infinite in a single act of perception (or thought to be infinite in a single, completed act of thought), the world can be thought to be infinite only through an act of synthesis in which completion is achieved via the addition of units. But an act of synthesis that achieved completion via the addition of units requires the lapse of an infinite amount of time – and we have already seen, in the argument for the first part of the thesis, that this is impossible. Consequently, an infinite world cannot be thought of – viewed, conceived, perceived – as a given whole or as simultaneously given. Whence it follows that the world is not infinite in extent, but is rather enclosed within spatial limits.

There are several things wrong with this argument. *First,* it relies on the argument for the first part of the thesis, yet we have already seen that that argument is defective. *Second,* it seems wrong to suppose that the world can be thought to be infinite only through an act of synthesis: For the content of the thought that the world is spatially infinite might be captured, for example, in the thought that, no matter how far I travel in *that* direction, I could travel further in *that* direction. *Third* – and most importantly – even if it were true that I could not form a proper or accurate conception – perception, view, thought, representation, whatever! – of an infinite world, it would not follow that the world is finite: Rather, what would follow is that I am unable to form a proper or accurate conception of the world.

(c) The World has no Beginning in Time

The first part of the antithesis is that the world has no beginning in time. The "proof" runs as follows. Suppose that the world has a beginning. Since something begins to exist only if there is a prior time at which it does not exist, there must have been an earlier time when the world did not exist, that is, an *empty* time. But nothing can come into existence in an empty time, since there is no sufficient reason for the thing to come into existence in one rather than another part of the empty time. Whence it follows that the world has no beginning in time.

There are several difficulties that come to light when one examines this argument.

First, there is a question about what Kant means by "the world". If "the world" is the physical universe – everything that belongs to the same spatiotemporal manifold as the visible universe – then it seems not to be ruled out *a priori* that there are things in time that are not part of the world. If, on the other hand, "the world" is the sum of all contingent existents, then it seems plausible to suppose that space and time are internal parts of the world, so that it is simply not possible for there to be an earlier, "empty" time. Moreover, even if "the world" is just the physical universe, it might still be that space and time are internal to the world, so that there is no earlier, "empty" time.

Second, the considerations just raised suggest that there is a problem with Kant's analysis of what it is for something to have a beginning. At least at first sight, there is no obvious difficulty in the thought that time is finite in the past, that is, that there has been only a finite lapse of time prior to the present. In that case, one might think, it would be perfectly appropriate to say that time had a beginning; and yet it would be absurd to suppose that Kant's analysis of what it is for something to have a beginning can apply in the case of time. Rather than say that something begins to exist only if there is a prior time at which it does not exist, say instead that something begins to exist iff either (1) there is a prior time at which that thing does not exist or (2) time is finite in the past, and that thing exists throughout some proper initial segment of time. On this analysis, it simply isn't true that, if the world begins to exist, then there is an earlier time at which the world does not exist. (If we suppose that time is composed from uncountably many instants, then it is possible for time to have finite measure in the past, and yet for there to be no first instant of time. Those who wish to maintain that this is a case in which there is no beginning of time will need to refine the account further: They will say that something begins to exist iff either (1) there is a prior time at which that thing does not exist or (2) there is a first instant of time, and that thing exists throughout some proper initial segment of time.)

Third, there are questions to be asked about the principle of sufficient reason on which the Kantian argument appears to rely. If we suppose that, whenever there is a range of events $E_1, \ldots, E_n$ that could have occurred, and one – E_i, say – does occur, there is a sufficient reason why E_i occurred rather than E_j, for each $j \neq i$, then it seems highly plausible to suppose that we shall be driven to the conclusion that there are no contingent events. On the assumption that "the world" is not necessary in every respect, we thus have good reason to reject the strong principle of sufficient reason that is here countenanced. But if this strong principle of sufficient reason is not the one to which Kant is appealing, then we need to be told more about the weaker principle to which he is appealing, and we need to be given good reasons to accept that weaker principle. Perhaps there is an acceptable weaker principle of sufficient reason that can carry the weight in this argument; the point that is being made here is just that the argument is plainly incomplete as it stands.

There are, of course, many further considerations that bear on our assessment of the truth of the conclusion of Kant's argument in the first part of the thesis and antithesis in the first antinomy. On the one hand, there is evidence from cosmology that suggests that the visible universe arose from a singularity in space and time: that evidence might be taken to be evidence that the universe did have a beginning in time (or with time). On the other hand, it is at least arguable that there is nothing in the mathematics of general relativity that prevents us from supposing that time extends back beyond the "initial" singularity, into a realm in which there are other contingent existents. If we suppose that "the world" is simply the sum of contingent existents, then it is at least arguable that the evidence that we have doesn't strongly support any conclusion about the status of hypotheses about the beginning of the world.

(d) The World is Spatially Infinite

The second part of the antithesis is that the world is not "limited as regards space", that is, that it has infinite spatial extent. The "proof" runs (more or less) as follows. Suppose that the world is spatially limited. Then the world must be contained in an unlimited empty space. Consequently, the objects in the world are not only related in space but also related to space. In particular, then the relation of the world to empty space would be a relation of the world to no object (since, roughly, empty space is just nothing). But there can be no such relation. So the world must be infinite in spatial extent.

The most obvious difficulty with this argument is the confident assumption that, if the world is spatially limited, then it must be contained in an unlimited empty space. It is unclear how to make sense of this assumption; in particular, it is unclear how to interpret the expression "the world" in a way that gives clear content to it. If we suppose that the world is a distribution of fields on a spatiotemporal manifold, then the assumption that the world is spatially limited is simply inconsistent with the assumption that the manifold extends spatially to infinity with all but some finite connected portion devoid of matter (and energy). Of course, Kant was not thinking of "the world" in exactly this way; but the example nevertheless serves to illustrate the difficulty that arises.

If we suppose that Kant's claim is that even a world that contains only a finite amount of matter (and energy) requires an infinite spatial container, then the proper reply is (1) that it is by no means obvious that this is so even in the case of Euclidean geometries and (2) that it seems clear that there can be worlds with non-Euclidean geometries that contain only a finite amount of matter (and energy) and that are spatially finite. Perhaps there are difficulties in the supposition that the spatiotemporal manifold of the world is both finite and Euclidean; but, at the very least, it is not obvious that this is so.

Moore (1990: 28) mentions that following argument, which he attributes to Archytas of Tarentum.[7] If the universe had an edge, then we could imagine someone, at the edge, trying to stretch out his or her hand. Success would show that there is at least empty space beyond; failure, that there is something preventing them. Either way, this would not, after all, be an edge. So the universe must be of infinite spatial extent. Arguing at this level, it seems that the proper response is to say that, if the person tries to stretch out his or her hand, then he or she must fail, simply because there is nowhere for his or her hand to go. There is a sense in which there is something that prevents him or her from stretching out his or her hand, namely, the absence of a space that the hand can occupy. Consequently, Archytas' argument against the possibility that the world is a finite Euclidean manifold fails. (Of course, as Earman (1995: 32) points out, there may be other kinds of reasons why one should not be satisfied with the postulation of an incomplete spatiotemporal manifold. For example, one might suppose that such a manifold would require an unacceptable violation

[7] Archytas was a Pythagorean friend of Plato. His argument can be found in many subsequent writers, such as Simplicius, Lucretius, Aquinas, Bruno, and Locke. Harrison (1987: 25) claims that this argument led, ultimately, to the discovery of Olber's paradox.

of a principle of sufficient reason. However, if there is a compelling objection to incomplete manifolds, it rests on something other than the argument that Archytas invented.)

Perhaps there is some other, telling objection to the suggestion that the spatiotemporal manifold of the world might be both finite and Euclidean; but if so, that objection is not even hinted at in the argument that Kant presents. So – even setting aside the more pressing concerns raised by the possibility that the geometry of the world is non-Euclidean – we should conclude that the argument of the second part of the antithesis fails, at least as it stands.

Apart from the difficulties already discussed, it should also be noted that it is doubtful that we should follow Kant in allowing that there can be no relationship between an object and surrounding empty space because the surrounding empty space is not an object. On the contrary, it seems that we should insist that an empty space is an object, at least in the sense that it can be named, described, quantified over, and so forth. An empty space has properties – for example, the possibility of occupancy by material objects, and so on – that would not be instantiated if there were no such empty space.

Conclusion

As advertised initially, I think that the above discussion shows that none of the arguments presented in Kant's first antinomy is any good. For all that Kant argues, it might be *possible* for the world to have a beginning in time, and *possible* for the world to have no beginning in time; and it might be *possible* for the world to be finite in spatial extent, and *possible* for the world to be infinite in spatial extent. Consequently, there is nothing in Kant's arguments that suggests that there are proofs of the conflicting theses for which he offers his defective "proofs". Neither friends nor foes of the possibility of physically instantiated infinities can take any comfort from the arguments that Kant develops.

There is, of course, much more to be said about the propositions that are the objects of the Kantian "proofs". If, for example, we were prepared to take a standard general relativistic – FRW – model of the universe with full ontological seriousness, then we would conclude that the universe is temporally finite in the past direction, temporally infinite in the future direction, and either spatially infinite at all times or spatially finite at all times. Since, however, it seems that there is an as yet unresolved conflict between general relativistic and quantum mechanical accounts of the universe, and since there is no alternative 'unified' theory that has gained widespread acceptance, we are left in a position of uncertainty by the current state of science. Even leaving aside the possibility of dispute about whether the universe is topologically open or topologically closed – both with respect to time and with respect to space – it seems to me that one should be *very* cautious about the conclusions that one draws in this area. However – as I have already noted – if one were inclined to throw caution to the winds, and were to cast in one's lot with the FRW models, then (at the time of writing!) one would end up concluding that the universe is temporally finite in the past direction, temporally infinite in the future direction, and either spatially infinite at all times or spatially finite at all times.

4.6 INFINITY MACHINES IN RELATIVISTIC SPACETIMES

So far, almost all of the discussion in this chapter has proceeded under the pretence that spacetime is Euclidean. However, if we suppose that the world has a fundamental spatiotemporal structure, then it seems clear that we should be considering the more general case of relativistic spacetimes $\langle \boldsymbol{M}, \boldsymbol{g} \rangle$ – where $\boldsymbol{M}$ is a connected differentiable manifold (without boundary) and $\boldsymbol{g}$ is a Lorentz metric defined throughout $\boldsymbol{M}$ – that are solutions to Einstein's field equations. One of the most interesting consequences of consideration of this more general case is that, at least *prima facie*, there are general relativistic spacetimes in which the relativistic nature of spacetime can be exploited to finesse the carrying out of an infinite number of operations in a finite amount of time. Following Earman and Norton (1993) and Earman (1995), we consider first the case of Pitowsky spacetimes, and then move on to consider the case of Malament-Hogarth spacetimes.

(a) Pitowsky Spacetimes

$\langle \boldsymbol{M}, \boldsymbol{g} \rangle$ is a *Pitowsky spacetime* iff there are future-directed timelike half curves $\gamma_1, \gamma_2 \subset M$ such that $\int_{\gamma_1} d\tau = \infty$, $\int \gamma_2 d\tau < \infty$, and $\gamma_1 \subset I^-(\gamma_2)$. A *half-curve* is a curve that has one endpoint and that is inextendible in the direction away from the endpoint. A *timelike curve* is, roughly speaking, a trajectory that a particle can follow. A *future-directed* timelike half-curve is a time like half-curve that is inextendible in the future direction. $I^{-}(\gamma)$ is the collection of points that lie on nontrivial past-directed timelike curves that intersect with γ. The intuitive sense of the definition of Pitowsky spacetimes is that these are spacetimes in which there are infinite trajectories that particles could follow that lie in the causal past of other trajectories that particles could follow. As Earman and Norton note, it seems plausible to conjecture that any relativistic spacetime that possesses a timelike half-curve of infinite proper length is Pitowskian. For example, simple Minkowskian spacetime is Pitowskian.

Given that a spacetime is Pitowskian, it is easy to see why one might think that the structure of this spacetime can be exploited to finesse the carrying out of an infinite number of operations in a finite amount of time. We suppose that, travelling along the trajectory γ_1, there is a Goldbach machine that carries out an infinite number of operations in an infinite amount of proper time. If, at any point, the machine produces a counterexample to Goldbach's conjecture, then a signal is sent that will be received by a mathematician travelling along trajectory γ_2. If there is no point at which the machine produces a counterexample to Goldbach's conjecture, then the mathematician receives no such signal, and dies content in the knowledge that Goldbach's conjecture is true.

There are various difficulties with this proposal. Most important, it seems that, even if there are no other difficulties, we have not managed to describe a situation in which the mathematician obtains knowledge of the truth of Goldbach's conjecture. For, at any point in the mathematician's life at which he or she has not yet received a signal that tells him or her that there is a counterexample to Goldbach's conjecture, he or she won't know whether this is because there is no counterexample to be found or whether it is because the signal telling him or her of the existence of a counterexample has not yet arrived. No matter how close we approach to the moment of the mathematician's death, it remains possible that the crucial signal is still on its way. Consequently, it isn't true that we have managed to describe a scenario in which the implementation of the Goldbach machine is finessed.

A second difficulty with this proposal concerns the acceleration that the mathematician will need to undergo in order to fit the demands of the story, that is, in order to be an "ultimate travelling twin". To have finite total proper time, when his or her stay-at-home twin has infinite total proper time, the travelling mathematician must have no upper bound to his or her acceleration. Consequently, in any physically realistic embodiment of the mathematician, he or she will be quickly crushed by the gravitational forces involved. While the structure of Pitowskian spacetime does allow for the possibility that there is a finite trajectory γ_2 in the "causal shadow" of an infinite trajectory γ_1, it seems doubtful that it allows for the possibility that an intelligent agent might travel along trajectory γ_1.

A final difficulty with this proposal concerns the possibility that one might make a Goldbach machine that operates successfully throughout an infinite amount of proper time. If one needs an infinite amount of hardware – for example, an infinite amount of storage capacity – in order to assess Goldbach's conjecture for ever larger numbers, then the mass of the "particle" that travels along the infinite trajectory γ_1 is unbounded. But if the mass of the particle is sufficiently large, then it will perturb the background metric. Yet it is one of the implicit assumptions of the story that the background metric is as we initially stipulated it to be. As things stand, no one has exhibited a Pitowskian spacetime $\langle M, g\rangle$ in which there is both space enough and material enough for a physically embodied computer to complete an exhaustive check of Goldbach's conjecture. Consequently, even apart from the first two objections given above, we have no reason to think that one can use Pitowskian spacetime to finesse the operation of a Goldbach machine.

(b) Malament-Hogarth Spacetimes

$\langle M, g\rangle$ is a Malament-Hogarth spacetime iff there is a timelike half curve $\gamma_1 \subset M$ and a point $p \in M$ such that $\int_{\gamma_1} d\tau = \infty$ and $\gamma_1 \subset I^-(p)$. The intuitive sense of the definition of Malament-Hogarth spacetimes is that these are spacetimes in which there are infinite trajectories that particles could follow that lie entirely in the causal past of particular locations that particles can occupy. In a Malament-Hogarth spacetime, the first two of the difficulties that arise for Pitowsky spacetimes do not arise: (1) There is a definite location at which any signal from the Goldbach machine will arrive, and this need not be towards the end of the mathematician's life, and (2) there is no need for the mathematician to be crushed by gravitational forces, since there is no need for the mathematician to have unbounded acceleration. However, there are some other difficulties that need to be addressed.

The first point that Earman and Norton make about Malament-Hogarth spacetimes is that they are not *globally hyperbolic,* that is, they do not possess Cauchy surfaces. (Some definitions: A *time slice* of a spacetime $\langle M, g\rangle$ is a spacelike hypersurface $\Sigma \subset M$ without edges. A *partial Cauchy surface* is an achronal time slice, that is, a time slice that is not intersected more than once by any future-directed timelike curve. A *Cauchy surface* is a partial Cauchy surface Σ for which the total domain of dependence $D(\Sigma) = D^-(\Sigma) \cup D^+(\Sigma) = M$. $D^-(\Sigma)$ – the *past domain of dependence* of Σ – is the collection of all points $p \in M$ such that every causal curve that passes through p and that has no future endpoint intersects Σ. $D^+(\Sigma)$ – the future domain of dependence of Σ – is the collection of all points $p \in M$ such that every causal curve that passes through p and that has no past endpoint intersects Σ.) In view of this consideration, we may think that Malament-Hogarth spacetimes are causally anomalous: They do not admit of the kind of predictability and causal determination of which well-behaved spacetimes ought to admit. However, it is not clear that we have sufficient grounds here to claim that Malament-Hogarth spacetimes are impossible: Even if, for example, we suppose that spacetime is Minkowskian – and, so, globally hyperbolic – it seems that we can also hold that spacetime could have had some very different structure.

The second point that Earman and Norton make about Malament-Hogarth spacetimes is that it is possible to prove the following result about them: If (1) $\langle \boldsymbol{M}, \boldsymbol{g}\rangle$ is a Malament-Hogarth spacetime that contains a timelike half-curve γ_1 and another timelike curve γ_2 from q to p such that $\int_{\gamma_1} d\tau = \infty$, $\int\gamma_2\, d\tau < \infty$, and $\gamma_1 \subset I^-(p)$; (2) the family of null geodesics from γ_1 to γ_2 forms a two-dimensional integral submanifold in which the order of emission from γ_1 matches the order of reception at γ_2; and (3) the photon frequency ω_1 as measured by the sender γ_1 is constant; then (4) the time-integrated photon frequency $\int^{p_2} \omega_2\, d\tau$ as measured by receiver γ_2 diverges as p_2 approaches p. It is tempting to suppose that this result entails that, in any Malament-Hogarth spacetime, there are divergent blue-shifts, that is, that any Malament-Hogarth spacetime is an arbitrarily powerful energy amplifier. However – as Earman and Norton note – there are some mathematically possible Malament-Hogarth spacetimes where γ_2 measures neither red-shift nor blue-shift on some sequences of points approaching p. Nonetheless, it seems that we are justified in concluding that, in physically nonpathological Malament-Hogarth spacetimes, γ_1 can only avoid destroying γ_2 by progressively reducing the energy of the photons that he or she sends out. Moreover, in such spacetimes, it seems that indefinite amplification of thermal noise would destroy γ_2's receiver; and, even if this were not so, the energy of the signal photons would eventually be reduced below that of the thermal noise photons. While we can perhaps imagine universes without thermal noise, we are surely moving to more remote possibilities when we do so; but it is hard to see that there is any other way of avoiding the difficulties just described.

The third point that Earman and Norton make about Malament-Hogarth spacetimes is that it is possible to prove the following result concerning them: If (1) $\langle \boldsymbol{M}, \boldsymbol{g} \rangle$ is a Malament-Hogarth spacetime that contains a timelike half-curve γ_1 such that $\int_{\gamma_1} d\tau = \infty$ and $\gamma_1 \subset I^-(p)$; and (2) $\Sigma \subset M$ is a connected spacelike hypersurface such that $\gamma_1 \subset I^+(\Sigma)$; then (3) p is on or beyond $H^+(\Sigma)$, where $H^+(\Sigma)$ is the future boundary of the future domain of dependence $D^+(\Sigma)$ of Σ. What this result says, more or less, is that events at p, or arbitrarily close to p, are subject to nondeterministic influences: There is nothing in the laws of physics to prevent a false signal conveying to γ_2 the misinformation that a signal has been sent by γ_1. To meet this difficulty, one might propose that the signals that are sent by γ_1 must encode the counterexample to Goldbach's conjecture, and not merely indicate that there is one. However, this will require that γ_2 be able to make arbitrarily fine discriminations – since ever larger numbers may need to be decoded in ever smaller time intervals – and thus returns us to the difficulties discussed in the preceding paragraph.

The upshot of our discussion is that there are various reasons for being sceptical about the claim that it is possible to *finesse* the operation of, for example, the Goldbach machine in suitable classes of relativistic spacetimes. If we allow that there is some sense in which the Goldbach machine is possible, then it seems doubtful that consideration of this machine in the context of relativistic spacetimes provides us with a *more robust* sense in which it is possible. As Earman and Norton stress, there is more work to be done before a fully definitive answer can be given; but, at the very least, we haven't yet been given reason to think that there are much closer possible worlds than we might previously have supposed in which there are machines that perform infinitely many operations in finite time.

4.7 SINGULARITIES

It is part of the folk wisdom of the twentieth century that general relativistic spacetimes contain points at which physical quantities take on infinite values. As Earman (1995) argues persuasively, this piece of folk wisdom is not, strictly speaking accurate: The truth about singularities in general relativistic spacetimes is more complex than this simple formulation allows. Nonetheless, any discussion of infinities in space and time that omitted some mention of singularities in general relativistic spacetimes would be seriously incomplete. So we shall follow Earman in trying to arrive at a more accurate view of the nature of singularities in general relativistic spacetimes.

As before, we suppose that a general relativistic spacetime is a pair $\langle \boldsymbol{M}, \boldsymbol{g} \rangle$, where $\boldsymbol{M}$ is a connected differentiable manifold (without boundary) and $\boldsymbol{g}$ is a Lorentz metric that is defined at every $p \in M$, and that is $C^k (k \geq 0)$ at every $p \in M$. (A metric is C^k iff partial derivatives of order k exist and are continuous. A metric is C^{k-} iff partial derivatives of order k exist and are locally bounded.) We shall say that $\langle \boldsymbol{M}_1, g_1 \rangle$ is an *extension* of $\langle \boldsymbol{M}_2, g_2 \rangle$ iff there is an isomorphic embedding of the latter into the former, that is, iff there is a diffeomorphism φ: $\boldsymbol{M}_2 \rightarrow \boldsymbol{M}_1$: $g_2 \,|_{\varphi(M2)} = \varphi^* g_1$. An extension is *proper* iff $\varphi(\boldsymbol{M})$ is a proper subset of $\boldsymbol{M}$. $\langle \boldsymbol{M}, \boldsymbol{g} \rangle$ is *properly extendible* iff it has a proper extension. $\langle \boldsymbol{M}, \boldsymbol{g} \rangle$ is *maximal* – with respect to continuity/differentiability condition C^β – iff there is no proper extension of $\langle \boldsymbol{M}, \boldsymbol{g} \rangle$.

It seems uncontroversial to require that a nonsingular spacetime is timelike geodesic complete, lightlike geodesic complete, and spacelike geodesic complete. It also seems relatively uncontroversial to require that, in a nonsingular spacetime, every timelike curve of bounded acceleration has infinite proper length. Both of these requirements are entailed by the condition that every half-curve has infinite generalised affine length. Say that a spacetime is *b-complete* iff every half-curve has infinite generalised affine length. Then a plausible suggestion is that a spacetime is *nonsingular* iff it is *b*-complete.

A *b*-incomplete curve in a spacetime $\langle \boldsymbol{M}, \boldsymbol{g} \rangle$ defines an ideal point on a boundary $\partial_b M$ of M. However, there is no appealing way to attach $\partial_b M$ to $\boldsymbol{M}$: In particular, the points in $\partial_b M$ are not Hausdorff separated from the points of $\boldsymbol{M}$. Given that the attempt to localise spacetime singularities requires such a high price, one might think it better to look for some other characterisation of singular spacetimes. On the other hand, the *b*-incompleteness criterion does provide an interesting classification of singular spacetimes.

A *regular point* p $\in \partial_b M$ is an inessential singularity: $\langle \boldsymbol{M}, \boldsymbol{g} \rangle$ can be extended to $\langle \boldsymbol{M}', \boldsymbol{g}' \rangle$ where the image of $p \in \boldsymbol{M}'$. *Singular points* are the nonregular points of $\partial_b M$. If $p \in \partial_b M$ is a singular point for which some of the physical components of the curvature tensor do not approach limits as the point is approached by parallel propagation along any *b*-incomplete curve that terminates in p, then p is a *curvature singularity*; else, p is a *quasi-regular point*. Curvature singularities divide into the following four cases: (1) *blow-up scalar polynomial singularities*, where a scalar curvature polynomial is unbounded as p is approached; (2) *oscillating scalar polynomial singularities*, where a scalar curvature polynomial fails to approach a limit as p is approached; (3) *blow-up nonscalar polynomial singularities*; and (4) *oscillating nonscalar polynomial singularities*. Further refinement is possible; but what we have is enough to show that, on the *b*-incompleteness approach, there are many singular spacetimes in which there are no unbounded quantities. It should be noted that the FRW big-bang singularities – and the Kruskal-Schwarzschild model – are examples of blow-up scalar polynomial singularities; that is, in these cases there are physical components of the curvature tensor that diverge.

While the *b*-incompleteness analysis captures the idea that singularities correspond to incompleteness, it fails to correspond to the idea that singularities correspond to missing points. Since a compact manifold cannot be a proper submanifold of a connected, Hausdorff manifold, the existence of *b*-incomplete compact manifolds gives us reason to be unhappy with the b-incompleteness analysis. Perhaps we should say that $\langle \boldsymbol{M}, \boldsymbol{g} \rangle$ is nonsingular iff every half-curve is either *b*-incomplete or else contained in a compact subset of $\boldsymbol{M}$. Or perhaps we should say that there are two different conceptions of singularities, and that we may avail ourselves of either. Or – as Earman indicates – perhaps there are other ways to proceed.

Even if we choose to retain the b-incompleteness analysis, our work is not done until we specify the completeness/differentiability conditions on the permissible extensions of $\langle \boldsymbol{M}, \boldsymbol{g} \rangle$. If we make the conditions too strong, then we shall exclude physically reasonable situations. But if we make the conditions too weak, then it will turn out that no spacetimes are essentially singular, and we won't be able to make use of well-known theorems about the existence of generic essential singularities in general relativistic spacetimes. If we insist that the metric is at least C^{2-} at all points, then we have the following results:

1. If $\langle \boldsymbol{M}, \boldsymbol{g} \rangle$ is a time-oriented spacetime satisfying the following four conditions:
   (a) $R_{ab}V^aV^b \geq 0$ for any nonspacelike V^a
   (b) the timelike and light-like generic conditions are fulfilled
   (c) there is no closed timelike curve
   (d) at least one of the following holds
      (i) there exists a compact achronal set without edge
      (ii) there exists a trapped surface
      (iii) there is a $p \in \boldsymbol{M}$ such that the expansion of the future (past) directed light-like geodesics through p becomes negative along each of the geodesics

   then $\langle \boldsymbol{M}, \boldsymbol{g} \rangle$ contains at least one incomplete timelike or light-like geodesic.
2. If $\langle m, g \rangle$ is a time-oriented spacetime satisfying the following three conditions:
   (a) $R_{ab}V^aV^b \geq 0$ for any nonspacelike V^a
   (b) there exists a compact spacelike hypersurface $\Sigma \subset M$ without edges
   (c) the unit normals to Σ are everywhere converging (or diverging)

   then $\langle M, g \rangle$ is timelike geodesically incomplete.

These results, due to Hawking and Penrose, tell us that, under plausible assumptions, there are generic essential singularities in general relativistic spacetimes. However, as noted above, it should not be supposed that these singularities must be places where physical components of the curvature tensor become unbounded. Moreover, as noted above, it is not obvious that we cannot suppose that the metric is only C^{1-}; and, in that case, it remains unknown whether results parallel to those of Hawking and Penrose obtain. As Earman says, there are various relative results about which we can be fairly confident: Essential singularities are more prevalent for negative values of the cosmological constant than when the value of the cosmological constant is zero, and essential singularities are more prevalent when the value of the cosmological constant is zero than for positive values of the cosmological constant. Again, essential singularities are more prevalent in spatially closed universes than in spatially open universes. And essential singularities are more prevalent when mass-energy is present than in vacuum solutions to the Einstein field equations.

In short: Taking general relativity seriously may well lead one to the conclusion that there are singularities in spacetime at which the physical components of the metric tensor become unbounded, but only if one makes further assumptions that it is not obviously compulsory to make. Those who wish to reject physically instantiated infinites, and who make those further assumptions, are then faced with a choice: Either refuse to take general relativity seriously or explain how taking that theory seriously is compatible with rejecting the claim that there can be physically instantiated infinities.

4.8 CONCLUDING REMARKS

There is at least some reason to suppose that any possible universe involves a system of external relations that bear at least some similarities to classical spatiotemporal relations.

If there are possible universes in which these external relations conform to classical Euclidean geometry, then – at least for all that we have learnt so far – it seems that it is possible for space to be infinite in volume and for time to be infinite both in the past and in the future in such universes. Certainly, there is nothing in the arguments of Kant's first antinomy to suggest otherwise. Moreover – at least for all that we have learnt so far – it seems that it is possible for space (and time) to be a mereological fusion of uncountably many points, or uncountably many regions, in such universes. Again, there is nothing in the arguments of Zeno of Elea to suggest otherwise.

If there are possible universes in which these external relations conform to classical general relativity, then, again – at least for all that we have learnt so far – it seems that it is possible for space and time to be infinite in both the large and the small in such universes. Moreover, it seems that it is possible for there to be various kinds of singularities in such universes even if we require that no physical components of the curvature tensor are unbounded as singular points are approached along appropriate trajectories. However, there is no good reason to suppose that it is possible to *finesse* the carrying out of an infinite number of operations in finite time in such universes.

If there are possible universes in which these external relations are of some other kind, then nothing that we have said so far in this chapter answers the question of whether there can be infinite aspects of those external relations in those universes. If, for example, there are possible universes in which there are nonmanifold external relations – discrete (lattice-based) relations, quantised relations, relations based on alternative algebraic fields, relations based on non-Archimedean geometries, relations based on topological fluctuations (as in spacetime foam models), relations analysable in terms of loop space representations, relations based on noncommutative geometries and quantum groups, relations based in quantum pre-geometries (as in twistor algebras), and so forth – then, for all that has been said here, it remains an open question of whether the external relations in these universes introduce large and small infinities.

Whether the system of external relations in the actual world involves large and small infinities depends on which system of external relations that is and on the ontology that is required to support such a system of external relations. Even if it is possible to give a relationalist construal of Euclidean spacetime – and perhaps even of some general relativistic spacetimes – it remains a further question whether it is possible to give a relationalist construal of the other possibilities canvassed in the previous paragraph. Since it remains a task for future science to determine the system of external relations that is instantiated in the actual world, we should be very cautious in making any proclamation about the finitude, or otherwise, of the system of external relations that provides the "frame" for the actual world.

5

Physical Infinities

Consideration of the structure of spacetime does not exhaust discussion of physical infinities. There are cases in which physical quantities take on infinite values that have nothing to do with either the small-scale or large-scale structure of spacetime. For example, following the discussion of Ehrlich (1982), we note that modern physics legitimates the notions of *negative, infinite,* and *hotter than infinite* temperatures. Understanding how this can be and yet not be problematic requires an understanding of the distinction between extensive and intensive magnitudes; so, after a brief discussion of thermodynamics, we shall conduct an exploration of the relevant parts of the theory of measurement.

Next, we turn our attention to what is, perhaps, the most bewildering role for the concept of the infinite in modern physics: namely, the discussion of the role of renormalisation in quantum field theory. At least initially, it seems that quantum field theories use methods of approximation that produce infinite terms that are then "thrown out" – though only after finite parts of these terms are removed – prior to the production of answers that are in better agreement with observation than are answers in any other branch of science. If there is any part of science that justifies belief in physical infinities, then at least, *prima facie*, it seems that it will be quantum field theory.

The third case study in this chapter involves the pretty problem of the dark night sky. If the universe contained infinitely many 'randomly distributed' stars, then it seems that, no matter the direction in which one looked, there would be light entering one's eye from a star. But if that's right, then surely the night sky shouldn't be dark; rather, it should be a dazzling blaze of light. Since simple observation tells us that the night sky is dark, it seems that we have here an argument for the conclusion that there are only finitely many stars.

In the last part of the chapter, we turn to some more general questions about the characterisation of physical infinities. While there is no doubt that each of our case studies does involve something that, at least *prima facie*, deserves to be called a physical infinity, there are various questions that arise when we try to give a more general account of what it is for there to be physical infinities.

For example, there are the questions that arise when we think about the different ways in which we can characterise a physical system. Consider, for example, the various different spaces that can be used in the characterisation of the system: configuration space, state space, phase space, and so forth. Should we worry equally about infinities in any of the spaces, or are there some spaces in which infinities would be more worrying than in others?

More generally, there are various interesting questions to be raised about different aspects of the physically infinite. For example, we might ask: Exactly which conceivable variations of our world should we suppose to be genuine physically possible worlds? To carry out an investigation of this question, we need to spend some time thinking about the nature of possibility and, in particular, the nature of physical possibility: There are, after all, theories of possibility that suggest very different answers to our question about the range of possible variation of our world.

5.1 HOTTER THAN INFINITE TEMPERATURES

A *temperature scale* is a function from the thermal states of objects to the real numbers. An *empirical temperature scale* assigns numbers to states on the basis of a chosen property of a chosen substance that is known to vary in continuous monotonic fashion when heated or cooled. So, for example, the Centigrade scale assigns the numbers 0 and 100 to the thermal states associated with the standardised height of a standardised mercury thread immersed in an ice bath at its melting point and in water at its boiling point. In principle, the properties of length on the real number line then determine the assignment of numbers to all other thermal states. In practice, things are not so simple: The described procedure clearly breaks down for temperatures below the freezing point of mercury and above the softening point of glass.

Kelvin's absolute temperature scale assigns numbers to states in a way that is independent of selected properties and selected substances. Carnot had discovered that heat engines obey the equation $Q_2/Q_1 = f(t_1, t_2)$, where Q_1 is the amount of heat absorbed at the hotter source, Q_2 is the amount of heat rejected at the colder source, t_1 and t_2 are the temperatures of the hotter and colder sources as measured on some arbitrarily selected empirical scale, and f is a function whose form depends on the chosen empirical scale. Kelvin showed that there is a function h whose form also depends on the chosen empirical scale, such that $f(t_1, t_2) = h(t_2)/h(t_1)$. Thus $Q_2/Q_1 = h(t_2)/h(t_1)$, and we can define the absolute temperature $T = Cg(t)$, where C is a constant. The value of C can be assigned either by assigning a number to an interval between two selected thermal states – as was done prior to 1954, when the difference between the ice point and the boiling point of water was set at 100°K – or by assigning a number to a selected thermal state – as has been done since 1954, when the triple point of water was set at 273.16°K. Thus, the current absolute temperature scale is defined by $T = -273.16\ Q/Q_{273.16}$.

From the first and second laws of thermodynamics, we have that $T = (\partial U/\partial S)x_1, \ldots, x_n$, where S is the entropy of a system and U is the internal energy of that system, and $x_1, \ldots, x_n$ are parameters that are held constant during the differentiation. It follows from this equation that a necessary condition for the existence of a system with an infinite or negative temperature is that the system has an upper bound with respect to energy. This condition can be satisfied, in particular, in systems that have only finitely many energy levels.

The systems standardly discussed in thermodynamics have an infinite number of energy levels; consequently, in these systems, infinite temperatures are unattainable. However, systems in which there are only finitely many energy levels are not uncommon, though often they occur as subsystems of systems in which there are infinitely many energy levels. To ascribe temperatures to these systems, it must be possible to isolate the subsystem from the system for sufficient time to allow the subsystem to enter thermal equilibrium. The first finite-level system in which this was found to be feasible is the set of nuclear spins of lithium ions in a lithium fluoride crystal. Several other sets of nuclear spins have since been found that meet the same requirement.

It may be easiest to understand what is going on here by considering a toy example. Suppose that we have a very simple system, each of whose elements can occupy only one of two energy levels. Since the elements of the system have only two energy levels, the system attains its upper bound with respect to energy when all of the elements are in the higher level. In this state of the system, $S = 0$ and $T = -0$. Similarly, the system attains its lower bound with respect to energy when all of the elements are in the lower level. Again, in this state of the system, $S = 0$ and $T = 0$. In intermediate states, in which some elements are in the higher level and some elements are in the lower level, $S > 0$, and there is some point at which S takes on a maximum value, S_{max}. At this point, $T = \pm\infty$. While the upper bound and lower bound states are not actually physically attainable, the state in which S takes on its maximum value is physically attainable, as are states with higher energy than this one.

It is perhaps surprising to learn that, on Kelvin's absolute temperature scale, temperatures range from coldest to hottest in the following order: $0, \ldots, \pm\infty, \ldots -0$. Negative temperatures are hotter than positive temperatures, and they are hotter than infinite temperatures! Moreover, there are systems in the world that have negative temperatures, and there are systems in the world that have infinite temperature! However, as Ehrlich goes on to argue, there is no good reason for fans of physically instantiated infinities to get excited by these results: These infinities are no more exciting than are regular points on the *b*-boundaries of general relativistic spacetimes. It will require a bit of a detour through the theory of measurement to explain why.

5.2 EXTENSIVE MAGNITUDES

A *measurement scale* is a function from the properties of objects and events to a number system. A useful measurement scale captures a homomorphism between structural features of the measured properties (and the empirical relations that obtain between them) and structural features of numbers (and the arithmetical relations that obtain between them). In the standard case, the system of numbers is the real numbers; we shall proceed under the assumption that our measurement scales are real-valued.

In the case of some properties of objects and events, there exists a natural empirical operation that corresponds to the arithmetical operation of addition over the real numbers. *Extensive* measurement scales capture this natural additivity. In consequence, extensive measurement scales conform to (something like) the following conditions.

1. There is a quasi-serial ordering of the elements of the domain of objects that possess the measured quantity q: For any a and b in the domain, either $a \sim b$ or $a > b$, or $a < b$, where $\sim$ is an equivalence relation, and $>$ is transitive and asymmetric.
2. There is a closed binary operation * over the elements of the domain of objects that satisfies the following properties
   (a) Associativity: $a^*(b^*c) \sim (a^*b)^*c$
   (b) Nonnegativity: Either $a^*b \sim a$ or $a^*b > a$
   (c) Monotonicity: $a \sim b$ iff $a^*c \sim b^*c$ iff $c^*a \sim c^*b$; $a > b$ iff $a^*c > b^*c$ iff $c^*a > c^*b$
   (d) Archimedeanism: If $a > b$, then for any c, d in the domain, there exists some positive integer n such that $na^*c > nb^*d$, where na is defined inductively by $1a = a$, $(n+1)a = na^*a$.

Intuitively, $\sim$ means "is equal in quantity q to" and $>$ means "is greater in quantity q than". * is an operation that concatenates elements of the domain. The first of the above conditions ensures that there is a real valued function S on the domain such that, for all elements in the domain, $a \sim b$ iff $S(a) = S(b)$ and $a > b$ iff $S(a) > S(b)$. The second of these two conditions ensures that $S(a^*b) = S(a) + S(b)$.[1]

It is clear that measures of temperature are not extensive: If we take two systems of a given temperature and combine them, the temperature of the composite system is equal to the temperatures of the two

[1] Mundy (1987) argues for a different conception of physical extensive measurement that does without any version of the Archimedean axiom and makes various other changes as well. Ehrlich (1982) does not allow that one can have $a^*b \sim a$ in 2(b), so that his requirement is properly called Positivity. There is no need for us to enter into dispute about these matters here.

systems that were combined. It is plausible to claim that a thermometric scale need satisfy only the following constraint:

There is a quasi-serial ordering of the elements of the domain of objects that possess temperatures: For any a and b in the domain, either $a \sim b$ or $a > b$, or $a < b$, where $\sim$ is the equivalence relation *is the same temperature as*, and $>$ is the transitive and asymmetric relation *has greater temperature than*.

Clearly, the Kelvin absolute temperature scale satisfies this requirement, provided that we take the range of our temperatures to be the extended real numbers **Я**. However, there are many other choices of a temperature scale that also conform to the above requirement. Consider, for example: $f(T) = 1/T$, which yields the range of values $-\infty, \ldots, \pm 0, \ldots, \infty$; or $f(T) = \text{Tanh}(1/T)$, which yields the range of values $-1, \ldots, \pm 0, \ldots, 1$. Since these scales are also perfectly acceptable, we can be sure that there is nothing problematic about the infinities that appear in the Kelvin absolute temperature scale; and we can also be quite sure that there is nothing problematic about the existence of systems that have infinite temperatures. While it is most convenient, all things considered, to adopt a system in which certain states are assigned infinite temperatures, the assignment of infinite temperatures is just a consequence of our choice of scale and does not indicate the existence of a genuinely problematic infinite quantity in the world.

5.3 INFINITE EXTENSIVE MAGNITUDES?

One of the most interesting features of Ehrlich (1982) is his attempt to defend the claim that there are possible worlds in which there are infinite extensive quantities. To make his case, Ehrlich begins with an example taken from the writings of Poincaré, and then adapts it to his own ends.

Poincaré's world is enclosed in a large sphere of radius R_2. The absolute temperature of the sphere varies as $R_2^2 - r^2$, where r is the distance from the centre of the sphere, R_1. Thus, the temperature is greatest at the centre and gradually decreases to zero at the surface of the sphere. Moreover, all bodies have the same coefficient of dilation, and this coefficient is proportional to temperature. Finally, a body transported from one point to another of different temperature is immediately in thermal equilibrium with its surroundings.

Ehrlich's world consists of a sequence of concentric spheres of radii R_i, $i \geq 2$, where $R_i > R_j$ for $i > j$. The innermost sphere, of radius R_2, is just like the sphere in Poincaré's world, except that the centre and surface of the sphere are at the same nonzero temperature, and all objects moving from the centre return to the size that they have at the centre as soon as they reach the surface of that sphere at R_2, with expansion away from the centre of the sphere. The nth concentric shell, consisting of the result of subtracting the nth sphere from the $n+1$th sphere, is much like the sphere of Poincaré's world, except that the inner and outer surfaces of the shell are at the same temperature as the centre of the innermost sphere, and the length of an object in the interior of this shell is proportional to the temperature that is, in turn, proportional to $(R_{n+2} - R_{n+1})^2 - (r - R_{n+1})^2$, where R_{n+2} and R_{n+1} are the radii of the $n+1$th and nth spheres. As in the innermost sphere, all objects return to the size that they have at the centre as soon as they reach the surface of any of the spheres. In the most general case, we can suppose that the series of concentric spheres is merely countable and well ordered.

Poincaré claimed that an attempt to measure the radius of his world using a standard measuring rod would yield the result that the radius is infinite, since the laws governing the shrinking of the object allow that an infinite number of 'identical' measuring rods can be placed end to end between the centre and the outer surface of the sphere or, alternatively, that a single measuring rod can be turned end-on-end infinitely many times in moving it between the centre and the outer surface. Ehrlich claims that, in his extended world, attempts to measure its radius will yield the result that there are greater than infinite lengths, because reaching the surface of any of the spheres requires a count of ω units since departure from the preceding surface of a sphere. Indeed, according to Ehrlich, the example shows that there can be a series of longer than infinite lengths that corresponds to the entire *countable* portion of Cantor's well-ordered universe of transfinite ordinals. (We are restricted to the countable portion because any collection of nonoverlapping nonzero three-dimensional regions of space is at most denumerably infinite.)

It seems to me that there are various difficulties with Ehrlich's claim. First, even if a measurer can complete a journey between two surfaces in Ehrlich's world, and even if that measurer claims that the distance between the two surfaces is actually infinite, the construction of the world shows that the measurer is mistaken: We were told at the outset that the distance between any two surfaces is finite. So it simply isn't true that we have an actually infinite extensive quantity: There are no two points in Ehrlich's world that are anything other than finitely far apart. However, if a measurer can complete a journey between two surfaces in Ehrlich's world, then – for all that has been argued so far – it seems that a measurer could have good reason to *suppose* that there are actually infinite extensive quantities, and it might be thought that that is trouble enough for those who reject the possibility of physically instantiated infinities.

Second, it is quite unclear what the grounds are supposed to be for insisting that, when the measurer reaches the second surface, the count of the distance will stand at ω. Since our measurer is making repeated use of a unit rule, and since – *ex hypothesi* – the measurer is not supposed to notice anything unusual when he or she reaches the second surface, what are we to suppose is the standing of the count immediately before he or she reaches ω? It is simply incoherent to suppose (1) that at any point before he or she reaches the second surface, the count is definitely finite, (2) he or she reaches the second surface by making one more use of the unit rule, and (3) that the count stands at ω when he or she reaches the second surface. Of course, there is nothing special about ω here. Pick any other infinite Conway number say, and the incoherence remains. The problem is that there is a *gap* between the finite numbers and the infinite numbers that cannot be bridged by the mere finite addition of units.

Third – for the reasons just given – it is not clear that we can make sense of the idea that the measurer does indeed reach the second surface. If we suppose that the amount of time that it takes for the measurer to lift and replace the unit rule is constant, then, at any finite time, the measurer will be short of the second surface. Consequently, it seems that we shall need to suppose that the speed with which the measurer works increases as he or she gets closer to the second surface. (Since the temperature approaches zero as the second surface is approached, we might suppose that he or she needs to work faster in order to keep warm!) If we think of the unit rule's motion on the model of a propeller that is moved transversely in the plane of rotation of the propeller, then I suspect that the velocity of the tip of the unit rule will then be unbounded as the second surface is approached; and, if that's right, we have good kinematical grounds for declaring that the envisaged scenario is not a logical possibility.

For the reasons given here, I think that Ehrlich's example does not establish that it is possible for there to be infinite extensive quantities; and neither does it establish that it is possible for a measurer to have good grounds to suppose that there are infinite extensive quantities. Perhaps we can make sense of the idea that a being can make infinitely many measurements of length in a finite period of time; but if so, the total length that is measured will have to be finite and will have to be taken by the measurer to be finite. Consider, for example, Grünbaum's staccato run, and suppose that the "runner" is measuring the distance that the Tortoise travels in a convergent infinite series of time intervals. At the very least, the kinds of considerations that have been rehearsed here fail to show that there is anything incoherent in *this* measurement scenario.

Even if we have reason to suppose that there cannot be infinite extensive quantities, and even if there is no reason to suppose that infinite nonextensive quantities are in any way problematic, there are other ways in which questions about infinity can intrude into thought about the physical world. We turn next to a discussion of the treatment of infinite quantities in quantum field theory. Since the nicest discussion that I know of these matters is provided in Teller (1989), we shall follow his presentation fairly closely.

5.4 RENORMALISATION

In the classical theory of electromagnetism, each electron produces an electric field. But, given an electric field and an electron, the electron must interact with the field. So, in the classical theory of electromagnetism, it must turn out that each electron interacts with its own electric field. The standard way of interpreting this interaction in the classical theory of electromagnetism is to suppose that the self-interaction of an electron – that is, the interaction of an electron with its own electric field – is a (not necessarily proper) part of the electron's mass. While this is fine if the electron has a nonzero radius, the self-interaction is infinite in the case of a point charge. But if the electron has a finite radius, then the electron has structure, and, in particular, the electron has a charge distribution. Why, then, doesn't the charge distribution cause the electron to fall apart under the influence of the repulsive charge?

This problem, which seems to have no satisfactory resolution in classical electromagnetism, carries over to quantum field theory. As in the classical case, in quantum field theory an electron interacts with its own field. This self-interaction gives rise to a quantity that can be taken to be part of the mass of the electron. The difficulty that arises is that the self-interaction quantity turns out to be infinite.

Our first task is to say a little bit more about where these problematic divergences arise in quantum field theory, and how quantum field theory deals with them. Since the exact description of quantum field theory is highly complicated, I shall follow Teller in introducing various simplifications that make no difference for the purposes of the present discussion.

We suppose that, associated with a particle of mass m, we have a propagator $S(m)$. $S(m)$ is a function of the mass of the particle and can be used in the calculation of many of the observable properties of the particle. Since no one knows how to calculate the value of $S(m)$ by exact, or analytic, methods, we can calculate its value only by a series of approximations, that is, by a perturbation expansion in a small parameter. That is, we calculate a first-order approximation $S_1(m)$, and then a series of corrections $C_i(m)$ that yield higher-order approximations $S_i(m)$. It turns out that the first-order approximation, $S_1(m)$, gives good results that agree quite well with experiment, but that the first correction term, $C_2(m)$ – the first point at which the self-interaction of the particle is taken into account – is divergent. While it might be thought that this divergence shows that there is something wrong with the underlying theory, with the scheme of approximation, or with the combination of these two, quantum field theorists have devised a method for dealing with the divergence.

The divergent quantities that appear in the second-order correction terms $C_2(m)$ are divergent integrals of the form $\int_0^\infty g(k)\,dk$, where $\int_0^L g(k)\,dk \approx \ln L$. Suppose that we choose a large value of L, and put $S(m)$ in the form $S(m - \int_0^L g(k)\,dk)$. When we expand $S(m - \int_0^L g(k)\,dk)$, we do not get any divergent terms, because we use L to "cut off" all of the divergent integrals. Moreover, if we take $m - \int_0^L g(k)\,dk$ to be an expression of the real, observable mass of our particle – so that we are free to take the value of the in principle unobservable m to be such that $m - \int_0^L g(k)\,dk$ is the actual value that we measure – we find that $\lim_{L\to\infty} S(m - \int_0^L g(k)\,dk)$ is well defined. (Think of m as the bare mass of the electron, i.e., the mass that it has when interaction and self-energy is ignored. Then m_r – the *renormalised* mass, the mass that is actually observed – is $\lim_{L\to\infty}(m(L) - \int_0^L g(k)\,dk)$ for an appropriately selected $m(L)$.)

The above account is a very crude approximation to the actual method of quantum field theorists. In particular, it makes no mention of the fact that there are finite "radiative corrections" that are not removed when renormalisation removes divergent integrals. Since these "radiative corrections" are needed to deal with the Lamb shift and anomalous magnetic moment, we need to be able to justify their inclusion. To do this, we begin by noting that mass measurement situations can be characterised by a parameter q that is small when the momentum exchanged in the mass measurement is small. Given q, we can write $\int_0^L g(k)\,dk = \int_0^L g_d(k)\,dk + q\int_0^L g(k)\,dk$. Consequently, the observed mass is $m_r = m - \int_0^L g_d(k)\,dk - q\int_0^L g_f(k)\,dk = m - \int_0^L g_d(k)\,dk$ when $q \approx 0$, as it is in any actual measurement situation. In situations in which we don't have $q \approx 0$, we need to add back in the "radiative correction" term $q\int_0^L g_f(k)\,dk$ in order to get the right answer. Thus – recalling that so far we have only been discussing the situation in which there is a finite cut-off – we can take the renormalised mass of our particle to be $\lim_{L\to\infty}(m(L) - \int_0^L g_d(k)\,dk) - q\int_0^L g_f(k)\,dk)$, and secure agreement with actual measurement for the Lamb shift, and so on.

The above discussion deals only with the second-order correction terms. When we move on to the third-order correction terms, we get new divergent integrals that we deal with in the same way. To show that a quantum field theory is renormalisable, what must be shown is that, at each order of correction, all of the divergent integrals can be absorbed. Of course, in the case of the electron, not all of the divergent integrals need to be absorbed into the electron's observed mass; for example, some could be absorbed into its observed charge. However, a renormalisable theory can contain no more than finitely many constants whose values are fixed by observation; and hence it is a highly nontrivial matter to show that a theory is actually renormalisable. Nonetheless, there are quantum field theories that have been shown to be renormalisable; and these theories yield the best agreement between theory and experiment that has been found anywhere in science.

There is another way in which the above discussion is a very crude approximation to the actual methods of quantum field theorists. There are various different ways in which one can introduce a parameter that leads to divergence as that parameter goes to infinity, but that yields finite values when it is finite. Cutting off the upper bound of integration is the crudest method (but the easiest to understand). There are methods that alter the integrand so that the integral is well defined over $(0, \infty)$, where this alteration depends on a parameter that can be allowed to go to infinity. There is also the method of dimensional regularisation, which begins by finding an expression for a problematic integral as a function of number of dimensions, and then considers the limit as the number of dimensions approaches 4. In general, the method of regularisation works by replacing the divergent integrals with nondivergent expressions that are a function of a parameter that yields back the expressions for the original divergent integrals in the limit as this parameter goes to infinity.

As Teller says, there are at least three different ways of thinking about renormalisation in quantum field theory.

The first is to adopt the regularisation approach presented above. This approach yields an unambiguous and mathematically consistent scheme for predicting the outcomes of measurements that is in excellent agreement with observation. However, some theorists reject this approach, because they object to the fact that the regularised theories – the intermediate theories before the limit of the parameter is taken – do not satisfy important theoretical constraints such as gauge invariance, unitarity, or Lorentz invariance. While, as Teller says, this does not seem to be a decisive objection – it is, after all, the theory that results after the limit is taken that is supposed to apply to the world – it is worth asking whether there are alternative approaches that can satisfy this further requirement.

A second way of thinking about renormalisation is to suppose that renormalisation really does have to be understood in terms of the mathematically inconsistent procedure of "throwing away" real infinities. On this view, there really are infinite self-interactions that are balanced by infinite bare masses and infinite bare charges. If we go this way, then we are supposing that our best-confirmed scientific theory commits us to the most dramatic actually infinite quantities, for example, points at which the magnitudes of fields are greater than any finite value. Since it seems doubtful that we so much as understand this proposal, it seems plausible to suggest that proponents of this approach should be taken to be putting their faith in a future conceptual revolution in mathematics.[2]

A third way of thinking about renormalisation is to suppose that quantum field theories are at best approximations to the truth and that, in a more correct theory of the world, all of the problematic divergent quantities disappear. This approach still has the resources to explain why renormalisability is a good thing: We want our theories to be renormalisable because we want to have tractable approximations to the truth. If we can renormalise, we can calculate; if not, not. Quantum field theories are in good agreement with observation; but a correct theory of the world would be thoroughly finite. Of course, this approach must incur the burden of explaining why it is that quantum field theory is in such good agreement with observation; but it can hardly be expected to provide this explanation in advance of the production of a more satisfactory theory.

Arriving at a satisfactory understanding of physical particles and their interactions with physical fields is a very difficult task, and one that is still beset with difficulties. Whether this fact should be taken as good news for friends of physical infinities remains a matter for dispute. My inclination is to follow Teller in thinking that it would be incautious to suppose that it is really good news: Either we can understand renormalisation in terms of regularisation or there will be no renormalisation in theories of the world better than those that we currently possess. As things stand, it isn't obvious that there is anything in quantum field theory to encourage friends of physical infinities.

[2] Teller suggests that it might be possible to use Conway's **No** as the basis for such a revolution. However, it seems to me that this suggestion is unpromising. As I have already noted, Conway himself is sceptical that **No** has any significance for analysis. Moreover, the familiar methods of nonstandard analysis – e.g., internal set theory – that involve "throwing away" of infinities do not give back anything other than the results of standard analysis.

5.5 THE DARK NIGHT SKY

The third of our case studies of the physical infinite is the interesting case of the dark night sky. If the universe contained infinitely many 'randomly distributed' stars or groupings of stars (galaxies, clusters of galaxies, or the like), then it seems that, no matter the direction in which one looked, there would be light entering one's eye from a star (or grouping of stars – but we shall suppress this qualification henceforth[3]). However, if that's right, then surely the night sky shouldn't be dark; rather, it should be a dazzling blaze of light. Since simple observation tells us that the night sky is dark, it seems that we have here an argument for the conclusion that there are only finitely many stars.

There are many different explanations that might be offered of why it is that the night sky is dark. Following Harrison (1987), we can divide these explanations into two classes: those that suppose that there are stars in any direction that we choose to look, but that there is some reason why we fail to see some of those stars; and those that suppose that there are not stars in every direction that we choose to look.

Examples of explanations of the first kind include the following: (1) that the light of distant stars is too faint to be seen (this solution was offered by Thomas Digges, the discoverer of the puzzle of the dark night sky, in 1576), (2) that the light of distant stars is slowly absorbed as it travels immense interstellar distances (this solution was offered by Jean-Philippe Loys de Chésaux in 1744, and again by Wilhelm Olbers in 1823), (3) that the vast majority of stars are nonluminous (this is one of the solutions that was suggested by Fournier d'Albe in 1907) (4) that there is a cycle in which stars decay into starlight and starlight transforms into matter that then aggregates into stars (this solution was offered by William MacMillan in 1925), and (5) that the light from distant stars is red-shifted into invisibility by the expansion of the universe (this solution was offered by Hermann Bondi in 1952).

[3] The qualification is strictly required. After all, it is well known that the stars are not uniformly distributed in the sky; rather, they cluster into galaxies, etc. Of course, this fact helps to explain why the stars do not *appear* to be uniformly distributed in the sky from our vantage point: The earth is in one of the spiral arms of a roughly disc-shaped galaxy, so that most of the stars that can be seen by the naked eye appear to be clustered in a narrow band (the Milky Way).

Examples of explanations of the second kind include the following: (1) that there aren't enough stars to cover the sky (this solution is suggested by the ancient Stoic cosmology in which the universe is a finite sphere located in infinite empty space, and by the neo-Aristotelian cosmology in which there is a cosmic wall that marks the outer limit of the universe), (2) that the universe consists of an appropriately organised infinite hierarchy of clusters, with stars grouped into clusters, star clusters grouped into galaxies, galaxies grouped into galactic clusters, galactic clusters grouped into superclusters, and so forth (this solution was proposed by John Herschel in 1848),[4] (3) that stars are not old enough for the light from distant stars to have yet reached us (this solution is offered by Edgar Allan Poe in 1848, and in quantitative form by Lord Kelvin in 1901), (4) that starlight cannot travel across intergalactic space but rather remains trapped within galaxies (this solution is offered by Simon Newcomb in 1878 and developed by John Gore in 1888), (5) that the light emitted from stars travels around a spherically curved universe and returns to the stars from whence it originated (this solution was given by Johann Zöllner in 1883 and endorsed by Stanley Jaki in 1969), and (6) that there is not enough mass/energy in the universe to make the night sky bright (this solution is the one defended by Harrison in 1987).

Almost all of these attempted explanations are flawed in one way or another. Amongst the explanations of the first kind, we can dismiss Digges's hypothesis on the grounds that the combination of enough weak signals will not itself be weak; we can dismiss the suggestion of de Chésaux and Olbers on the grounds that an absorptive medium will heat up until it reaches thermal equilibrium, in which state it reradiates as much energy as it absorbs; we can dismiss Fournier d'Albe's solution on the grounds that we have solid independent reasons for denying that the universe contains so many nonluminous stars; we can dismiss MacMillan's proposal on various grounds, not least that there is no way of transforming light into matter in the way that his solution requires;

[4] Fournier d'Albe proposed a much simpler variant of this solution, with the stars arranged in rows leading away from the earth. (As Alan Hájek pointed out to me, it is logically possible that the universe contains infinitely many stars even though only one is visible from earth, if the stars are all arranged in a single row.) But we have good physical grounds for refusing to take d'Albe's proposal seriously given that we are seeking to explain why it is *actually* the case that the night sky is dark.

and we can dismiss Bondi's hypothesis on the grounds that, while it is an adequate solution for an expanding steady state universe, we have good independent reasons for denying that ours is an expanding steady state universe. It seems, then, that none of these proposals of the first kind is satisfactory: It is not true that we can explain the darkness of the night sky by adverting to any of these versions of the claim that, even though there are stars in any direction that we choose to look, there is a reason why we fail to see some of those stars.

Amongst the explanations of the second kind, we can dismiss those based on Stoic and neo-Aristotelian cosmology on the grounds that there are good, independent grounds for rejecting those cosmologies; we can reject the Newcomb/Gore hypothesis on the grounds that the radiation level will rise inside the cavity that surrounds a galaxy to produce a bright night sky; and we can dismiss the Zöllner/Jaki suggestion on the grounds that, in fact, spherical space will not act as a perfect lens, which means that the level of reabsorption of light by sources will be much less than is required to make this proposal fly. To assess the remaining proposals properly, we need a modest amount of theory.

In his discussion of the problem, Lord Kelvin noted, roughly, that the fraction of sky covered by stars = the brightness of the starlit sky/the brightness of the sun's disk = the size of the visible universe/the background limit, where the background limit, or mean free path, is the average distance of visible stars in a universe populated uniformly with stars. Given this result, it follows that the night sky is dark iff the size of the visible universe is less than the background limit. From observation, we can determine that the background limit is about 1,000 trillion light years. So, unless the size of the visible universe is also about 1,000 trillion light years or more, the night sky will be dark. But the size of the visible universe is much less than 1,000 trillion light years.

So, why is the night sky dark? Well, there are several ways of answering this question. If what you want to know is why the size of the visible universe is less than the background limit, then a plausible answer is that the mass-energy density of the universe is too small. (This is Harrison's answer.) If what you want to know is why the size of the visible universe is less than 1,000 trillion light years, then a plausible answer is that it is not true that luminous stars have been shining for 1,000 trillion years. (This is the Poe/Kelvin answer.) There are, of course, other considerations that might be raised here: for instance, that, given the finite speed of light and the finite age of the universe, the size of the visible universe is determined to be a particular value that is less than 1,000 trillion light years.

Which explanation we adopt depends on what else we are prepared to assume and which facts about the universe we are prepared to take for granted. It seems to be true that, if there are only finitely many stars, and those stars are not crammed too closely together, then the night sky will be dark. However, it is not true that having less than infinitely many stars guarantees that the night sky is dark. So, roughly, appealing to the finitude of the number of stars works as an explanation only if we hold fixed facts about the actual distribution of the stars in space. Likewise, it seems to be true that, if the universe has the right kind of hierarchical structure, then the night sky will be dark even if there is no upper bound on the speed of light. Given that we hold fixed facts about the finite speed of light, there is no need to appeal to any such kind of structure in order to explain the darkness of the night sky; but it may nonetheless be true that the universe has such a structure and that, because it does so, there is a guarantee that the night sky would be dark even if light could travel arbitrarily fast.

Returning to the argument that was set out at the beginning of the current section, we see that there is no good argument from the darkness of the night sky to the finitude of the number of stars in the universe. Both the Harrison answer and the Poe/Kelvin answer work whether the universe is finite or infinite, and whether the number of stars is finite or infinite. Moreover, it seems that there are nearby possible universes in which there are only finitely many stars in which the night sky is bright, even though the speed of light is finite and the laws of thermodynamics are such as to require stars to burn out after a finite lifespan; and it seems that there are nearby possible universes in which there are infinitely many stars in which the night sky is dark, and in which the speed of light is as large as you please and the laws of thermodynamics are such as to permit stars to burn forever. In our world, and in worlds like ours, the darkness of the night sky gives no encouragement to either friend or foe of physically instantiated infinities.

5.6 SOME MORE GENERAL CONSIDERATIONS

Our three cases, and the discussion thereof, barely begin to scratch the surface of the topic of physical infinities. There are many different ways that discussions of infinities turn up in the physical sciences, and many different considerations that must be borne in mind in trying to assess what are the implications of these discussions. Here, we shall try to survey some of the most important questions that arise when one thinks in general terms about the possibility of physical infinities.

First, there are different kinds of infinitary assumptions that can be made in physical theories. One might suppose that one has infinitely many *objects* of a given kind (e.g., that there are infinitely many stars, electrons, or the like). One might suppose that there are infinitely many distinct *states* that it is possible for objects to occupy (e.g., infinitely many energy levels for electrons in an ideal gas). One might suppose that there are divergent (or infinite) physical *magnitudes* (e.g., divergent (or infinite) temperatures in systems in which there are infinitely many energy levels). One might suppose that there are *continuous* field distributions (e.g., a continuous gravitational field). One might suppose that there are *point* objects, that is, objects that are instantiated at single spatiotemporal points (e.g., electrons, when these are thought of as point particles). One might think that there are *infinitesimal* physical magnitudes (e.g., infinitesimal changes in an electromagnetic field distribution). And so forth.

Second, there are different views that one can take about what it is that one is committed to by the adoption of a given physical – or, more generally, scientific – theory.

One can construct scientific models in which the large is *approximated* by the infinite, and/or the small is *approximated* by the infinitesimal, in order to obtain an advantage of some kind, for example, computational tractability. As Segel (1991) notes, there are problems about, for example, pendulums, chemical decay, coagulation kinetics, diffusion, convection, economic equilibrium, and fluid flow in which progress has proven to rely on the approximation of the large by the infinite and/or the small by the infinitesimal. In these cases, there is no commitment to the existence of infinite or infinitesimal quantities in nature, for the theory is merely a convenient approximation to reality in which everything is finite.

One can construct scientific theories in which infinities and/or infinitesimals appear, and for which there is no underlying theory in which these infinities and infinitesimals are replaced by finite quantities, and yet insist that these theories should be given a merely *instrumentalist,* or otherwise *antirealist,* interpretation. If we think that acceptance of a scientific theory does not require commitment to the truth of that theory – so that, in particular, acceptance of that theory does not require commitment to the existence of the entities over which the theory quantifies – then we shall think that references to infinities and infinitesimals in our accepted scientific theories have no serious implications for questions about the existence of physical infinities. Of course, it is a hotly contested question whether one can be, or should be, an antirealist about accepted scientific theories; to mention that this is an option on the philosophical menu is not to endorse it.

Third, there are different views that one can take about how one works out what it is that one is committed to by the adoption of a given physical – or, more generally, scientific – theory. We might follow Quine in thinking that quantification (in canonical notation) is a mark of ontological commitment: Wherever we quantify over a domain of objects, we are committed to the existence of objects of that kind. Or we might have a discriminating view, according to which only some instances of quantification (in canonical notation) are ontologically committing, while others are not. On the latter kind of view, we might hold that, even though physical theories in canonical notation quantify over the real numbers, it does not follow that acceptance of those theories brings with it ontological commitment to the existence of uncountably many objects.

Fourth, there are different views that one might take about the nature of the canonical notation in which scientific theories should be framed. In particular, there is a question about how one should view possible trade-offs between ontological commitments and ideological commitments. If we suppose that it is possible to trade in ontological commitments for ideological commitments – as, perhaps, in the move from a substantivalist to a relationalist treatment of spacetime – then we might suppose that we can avoid any problematic commitment to an infinite realm of objects by recasting all of our theories in terms of, for example, the instantiation of properties. On the other hand, one might think that an infinity of property instantiations – or, at any rate, an infinity of more or less natural property instantiations – is no better than an infinity of objects.

Fifth, there are different views that one might take about how to characterise the *physical*: physical objects, physical states, physical properties, physical magnitudes, and the like. While the characterisation of physical objects may be relatively straightforward – physical objects are those objects that have spatiotemporal locations or, at any rate, those objects that stand in a system of external relations that is relevantly similar to the system of spatiotemporal relations and that possess the property (or properties) that corresponds to possession of spatiotemporal location – it is not at all easy to demarcate the physical properties from the nonphysical properties. If we are prepared to assume that current physics is at least in the ballpark of correct physics, then we might try saying that the physical properties are all of the properties that belong on the following list: mass, charge, spin, colour, strangeness, and so on. However, if we are prepared to suppose that it may turn out that none of these properties is actually instantiated, then it is not clear where to turn to look for an informative account, that is, for an account that says something more than that the physical properties are those contingently instantiated properties of physical objects that figure in a complete true theory of the universe. (In the end, the possible differences of opinion here may not be overly important. While we have been focusing on the physical, it is actually the category of the contingent – and/or, perhaps, the nonabstract – that will be most important when we move on to apply the results of our discussion of the infinite.)

Sixth, even if one supposes that the difficulties involved in the characterisation of the physical are overstated, one might well suppose that there are very serious difficulties that confront any attempt to explain the notion of physical possibility. If we are interested in the question of whether it is possible for there to be physically instantiated infinities, then we need to have some idea of the bounds of physical possibility. This question divides into two parts. First, there are some general questions about possibility, for instance, how do we determine what is, and what is not, a genuine possibility? Second, there are particular questions about physical possibility: Supposing that we have a fairly good understanding of the notion of possibility, how should we go about delimiting the class of physical possibilities within the larger class of possibilities? In the next two sections of this chapter, we shall consider each of these questions in turn.

5.7 POSSIBILITIES

Much work has been done in the past half-century on the logic, metaphysics, and epistemology of modality – that is, roughly, on the logic, metaphysics, and epistemology of necessity and possibility. As is typically the case in philosophy, this vast effort has not led to much in the way of consensus: There is a vast array of different preferred modal logics, and there is a great diversity of views about the metaphysics and epistemology of modality.

If we begin by thinking about modal talk, then we can distinguish between those who hold that there are sentences of the form "Necessarily, *p*" and "Possibly, *p*" that are literally – though perhaps derivatively – true, and those who deny that there are sentences of the form "Necessarily, *p*" and "Possibly, *p*" that are literally true. Among those who deny that there are sentences of the form "Necessarily, *p*" and "Possibly, *p*" that are literally true, there are *modal instrumentalists* who allow that utterances of sentences of these forms may nonetheless properly serve some useful purpose, and *modal eliminativists* who deny that utterances of sentences of these forms may properly serve some useful purpose.

Among those who hold that there are sentences of the form "Necessarily, *p*" and "Possibly, *p*" that are literally – though perhaps derivatively – true, there are those who suppose that, when a sentence of one of these forms is true, the truth of that sentence is to be explained in terms of the properties of a domain of possibilia (possible objects); and there are those who suppose that, when a sentence of one of these forms is true, the truth of that sentence is not to be explained in terms of the properties of a domain of possibilia (possible objects). Among those who deny that, when a sentence of one of these forms is true, the truth of that sentence is to be explained in terms of the properties of a domain of possibilia (possible objects), there are those who suppose that the truth of the sentence should be explained in terms of the properties of the mental states of actual human agents; there are those who suppose that the truth of the sentence should be explained in terms of the properties of the mental states of idealised human agents; and there are those who suppose that there is no explanation to be given of why it is that one of these sentences is true. The last of these positions is a kind of *modal primitivism;* the first two are varieties of *modal conceptualism.*

Among those who suppose that, when a sentence of one of these forms is true, the truth of that sentence is to be explained in terms of the properties of a domain of possibilia (possible objects), there are those who suppose that the objects in question are concrete particulars – for example, Lewisian possible worlds – and there are those who suppose that the objects in question are abstract particulars – for example, maximal consistent sets of propositions or the like. Both of these views are varieties of *modal realism,* but the latter might be said to be committed to ersatz possibilia.

The various different views that one might take concerning the ontology – or metaphysics – of modality are naturally associated with different questions concerning the epistemology – or doxology – of modality. If one is an eliminativist, then an important question that one faces is why it is that we so naturally suppose that our modal talk does serve some properly justified purpose, and how it might be that we could get by without it. If one is an instrumentalist, then an important question that one faces is how to explain the fact that modal talk does serve some properly justified purpose given that none of that talk turns out to be literally true. If one is a primitivist, then an important question that one faces is how to give a plausible account of the (evident) constraints on reasonable modal belief: If modal truth is primitive, then what is it about human subjects that allows them to be good trackers of modal truth (if, indeed, they are good trackers of modal truth)? If one is a conceptualist, then one major difficulty that one faces is to get the deliverances of one's theory to match up with pretheoretical intuitions about which modal sentences are in fact true. If one is a modal realist, then an important question that one faces is how to answer the objection that it seems impossible to see how the properties of the objects in question could play any role in *constraining* reasonable modal belief.

The discussion to this point is very imprecise and impressionistic; there is much more detail that can be added, and there are many arguments for and against each of these kinds of views that could be examined. While, for our purposes, we shall not need to pursue *that* kind of investigation here, there are some further points and distinctions that we need to note.

First, following Quine (1953), one can distinguish between modal sentences in which modal operators take widest scope and sentences in which modal operators occur within the scope of quantifiers and other sentential operators. At least at the outset, there is no obvious reason why one cannot take a different view about these two kinds of modal sentences, for example, by being an eliminativist only about sentences of the second kind. More generally, it seems that the categories that we distinguished above for the case of sentences in which modal operators take wide scope with respect to all nonmodal operators might be specialised to various different subclasses of sentences that involve modal vocabulary.

Second, whether or not one is a modal realist, it seems that one can accept that modal talk can be 'replaced' by talk about possible worlds (and possible objects), in the following sense: We can specify a scheme of translation that takes us from modal sentences to possible worlds sentences, and from possible worlds sentences to modal sentences. True enough, some people have thought that the expressive power of possible worlds talk outruns the expressive power of modal talk – see, for example, Hazen (1976) – but I think that the argument in Nolan (2002) makes it plausible to hold that this alleged difficulty is merely apparent. If this is right, then, no matter what views one takes about the metaphysics and epistemology of modality, one should not be afraid to indulge in the idiom of possible worlds: For either one will think that that idiom wears its ontological commitments on its sleeve or one will be able to translate back into what one takes to be the more ontologically sober vocabulary of orthodox modal talk.

Third, while I have hitherto talked blithely about 'modal talk', one might well think that there are many different kinds of modal talk that need to be distinguished. For instance, one might think that there are various kinds of restricted modalities: "logical possibility", "metaphysical possibility", "physical possibility", "epistemic possibility", "doxastic possibility", and the like, all of which can be explained in terms of restrictions on quantification over the same underlying domain of possible worlds. Or, alternatively, one might think that at least some of these should be explained in terms of (restricted or unrestricted) quantification over distinct domains of possible worlds. While we are keen to insist on the distinction among alethic, epistemic, and doxastic modalities, we shall not try to settle here any of the further issues that arise about different kinds of alethic modalities; in particular, we shall leave it open whether there is a kind of metaphysical possibility that is distinct from broadly logical possibility.

Fourth, one of the key questions that arises for any theory about the metaphysics and epistemology of modality concerns the connection between imagination – conception – and modality. Many theorists have supposed that there is a very strong link between a certain kind of imagination and possibility, for example, that whatever one can clearly and distinctly imagine is at least possible, in a quite strong sense of 'possible'. So, for example, there are many theorists who are prepared to suppose that talking donkeys are possible – that there are possible worlds in which there are talking donkeys – on the grounds that we can clearly and distinctly imagine talking donkeys. However, there are other theorists who are not prepared to make the supposition that talking donkeys are possible and who maintain that there are very severe restrictions to be placed on reasonable modal theorising precisely because clear and distinct imagining is such a poor guide to possibility. (Sometimes, the view is not so much that clear and distinct imagining is a poor guide to possibility, but rather that it is so difficult to tell whether or not what one is indulging in is clear and distinct imagining.) While it seems plausible to suppose that conceptualists may be better placed to insist on a strong link between imagination and possibility, it is not clear that this kind of strong link is desirable, at least in the case of alethic (and epistemic) modalities.

Fifth, whatever else is controversial in the analysis of modality – and, in particular, in the theory of what is possible – there is one principle that seems absolutely solid: Whatever is actual is possible.[5] No matter how sceptical we might be about the connection between clear and distinct imagining and possibility – or about our ability to tell whether our imaginings are clear and distinct – it seems that we can be quite sure that whatever is true of the actual world is true of at

[5] Of course, we can get apparent counterexamples to the principle if we mix our modalities: For example, the alethically actual world typically will not be doxastically possible for human believers. I claim only that 'unmixed' readings of this claim are uncontroversial.

least one possible world. Even if we are sceptical about the reliability of principles of recombination – for example, the principle that says that any recombination of parts of a possible world is itself a possible world – we can hardly doubt that the actual combination of objects and properties that is to be found in the actual world is to be found in a possible world.

As we noted earlier, the very sketchy remarks that have been made in this section admit of almost indefinite extension. However, we shall not need greater precision or depth for the purposes that we shall be pursuing.

5.8 PHYSICAL POSSIBILITIES

Given that we fix an account of modality and, in particular, that we fix an account of possibilities, we can then turn our attention to the question of the characterisation of the *physical* possibilities. Making use of the idiom of *possible worlds*, we might say that the question to be addressed is the question of the characterisation of the class of physically possible worlds. What distinguishes the physically possible worlds from the possible worlds that are not physically possible worlds?

Given our absolutely foundational modal principle – namely, that the actual world is a possible world – and given that the world in which we live is a physical world, we can be sure that there is at least one physically possible world. Moreover – whether or not we accept a fundamental modal recombinatorial principle – it seems that we can be sure that any possible world that is sufficiently similar to the actual world in certain respects is also a physically possible world. The key question, of course, concerns the dimensions along which relevant similarity preserves physical possibility when all else is held constant.

First, it seems that we are on fairly solid ground if we suppose that there are physically possible worlds that obey exactly the same physical laws that hold in the actual world, but in which some of the "initial" conditions – or the conditions that hold "at infinity" – in the actual world take on different values in those other physically possible worlds. If, for example, we suppose that the actual world is globally hyperbolic, and we consider a Cauchy surface for the actual world at some very early point in the history of the actual world, then it seems reasonable to suppose that there are other physically possible worlds in which, at that same early point in the history of those worlds, some of the values on the Cauchy surface for that world differ from the values on the Cauchy surface for the actual world.

Second, it also seems that we are on fairly solid ground if we suppose that there are physically possible worlds in which the physical laws have exactly the same form that they have in the actual world, but in which the values of some of the parameters that appear in these laws are different from the values that those parameters take in the actual world. So, for example, it seems reasonable to suppose that, if there are different fundamental forces in the actual world, then there are physically possible worlds in which the ratios of the strengths of the various fundamental forces take different values from the ratios of those strengths in the actual world.

Third, it seems plausible – though rather more controversial – to suppose that there are physically possible worlds in which the physical laws take on a form that differs from the form that the laws of physics take in the actual world. If, for example, we can think of the world as a distribution of physical properties across a manifold, and if, further, we can suppose that the physical laws govern – or describe – the evolution of the distribution of these properties along one of the dimensions of the manifold, then we might think that it is reasonable to suppose that there are many possible ways in which distributions of physical properties on a manifold can evolve. Of course, it might not be the case that our world does consist of a distribution of properties on a manifold; but there is some correct account of the basic physical structure of our world, and it seems plausible to suppose that the same kind of idea can be made to apply no matter what form that correct account takes.

Even if it is conceded that there are physically possible worlds in which the initial conditions, conditions at infinity, values of physical constants, and physical laws differ from the initial conditions, conditions at infinity, values of physical constants, and physical laws that obtain in the actual world, it is unclear what follows for the cases that were discussed in chapter 3 above. Can we suppose that there is a physically possible world in which matter is infinitely divisible? Can we suppose that there is a physically possible world in which there is no upper limit to the speed of signals? Can we suppose that there is a physically possible world in which there is no thermodynamic noise?

Can we suppose that there is a physically possible world in which there is no lower limit to the accuracy with which agents can make physical discriminations, such as measurements of lengths? The discussion to this point seems to be of almost no help when we turn to address these kinds of questions.

If we are prepared to suppose that conceivability is a defeasibly reliable guide to possibility, then we can go much further. We can surely imagine worlds in which, for each finite speed, there are signals that travel at that speed. We can surely imagine worlds in which, for each degree of precision of measurement, there are measurements that have more than that degree of precision. Since we can devise logically consistent models in which there is no thermodynamic noise, it seems that we can imagine worlds in which there is no thermodynamic noise. Since we can devise logically consistent models in which there is gunk, it seems that we can imagine worlds in which there is gunk. And so forth. What we should conclude from these observations depends on the view that we take about the connection between imagination and possibility.

6

Probability and Decision Theory

Decision theory – the theory of decision making under risk – raises various questions about large infinities (infinite utilities) and about small infinities (infinitesimal probabilities). There are various puzzle cases – for example, the St. Petersburg Game and the Two-Envelope Paradox – which put pressure on the suggestion that we can allow infinite utilities into decision theory. There are other puzzle cases – for example, the case of an infinite fair lottery – which might be taken to suggest that we should be cautious about supposing that probability measures are more than finitely additive.

We shall begin with the mathematics of probability theory and with a discussion of additivity principles for probability measures. Next, we shall turn to decision theory and a discussion of infinite utility. With that discussion behind us, we shall move on to a discussion of some hard cases that bring out the potential costs of various assumptions about the infinitely large and the infinitely small in the theories of probability and decision.

6.1 PROBABILITIES

We begin with some mathematical preliminaries.

If **¥** is a nonempty set of subsets of a nonempty set *X*, then **¥** is an *algebra of subsets* of *X* iff **¥** is closed under finite unions and complementation. An algebra of subsets **¥** is a *σ-algebra* iff **¥** is closed under countable unions. If $\mathfrak{C}$ is a nonempty set of subsets of a nonempty set X, then the algebra (σ-algebra) *generated by* $\mathfrak{C}$ is the intersection of all algebras (σ-algebras) that include $\mathfrak{C}$. An algebra ¥ is *finite* iff ¥ is finite.

If ¥ is an algebra of subsets of X, then a *probability measure* on ¥ is a real-valued function p on ¥ that satisfies the following three axioms:

1. $p(A) \geq 0$ for all A
2. $p(X) = 1$
3. $p(A \cup B) = p(A) + p(B)$ for all A, $B \in$ ¥ such that $A \cap B = \varphi$.

A probability measure p on an algebra ¥ is *simple* iff there is a finite $A \in$ ¥ for which $p(A) = 1$. If p is simple, and $\{x\} \in$ ¥ for all $x \in X$, then $p(x) = 0$ for all but finitely many $x \in X$. Moreover, if p is simple, and $\{x\} \in$ ¥ for all $x \in X$, then, for all $A \in$ ¥, $p(A) = \sum_{x \in A} p(x)$.

A probability measure p on an algebra ¥ is *countably additive* iff for any pairwise disjoint sets $A_1, \ldots, A_n, \ldots \in$ ¥, $p(\cup_n A_n) = \sum_n p(A_n)$. It is standard practice to suppose that σ-algebras are equipped with countably additive measures and to say that, according to the standard Kolmogorovian account of probability, a probability measure on a σ-algebra – or *Borel field* – of sets is nonnegative, normalised, and countably additive. However, we shall not assume that measures on σ-algebras must be countably additive.

A probability measure p on an algebra ¥ is *discrete* iff ¥ is a σ-algebra, p is countably additive, $\{x\} \in$ ¥ for every $x \in X$, and $p(A) = 1$ for some countable $A \in$ ¥. If p is discrete, then $p(x) = 0$ for all but a countable number of $x \in X$. Moreover, if p is discrete, then $p(A) = \sum_{x \in A} p(x) = \sup\{\sum_{x \in B} p(x)$: B is a finite subset of $A\}$, that is, the least upper bound on $\{\sum_{x \in B} p(x)$: B is a finite subset of $A\}$.

We shall say that a triple $\langle X$, ¥, $p\rangle$ is a *probability space* iff X is a nonempty set, ¥ is an algebra of subsets of X, and p is a probability measure on ¥. If $\langle X$, ¥, $p\rangle$ is a probability space, and $p(A) > 0$ for some A, then $p_A(B) = p(B \cap A)/p(A)$ for all $B \in$ ¥ is the *conditional probability measure* of p given A. If $\langle X$, ¥, $p\rangle$ is a probability space, and $p(A)p(B) > 0$ for A, $B \in$ ¥, then $p(A)p_A(B) = p(B)p_B(A) = p(A \cap B)$, and $p_B(A) = p(A)p_A(B)/p(B)$. The latter result is known as *Bayes' Theorem* .

R is a *random variable* on a probability space $\langle X$, ¥, $p\rangle$ iff R is a real-valued function on X such that, for each $I \in \boldsymbol{R}$, $\{x \in X$: $R(x) \in I\} \in$ ¥.

A *univariate distribution* is a probability measure whose domain consists of subsets of the real line. If p is a univariate distribution, then $F(b) = p(-\infty, b]$ for each b is a *univariate distribution function* of the distribution p. The univariate distribution $p_X(I) = p\{x \in X\colon R(x) \in I\}$ for each interval $I \in \boldsymbol{R}$ is the *distribution of the random variable R*. It is easy to show that any univariate distribution function is monotone nondecreasing, right continuous, and such that $\lim_{b\to-\infty} F(b) = 0$ and $\lim_{b\to\infty} F(b) = 1$.

If p is a univariate distribution, and there is a set $\{x_0, \ldots, x_n, \ldots\}$ such that $p(A) = \sum_{x_i \in A} p\{x_i\}$ for each A, then the restriction of p to $\{x_0, \ldots, x_n, \ldots\}$ is a *discrete probability function* for p. A sequence $p_1, \ldots, p_n, \ldots$ is a discrete probability function iff $p_k \geq 0$ for each k and $\sum_{k=1}^{\infty} p_k = 1$. An example of a discrete probability function is the *binomial distribution* function $p_k = \binom{n}{j} p^j (1-p)^{n-j}$, if $j = 0, 1, \ldots, n$, and 0 otherwise. A second example is the *Poisson distribution* with mean μ, $p_k = e^{-\mu} \mu^k / k!$, $k = 0, 1, 2, \ldots$.

If p is a univariate distribution, and we can represent the distribution function F of p in the form $F(x) = \int_{k=1}^{\infty} f(t)\, dt$ for all real x, then f is the *density of the distribution p*. The density of the distribution p_R of a random variable R, f_R, is the *density* of R. A real-valued function f of a real variable is a probability density iff $f(t) \geq 0$ for all real t, and $\int_{-\infty}^{\infty} f(t)\, dt = 1$. An example of a density function is the *normal distribution* with mean μ and variance σ, $f(r) = (1/\sqrt{2\pi\sigma^2}) e^{-(r-\mu)^2/2\sigma^2}$ for $r \in \boldsymbol{R}$. A second example is the *uniform* – or *rectangular* – density on $[a, b]$, $f(r) = 1/(\mathrm{b}-\mathrm{a})$ for $a \leq r \leq b$, and 0 otherwise.

The definitions of discrete probability functions and densities can be generalised to the case in which there are n real-valued variables, and *conditional density* can be defined by generalising the notion of conditional probability. Since we won't require these generalised definitions, we omit to give them here.

If R is a random variable, with $p(R = b_j) = p_j$, $j = 1, \ldots, k$, and $\sum_{j=1}^{k} p_j = 1$, then the *expectation – expected value, mean* – of R, $E(R) = \mu = \sum_{j=1}^{k} b_j p_j$. Moreover, the *variance* of R, $\mathrm{Var}(R) = \sigma_R^2 = \sum_{j=1}^{k} (b_j - \mu)^2 p_j$, and the *standard deviation* of R, σ_R, is the nonnegative square root of the variance.

If R is a random variable with $p(R = b_j) = p_j$, and $\sum_{j=1}^{\infty} p_j = 1$, and $\sum_{j=1}^{\infty} |b_j| p_j$ is finite, then the *expectation* of R, $E(R) = \mu = \sum_{j=1}^{\infty} b_j p_j$.

Moreover, if $\sum_{j=1}^{\infty} (b_j - \mu)^2 p_j$ is finite, then the *variance* of R, Var $(R) = \sigma_R^2 = \sum_{j=1}^{\infty} (b_j - \mu)^2 p_j$, and the *standard deviation* of R, σ_R, is the nonnegative square root of the variance.

If R is a random variable with density f_R, and $\int_{-\infty}^{\infty} |r| f_R(r)\, dr$ is finite, then the *expectation* of R, $E(R) = \mu = \int_{-\infty}^{\infty} r f_R(r)\, dr$. Moreover, if $\int_{-\infty}^{\infty} (r-\mu)^2 f_R(r)\, dr$ is finite, then the *variance* of R, Var $(R) = \sigma_R^2 = \int_{-\infty}^{\infty} (r-\mu)^2 f_R(r)\, dr$, and the *standard deviation* of R, σ_R, is the nonnegative square root of the variance.

Given these definitions, we can go on to define *conditional expectation, conditional variance,* and so forth, on analogy with the definition of conditional probability and conditional density. But, again, we won't require these further definitions in our subsequent discussion.

While the fundamental mathematical theory of probability is *mostly* relatively uncontroversial, there is a vast debate about how the notion of probability should be understood. We shall merely gesture at some of the more prominent interpretations of the notion of probability in what follows. (One important controversy in the fundamental mathematical theory of probability is whether we should accept the definition of conditional probabilities in terms of unconditional probabilities, or whether we should suppose that the notion of conditional probability is fundamental. We shall not need to worry about this dispute in our subsequent discussion.)

According to *subjective* or *doxastic* interpretations of probabilities, probabilities are credences or rational degrees of belief. Roughly speaking, the idea here is that, in an ideally rational belief system, degrees of belief admit of numerical representations that conform to the mathematical definition of probability. This rough idea admits of many different precisifications. Few subjectivists suppose that an ideally rational believer must have nothing but precise real-valued degrees of belief; rather, the typical view is that the doxastic state of a rational believer is accurately represented by a family of assignments of precise real-valued degrees of belief, or perhaps by a family of assignments of intervals whose endpoints are precise real numbers. This suggests, perhaps, that subjectivists suppose that ideal rationality is concerned only with the relationships between beliefs, and not at all with the contents of individual beliefs. However, it is perfectly possible for subjectivists to insist that there are constraints on ideal rational belief that go beyond rules that govern the updating of beliefs in the light of new evidence.

According to *statistical* interpretations of probabilities, probabilities are relative frequencies: long-run frequencies, limiting relative frequencies, hypothetical relative frequencies, or the like. There are problems that confront statistical interpretations of probabilities. If probability is limiting relative frequency in an infinite sequence of trials – or, perhaps, limiting relative frequency in an infinite sequence of uniform trials – then one might well think to object that there are no probabilities, since there are no infinite series of trials. If probability is hypothetical relative frequency – what the limiting relative frequency would have been if there had been an infinite sequence of (uniform) trials – then one might suspect that, again, there are very few probabilities, since there are very few cases in which there is an answer to the question of what the limiting relative frequency *would* have been if there had been an infinite sequence of (uniform) trials.

According to *objective* interpretations of probabilities, probabilities are chances or propensities: objective features of the world. In deterministic worlds – for example, universes in which there are Cauchy surfaces on which data determines all past and future data – there are no nontrivial chances or propensities: Events that occur have probability 1 and events that do not occur have probability zero.[1] However, in nondeterministic worlds, there may be nontrivial chances: It may, for example, be a fundamental fact about a given radioactive particle that it has a given chance of decaying in a given time interval (where this fact does not supervene on facts about the decay behaviour of similar radioactive particles and the like).

It should not be thought that one is necessarily required to choose between these different interpretations of probability. While it is controversial whether there are chances, it seems relatively uncontroversial that there are both credences and frequencies. Moreover, while it seems highly questionable whether frequencies really are a kind of probability, it seems very plausible to suppose that chances and rational credences will obey the fundamental mathematical theory of

[1] Or, at least, so I'm tempted to say. But this claim has been controverted, e.g., by Levi (1980).

probability. If there are chances, then it seems clear that knowledge about chances must constrain rational credences: If one knows that the chance that a particle will decay in an interval *T* is *x*%, then – except perhaps in a small range of exceptional cases – one ought to believe to degree *x*% that the particle will decay in interval *T*. Similarly, if there are chances and if one has statistical data about the decay of particles of a given kind, then this data will surely constrain the beliefs that one has about the chance that a given particle will decay in a given time interval.

There is, of course, much more that can be said about the interpretation of probability. However, with these brief introductory remarks behind us, we turn now to the one controversial aspect of the mathematical theory of probability that will be important for subsequent discussion, namely, the question of additivity principles.

6.2 ADDITIVITY PRINCIPLES

There are various places where infinities intrude into the mathematics of standard probability theory. It is standard to allow probability spaces in which ¥ is a σ-algebra, that is, to consider a set of subsets that is closed under countable union. It is standard to suppose that random variables are real-valued functions. And so forth. But the most controversial questions about the role of infinities in standard probability theory arise when we consider the additivity principles that are obeyed by probability measures.

The key question is whether we should suppose that probability measures can be countably additive – that is, whether we can accept measures in which it is true that, for any pairwise disjoint sets $A_1, \ldots, A_n, \ldots \in$ ¥, $p(\cup_n A_n) = \sum_n p(A_n)$ – or whether we should insist that any acceptable probability measure must be merely finitely additive – that is, whether we should insist that all that is true is that, for any pairwise disjoint sets $A_1, \ldots, A_k \in$ ¥, $p(\cup_{n=1}^{k} A_n) = \sum_{k=1}^{k} p(A_n)$.

Perhaps the most obvious – though by no means the only – consideration in favour of allowing that probability measures can be countably additive is that there are central results in modern statistical theory whose proof relies on the assumption of countable additivity. Consider, for example, the Central Limit Theorem. There are many cases in which one has a collection of independent random variables $X_1, \ldots,$

X_n, with a common distribution function $F_{X_1 \ldots X_n} = F$, finite expectation μ, and finite variance σ^2. (Simple examples include cases in which one wishes to compute accumulated timing errors or round-off errors in calculations.) The Central Limit Theorem says that, for each real t:

(1) $\lim_{n\to\infty} p\{(1/\sqrt{n})\sum_{j=1}^{n}((X_i-\mu)/\sigma) \leq t\} = \int_{-\infty}^{t}(1/\sqrt{2\pi})\, e^{-\mu 2/2}$ du; and
(2) $|p\{(1/\sqrt{n})\sum_{i=1}^{n}((X_i - \mu)/\sigma) \leq t\} - \int_{-\infty}^{t} (1/\sqrt{2\pi})e^{-\mu 2/2}\, du| \leq$ $(2/\sqrt{n})\ \mathrm{E}\ [|(X_i - \mu)/\sigma|^3]$.

But this theorem can be established only if we suppose that our probability measure is countably additive. If we give up countable additivity and insist only on finite additivity, then, plausibly, we forfeit the right to use this valuable statistical tool. And this is not an isolated case: There are many tools in the modern statistical kitbag whose justification depends on the assumption that probability measures are countably additive. Of course, it has not yet been ruled out that one might fashion a collection of satisfactory replacement tools using nothing but finitely additive probability measures – but, at the very least, it has not yet been shown that this can be done.

There are various arguments that might be given in favour of the view that we should *not* countenance countably additive probability measures.

First, one might argue that, contrary to the demands imposed by countable additivity, it can be rational to be certain of each given member of an infinite class of events that that member will not occur, while nonetheless being certain that one of the events from that class will occur. So, for example, if there were a fair infinite lottery – that is, a fair lottery in which there were countably many tickets – then it can be rational to hold both (i) that it is certain that one of the tickets is going to win and (ii) that, for any given ticket T_i, it is certain that T_i will not win. Since the only way to model this is to suppose that $p(T_i \text{ wins}) = 0$ for each T while $p(V_i\ (T_i \text{ wins})) = 1$, we have here a direct argument against countable additivity.

This argument depends on the highly dubious assumption that there could be a fair infinite lottery (or, perhaps, on the still highly dubious assumption that one could reasonably believe that there is a fair infinite lottery). But let's defer discussion of this assumption here. If we allow that there *could* be a fair infinite lottery, then it seems entirely obvious that we are required to suppose that $p(V_i\ (T_i$ wins)/plausible assumptions) = 1. (The plausible assumptions here are, for example, that a winning ticket is drawn in the lottery.) However, given that this is so, it is quite unclear why we should allow that, in a fair infinite lottery, $p(T_i$ wins) = 0 for any given T_i. At least *prima facie*, it sounds incoherent to suppose that it is certain that there will be a winner in the lottery and that each ticket in the lottery is certain not to win. What is true is that, for any $\varepsilon > 0$, you cannot believe that $p(T_i$ wins) = ε for each T_i. Moreover, given that the lottery is fair, you are constrained to suppose that $p(T_I) = p(T_j)$, for all i and j, if you assign values to $p(T_I)$ and $p(T_j)$. So it seems that, if there were a fair infinite lottery, one ought to refrain from assigning any value to the probability that a given ticket wins. At the very least, given the *prima facie* incoherence of the claim that it is certain that there will be a winner in the lottery and that each ticket in the lottery is certain not to win, it seems that those who suppose that there could be a fair infinite lottery should seriously consider the suggestion that there is just no way to apply the theory of probability directly to propositions of the form T_i *wins* in this case.

Just to fix intuitions a bit further, suppose that God runs a lottery for entry to Heaven. Infinitely many tickets are made up, and one ticket is given to each person on earth. Then finitely many numbers are drawn at random from amongst the natural numbers, and, if there are people who have those numbered tickets in their possession, then those people are admitted to Heaven. To gain admission to Heaven, one must still have the ticket that one has been given in one's possession; if one has torn up the ticket or given it to someone else, then one is not a winner of the lottery. (Since God is running the lottery, we can suppose that no one can illicitly obtain someone else's ticket without detection.) If you had a ticket in this lottery, would you tear it up? If you really think that, in an infinite lottery in which there are guaranteed to be finitely many winners, there is no chance that a given ticket will win, then you should be prepared to say that it would make no difference to you whether or not you tore up your ticket. After all, no chance of winning is *no* chance of winning. If you have any reluctance about tearing up your ticket, then surely that shows that you don't really think that you have *no* chance of winning a fair infinite lottery in which you hold no more than finitely many tickets.[2]

Second, one might try to argue that any intuitive support for countable additivity is bound to be intuitive support for uncountable additivity. Yet we can be quite certain that uncountable additivity is an unacceptable requirement: We know, for example, that it is possible to have a rational uniform distribution over the interval [0,1] such that $p\{r\} = 0$ for all $r \in [0,1]$. So there can hardly be *reliable* intuitive support for countable additivity. Consider, for example, the claim that I made earlier that it sounds incoherent to suppose both that it is certain that there will be a winner in the infinite fair lottery and that each ticket in the lottery is certain not to win. If we have a uniform distribution over the interval [0,1], then it seems that we are both certain that our variable takes a value in the interval [0,1], and that $p(R = r) = 0$ for each point r in the interval, that is, that, for each point in the interval, we are certain that the variable does not take a value at that point. So, the argument that we gave previously in defence of countable additivity is no good, since it would work just as well as a defence of the indefensible uncountable additivity.

There are several ways that one might respond to this argument. For example, one might reformulate one's theory so that it does not have the consequence that $p(R = r) = 0$ when r is a point in a bounded continuous interval over which a (uniform) density function has been defined. Just as one can develop theories of physical space in which regions are fundamental, so, too, one can develop theories of probabilistic space in which regions are fundamental. Since such an approach will lead to changes to the underlying logic, there are reasons to be cautious about adopting it, but it is clearly an option worth exploring at this point.

Another response that one might give at this point is to insist the interpretation of $p(R = r) = 0$ in the continuous case is relevantly different from the interpretation of $p(X = x) = 0$ in the discrete case. While we can be happy to allow that $p(X = x) = 0$ should be taken

[2] Cf. Skyrms (1966).

to mean that it is *certain* that $X \neq x$, we should not be prepared to accept that $p(R = r) = 0$ can be taken to mean that it is *certain* that $R \neq r$ in the continuous case. Rather, in the continuous case, we should say that it can only be certain that $R \neq r$ if there is a subinterval I – or, more generally, a subregion – with nonzero measure such that $r \in I$ and for which $p(R \subset I) = 0$. It seems to me that this response preserves the intuition, that it is incoherent to suppose both that it is certain that a variable takes a value at some point in a region and that each point in the region is such that it is certain that the variable does not take a value at it, without resorting to an *ad hoc* modification of the interpretation of the classical theory of probability. However, I am sure that there will be many who disagree.

A final response that one might countenance is to consider what happens to conditional probabilities in the two cases. As I noted above, there is a perfectly good definition of conditional densities that can be given in the continuous case, which makes use of the possibility of taking limits as quantities are continuously approached. Having $p(\{r\}) = 0$ for all $r \in R$ is no barrier to this definition of conditional densities. However, if we suppose that $p(\{x\}) = 0$ for all $x \in X$, then it seems that there will be no conditional probabilities at points or at finite sets of points. Since this is a technical problem, it is perhaps unsurprising that it is amenable to a technical fix;[3] I mention it merely to draw attention to the fact that there are obvious differences between the discrete case and the continuous case that may be relevant to the present discussion.

Third, one might try to argue that it must be *prima facie* unpromising to suppose that intuitions about reasonable credences could be sensitive to the difference between countable and uncountable infinities, since that distinction belongs to the recondite domain of higher mathematics, while intuitions about reasonable credences are widespread and resilient even amongst those who have little or no knowledge of higher mathematics. I think that there are various reasons why little weight should be given to this argument. Since it often seems plausible to say that our behaviour is guided by theories of which we have an implicit grasp but for which we find extraordinarily difficult to give

[3] Kolmogorov provides the fix by appealing to the Rodon Nikodyn theorem, and the notion of probability conditional on a sigma algebra.

explicit formulation, it is doubtful that there would be much support supplied to the opponents of countable additivity if it were true that intuitions about reasonable credences are widespread and resilient amongst those who have little or no explicit knowledge of mathematics. But, in any case, it is not clear why we should suppose that it is true that intuitions about reasonable credences are widespread and resilient amongst those who have little or no explicit knowledge of mathematics. There is plenty of psychological data that tells us that people are not very good at probabilistic and statistical inference, so we should be cautious in supposing that there *are* widespread resilient reliable intuitions about reasonable credences without undertaking studies that establish that this is so.

Perhaps there are yet other ways in which one might try to argue against countable additivity. I do not know of any argument stronger than those that I have presented here, but this certainly does not mean that such arguments are not to be found. In the absence of such arguments, however, I think that it is plausible to claim that there is no particularly good reason to suppose that one ought to give up on countable additivity, and to accept only finite additivity, in one's theory of probability.

6.3 DECISION THEORY

Decision theory takes as its subject matter situations in which agents choose between alternatives. We assume that each possible choice that an agent might make – each alternative for which the agent might opt – has consequences or outcomes and that the agent has a preference ranking for these consequences or outcomes.

We distinguish between *descriptive* decision theory – which is concerned with what agents actually do in choice situations – and *normative* decision theory – which is concerned with what rational agents ought to do in choice situations. Our focus here will be entirely on normative decision theory.

We suppose that the outcome of a choice or decision depends on two factors: (1) the choice that is made and (2) the state of the world at the time that the choice is made. Since we are supposing that an agent in a choice situation has a preference ranking for outcomes, we can suppose that the preference ranking of an agent can be represented by a table of the following form:

	S_1	S_2	...	S_j	...	S_n
A_1	u_{11}	u_{12}	...	u_{1j}	...	u_{1n}
A_2	u_{21}	u_{22}	...	u_{2j}	...	u_{2n}
...	...	...	...	...	...	...
A_i	u_{i1}		...	u_{ij}	...	u_{in}
...	...	...	...	...	...	...
A_m	u_{m1}		...	u_{mj}	...	u_{mn}

Here, the A_i are the alternatives between which the choice is to be made, and the S_j are the states of the world that might obtain at the time of the choice decision. (At least until further notice, we shall suppose that there are only finitely many alternatives, and finitely many possible states of the world.)

We distinguish between *decisions under uncertainty* – in which we suppose that the agent does not assign probabilities to all of the S_j – and *decisions under risk* – in which we suppose that the agent assigns probabilities to all of the S_j. While we shall be principally concerned with decisions under risk, we begin with a few brief remarks about decision under uncertainty.

(a) Decisions under Uncertainty

There are various decision rules that one might propose to use in cases of decision under uncertainty, and various criteria that one might suppose that such decision rules ought to obey. We shall begin by listing criteria, and then mention a few rules that have been countenanced.

1. *Ordering of alternatives*: The rule should yield an ordinal ranking of the alternatives.
2. *Dominance*: If every utility u_{ij} associated with alternative A_i is greater than the corresponding utility u_{kj} associated with alternative A_k, then A_i should have a higher preference ranking than A_k.

3. *Symmetry*: Relabelling the rows or the columns of the matrix should not affect the result of applying the rule.
4. *Linearity*: The result of applying the rule should be invariant under positive linear transformations of the utilities.
5. *Column linearity*: Adding a constant value to all of the utilities in a column should not affect the result of applying a rule.
6. *Redundancy*: Duplicating a column or removing one of two identical columns should not affect the result of applying a rule.
7. *Addition*: The addition of a row should leave the relative ranks of the original rows unaltered.
8. *Convexity*: If an agent is indifferent between two alternatives A_i and A_j, then that agent should be indifferent between either of them and their equiprobable mixture $(\frac{1}{2}A_i, \frac{1}{2}A_j)$, that is, flipping a fair coin and letting the result of the toss decide between them.

Some rules that have been considered for decision under uncertainty include:

1. *Maximin*: Choose the alternative of which the worst possible outcome is the best of all of the worst outcomes associated with the alternatives.
2. *Maximax*: Choose the alternative that has the best of the best possible outcomes amongst the alternatives.
3. *Hurwicz-α*: Suppose that $u_i^{\min}$ and $u_i^{\max}$ are the worst and best outcomes associated with alternative A_i. We compute $\alpha u_i^{\min} + (1-\alpha)\, u_i^{\max}$, for some $0 \leq \alpha \leq 1$, and choose the alternative for which this quantity is a maximum. Here, α is a parameter that is characteristic of the agent: When $\alpha = 0$, we get back Maximax; and when $\alpha = 1$ we get back Maximin.
4. *Minimax Regret*: Given the preference table for an agent, we construct a regret table by replacing each entry in the preference table by the difference between it and the largest entry in the column in which it lies. We then choose by applying the minimax rule to the regret table, that is, we choose the alternative on which the largest entry in the regret table is minimised.

Inspection shows that none of these rules satisfies all of the stated criteria. (For example, Maximin, Maximax, and Hurwicz-α violate

Column Linearity; Minimax Regret violates Addition; and Hurwicz-α also violates Convexity.) Thus, either we don't yet have a satisfactory rule for decision under uncertainty on our list or some of the stated criteria are unacceptable.

It is an interesting question whether we should suppose that there is a satisfactory rule for decision under uncertainty, or whether we should suppose that rationality requires that every decision problem be treated as a problem of decision under risk. If we could help ourselves to a *principle of indifference* – that is, a principle that allows us to assign equal probabilities to outcomes in situations in which we have no reason to assign other values to them – then we would surely be able to treat decisions under uncertainty as decisions under risk. However, it seems doubtful that there is any generally acceptable principle of indifference.

(b) Decisions under Risk

In the case of decision under risk, we suppose that the agent associates a probability p_i with each of the possible states of the world S_i such that $\sum_{j=1}^{n} p_j = 1$. We define the *expected utility* of an alternative A_i to be $\text{EU}(A_I) = \sum_{j=1}^{n} p_j u_{ij}$. Our decision rule then says that a rational agent acts so as to *maximise* expected utility; that is, a rational agent chooses the alternative that has the greatest expected utility.[4]

While the decision rule of maximising expected utility is easy to state, there are many questions that it prompts. The claim that is made by those who endorse this decision rule is that an ideally rational agent will act always so as to maximise expected utility. This claim from normative decision theory is intended to make some kind of contact with descriptive decision theory and with our prior conception of how ideally rational agents would behave. Many people have thought

[4] Of course, as it stands, our rule is incomplete. In case of a tie, our rule requires an arbitrary choice: A rational agent arbitrarily selects one of those alternatives that has greatest expected utility. In the case that there is no alternative that has greatest expected utility, our rule is silent. Perhaps our rule should say that, in such a case, a rational agent arbitrarily selects an alternative that has 'sufficiently large' expected utility. Trying to sort this out would take us far beyond the bounds of the current discussion.

that there are reasons for rejecting the suggestion that ideally rational agents act always so as to maximise expected utility.

Some objections to the decision rule of maximising expected utility are arguably based on straightforward misunderstandings. We have already seen – in our discussion of subjective interpretations of probability theory – that we need not suppose that an ideally rational agent ascribes precise real-valued probabilities to possible states of the world. Rather, what we suppose is that the beliefs of an ideally rational agent can be represented by a family of assignments of precise real-valued degrees of belief or, perhaps, by a family of assignments of intervals whose endpoints are precise real numbers. In a similar way, we need not suppose that an ideally rational agent ascribes precise real-valued utilities to the alternatives among which he or she is to choose. Rather, what we suppose is that the preferences – desires, values – of an ideally rational agent can be represented by a family of assignments of precise real-valued utilities or, perhaps, by a family of assignments of intervals whose endpoints are precise real numbers. While this still represents a considerable degree of idealisation, it is much less obviously absurd than the supposition that the degrees of belief and strengths of preferences of ideally rational agents can be calibrated directly using precise real values.

In our discussion of decision under uncertainty, we suggested that strength of preferences should constitute an *ordinal* scale. A bunch of preferences $p_1, \ldots, p_k$ lie on an ordinal scale – that is, a bunch of preferences $p_1, \ldots, p_k$ are *weakly ordered* – iff the following conditions obtain: (1) *Irreflexivity of Preference*: It is not the case that p_i is preferred to p_i; (2) *Asymmetry of Preference*: If p_i is preferred to p_j, then it is not the case that p_j is preferred to p_i; (3) *Transitivity of Preference*: If p_i is preferred to p_j, and p_j is preferred to p_k, then p_i is preferred to p_k; (4) *Transitivity of Indifference*: If it is not the case that p_i is preferred to p_j, and it is not the case that p_j is preferred to p_i, and it is not the case that p_j is preferred to p_k, and it is not the case that p_k is preferred to p_i, then it is not the case that p_i is preferred to p_k and it is not the case that p_k is preferred to p_i. (If we drop the requirement of transitivity of indifference, then the preferences would obey a *strict partial order.*)

However, for the application of the decision rule of maximising expected utility, we need more: It isn't enough that numbers are assigned to preferences in such a way as to order the preferences weakly, with stronger preferences being assigned larger numbers. Rather, for the purposes of the decision rule of maximising expected utility, we need the assigned numbers to indicate *how much* one alternative is preferred to another. If we follow the standard practice of characterising measurement scales in terms of the magnitudes that are invariant under admissible transformations of those scales, then our ordinal scale admits positive monotone transformations under which all that is invariant is the relative magnitudes of the numbers assigned to the alternatives. However, it seems that what we need is a scale that admits only transformations of the form $x' = \alpha x$, $\alpha > 0$, that is, a *ratio scale.* (An intermediate possibility is to adopt an *interval scale* that admits only transformations of the form $x' = \alpha x + \beta$, $\alpha > 0$. A weaker intermediate possibility is to adopt a *difference scale* that admits only transformations that are positive monotone on both the magnitudes and the differences between magnitudes.)

There are various methods that have been proposed for establishing the utilities of rational agents. One can establish an interval scale based on an agent's preferences amongst lotteries; and one can establish a ratio scale based on choice experiments in which an agent is invited to make pairwise comparisons of alternatives. We shall not need to pursue the details of these constructions here.

Among the assumptions of the decision theory presented here that can be questioned, some of the most important are the assumption that rational preferences are transitive, the assumption that decision under uncertainty obeys a principle of dominance, and the assumption that probability is countably additive. There are various levels of structure in decision theory, and the assumptions at each level of structure require careful examination.

6.4 APPROACHING INFINITE DECISION THEORY

So far, we have proceeded under the assumptions (1) that there are finitely many alternatives, (2) that there are finitely many relevant different possible states of the world, and (3) that there is an upper bound to the utilities that appear in any given decision problem. When we model rational human agents, it seems that these assumptions are reasonable. Nonetheless, we might want to consider whether we can extend our theory to accommodate cases in which one or more of these assumptions is dropped.

Supposing that there might be infinitely many alternatives among which an agent must choose is uninteresting if we suppose that there are only finitely many relevant states of the world and finitely many different utilities that can be assigned to outcomes. Under these assumptions, decision theory becomes intractable in all but the most special of cases: Often, our "decision rule" will do no better than to enjoin us to make an arbitrary choice from amongst infinitely many equally good alternatives. However, if we allow that there are infinitely many different utilities that can be assigned to outcomes, then we needn't worry about this kind of consideration.

Supposing that there are infinitely many different relevant states of the world between which the agent must choose can be interesting even if we suppose that there are only finitely many alternatives between which an agent must choose, and even if we suppose that there is a fixed upper bound to the utilities of outcomes. Consider, for example, a case in which $p(S_j) = (\frac{1}{2})^j$, and $u_{ij} = f_i(j)B$, $0 \leq f_i(j) \leq 1$ for all $i, j \in N$, and $B \in N$. In this case, $\text{EU}(A_i) = \sum_j (\frac{1}{2})^j f_i(j)B < \text{B}$. So, at least for all of the considerations that have been raised thus far, there is no barrier to getting unequivocal decisions from infinite decision theory in cases in which there are infinitely many different relevant states of the world. Moreover, this remains true even if we suppose that there are infinitely many alternatives among which the agent must choose: We could have an array of utilities bounded by B such that $\text{EU}(A_i) \neq \text{EU}(A_j)$ whenever $i \neq j$ for all $i, j \in N$. Finally, we can see that there is no danger that any calculations of expected utility will diverge under the assumptions now under consideration: No matter how the agent distributes probabilities over the different relevant states of the world, if there is a finite upper bound B to utility, then the expected utility of any alternative course of action can be no greater than B.

If we suppose that there is no upper bound to utility, and we suppose that there are infinitely many alternatives, then we can easily describe situations in which $\text{EU}(A_i)$ diverges as i increases. Consider, for example, a case in which there are only two equiprobable relevant states of the world, and in which $u_{i1} = u_{i2} = i$. Under these assumptions, $\text{EU}(A_i) = i$. In this kind of case, one might suggest that an appropriate "decision rule" is to select arbitrarily any sufficiently large A_i;

alternatively, one might say that, in this case, there is no reasonable decision to be made.

If we suppose that there is no upper bound to utility, and we suppose that there are infinitely many relevant states of the world, then, again, we can easily describe situations in which $\mathrm{EU}(A_i)$ diverges for some, or all, values of $\mathrm{EU}(A_i)$, regardless of whether the number of alternatives is finite or infinite. Consider, for example, a case in which there are only two alternatives A_1 and A_2, $p(S_j) = (\frac{1}{2})^j$, and $u_{ij} = i2^j$, for all $i \in \{1, 2\}$ and $j \in N$. In this case, $\mathrm{EU}(A_1) = 1 + 1 + 1 + \ldots$ and $\mathrm{EU}(A_2) = 2 + 2 + 2 + 2 + \ldots$. In this case, the expected utility of the two options is equal, even though there seems to be a good intuitive sense in which the second option is better than the first. To cope with this case, one might propose a modified "decision rule": If two alternatives have the same expected utility, but one option dominates the other – that is, has higher utility on each possible relevant state of the world – then one ought to select the dominant option; alternatively, one might say that, in this case, there is no reasonable decision to be made, and that any arbitrary choice will do.

While the extension of finite decision theory that arises by allowing (1) infinitely many alternatives, (2) infinitely many possible states of the world, and (3) unbounded utilities, and adopting the standard decision rule is mathematically unproblematic, there may be cases that arise in which we feel that further rules should be added to break ties in some cases in which there are many alternatives that have infinite expected utility. We have noted some of the kinds of cases in which this sort of pressure might arise, and some of the kinds of responses that might be made to it. A further – and more detailed – investigation of these matters lies beyond the scope of the present inquiry.

6.5 INFINITE UTILITY STREAMS

Depending on the further assumptions that we are prepared to make, we may think that we can make sense of the idea of infinite utilities, that is, utilities that take on an infinite value. We shall consider the consequences of this suggestion after we have considered an example in which infinite utilities arise. Since it seems to be the least problematic suggestion, we shall consider a case in which one must choose between different infinite utility streams, that is, streams of finite daily utility that accumulate over an infinite future.

Suppose that a day spent in Heaven has utility 1 and that a day spent in Hell has utility -1. Suppose further, that for all n, n days in Heaven has utility n, and n days in Hell has utility $-n$. Suppose still further, that for all n and m, any combination of m days in Heaven and n days in Hell has utility $m - n$, and any combination of n days in Heaven and m days in Hell has utility $n - m$. Then consider the following alternatives:

(a) an infinite number of days in Heaven (with no days in Hell);
(b) an infinite number of days in Hell (with no days in Heaven);
(c) an infinite number of days in Heaven (with no days in Hell), preceded by a finite number of days in Hell (with no days in Heaven);
(d) an infinite number of days in Hell (with no days in Heaven), preceded by a finite number of days in Heaven (with no days in Hell);
(e) an infinite number of alternating days, first in Heaven and then in Hell;
(f) an infinite number of alternating days, first in Hell and then in Heaven;
(g) a day in Heaven, followed by an infinite number of alternating days, first in Heaven and then in Hell;
(h) a day in Hell, followed by an infinite number of alternating days, first in Hell and then in Heaven.

Straightforward arithmetic considerations suggest, first, that scenarios (a) and (c) have positive infinite utility and that scenarios (b) and (d) have negative infinite utility. One might think that (a) should be preferred to (c) – on the grounds that, on any day, the sum of utility to that day is greater on option (a) than on option (c) – or one might think that one should be indifferent between (a) and (c) – on the grounds that it is only the total utility that matters, and this is the same in each case. Similarly, one might think that (d) should be preferred to (b) – on the grounds that, on any day, the sum of utility to that day is greater on option (d) than on option (b) – or one might think that one should be indifferent between (b) and (d) – on the grounds that it is only the total utility that matters, and this is the same in each case.

Since the series of partial sums in scenarios (e) to (h) are oscillating, it is less straightforward to determine what to say about the total utility in these cases. As before, one might think that (g) should be preferred to (e) and that (f) should be preferred to (h), because, on any day, the sum of utility to that day is greater on the former option than it is on the latter option. However, if you suppose that the order of the days shouldn't make any difference to your preference – that is, if you suppose that you should be indifferent to permutations of the utilities that are assigned to days – then it seems that you should be indifferent between all four of these options. After all, if we represent option (g) by $\{1, 1, -1, 1, -1, 1, -1, \ldots\}$, then one permutation – that is, exchange of adjacent options – yields $\{1, -1, 1, -1, 1, -1, 1, \ldots\}$, that is, option (e). Then, a second permutation yields $\{-1, 1, -1, 1, -1, 1, -1 \ldots)$, that is, option (f). And a final permutation yields $\{-1, -1, 1, -1, 1, -1, 1, \ldots\}$, that is, option (h).

The considerations that apply if one is to choose between (e) and (f) – or between (g) and (h) – seem to be even more delicate. On any day, the sum of utility to that day in scenario (e) is never less than the sum of utility to that day in scenario (f), and it is greater on every other day. Moreover, on any day, the sum of utility to that day in scenario (g) is always greater than the sum of utility to that day in scenario (h). So, if we think that these partial sums determine choice, it seems that we shall be obliged to say that (e) is to be preferred to (f), and that (g) is to be preferred to (h). However, at least the first of these recommendations seems evidently wrong: There cannot be a good reason to prefer (e) to (f). Of course, this conclusion could be bolstered by appeal to considerations about permutation – (e) is a single permutation of (f) – but it seems to me that it could also be based in independent symmetry considerations: Each case is an infinite alteration between two options; they differ only in which is the initial option; and you are stipulated to be indifferent to the ordering of pairs of options.

In the case of choice between (f) and (g) – and in the case of choice between (e) and (h) – there is another kind of consideration to which one might appeal. If one compares utilities day by day, one sees that (g) dominates (f): There is no day on which the utility of (f) is greater than the utility of (g), and there is a day on which the utility of (g) is greater than the utility of (f). So, in this case, one doesn't need to appeal to the partial sums of the utilities: One can argue directly that (g) should be preferred to (f) on grounds of dominance. And, of course, the same kind of argument establishes that (e) should be preferred to (h). It should be noted that, if there is day-by-day domination of one alternative by another, then there will also be partial sum domination of the one alternative by the other; and it should also be noted that the reverse claim is not true: There can be partial sum domination of one alternative by another even though there is not day-by-day domination of the one alternative by the other.

Collecting the threads of the discussion to this point, we have the following candidate principles for the comparison of alternative future utility streams:

1. Prefer the possible future utility stream that has maximal total utility, if there is one.
2. If more than one possible future utility stream has divergent utility, prefer the divergent future utility stream whose partial sum is dominant, if there is one.
3. If more than one possible future utility stream has divergent utility, maintain indifference between divergent future utility streams that are permutations of one another.

Since – as we have seen above – (2) and (3) give contradictory advice, we cannot accept them both. Moreover, there seem to be clear cases in which (2) gives the wrong advice – for example, in the comparison between (e) and (f) above – and there seem to be clear cases in which (3) gives the wrong advice – for example, in the comparison between $\{1, -1, 1, -1, 1, -1, \ldots\}$ and $\{1, -1, 1, 1, -1, 1, 1, 1, -1, 1, 1, 1, 1, -1, \ldots\}$. In the face of these difficulties, one might propose replacing (2) and/or (3) with the weaker principles:

2′. If more than one possible future utility stream has divergent utility, prefer the divergent future utility stream that is day-by-day – or, more generally, step-by-step – dominant, if there is one.

3′. If more than one possible future utility stream has divergent utility, maintain indifference between divergent future utility streams that are finite permutations of one another (i.e., that can be derived from one another by finitely many exchanges at neighbouring days or, more generally, steps).

However, there are two difficulties with this proposal. First, there are cases where these principles fail to yield the advice that one might expect to receive – consider, again, the case of the comparison between $\{1, -1, 1, -1, 1, -1, \ldots\}$ and $\{1, -1, 1, 1, -1, 1, 1, 1, -1, 1, 1, 1, 1, -1, \ldots\}$. Second, and more important, there are still anomalies. Intuitively, it may seem reasonable to suppose that one ought to prefer an infinite series of alternating days in Heaven and Hell preceded by any finite number of days in Heaven to an infinite series of alternating days in Heaven and Hell preceded by any finite number of days in Hell. However, while our principles licence preference of $\{1, 1, -1, 1, -1, 1, -1, \ldots\}$ to $\{-1, 1, -1, 1, -1, 1, \ldots\}$ – by (2′) – they fail to licence preference of $\{1, 1, -1, 1, -1, 1, -1, \ldots\}$ to $\{-1, -1, 1, -1, 1, -1, 1, \ldots\}$. While I do not suppose that these objections are decisive, I think that they show that we are far from the development of a satisfactory account of comparison of alternative infinite utility streams – and, in particular, that it is far from clear that we have good reason to endorse (2′) and (3′).

Clearly, there is *much* more to be said about the assessment of alternative infinite utility streams. Nonetheless, the little that has been said here may be enough to motivate the suggestion that there are good grounds for pessimism about the prospects of developing a satisfying account of infinite utility streams. At the very least, those who think that it ought to be possible to accommodate infinite utility streams in decision theory have work to do to develop a satisfactory set of principles that the envisioned account can endorse. Moreover, since infinite utility streams are pretty clearly the least problematic way of generating infinite utilities, the pessimism – and the need for work on the part of those who wish to kick against that pessimism – extends to infinite utilities in general.[5]

6.6 INFINITE DECISION RULES

Suppose that we *do* think that we can construct a satisfying account of infinite utility streams, and suppose that we think that we can make

[5] This discussion of infinite utility streams mirrors a debate about "infinite utilitarianism". See, e.g., Diamond (1965), Segerberg (1976), Jeffrey (1983), Nelson (1991), Vallentyne (1993; 1995), Cain (1995), Ng (1995), Van Liederkerke (1995), Lauwers (1997), Vallentyne and Kagan (1997), and Dreier (2003).

sense of the idea that one might be in a choice situation in which one of the options is to enter into an infinite utility stream. If we think this way, then we shall want a decision theory that works when the utilities u_{ij} in our decision matrix take values from $\mathfrak{R}$, that is, from the extended real line. To keep things simple, let's suppose that there is only one candidate infinite utility stream and that there is exactly one open alternative A that lands one in that utility stream on at least one possible state of the world (to which nonzero probability is assigned). Under these assumptions, it may seem that one ought to be able to conclude that the choice of A maximises expected utility. For instance, if there are only two alternatives, A_1 and A_2, and two possible states S_1 and S_2, with probabilities p_1 and $1 - p_1$, $p_1 \neq 0$ and $u_{11} = \infty$ while u_{ij} is finite for i, j, not both equal to 1, then $\text{EU}(A_1) = \infty$, and $\text{EU}(A_2)$ is finite.

While this may sound fine, there are various considerations that suggest that there are potholes along the road to application. In a genuine decision situation, one ought to take all relevant alternatives into account. But in a genuine decision situation, there are always 'mixed' alternatives. If A_1 and A_2 are alternatives, then so is $1/2(A_1, A_2)$: If the toss of a fair coin comes down Heads, choose A_1; if it comes down tails, choose A_2. But in our previous example, $\text{EU}(1/2(A_1, A_2)) = \infty$. Unless we revise our decision rule, it seems plausible to suppose that infinite decision theory is not going to yield much in the way of decisions.

Perhaps it might be proposed that we add to our decision theory the rule that, in the kind of case that we have just been considering, one ought to select the alternative that is most likely to lead one to end up in an infinite utility stream.[6] At least roughly, what this proposal amounts to is to treat cases of decision under risk in which there are infinite utilities as cases of decision under uncertainty and to adopt the Maximax rule. However, there are obvious objections to *that* proposal: If there can be positive infinite utility streams, then surely there can also be negative infinite utility streams. But in circumstances in which one is choosing between alternatives, some of which are positive infinite utility streams and some of which are negative infinite utility streams,

[6] This proposal has been made by Schlesinger (1994), and discussed by, e.g., Sorenson (1994).

the Maximax rule has all of the evident disadvantages that the Maximax rule has in cases in which all utilities are finite. If we are to incorporate consideration of infinite utility streams into decision theory, then we need *generally* applicable rules to regulate our treatment of them. I do not think that the proposed Maximax rule should find wide acceptance.

Moreover, it is not clear that there is any good justification for treating cases of decision under risk involving infinite utility streams as cases of decision under uncertainty. We have already seen that there are severe theoretical difficulties that face theories of decision under uncertainty and that there is at least some reason to suppose that we should treat all decision problems as cases of decision under risk. Furthermore, if we are to suppose that there can be infinite utility streams – and hence the possibility of infinite utilities – then it seems that we ought also to be able to make sense of the idea that there are infinitesimal probabilities. If we are prepared to work with ∞, then surely we should be prepared to countenance $1/\infty$ as well. But if we are prepared to countenance infinitesimal probabilities, then we shall again have cases of decision under risk – though perhaps we shall find that almost all such cases are now computationally intractable. (Just as we have *trivial* finite additivity for ∞ in **Я**, we have *trivial* finite additivity for $1/\infty$ in the extension of **Я** that also contains $1/\infty$. If we suppose that a number is sampled uniformly from the natural numbers, then the probability that that number is in *any* finite set of size $n \in N$ is $1/\infty$.)

Furthermore, one might well think that there are other grounds for maintaining that thoughts about possible addition of further decision rules in cases in which there are infinite utility streams into which one might fall are premature. Suppose that there is an infinite utility stream. Suppose, further, that for any alternative that one might select at any time – in any choice situation – prior to entry into the infinite utility stream, there is some chance – however small – that choosing that alternative will lead to entry into the infinite utility stream. In those circumstances, it is tempting to suggest that every alternative will have infinite expected utility. To see this, suppose that we begin with a standard decision problem, with alternatives A_i, possible states S_j with probability p_j, and utilities u_{ij}. Suppose we are then told that there is an infinite utility stream and that there is some chance that one might obtain entry to this stream by performing any given one of the A_is. It seems that we should then reassess our formulation of the decision problem. The alternatives are still the same A_i, but each S_j should be replaced by two states S_{j_1} and S_{j_2} with probabilities p_{j_1} and p_{j_2}, $p_{j_1} + p_{j_2} = p_j$, where $S_{j_1} = S_j +$ you gain entry to an infinite utility stream, and $S_{j_2} = S_j +$ you do not gain entry to an infinite utility stream. If we suppose, as seems plausible, that $u_{ij_1} = \infty$, then we do indeed get the result that each alternative has infinite expected utility. If each alternative *might* lead to entry into an infinite utility stream, then you have no way of choosing between alternatives on any other grounds.

Against the argument in the last paragraph, it might be suggested that, if this reasoning were cogent, then it would show that ordinary, finite decision theory is unworkable. After all, there are large but finite utility streams and large but finite disutility that one might fall into whenever one makes a decision: It is possible – though, of course, massively unlikely – that the fate of the next federal election turns on what I choose to have for breakfast tomorrow. (The world is chaotic; a butterfly effect cannot be ruled out.) But in that case, surely I am required to partition states of the world and assign probabilities, in the same manner as was suggested for the infinite case. Well, yes and no. If the probabilities were high enough, and the utilities and disutilities were large enough, then, indeed, this is what one would need to do. If there is a high enough chance that the outcome of the next federal election hinges on my choice of breakfast cereal, then I should try to take that into account when I am deciding what to do. But, of course, it is entirely reasonable to suppose that the probability that the outcome of the next federal election hinges on my choice of breakfast cereal is so small that redoing the calculation of expected utility along the suggested lines would make no difference to the result of the calculation. But the case that we described in the previous paragraph is relevantly different: Whereas large but finite utilities and disutilities can be ignored when the probabilities are small enough, any finite probability demands that infinite utilities and disutilities must be considered. So this response fails to show that we do, after all, have good grounds for supposing that we can construct a tractable infinite decision theory.

In sum, then, we see that the development of an infinite decision theory – where that theory doesn't merely consider infinitely many alternatives, infinitely many states of the world, and the absence of an upper bound on utilities, but rather extends to consideration of infinite utilities – is fraught with difficulties. While, for all that has been argued so far, it seems that we can happily countenance countably additive probabilities, countably many alternatives, countably many states of the world, and the absence of an upper bound on utilities, the introduction of infinite utilities promises to wreak havoc with the theory of decision.[7]

6.7 TWO ENVELOPES

Despite the slightly optimistic conclusion of the previous section, there might be reasons for worrying about the development of decision theory in contexts in which there is no upper bound on utilities. In the next two sections of this chapter, we present two well-known cases in which decision-theoretic reasoning seems to go awry once we countenance unbounded utility functions. We begin with various versions of the Two-Envelope Paradox, and then move on to discuss the – in some ways simpler and yet even more puzzling – case of the St. Petersburg Game.

There are many different versions of the two-envelope – 'exchange', 'trading' – paradox.[8] We begin with a simple version, and then go on to consider some of the more complex cases. Along the way, I shall argue that one of the advantages of supposing that probability measures are countably additive – and not merely finitely additive – is that this affords a ready solution to certain versions of the two-envelope paradox. I shall also defend the view that one can respond to the two-envelope paradoxes without rejecting unbounded utility functions out of hand.

Version 1. A person is offered a choice between two envelopes, A and B. She is told that one envelope contains twice as much money as the other, but she has no further information (e.g., information about

[7] For more in this pessimistic vein, see McClennen (1994), and Hájek (2003).

[8] For other presentations and discussion of the two envelope paradox, see Littlewood (1953), Nalebuff (1989), Cargile (1992) Christensen and Utts (1992), Castell and Batens (1994), Jackson, Menzies, and Oppy (1994), Broome (1995), Arntzenius and McCarthy (1997), McGrew, Shier, and Silverstein (1997), Scott and Scott (1997), Wagner (1999), Clark and Schackel (2000), Horgan (2000), Chalmers (2002), and Chase (2002).

which envelope contains the higher amount). She chooses A, say. Before opening A, she asks herself whether she ought to have taken B instead. There is a line of reasoning that suggests that she should. Suppose that the amount of money in A is \$$x$. Then either B contains \$$2x$ or B contains \$$0.5x$. Each possibility is equally likely, so the expected value of taking B is $0.5\$2x + 0.5\$0.5x = 1.25\$x$, that is, an increase of $0.25\$x$. This conclusion cannot be right. The mere choosing of A cannot give her a reason to say that she ought to have picked up B instead. For the situation is symmetrical: There is nothing to favour choice of A over choice of B, at least until one of the envelopes is opened. Had she chosen B initially, the same line of reasoning would suggest to her that she ought to have chosen A, instead. Since, no matter which choice she makes, the line of reasoning leads her to the conclusion that she ought to have made the other choice instead, there must be something wrong with the line of reasoning. But what?

At least initially, I'm tempted to say that one mistake in this line of reasoning lies in the assumption that a reasonable person might reasonably believe that, for all \$$x$, it is equally likely that there is \$$2x$ and \$$0.5x$ in the other envelope. No reasonable person could reasonably have a 'flat' distribution for the random variable x. After all, any reasonable person will believe that there is a minimum unit of currency – for example, if the envelope she holds contains 1 cent, then, if the other envelope either contains half or double the contents of her envelope, then the other envelope certainly contains 2 cents. And any reasonable person will believe that there is a limit to the amount of money that could have been placed in the envelopes – for example, to take a really extravagant upper bound, if more than half of the money in the world economy is in the envelope she holds, then, if the other envelope either contains half or double the contents of her envelope, then the other envelope certainly contains half of the amount that is contained in the envelope she holds. While there is, perhaps, very little that we can say in advance about the shape of the 'prior' distribution that the person who undertakes the line of reasoning possesses, we can be quite sure that no reasonable person will have the 'flat' distribution that is assumed in the statement of the paradoxical reasoning.

There are at least two reasons why one might be dissatisfied with this initial response. As we shall go on to see, there are ways in which our first version of the two-envelope paradox can be varied, producing lines of reasoning that seem immune to this particular style of criticism. True enough, this version of the paradox involves a flat probability distribution over an infinite domain, and may be criticisable on that account. But other variants of the puzzle that involve nonflat probability distributions (and, perhaps, nonstandard or peculiar utility functions) will have to be criticisable on other grounds. If there is a more general criticism that takes in all of the variants of the initial version of the puzzle, then there are good grounds for claiming that it identifies *the* (fundamental) mistake in the line of reasoning. While this would not undermine the claim that our initial response identifies *a* mistake in the line of reasoning in the initial version of the paradox, it could be taken to show that that initial response is, in a certain sense, too superficial.

A second reason for dissatisfaction with my initial response is that it is not obviously correct to claim that no reasonable person could reasonably believe that, for all $\$x$, it is equally likely that there is $\$2x$ and $\$0.5x$ in the other envelope. On the one hand, if we suppose that it is logically possible for there to be a world in which there is no minimum unit of currency and no upper bound on the amount of money that could be contained in an envelope, then, at the very least, it isn't clear why we shouldn't also suppose that it is logically possible for there to be a reasonable person who reasonably believes that, for all $\$x$, it is equally likely that there is $\$2x$ and $\$0.5x$ in the other envelope. And on the other hand, even if it is logically necessary that there is a minimum unit of currency, it is not clear that this fact entails that no reasonable person can reasonably believe that, for all $\$x$, it is equally likely that there is $\$2x$ and $\$0.5x$ in the other envelope. Perhaps, for instance, someone could reasonably come to hold this belief on the basis of a trusted informant. If decision theory is to provide 'the logic of decision', then it ought to apply to the deliberations of all rational agents in all logically possible worlds.

To probe these suggestions a bit further, I turn now to the next of the versions of the two-envelope paradox that I propose to discuss.

Version 2. You are rotting in Hell. Because you have been good, God decides to offer you a temporary stay in Heaven. He offers you two envelopes, one of which will entitle you to N days in Heaven, and the other of which will entitle you to $2N$ days in heaven, where N is a natural number that God tells you he has chosen uniformly from the set of all of the natural numbers. In your position, you are desperate to spend as much time in Heaven as you can. You choose one of the envelopes, and then God offers you the chance of taking the other envelope instead. You reason as follows: Suppose that the envelope you have chosen entitles you to D days in Heaven. Then either the other envelope entitles you to $2D$ days in Heaven, or the other envelope entitles you to $0.5D$ days in Heaven. Moreover, since God has chosen the amount by uniformly sampling the entire set of the natural numbers, you are required to suppose that these two possibilities are equally likely. So the expected utility of holding the other envelope is $0.5 \times 2D + 0.5 \times 0.5D = 1.25D$. So, by the principle of maximising expected utility, you should trade envelopes. Of course – for the same reasons as in the previous case – there is something wrong with this line of reasoning. But what?

In this case, it seems *prima facie* that we cannot make the same initial objection that we made in the previous case. After all, it is built into the story that you have good reason to have a 'flat' distribution for the random variable that ranges over amounts of money in the envelope that you choose first: If an omnipotent, omniscient and omnibenevolent being tells you that he has brought it about that *p*, and if you correctly and reasonably believe that this being is omnipotent, omniscient, and omnibenevolent, then you have the best possible reason for believing that *p*. Nonetheless, I do not think that we should suppose that the background information in this scenario establishes that it is at least possible that a reasonable agent have a 'flat' distribution over a countably infinite domain. Rather, I think that we should insist that not even God could choose a number uniformly from the set of all of the natural numbers: This version of the two-envelope paradox does not describe a logically possible scenario, and so, in particular, it does not describe a logically possible scenario in which a rational agent has a 'flat' distribution over a countably infinite domain.

If we are prepared to endorse the principle of countable additivity, then we might give the following argument in defence of our rejection of the possibility of this scenario. If we have a 'flat' distribution over a countably infinite domain, then either each of the elements in the domain is assigned probability zero, or each of the elements in the domain is assigned a finite value, ξ, say. If each of the elements in the domain is assigned probability zero, then, by countable additivity, the sum of probabilities over the entire domain is 0 (which contradicts the axiom that the measure of probability on the entire domain is 1). If each of the elements in the domain is assigned probability ξ, for some finite ξ, then, again by countable additivity, the sum of probabilities over the entire domain diverges (which again contradicts the axiom that the measure of probability on the entire domain is 1). Given countable additivity, it is impossible to have a 'flat' distribution over a countably infinite domain. However, if a being could sample uniformly from a countably infinite domain, then one would have a probability distribution that is 'flat' over a countably infinite domain. Whence it follows that it is logically impossible for a being to sample uniformly from a countably infinite domain.

If we are not prepared to endorse the principle of countable additivity, but maintain instead that probability measures need only be finitely additive, then the above route to the rejection of the possibility of the case under consideration is blocked. If we suppose, under this new assumption, that each of the elements in the domain is assigned probability ξ, for some finite ξ, then, as before, we shall find that we do not have a well-defined probability measure: For we can choose $n \in \boldsymbol{N}$ such that the product $n\xi$ is as large as we please (and certainly greater than 1). However, if we suppose that each of the elements in the domain is assigned probability zero, then the only conclusion that we can draw is that any finite subset of the domain also gets assigned probability zero: Without the assumption of countable additivity, we cannot go on to conclude that the measure of the entire domain is also zero. At the very least, there is a challenge here for those who are only prepared to endorse finite additivity: How is the plainly mistaken line of reasoning to be blocked in the version of the two-envelope paradox that is here under consideration?

To help with the development of other lines of criticism of the first two versions of the two-envelope paradox, I turn now to a third version, which brings up a new range of issues.

Version 3. A person is told that money has been placed in two envelopes using the following method. A coin that has a 1/3 probability of falling heads and a 2/3 probability of falling tails is tossed. If it falls heads, then \$1 is placed in one envelope and \$2 is placed in the second envelope. If the coin falls tails, it is tossed again. If it falls heads, then \$2 is placed in one envelope and \$4 is placed in the second envelope. If the coin falls tails, it is tossed again.... If the coin falls heads on the nth toss, then $\$2^{n-1}$ is placed in the first envelope, and $\$2^n$ is placed in the second envelope.... Since the person is rational, he or she believes that the probability that the smaller of the two amounts in the envelopes is $\$2^n$ is $2^n/3^{n+1}$. The person chooses one of the envelopes, and then is offered the opportunity to switch. The person reasons as follows. Suppose that the amount of money in the envelope I hold is $\$x$. Then the expected value of holding the other envelope is $3/10\$x + 8/10\$x = 11/10\$x$ (unless, of course, my envelope contains \$1, in which case the expected value of holding the other envelope is \$2). So, by the principle of maximising expected utility, I should trade envelopes. Once again, it seems that there must be something wrong with the line of reasoning in this case. But what could the mistake be?

We might think that, even if we have been told the truth about the method that was used to place money in the envelopes, we could hardly be justified in adopting the proposed probability distribution, since it conflicts with what any reasonable person will believe about large amounts of money: At the time of writing there is, for example, no chance that there is more than $\$10^{1000}$ available to place in the envelopes. However, we can retell the story so that God chooses from the natural numbers, with a 1/3 chance of choosing $2^0 = 1$, a 2/9 chance of choosing $2^1 = 2$, a 4/27 chance of choosing $2^2 = 4$, an 8/81 chance of choosing $2^3 = 8$, and so on, and uses this as the basis for a gift of days in Heaven. There is nothing obviously incoherent about that version of the story. So we can set this kind of objection aside.

The distribution that we have described has unusual features. In particular, as Broome (1995) points out, this distribution does not have a (finite) mean: $\sum_{n=1}^{\infty} 2^n \cdot (2^{n-1}/3^n) = \frac{1}{2}\sum_{n=1}^{\infty}(4^n/3^n)$, which diverges. Moreover, as Broome proves, one can get the apparently paradoxical reasoning to run only if one has a distribution that lacks a finite mean: No distribution with a finite mean will support the paradoxical reasoning. Given this result, one might think that the solution to the version of the paradox now under consideration is to ban distributions without finite means: If no rational agent can have a distribution that lacks a finite mean, then no rational agent can become embroiled in the paradoxical line of reasoning.

Of course, as in our previous discussion, one might wonder whether it is correct to claim that no reasonable person could reasonably have a distribution that lacks a finite mean. On any ordinary account of reason, there are grounds for suspicion of this claim. So it is unclear whether we should put much faith in the above analysis. But there are alternatives. I shall consider two.

First, as various authors have noted, the distribution that we are discussing belongs to a special class of distributions that lack a finite mean. Suppose that we take the total outcome space of envelope possibilities to be $\{[1, 2], [2, 1], [2, 4], [4, 2], [8, 4], [4, 8], \ldots\}$, where $[x, y]$ means \$$x$ in envelope 1 and \$$y$ in envelope 2.

Plainly enough, there is a partition $\prod$ of this outcome space according to the amount of money in envelope 2: $\{\{[2, 1]\}, \{[1, 2], [4, 2]\}, \{[2, 4], [8, 4]\}, \ldots\}$. For any element $\{[k/2, k], [2k, k]\}$ of this partition, if you hold a Broome-paradoxical probability distribution, then the expected value of holding envelope 1 at this element ($\frac{11}{10}\$k$) is greater than the expected value of holding envelope 2 at this element ($\$k$). Consequently, we have the line of argument that concludes that it is irrational to hold envelope 2: No matter which element of the partition we consider, you prefer to hold envelope 1 at that element.

Equally plainly, there is a partition Γ of this outcome space according to the amount of money in envelope 1: $\{\{[1, 2]\}, \{[2, 1], [2, 4]\}, \{[4, 2], [4, 8]\}, \ldots\}$. For any element $\{[k, k/2], [k, 2k]\}$ of this partition, if you hold a Broome-paradoxical probability distribution, then the expected value of holding envelope 2 at this element ($\frac{11}{10}\$k$) is greater than the expected value of holding envelope 1 at this element ($\$k$). Consequently, we have the line of argument that concludes that it is irrational to hold envelope 1: No matter which element of the partition we consider, you prefer to hold envelope 2 at that element.

However, the reasoning to this point really only talks about conditional expected values: We calculated our expectation in the problematic line of reasoning conditional on a particular partition of the outcome space. In order to draw a conclusion, we need to be able to discharge our assumption, that is, we need to be able to conclude that we would get the same answer no matter which partition we chose. But this we cannot do: We have already seen that different partitions on the space of outcomes yield different answers in our calculation of expected value. (Strictly speaking, the series that we have used for the calculation of the expected value is: $1/6 \cdot (-1) + 1/6 \cdot (1) + 1/9 \cdot (-2) + 1/9 \cdot (2) + 2/27 \cdot (-4) + 2/27 \cdot (4) + \ldots$. This series does diverge, but not merely because the absolute values of the terms are unbounded; for there is also the matter of the oscillation of the signs of the terms.) The upshot is that, even if we admit distributions that lack finite means, we can bar the paradoxical reasoning on the ground that it depends on the unjustified choice of a particular partition of the space of possible outcomes.

If we allow that a rational agent can have a Broome-paradoxical distribution, then a rational agent might find herself in the following interesting situation: While she doesn't have a good reason for trading if she has no asymmetrical information about the envelopes, if she is allowed to open one of the envelopes to see what is in it, then she will immediately want to swap for the other envelope, no matter what amount she sees! On the one hand, there is no good *a priori* argument for swapping without looking. On the other hand, there is a good *a priori* argument for the conclusion that, no matter which envelope one opens, and no matter what one sees, one will want to swap after one has looked. If one thinks that there is something *pathological* about this state of affairs, then one might prefer to return to the blanket ban on distributions that lack finite means. But we have already found some reason for dissatisfaction with that proposal.

Second, some philosophers – for example, Adam Elga and Alan Hájek – have recently suggested a different analysis that shares some of the features of the analysis just discussed. On this analysis, the key step in the two-envelope reasoning is the move *from* the claim that for all $\$x$, the conditional expectation for swapping, given that the amount in the envelope you hold is $\$x$, is $\$1.25x$ *to* the conclusion that you should swap envelopes. How is this move to be justified? After all, in general, decision theory tells us to maximise expectation; it says nothing at all about what to do given various kinds of conditional expectations.

What is needed, it seems, is something like the following principle: If there is a partition of an outcome space such that for every element *Pi* of the partition $E(Y/PI) > E(X/PI)$, then $E(X) > E(Y)$. But the problem is that this principle is evidently false. On the one hand, as we've already seen, there are cases where this principle simply leads to contradiction, since there is one partition that would licence the conclusion that $E(X) > E(Y)$, and another partition that would licence the conclusion that $E(Y) > E(X)$. And, on the other hand, there are (not necessarily distinct) cases where the unconditioned expectations $E(X)$ and $E(Y)$ are infinite. In those cases, whether we say that $E(X)$ and $E(Y)$ are both undefined or we say that $E(X)$ and $E(Y)$ are both infinite, we do not have that $E(X) > E(Y)$. However we argue that case, there is no doubt that it is not true, in general, that if there is a partition of an outcome space such that for every element *Pi* of the partition $E(Y/PI) > E(X/PI)$, then $E(X) > E(Y)$. But how else are we to get to the conclusion that we should swap envelopes from the claim that for all \$*x*, the conditional expectation for swapping, given that the amount in the envelope you hold is \$*x*, is \$1.25*x*?

It is worth noting that the analysis that we have just rehearsed applies equally well to all three versions of the two-envelope paradox that have been considered here. So, even if we suppose that, in our first version of the puzzle, no reasonable person could believe that, for all \$*x*, it is equally likely that there is \$2*x* and \$0.5*x* in the other envelope, our latest analysis suggests that we should nonetheless suppose that this observation does not identify the most fundamental flaw in the paradoxical reasoning.

In some ways, the discussion to this point barely scratches the surface of recent discussions of the two-envelope paradox. There are many variants of the puzzle that have not been mentioned here. There are more sophisticated formulations of the relevant mathematics that have been ignored. There are quite different proposals for resolution of the paradox that have not been considered. However, discussion of all of these matters must be deferred to some other occasion. The one conclusion that I will draw here is that, while one might take the various versions of the two-envelope paradox to give one some reason to refuse to countenance unbounded distributions of utility, there are other possible responses to these cases that might well be preferred.

If you think – for example – that it is possible that God might give you a gift of any finite number of days in Heaven, there are other points at which you can fault the plainly problematic reasoning.

6.8 ST. PETERSBURG GAME

Daniel Bernoulli introduced and studied the St. Petersburg game while he was working in St. Petersburg (hence the name). It works like this:[9] A fair coin is tossed. If the coin comes up heads, you get \$2. If the coin comes up tails, it is tossed again. If the coin now comes up heads, you get \$4. If the coin comes up tails, it is tossed again. If the coin now comes up heads, you get \$8. If the coin comes up tails, it is tossed again. And so on. A play of the game continues until the coin comes up heads. If this takes n throws, then you get $\$2^n$. The question is: How much should you expect to pay to be allowed to play this game? Plainly enough, you have a 1/2 chance of winning \$2, a 1/4 chance of winning \$4, a 1/8 chance of winning \$8, ..., a $1/2^n$ chance of winning $\$2^n$, ..., and so your expected gain for playing the St. Petersburg game is infinite. There is no finite amount of money that should entitle you to a single play of this game! That is, you should be prepared to pay any finite amount of money to play the game just once. Indeed, you should be prepared to pay any finite amount of money for a one in a million chance to play the game just once.

Bernoulli himself noted that, if the utility of money decreases at an appropriate (logarithmic) rate as one obtains more of it, then the expected utility of playing the game may well be finite even though your expected monetary gain is infinite. However, we can run though the same argument in the case of a game that is played for *utils* rather than for cash, that is, for a game in which declining marginal utility is irrelevant. So, while Bernoulli's proposal may have satisfied him in the case of gambling for money, there is a theoretical problem here that remains unresolved. Moreover – and perhaps even more tellingly – if you have an unbounded utility function, then the problem that Bernoulli sought to avoid can be reinstated simply by stepping up the

9 For other presentations and discussions of the St. Petersburg game, see Samuelson (1977), Jeffrey (1983), Weirich (1984), Cowen and High (1988), Jordan (1994), and Chalmers (2002).

payoffs: Consider a super St. Petersburg game in which the payoffs escalate superexponentially.

If we suppose that there is no limit to the number of days in Heaven that could be granted to us by God, then the line of reasoning sketched above suggests that one ought to be prepared to give up any finite amount of utils in order to play a St. Petersburg gamble on days in Heaven with God. What response can one make?

One suggestion that is often made is that there are further reasons why it is reasonable for us to decline the St. Petersburg gamble even though to accept it is to maximise expected utility. In particular, there are consideration about *risk* and aversion to risk. Consider a truncated St. Petersburg game, in which there will be at most N throws of the coin, and in which one wins $\$2^{n+1}$ if one throws N consecutive tails. In this case, the expected value of the gamble is $\$N + 1$. However, one will find very few people who are prepared to wager $10,000 to play a St. Petersburg game in which there will be at most 1,000,000 throws, even though the expected value of the gamble is $1,000,001. Rather than suppose that people are typically irrational – for refusing a gamble at such attractive rates – we do better to suppose that people are risk-averse: It is better to have the $10,000 for sure than to have one chance in a hundred of winning $1,000,000.

Another suggestion that is sometimes made is that – despite appearances – it is rational to give up any amount of utils for a single play of the St. Petersburg game. However, this response is not obviously attractive. If we suppose that the result is to be determined by the regular tossing of a coin – and not by the use of an infinity machine that can perform an infinite number of tosses in a finite amount of time – then it seems that, if you receive a pay-off for playing the game, then you can be sure that the amount that you receive is finite: You cannot receive an infinite payout from a single play of the St. Petersburg game. But in that case, the expected value of the gamble is clearly greater than any amount of money that you can actually receive from playing the game. (If, perhaps *per impossible*, you had an infinite amount of utils to wager, then it would be irrational for you to bet everything you have on a single play of the St. Petersburg game: You *cannot* get your infinite stake back if you play. Of course, if you have an infinite amount of utils to wager, then you can play at more or less no cost, since an infinite number of utils can be partitioned into an infinite collection of infinite numbers of utils – but that's another story.)

If we are unmoved by considerations concerning risk, but do not want to accept that it is rational to give up any amount of utils for a single play of the St. Petersburg game, then what else can we say? If we aren't to give up on decision theory altogether – and that would indeed be counsel of despair – then it seems to me that, if we are unmoved by considerations of risk, we ought to accept that we do not have – and perhaps will never have – a good theory about what to do in cases in which there are distributions that lack finite mean, finite variance, or both. While decision theory can be extended to cases in which there is unbounded utility, we can trust the results of decision-theoretic calculations only in cases in which the expectation has finite mean, finite variance (and, one might expect, finite moments of all higher orders as well). As before, this conclusion might be taken to be too strong. However, those who would like to embrace a decision theory that tolerates infinite moments have work to do to develop a satisfactory theory of this kind.[10]

6.9 HEAVEN AND HELL

There are many other puzzle cases that might be discussed at this point. Consider, for example, the following (from Arntzenius and McCarthy (1997)).

Suppose that your utilities for one day in Heaven, Purgatory, and Hell are 1, 0, and −1, respectively. God reliably informs you that you have an infinite amount of time in Purgatory to which to look forward. God then offers you a St. Petersburg gamble where the payoffs are days in Heaven: a probability of a half of the next day in Heaven and then back to Purgatory; a probability of one-quarter of the next two days in Heaven and then back to Purgatory; a probability of one-eighth of the next four days in Heaven and then back to Purgatory; and so on. You accept the gamble, and win 2^n days in Heaven, for some $n \in N$. Next

[10] Other proposals for dealing with the St. Petersburg game include disallowing unbounded utility functions, disallowing utility/probability profiles on which expectations are unbounded, and disallowing infinite state spaces. Given that decision theory is to provide "the logic of decision", there is reason not to be happy with any of these suggestions.

morning, God meets you at the entrance to Heaven and offers you a deal. If you abandon the days in Heaven that you have won, and spend today in Hell, you can have another shot at the St. Petersburg gamble. But if you decline to play again, after your n days in Heaven, you will spend the rest of your days in Purgatory. Since it seems reasonable to you to accept this deal, you do so. You win 2^m days in Heaven, for some $m \in N$, and then spend the day in Hell. Next morning, God again meets you at the entrance to Heaven, and makes the same deal. Again, it seems reasonable to you to accept, so you do. However, you note that it now seems that you may have an unending life in Hell to look forward to! And that makes you suspect that something must have gone wrong with your reasoning.

Arntzenius and McCarthy consider the suggestion that you might think that what has gone wrong is that you have been offered a gamble with infinite expectation. They respond with the observation that it seems that God could secure you unending life in Hell by first offering you one day in Heaven, and then three days in Heaven in exchange for one day in Hell, and then five days in Heaven in exchange for one day in Hell, and so forth. Consequently, it seems that your difficulties aren't due to the fact that you've been offered a gamble with infinite expectation; the mere fact that there is no limit to how many days in Heaven can be offered to you by God is enough to trap you.

In the original scenario, it seems to me that it might matter how the winnings are determined. If the winnings are determined by regular throws of a coin, then there will be plenty of days – and weeks, and years – that are spent tossing a coin with God (and hence in which one spends no time in either Hell or Purgatory). Moreover, in this case, there really is no chance that one can maximise one's winnings: If one wins at all, one wins only a finite number of days in Heaven; and, no matter how much one wins, it is possible for one to win more. On the other hand, if the winnings are determined by an infinity machine, then there is the (unlikely) possibility that one will win an infinite number of days in Heaven: even if the chance is strictly zero, there is at least the *possibility* of maximising one's winnings. Moreover, in this case, the time spent with God on any given day can be negligible.

If, at the outset, one were given a choice between: (a) an infinite series of days in Hell, on each of which, as the result of a St. Petersburg gamble, one wins – but subsequently renounces – a finite number of days in Heaven; and (b) an infinite series of days in Purgatory prefaced by the number of days in Heaven that one wins in a one-off St. Petersburg gamble, then one would certainly opt for the latter. However, it is not clear that this fact somehow shows that it is irrational to accept – and then renounce – each of an infinite series of St. Petersburg gambles in the manner described: For it isn't written into the story that God will continue to offer you more chances at a St. Petersburg gamble. To take the most dramatic example, suppose that, on any given day, you have no way of estimating how likely it is that God will offer you another St. Petersburg gamble on the following day: In that case, the fact that you end up spending an infinite number of days in Hell need not impugn your rationality at all. (True enough, you will acquire some inductive evidence as time goes by. But that inductive evidence could be overridden by other considerations.)

Suppose, on the other hand, that you come to have good reason to think that God will continue to offer you St. Petersburg gambles forever. Then – at least in the version of the scenario in which one cannot win an infinite number of days in Heaven, and in which the utility of time spent tossing a coin with God is less than the utility of Purgatory – it seems clear that one has good reason arbitrarily to accept the result of the next St. Petersburg gamble. Whatever amount is won in that gamble, one could win more – and, if one waits long enough, one will win more. But this will be true of every future gamble as well. So, if one reasons in *that* way, one will spend all of one's future in Hell.

Setting aside cases in which the utility of tossing a coin with God is high enough to ensure that you prefer time spent in Hell plus time spent tossing the coin to time spent in Purgatory, the only case left to consider is that in which one *can* win an infinite number of days in Heaven. In this case, it is hard to know what to say – for now we are back in the realm of decision theory with infinite utilities (and not merely decision theory with unbounded utilities). At the very least, there seems to be little reason to rely on intuitions that are generated by this case.

In the modified scenario – in which God offers ever-increasing but finite numbers of days in Heaven – the same kinds of considerations apply. If you know for sure that God will offer you $n + 2$ days in Heaven on the day after the day on which he offers you n days in Heaven, for all $n \in N$, then it is hard to know what to recommend to you to do. If you don't accept any of God's offers, then you will spend an eternity in Hell: the worst outcome of all. But if you accept one of God's offers, then you will have an eternity in Purgatory in which to reflect on the fact that, had you waited longer, you would have been able to spend more time in Heaven. Moreover, each day that you spend in Hell earns you two days in Heaven; so, provided that you do take up God's offer at some point, the longer you delay, the greater your overall utility.

If we allow that one can choose between infinitely many alternatives in circumstances in which utilities are unbounded, then one can face a decision problem with the following structure: There is just one relevant state of the world – God fulfills the conditions of your choice – and infinitely many alternatives A_i, $1 \leq i \leq \infty$, where $u_{i1} = i$, for $2 \leq i \leq \infty$, and $u_{11} = -\infty$. In this case, one cannot choose so as to maximise one's expected utility; and there is no simple decision rule that leads to an intuitively acceptable result, since, in the envisioned circumstances, there is no intuitively acceptable result. However, it is clear that any arbitrary choice of an A_i, $2 \leq i \leq \infty$, is better than the choice of A_1; so, as before, it seems most reasonable to suggest that you arbitrarily select some large j, and go with A_j. (Perhaps, for example, you could first arbitrarily select the resources that you will allow yourself to use in choosing a number – so many days of calculation, so much paper, and so forth – and then spend your time constructing the largest number that you can express given the resources that you have arbitrarily selected. No matter what you do, you could do better: But if failing to select one of the A_i, $2 \leq i \leq \infty$, entails that one selects A_1, then *any* selection is better than none at all.)

6.10 CONCLUDING REMARKS

As the discussion in the previous section makes clear, decision theory with unbounded utilities and infinite alternatives makes no recommendations in a wide range of cases unless new decision rules are formulated. While the project of developing such decision rules is interesting, it seems clear that there is room for scepticism about the prospects of developing a really compelling infinite decision theory of this kind. Moreover, even if one supposes that there is no reason to be sceptical about the possibility of developing a decision theory that can handle unbounded utilities and infinite alternatives, there is even stronger reason to be sceptical about the prospects for developing a compelling decision theory that permits infinite utilities.

7

Mereology

Mereology is the theory of the part/whole relation. The basic principles of the theory of the part/whole relation may seem to be utterly straightforward. However, as we shall see, there are various different ways in which questions about infinity impose themselves on the investigation of the general nature of part/whole relations.

We begin with the "proofs" in Kant's *Second Antinomy,* which concern the part/whole structure of the world. On the one hand, he offers a "proof" of the claim that the world – and everything in it – either is something that has no parts (i.e., a simple) or is composed without remainder from things that have no parts. On the other hand, he offers a "proof" of the claim that there are no simples, that is, there are no things that have no parts. In each case, the object of "proof" is a strong modal thesis – that it is necessary that any object either has no parts or else is composed without remainder of objects that themselves have no parts, that it is necessary that there are no things that have no parts – from which the desired results can be inferred by a simple application of the T-axiom (if it is necessary that *p*, then *p*).

After this warm-up, we turn to a formal presentation of the basic concepts and axioms of mereology, and then to a discussion of the various ways in which questions about infinity bear on these concepts and axioms. We shall follow the discussion of mereology in Lewis (1991) – partly on account of its simplicity and succinctness – but we shall not be supposing that there is any particularly clear reason to prefer that account to, say, the one offered in Simons (1987). A full discussion of mereological principles would require far more space than we can afford here.

7.1 SECOND KANTIAN ANTINOMY

In the *Second Antinomy of Pure Reason*, Kant offers "proofs" of conflicting theses about the ultimate constituents of the world. On the one hand, there is the view that every composite entity is ultimately constituted from simple parts: Nothing exists apart from simples, and things that are composed of simples. On the other hand, there is the view that no composite entity is ultimately constituted from simple parts: There are no simples from which composite entities could be ultimately constituted.

(a) On Behalf of Simples

The thesis of the second antinomy is that nothing exists but simples and fusions of simples: "Every composite substance in the world is made of simple parts, and nothing anywhere exists save the simple or what is composed of the simple". The "proof" runs more or less as follows. Suppose that there is a composite substance C that is not ultimately composed of simple parts. If we imagine that all composition is removed from C, then clearly we will be left imagining nothing. So it must be impossible to imagine that all composition is removed from C. But there is nothing impossible in imagining that all composition is removed from any object. Whence it follows that C is impossible: There cannot be a composite substance that is not ultimately composed of simple parts.

The strategy behind this "proof" is peculiar. Perhaps the simplest model for a composite entity that is not ultimately composed of simples is an infinite Russian doll: Inside each part of the Russian doll, there is another part of the Russian doll occupying a smaller, but nonetheless finite spatial volume. If we start with our infinite Russian doll, and imagine that "all composition is removed" – that is, that every one of the parts is taken away – then, of course, there is nothing left. But how does that in any way show that it is impossible to imagine that "all composition is removed" from an infinite Russian doll or that it is impossible for there to be an infinite Russian doll? A proof that there can be only simples and fusions of simples has to be able to establish that there cannot be things that have the structure of an infinite Russian doll. I think that it is quite clear that there is nothing in the argument of the "proof" of the thesis of Kant's second antinomy that does any such thing.

(b) Against Simples

The antithesis of the second antimony is that there are neither simples nor fusions of simples: "No composite thing in the world is made up of simple parts, and there nowhere exists in the world anything simple". The "proof" runs very roughly as follows. Suppose that a composite substance C is ultimately composed of simple parts. Clearly, C must occupy a space that has as many parts as C itself possesses: Each part of C must occupy a space. Hence, each of the simples of which C is composed must occupy a space. But anything that occupies a space must "contain a manifold of constituents external to one another" and hence be composite. Whence it follows that C is impossible: There cannot be a simple that has no further constituents.

If anything, this argument on behalf of the antithesis is even worse than the "proof" of the thesis. Suppose that we grant that simples are required to be point particles, that is, particles that occupy a single spatial point. Then the "space" that is occupied by a simple will be a single spatial point, that is, it will not be a space that "contains a manifold of constituents external to one another". Kant's argument provides no grounds for denying that composite objects are ultimately composed of simples that occupy single spatial points. To establish the desired conclusion, Kant would need to show that there cannot be point particles; but nothing in the "proof" of the antithesis of the second antinomy supports this claim.

Apart from worries about the arguments that Kant marshals in defence of his "thesis" and "antithesis", one might also have worries about the formulation of these two claims. Plainly enough, if there are neither simples nor fusions of simples, then it cannot be the case that there is nothing in the world but simples and fusions of simples. However, it can be true that there are both simples and fusions of simples even though it is not true that there is nothing in the world but simples and fusions of simples. If, for example, the world contains some simples, and also some things that have the structure of an infinite Russian doll, then neither the "thesis" nor the "antithesis" is true. So there can hardly be any affront to reason in rejecting both the "thesis" and the "antithesis" as formulated. (Of course, given the way that I have formulated the arguments, they do yield something close to contradictory conclusions: It cannot be both that it is necessary that there are neither simples nor fusions of simples and that it is necessary that there is nothing in the world but simples and fusions, *unless* it is necessary that there is nothing at all. But the point that I have emphasised is that it should not be thought that these modal claims exhaust logical space.)

7.2 SOME POSTULATES

In the previous section, I introduced various terms from mereology without explaining them. As Lewis (1991) observes, there is a choice of which terms to take as mereological primitives. We might say: x and y *overlap* iff they have some common part; and that x and y are *disjoint* iff x and y do not overlap. Or we might say that something is a *fusion* of some things iff it has all of those things as parts and has no part that is disjoint from each of them. Or we might say that x is a *part* of y iff everything that overlaps x also overlaps y; or iff everything that is disjoint from y is also disjoint from x; or iff y is a fusion of x and something z. Given this circle of interdefinition, we can then go on to say that x is a *proper part* of y iff everything that overlaps x also overlaps y, but not everything that overlaps y also overlaps x; or iff everything that is disjoint from y is also disjoint from x and everything that is disjoint from x is also disjoint from y; or iff y is a fusion of x and something that is disjoint from x. (There are further terms for which definitions could be provided: 'binary sum', 'binary product', 'difference', 'universe' and 'complement' – see Simons (1987: 13–16). However, we shall not need these terms in our discussion.)

Following Lewis (1991: 74), we might say that there are three *basic* axioms of mereology (together with whatever axioms one chooses in order to close the circle of interdefinition of terms exhibited above):

Axiom 1: (*Transitivity*) If *x* is a part of some part of *y*, then *x* is a part of *y*.

Axiom 2: (*Uniqueness of Composition*): It cannot be that the same things have two different fusions.

Axiom 3: (*Composition*): Whenever there are some things, there is a fusion of those things.

While we shall consider alternatives to Axiom 3 – in particular, while we shall consider alternatives according to which it is only true that when we have fewer than a certain cardinal number of things, there is a fusion of those things – we can follow Lewis in noting that Axiom 2 and Axiom 3 jointly licence talk of *the fusion* of a collection of things. If there are more things indicated than the limit imposed in alternatives to Axiom 3, then it may turn out that those things are permitted not to have a fusion by theories based on those alternative axiomatisations.

Whether we should follow Lewis in saying that these are the basic axioms of mereology depends on the answers to two questions. First, there are many matters on which these axioms are silent, but on which one might suppose that the fundamental axioms of mereology ought to speak. So, for instance, the questions that are addressed in Kant's second antinomy are not answered by Lewis's axioms. Second, there are objections that can be made to each of the axioms that Lewis presents: It simply isn't obvious that there is a topic-neutral conception of part and whole that conforms to these – or any other – collection of axioms.

Enemies of the infinite must, I think, suppose that there are just finitely many atoms, that is, things that have no parts; and they must suppose that there is nothing that is not made up, without remainder, from those finitely many atoms. If this is right, then finitist mereologies require an axiom like the following: For some $n \in N$, there are exactly n atoms. Further, I think that enemies of the infinite will most plausibly allow that the number of atoms can change over time: that is, rather than hold that there is some $n \in N$ such that, for all times t, there are n atoms at t, they will hold that, for each time t, there is some $n \in N$ such that there are n atoms at t. Finally, it seems to me that enemies of the infinite will suppose that it is a necessary truth that there are always only finitely many atoms: Necessarily, for each time *t*, there is some $n \in N$ such that there are *n* atoms at *t*.

Friends of the infinite have more options. They might suppose that there are only finitely many atoms; or they might suppose that there are infinitely many atoms. They might suppose that there can be only finitely many atoms, or they might suppose that there can be infinitely many atoms. Moreover, if they suppose that there are, or can be, infinitely many atoms, they might suppose that the infinity in question is $\aleph_0$, or $\aleph_1$, or some higher cardinality. Furthermore, friends of the infinite might suppose that there are possible worlds in which, at some times, there are only finitely many atoms but in which, at other times, there are infinitely many atoms; or they might suppose that *this* kind of variability in the number of atoms is impossible.

Apart from considerations about the number of atoms, friends of the infinite might also suppose that there are objects that are not composed from atoms: objects that have parts, whose parts have parts, and so on *ad infinitum.* They might suppose that everything is composed, without remainder, from atoms; they might suppose that nothing is composed, without remainder, from atoms; or they might suppose that some, but only some, things are composed, without remainder, from atoms. Moreover, they might suppose that it must be that everything is composed, without remainder, from atoms; or they might suppose that it must be that nothing is composed, without remainder, from atoms; or they might suppose that it must be that some, but only some, things are composed, without remainder, from atoms; or they might suppose that it can be that everything is composed, without remainder, from atoms, and it can be that nothing is composed, without remainder, from atoms, and it can be that some, but only some, things are composed, without remainder, from atoms. And so on.

If we suspect that we need different accounts of the part/whole relation for concrete individuals (occurrents and continuants) and for abstract individuals (classes), then we might also think that questions about atoms and gunk can be answered differently in these different cases. So, for example, those who are prepared to countenance abstract infinities but who are opposed to physically instantiated infinities might hold that, while there are infinitely many abstract atoms and there is abstract gunk, there can be only finitely many concrete atoms at any time, and there cannot be concrete gunk. More generally, those who suppose that there are many different part/whole relations that apply in different domains may have a series of questions about atoms and gunk to answer concerning each of the domains that they recognise.

Among the axioms that Lewis gives, the first is clearly the least controversial. While there are *prima facie* counterexamples to transitivity – for example, a handle is part of a door, and a door is part of a house, but a handle is not part of a house – these counterexamples work by introducing a qualified part/whole relation in which the qualification involves functional contribution, causal contribution, lines of command, or the like. A handle makes a direct functional contribution to a door; and a door makes a direct functional contribution to a house; but a handle makes only an indirect functional contribution to a house. While there might be some interest in pursuing the theory of this or that qualified part/whole relation, it seems that there is no reason here to deny that fundamental mereology should focus on a transitive part/whole relation.

Lewis's Axiom 2 is plainly controversial. To begin with, there are cases in which it might be said to be evidently violated, namely, cases in which two individuals have the very same parts, but the organisation of the parts differs in the two cases. So, for example, the Promotions Committee and the Exclusions Committee may have the very same membership, even though these are very different committees; and I and my body may have the very same parts, even though, unlike my body, I exist only when there are certain kinds of processes going on in my body. Since it is unclear what are the parts of a committee – at the very least, one might suspect that the charter is part of the committee – there is reason to be sceptical about the first kind of case. Moreover, since I am inclined to the view that, when the relevant processes are no longer going on in my body, I shall be dead and buried, I do not think that the second case is any more compelling: When I am buried, the processes will have ceased, but there is a perfectly good sense in which I shall continue to exist – though, of course, I won't be *alive.* While it is possible to exhibit cases – both about collectives and about individuals – in which there is some intuitive pull to the idea that Axiom 2 is violated, I do not know of any cases of these kinds that could reasonably be taken to be decisive. In general, as Lewis says, the problems that arise in connection with Axiom 2 are problems about temporary intrinsic properties and accidental intrinsic properties that are hard problems for everyone. While there are undoubtedly (weakened) alternatives to Axiom 2 that merit serious consideration – see, for example, the discussion in Simons (1987) – it is beyond the scope of the present study to examine them.

There are two different ways in which Axiom 3 might be thought to be controversial. On the one hand, it is controversial because it allows that any arbitrary fusion of (parts of) objects is itself an object. If we have a trout and a turkey, then we also have the object that consists of the fusion of the trout and the turkey. If we suppose that there is such a thing as the top half of the trout and that there is such a thing as the bottom half of the turkey – under any way of dividing the trout and the turkey that is sufficiently determinate – then there is such a thing as the fusion of the top half of the trout and the bottom half of the turkey. If we suppose that all objects are just fusions of atoms, then Axiom 3 entails that any fusion of atoms – no matter how spatially scattered the atoms may be – is an object. While, on this view, the vast majority of objects turn out to be "inhomogeneous, disconnected, not cohesive, not causally integrated," and so forth, it is unclear whether this is a weighty objection. After all, one might think that, for most purposes, it is fine if one's attention is fixed only on interesting subcollections of all of the objects that there are. Why should we insist that *all* objects fall under natural sortals?

On the other hand, there is an objection that remains even if we suppose that there is nothing objectionable in the arbitrariness of mereological composition. For, as noted above, if we suppose that there are infinitely many atoms – or if we suppose that there is gunk – Axiom 3 will commit us to the existence of infinite arbitrary fusions, that is, arbitrary fusions that have countably many, or even uncountably many, parts. To see why this might be taken to be additionally problematic, we turn to an argument that is due to Forrest (1996).

7.3 FORREST'S CHALLENGE

One of the key claims that Lewis makes about his version of mereology is that it is *ontologically innocent*: Commitment to fusions is nothing over and above commitment to the objects fused. This claim about ontological innocence is then an important component of the further thesis that the identity relation is a special, limiting case of a family of mereological relations: the composition relation, the overlap relation, and the part/whole relation. Lewis calls this further thesis "Composition as Identity". If mereology were not ontologically innocent, then that would undermine the claim that composition is a kind of identity.

Forrest (1996) objects to the claim that Lewis's version of mereology is ontologically innocent on the grounds that it entails the falsity of a theory of space that cannot be known *a priori* to be false.

The theory of space in question is Whiteheadian, and is committed to the following claims:

1. Regions are the fundamental spatial entities.
2. Regions have no parts other than regions and are parts of nothing other than regions.
3. All regions have the same dimension.
4. Regions may be represented by sets of points in such a way that each representing set contains a sphere – that is, all the points less than some distance z from some point Z.
5. There are spherical – or at least approximately spherical – regions of arbitrarily small diameter; that is, for any point X and any positive real number y, there is a region represented by a set of points including all those of distance less than y from X and none of distance greater than $2y$ from X.
6. The representation of regions as sets of points preserves volumes; that is, the volume of a region equals the Lebesgue measure of the corresponding set of points.

Forrest's main argument proceeds as follows. Lewis's Axiom 3 entails countable fusion: Any countable collection of objects has a fusion. In the context of the Whiteheadian theory that we have just sketched, we then have – in particular – that any countably many regions of space have a fusion that is itself a region of space. But consider. The points in space with rational coordinates are countable. Let them be the points A_i, $i \in N$. Then there are approximate spheres R_i, such that R_i includes all points less then $(1/2)^{i+1}$ from A_i, and no points of distance greater than $(1/2)^i$ from A_i. Suppose that the R_i have a fusion. If this fusion is less than the whole of space, then there is a region T disjoint from the fusion of the R_i. Moreover, T can be represented by a set of points containing all points within $2z$ of Z for some positive z. So there must be a point with rational coordinates within z of Z. Suppose that it is A_k. Then T is not disjoint from R_k. So, if the R_i have a fusion, then that fusion is the whole of space. But the sum of the volumes of the R_i is 1, whereas we can choose units so that the volume of space is much greater than one. Whence it follows that the R_i do not have a fusion.

Forrest maintains that, since Countable Fusion entails the falsity of a theory that we do not have *a priori* reason to reject, we have good reasons to suppose that Lewis's mereology is not ontologically innocent: We do not have enough *a priori* knowledge about the true nature of space to reject the Whiteheadian account of space in almost *a priori* fashion.

Forrest also provides a subsidiary argument – a "further illustration of his case" – that goes as follows. It follows from the alleged innocence of mereology that, if a region S is the fusion of countably many regions R_i, then there is no number v such that the volume of every finite fusion of the R_i is less than v but the volume of S is greater than v. (Why? Because the whole is no greater than the sum of its parts: There is nothing more to the fusion than the regions fused.) But now suppose that all regions of space are either empty or filled with a homogeneous fluid of density 1 g/cm^3. Suppose, further, that region R_i is filled at time $t_i = 1-(1/2)^i$, $i \in N$, so that the t_i converge to time 1. If both Countable Fusion and the Whiteheadian account of space hold, then at time 1, the whole of space is filled with matter at density 1 g/cm^3. Yet it seems absurd to say that this counterintuitive result is just what one ought to expect if space is Whiteheadian and there are arbitrary countable fusions: Surely, we would need a better explanation than that of the spontaneous appearance of matter, if we are to be offered any explanation at all.

While Forrest's *reductio* arguments do make use of the assumption of countable fusion, it seems that it is possible to derive more or less equally counterintuitive consequences from the Whiteheadian theory of space alone. For simplicity, we shall focus on the case of one-dimensional space that is, the real number line – but nothing but computational ease hangs on this choice. We consider the line segment (0, 10), and assume – with our Whiteheadian account – that, while there are line segments, there are no points, so that there is no distinction among the intervals (0, 10), [0, 10), (0, 10], and [0, 10]. We assume, also, that all of the parts of space are perfectly precise – there are no fuzzy regions, or the like.

Consider, now, the line segment (0, 1), that is, an arbitrary line segment of unit length. We can use this line segment to construct a 'cover' of the line segment (0, 10), following the recipe that Forrest provides for deducing a contradiction from the conjunction of Countable Fusion and the Whiteheadian account of space. The rational points in the line segment (0, 10) are countable. Let them be the points, A_i, $i \in N$. There are line segments R_i such that R_i includes all and only the points of distance less than $(1/2)^{i+1}$ from A_i. Thus, we can use our line segment (0, 1) to construct a 'cover' of the R_i, using the sequence of intervals $(0, \frac{1}{2})$, $(\frac{1}{2}, \frac{1}{4})$, $(\frac{1}{4}, \frac{1}{8})$, and so on. Under this 'cover', there is no interval in – hence, according to our Whiteheadian account, no part of – the interval (0, 10) that is not overlapped by at least one of the R_i.

To make this vivid: Suppose that you have a stick of length 10 metres, and a stick of length 1 metre. Suppose that you break the stick of length 1 metre in half infinitely often and that you can arrange the resulting parts on top of the stick of length 10 metres with perfect accuracy. Then, on the Whiteheadian account of space, you will be able to arrange the pieces of the stick of length 1 metre so that no part of the stick of length 10 metres is fully uncovered, that is, fully visible, even to infinitely discriminating vision. Remember: The Whiteheadian account of space says that the only parts of a line segment are line segments. There are no points, nor anything corresponding to kinds of fusions of points other than line segments. So the fact that, in non-Whiteheadian space, there would be many points – and, indeed, entities that are neither points nor line segments – not covered is irrelevant: No part of the 10 metre stick that the Whiteheadian says exists can be seen in its entirety.

Suppose, further, that line segments can be assigned a colour. Suppose that all line segments with which we work initially are either entirely black or entirely white. Suppose that the line segment (0, 10) is initially all white – that is, it, and all of its subsegments – are entirely white. Suppose that region R_i – and the corresponding part of the interval (0, 10) – is blackened at time $t_i = 1-(1/2)^i$, so that the t_i

converge to 1. At time 1, there is no region – however small – of the 10 metre stick that is totally white – that is, white throughout – even though we only blackened regions with a total length of 1 metre. Now suppose that, over a finite period of time, we remove regions that are entirely black, until all of the entirely black regions are removed. For definiteness, we can suppose that larger regions are removed earlier, with the further provision that, where there are regions of the same size, they are all removed together. Let regions of measure α – where, by construction $0 < \alpha < 10$ – be removed at time $10 - \alpha$. Then, at time 10, the process of removal of entirely black parts will be complete. What will be left? Well, according to the Whiteheadian, we shall have a pile of black line segments . . . and nothing else! What has happened to all of the white colour in the line segment (0, 10)? And what will happen if we put the black regions back together again to reconstruct a line segment isomorphic to (0, 10)? Will the white colour magically reappear? Will some other colour magically appear? Or what?

I don't think that it should be denied that the combination of Countable Fusion and the Whiteheadian theory of space leads to counterintuitive results. But the Whiteheadian theory of space all by itself leads to equally counterintuitive results. It seems entirely plausible – if not more or less knowable *a priori* – that, at least in cases in which 'F' is restricted to spatially distributed properties such as volumes of colours – something that is partly F must have some parts that are entirely F. Since the Whiteheadian account of space violates this principle, we have good reason for thinking that the Whiteheadian theory of space can be rejected on more or less *a priori* grounds. If Forrest is happy to say that one should just expect that magical appearance of colour when one puts together regions according to the prescription at the end of the last paragraph, then what real grounds does he have for rejecting the suggestion that one should just expect the magical filling of space with matter of density $1g/cm^3$ in the case that he claims casts doubt on the *a priori* knowability of Countable Fusion?

In closing, it is perhaps also worth noting that the reasons that Forrest gives – on behalf of the claim that it follows from the ontological innocence of mereology that, if a region S is the fusion of countably many regions R_i, then there is no number v such that the volume of every finite fusion of the R_i is less than v but the volume of S is greater than v – are specious. According to Forrest, the entailment claim is justified by the observation that our intuitive claim that the whole is no greater than the sum of its parts can be encapsulated in the more formal claim that a whole cannot have a volume in excess of the sum of the volumes of its parts. But if this justification were any good, it would establish that space cannot be taken to be a fusion of points. After all, the volume of a point is zero, as is the volume of a finite fusion of points. Space is a fusion of points. The volume of space can be nonzero. Wherefore, if a region S is the fusion of uncountably many points R_r, $r \in R$, there is a number – 0 – such that the volume of every finite fusion of the R_r is no greater than that number, but the volume of S is greater than that number. So, if the justification that Forrest gives for the alleged entailment were good, then the detour through Whiteheadian space would be unnecessary – the innocence of mereology would be refuted by considerations concerning standard space alone. (It is no part of Lewis's mereology that the volume of a fusion of nonoverlapping regions is the sum of the volumes of those regions. There is nothing in Axioms 1 to 3 to support this suggestion.)

7.4 TAKING STOCK

Even if we are persuaded that Forrest's objection to Lewis's thesis of the ontological innocence of (his version of) mereology can be met, there are still further worries that one might have about the claim that Lewis's axioms provide the *basic* axioms for mereology. A useful point of comparison at this point is the fundamental theory of Simons (1987).

If we ignore time and modality, then Simons (1987: 362) proposes that the following are the basic mereological principles:

1. *Falsehood*: If x is a proper part of y, then x and y both exist.
2. *Asymmetry*: If x is a proper part of y, then y is not a proper part of x.
3. *Transitivity*: If x is a proper part of y, and y is a proper part of x, then x is a proper part of z.
4. *Supplementation*: If x is a proper part of y, then there is some z such that z is a proper part of y, and z does not overlap x.

If we do not ignore time and modality, then Simons proposes that the following are the basic mereological principles:

1. *Falsehood*: Necessarily, for all *t*, if *x* is a proper part of *y* at *t*, then *x* exists at *t* and *y* exists at *t*.
2. *Asymmetry*: Necessarily, for all *t*, if *x* is a proper part of *y* at *t*, then *y* is not a proper part of *x* at *t*.
3. *Transitivity*: Necessarily, for all *t*, if *x* is a proper part of *y* at *t*, and *y* is a proper part of *z* at *t*, then *x* is a proper part of *z* at *t*.
4. *Supplementation*: Necessarily, for all *t*, if *x* is a proper part of *y* at *t*, then there is some *z* at *t* such that *z* is a proper part of *y* at *t*, and *z* does not overlap *x* at *t*.

Setting aside Transitivity, we might try supposing that the remaining axioms are selected merely to "close the circle of interdefinition" between the basic terms of mereology. But that doesn't seem right. On the one hand, Simons includes Falsehood so that he can introduce free logic into the base of mereology. On the other hand, Asymmetry is included because this seems to be a fundamental constraint on the meaning of 'proper part'. Perhaps Supplementation can be put on the list of axioms "required to close the circle of interdefinition", but even this is not entirely obvious.

I suspect that the right thing to say at this point is that Lewis requires further axioms than those needed to "close the circle of interdefinition", but that many of these further axioms are relatively uninteresting. Since Lewis is not prepared to allow cross-world fusions, he accepts something like Falsehood. Moreover, he accepts something like Asymmetry and Supplementation as well. However, because he is prepared to make much stronger assumptions about the basic, topic-neutral conception of part and whole, there may well be further axioms that must be added in order to provide a fully explicit development of Lewis's mereology. While those further axioms might have implications for the treatment of infinity in the general theory of mereology, I think that we can leave this matter here.

As Lewis (1987: 76) notes, there is a different range of matters on which his version of mereology is silent. His theory says nothing on the question of whether all objects are spatiotemporal. His theory is silent on the question of whether an object can have proper parts that occupy no less spatial volume than is occupied by the whole. His theory is silent about the possibility of bilocation: For all that the theory says, it may be possible for one object to be wholly present in two disjoint locations. And his theory is silent on the question of whether, if an object occupies a region, each part of the occupied region must be occupied by a – perhaps improper – part of the object: For all that the theory says, there may be mereological atoms that occupy finite spatial volumes.

Some of these matters are of interest to us. If, for example, we suppose (1) that if an object occupies a region, each part of the occupied region must be occupied by a – perhaps improper – part of the object, and (2) that space is a fusion of points, then we immediately get the consequence that finite spatially located objects have uncountably many parts. Moreover, we shall also get the immediate consequence that any finite spatially located object has countably many disjoint parts, that is, countably many parts that are such that no one of these parts overlaps any other of these parts. Of course, the supposition that space is Whiteheadian would not help to avoid infinitary consequences: Even if space is Whiteheadian, our main supposition yields the result that finite spatially located objects have countably many disjoint parts. (If we start with a finite region of Whiteheadian space, divide it in half, divide one of the resulting regions in half, divide one of the resulting regions in half, and so on, we shall partition our finite region into infinitely many disjoint subregions. Now suppose that there is an object that occupies all of the finite region with which we began: Under our assumption, that object clearly has countably many disjoint parts.)

7.5 ATOMS AND INDISCERNIBLE PARTICLES

In section 7.2, I discussed the range of views that it is possible to take about atoms and gunk. In the present section, I want to consider the possibility that that earlier taxonomy was incomplete: There may be views that one could have about the fundamental part/whole structure of the world other than the views countenanced in that earlier taxonomy.

Consider, for example, the theory of indistinguishable particles that is offered in Lavine (1991). According to Lavine, the standard account of quantum mechanics is that it is an atomistic theory, that is, a theory that obeys at least the following four principles:

1. Objects in a system are represented as being composed of simplest elements – the atoms of the theory.
2. Properties, relations, and behaviour of objects in a system are connected to properties, relations, and behaviour of the atoms of which they are composed.
3. A theory of the properties, relations, and behaviour of atoms is given.
4. Properties, relations, and behaviour of complex systems are explained or predicted by (1) using the general theory of the properties, relations, and behaviour of atoms to infer the properties, relations, and behaviour of the particular atoms of which the systems in question are composed, and then (2) using the connections among the properties, relations, and behaviour of atoms and the properties, relations, and behaviour of the objects they compose to go from statements about atoms to statements about systems

A standard model that justifies the claim that these postulates accurately characterise atomistic theories is that they accurately characterise the connection between the temperature of an ideal gas in nonextreme conditions and the mean kinetic energies of the atoms that compose the ideal gas.

The assumption that quantum mechanics is an atomistic theory leads to difficulties when we come to the characterisation of indistinguishable particles in quantum mechanics. The problem is generated by the presence of the following fundamental postulate in quantum mechanics:

Indiscernibility Postulate: If a system in atomic physics contains a number of particles of the same kind, then these particles are indiscernible with respect to all of the physical properties used in quantum mechanics.

If we suppose that one particle is in a state represented in a suitable Hilbert space by the vector $|a\rangle$, and another particle is in a state represented in a suitable Hilbert space by the vector $|b\rangle$, then, if the particles are of different kinds, the state with the first particle in the state represented by $|a\rangle$, and the second particle in the state represented by $|b\rangle$, is itself represented in the product Hilbert space by $|a_1\rangle\,|b_2\rangle$. However, if the particles are of the same kind, the analogous state is represented by the state $|a_1\rangle\,|b_2\rangle \pm |a_2\rangle\,|b_1\rangle$. The state $|a_1\rangle\,|b_2\rangle$ is disallowed because it is not symmetric. Moreover, the state $|a_1\rangle\,|b_2\rangle\ \pm\ |a_2\rangle\,|b_1\rangle$ is not decomposable into separate states for each of the two particles.

Given that we admit that there are particles that are indiscernible with respect to all of the physical properties used in quantum mechanics, it seems that there are just three options open to us.

1. *Hidden Identities*: We can claim that quantum mechanics is incorrect and that the individual particles differ in some not yet discerned physical aspect; or
2. *Metaphysical Identities*: We can claim that the particles are different, but the difference is nonphysical: There is the property of being identical to particle a despite the fact that – even in principle – we cannot tell which particle has this property; or
3. *No Identities*: We can cast aside our Quinean heritage and claim that there can be quantum mechanical entities without quantum mechanical identities.

Each of these proposals is problematic. However, as just noted, it appears that they constitute exhaustive alternatives under the assumption that quantum mechanics is an atomistic theory. Lavine's proposed alternative to these three problematic views is to give up the claim that quantum mechanics is an atomistic theory. Instead of supposing that quantum mechanics treats of atomic particles, suppose instead that quantum mechanics treats of substances – kinds of stuff – for which there are smallest possible amounts. Instead of the principles characteristic of atomic theories, suppose instead that basic quantum mechanical stuff obeys the following four principles:

1. Objects are made of simple stuff that has smallest possible amounts in which it can occur.
2. Properties, relations, and behaviour of complexes are connected with properties, relations, and behaviour of the simple kinds of stuff from which they are composed.
3. A theory of the properties, relations, and behaviour of the smallest amounts of simple stuff is given; and a theory of how the

smallest amounts of stuff combine to make larger quantities is given.

4. The properties, relations, and behaviour of complex systems are explained or predicted by applying the theory of the properties, relations, and behaviour of the smallest amounts of the simple kinds of stuff and the theory of how these amounts combine to infer the properties, relations, and behaviour of the particular configurations of kinds of stuff that occur in the systems in question.

On Lavine's theory, it seems that one could have a system in which there are n units of some quantum mechanical stuff – light, say – and yet in which there are no parts of that quantum mechanical stuff – no photons that together make up the n units of light. Of course, if one has n units of this quantum mechanical stuff, then, under appropriate circumstances, one may be able to make it yield up n photons; but one should not suppose that this entails that the stuff is composed from n photons that exist prior to the procedures that cause the n photons to be yielded up. Rather, the situation is that one has some stuff that is potentially divisible, and yet which does not have parts – or, at least, does not have parts of the kind into which it can be divided. But doesn't this possibility make difficulties for the taxonomy that was produced in section 7.2?

I don't think so. There is nothing in the theory of mereology that says that mereological atoms are required to obey all of the postulates that Lavine sets down for atomic theories. All that is required of a mereological atom is that it has no parts. If it is truly the case that there is a quantity of quantum mechanical stuff that has no parts, then that quantity of quantum mechanical stuff constitutes a mereological atom. Of course, for all that we have argued, it could be that our quantity of quantum mechanical stuff has parts other than units of the quantum mechanical stuff in question – and, in that case, we shall have independent reason for saying that our quantity of quantum mechanical stuff does not constitute a mereological atom. But if we suppose that there are no other kinds of parts that our quantity of quantum mechanical stuff can have, then there is nothing to prevent us from supposing that our quantity of quantum mechanical stuff is a mereological atom.

Perhaps this does suggest a wrinkle on our earlier taxonomy. I claimed that enemies of the infinite are required to suppose that there are only finitely many mereological atoms. However, I think that enemies of the infinite should not be happy with the suggestion that there is an infinite quantity of quantum mechanical stuff – that is, a quantity of quantum mechanical stuff from which infinitely many units of quantum mechanical stuff could be distilled – even in the case in which that infinite quantity of quantum mechanical stuff constitutes a mereological atom. At the very least, it seems that there are two cases that need to be distinguished. Perhaps some enemies of the infinite will tolerate infinite potential divisibility; if so, then we can distinguish between the case in which there are only finitely many mereological atoms, none of which is potentially infinitely divisible, and the case in which there are only finitely many mereological atoms, but at least one of these atoms is potentially infinitely divisible.

In closing this section, it is perhaps worth noting that standard theories of mereology are silent on questions about divisibility, unless one adds to them the assumption that there can only be division – partition – where there are already parts. When Lewis discusses the trout-turkey, he discusses an object that is a fusion of two unproblematic objects: a trout and a turkey. He does not assume that there is such an object as the – or, at any rate, a – top half of the trout; and perhaps there isn't, at least until the trout is actually cut in half. Of course, this line of thought leads us back to the question of whether, if an object occupies a region, each part of the occupied region must be occupied by a – perhaps improper – part of the object.

7.6 VAGUENESS AND INFINITE DIVISIBILITY

There is, perhaps, another way in which someone might think to question the taxonomy of section 7.2, and, indeed, a number of the analyses that have been presented in earlier sections of this book. I shall begin by addressing the question in the context of infinite divisibility, and then turn to the application of this discussion in other contexts.

Sanford (1975: 528ff.) argues that, when we come to the question of the infinite divisibility of (classical) space, we are not faced with two exhaustive options: We need not opt either for the view that space has infinitely many parts or for the view that space has only finitely many quantised parts of some fixed minimum extension. Similarly, in the case of (classical) time, Sanford argues that we are not faced with two exhaustive options: We can reject the view that space has infinitely many parts while also consistently rejecting the view that time has only finitely many quantised parts of some fixed minimum duration. If Sanford is right about these cases, then one might think that we were too quick to suppose that enemies of the infinite must suppose that there are only finitely many mereological atoms; perhaps enemies of the infinite can avail themselves of Sanford's *tertium quid* in the more general case as well.

Following Sanford, we might suppose that the most plausible argument for the conclusion – that either we suppose that there are infinitely many intervals or else there are only finitely many quantised intervals of some fixed minimum extension – begins with the observation that, for any relation R, the following five claims are inconsistent:

1. *Existence*: There are R-related things. $((\exists x)(\exists y)Rxy)$
2. *Asymmetry*: The R-relation is asymmetric. $((\forall x)(\forall y)(Rxy \rightarrow {\sim}Ryx))$
3. *Transitivity*: The R-relation is transitive. $((\forall x)(\forall y)(\forall z)((Rxy \,\&\, Ryz) \rightarrow Rxz)))$
4. *Existential Heredity*: Anything that has an occurrence as the first term of the R-relation also has an occurrence as the second term of the R-relation. $((\forall x)(\forall y)(Rxy \rightarrow (\exists z)Rzx)$
5. *Finitude*: There are only finitely many R-related things. $((\exists n \in N)(\exists X\colon \mathrm{card}(X) < n)(\forall x)[\{(\exists y)Rxy \vee (\exists y)Ryx\} \rightarrow x \in X])$

Still following Sanford, suppose that we accept the following principle of *homogeneous divisibility* for intervals: If some interval of extent e exists, then every interval of an extent greater than e contains a subinterval of extent e. Suppose, further, that we interpret Rxy to be the relation x is a proper part of y, and that we take the variables x and y to range over intervals. Then, since it is clear that the relation R satisfies (1) to (3) when interpreted on a domain of intervals, we are left with a choice between (4) and (5) Either we accept that there are only finitely many intervals – and, in that case, given homogeneous divisibility, we must accept that there are only finitely many quantised intervals of some fixed minimum duration – or else we must accept that every interval contains a smaller interval – and, in that case, we must accept that there are infinitely many intervals.

To defuse this argument, Sanford observes that the argument does not go through if we are prepared to suppose that the relation R – or, at any rate, the predicate 'R' that is used to express the relation R – is *vague.* If the relation R is vague, then it can be true both that there are only finitely many R-related things and that there is no identifiable "first member" of the R-related things. To see this, consider what happens when we interpret 'Rxy' to mean 'x is a mammalian ancestor of y'. Clearly, says Sanford, we believe both that there have been only finitely many mammals and that it is not true that there is something that is definitely a mammalian ancestor of ours but that does not have parents that are definitely mammals. The conclusion that we should draw is that, if the R-relation is vague, then the reasoning to the conclusion that (1) to (5) are inconsistent fails: In the case that the R-relation is vague, the reasoning in question is soritical and, hence, notoriously unreliable.

Suppose that we agree with Sanford that (1) to (5) are not inconsistent when the R-relation is vague. Then, whether or not his strategy provides a *tertium quid* in the case of intervals seems to depend entirely on whether or not it is plausible to claim that the R-relation *is* vague. In the case at hand, then, the key question is whether it is – or, at any rate, can be – a vague matter whether one interval is a proper part of another.

Initially, it does not seem plausible to suppose that it can be a vague matter whether one interval is a proper part of another. Certainly, there is no vagueness in the mathematical theory of intervals. And while it seems plausible to suppose that one could be uncertain whether or not one interval is a proper part of another, it is also at least initially plausible to suppose that this merely reflects our epistemic limitations and tells us nothing at all about the nature of the intervals themselves.

Sanford suggests that we might suppose that there is a very small number n such that there is no interval with magnitude less than n, even though there is no small number m such that there is an interval of magnitude m and no interval of magnitude less than m. I think that this suggestion amounts to the proposal that there is a very small number n such that there is no interval of magnitude n, but there are intervals of magnitude $n + \varepsilon$ for all $\varepsilon > 0$, for ε belonging to an at least dense ball around 0. But in that case, while we may have averted one kind of infinite divisibility – converging on points – we find that there is a new kind of infinite divisibility – converging on intervals of magnitude n. It is hard to believe that this is progress.

Perhaps Sanford's proposal should be reconstrued in the following way. Space divides not into precise intervals, but rather into vague ones. The correct way to represent the measure of an interval is to include an error term: The measure of an interval has the form $m \pm \delta$, where $m > n$ and $\delta > \varepsilon$ for all m and δ. In that case, $n - \varepsilon$ is an absolute lower bound on the measure of intervals, but one cannot say that any interval has measure $n - \varepsilon$. So far, so good. But under these assumptions, when are we to say that one interval is a proper part of a second? If we say that the interval $(m_1 \pm \varepsilon_1, m_2 \pm \varepsilon_2)$ is a proper part of the interval $(n_1 \pm \delta_1, n_2 \pm \delta_2)$ iff $n_1 - \delta_1 < m_1 - \varepsilon_1$ and $m_2 + \varepsilon_2 < n_2 + \delta_2$, then there is no uncertainty about when one interval is a proper part of another. While this proposal is plainly unsatisfactory, it is hard to see what alternative might be offered in its stead.

There are reasons for thinking that we do not face an easy task here. We have already noted Lewis's proposal that we should think of the identity relation as a special, limiting case of a family of mereological relations: the composition relation, the overlap relation, and the part/whole relation. But there is at least strong *prima facie* reason to suppose that the identity relation cannot be vague – see, for example, Evans (1978). Moreover, there is good reason to suppose that, if the composition relation, the overlap relation, or the part/whole relation could be vague, then the identity relation could be vague. (How can it be determinate whether *a* is identical to *b* if it is not determinate whether *a* is a proper part of *b*?) So there is strong *prima facie* reason to suppose that none of the mereological relations can be vague.

Even if we are prepared to suppose that the proper part relation can be vague, the most that we are entitled to conclude, on the basis of Sanford's argument, is that there is no direct argument, for the joint inconsistency of the claim that there are only finitely many proper parts of objects and the claim that anything that has a proper part is itself a proper part of something else, that starts from the observation that (1) to (5) are formally inconsistent. But this leaves it open that there is some other inferential route that will lead us to the conclusion that either there are finitely many mereological atoms or the world is infinite in some respects. Moreover, even if there is no other way that we can find to establish the claim that either there are finitely many mereological atoms or the world is infinite in some respects, there are still difficulties that must be faced in the application of Sanford's proposal to particular cases.

Consider, for example, the question of whether the measure of past time is finite or infinite. Sanford suggests that, if the concept of an event's occurring at least an hour before another event is vague, then there may be borderline cases, and hence, there may be series of events that are finite, and yet contain no event that definitely is not preceded by an event that occurred at least an hour earlier. On this suggestion, even if there was no first eventful hour, it could be that the number of eventful hours in the past is less than some finite bound $n \in N$. But why might we suppose that the concept of an event's occurring at least an hour before another event is vague? Sanford says:

> The measurability of time is presumably a necessary condition of one event's occurring an hour or more before another. If a systematic correlation of cyclic processes is a necessary condition of the measurability of time, then such a systematic correlation is a necessary condition of one event's occurring an hour or more before another. And if such a systematic correlation did not always exist, it need not have come about suddenly. A gradual evolution from chaos to a systematic correlation of cyclic processes would result in the gradual realisation of the possibility of time measurement.

In other words, Sanford's proposal is that it might be a vague matter whether time is measurable – because it might be a vague matter whether there is sufficient correlation between cyclic processes in the universe – and hence that it might be a vague matter whether one event occurs at least an hour before another. However, it is at the very least highly contentious whether we should suppose that there cannot be (metrical) time in the absence of cyclic processes; and it is perhaps even more contentious whether we should suppose that there cannot be (metrical) time in circumstances in which it is impossible for observers to measure time. If Sanford's proposal can be supported only by contentious subsidiary assumptions such as these, then it seems to me that it loses much of its interest.

While – as always – there is room for further discussion, it seems to me to be reasonable to conclude that Sanford's *tertium quid* does not pose a serious challenge to the claim that either we should suppose that there are finitely many mereological atoms or we should suppose that the world is infinite in some respects.

7.7 CONTINUITY

There are various ways in which one might test out the hypothesis that there are only finitely many mereological atoms. In this section of the present chapter, I shall explore the consequences that this hypothesis has for the claim that there are *continuous* processes in the world.

Consider any property that varies across mereological atoms. Plausibly, no property of this kind can vary across a single mereological atom. For how are we to make sense of the idea that a mereological atom m possesses the property p both to degree d_1 and degree d_2 without contradicting ourselves? If there is an object that possesses the property p both to degree d_1 and degree d_2, this can be only because the object has disjoint parts p_1 and p_2, where p_1 possesses property p to degree d_1, and p_2 possesses property p to degree d_2. Hence, we can conclude that, if m possesses a degreed property p, then there is some unique degree d_m to which m possesses p.

Now, suppose that there are only finitely many mereological atoms, $m_1, \ldots, m_k$, and that each atom m_i possesses a property p to degree d_{in}. Then, when we consider the variation of the property p across any object that is a fusion of the m_i, it is clear that the property p must vary discontinuously across the parts of that fusion, unless the quantities d_{ij} form an order $d_{ij_1} < d_{ij_2} < \cdots < d_{ij_k}$ with the property that there are no other possible degrees of property p that are intermediate between d_{ij_1} and d_{ij_k}.

Suppose, for example, that a temporal interval of 1 minute between t_1 and t_2 is composed of finitely many subintervals, each of which has no further subintervals as parts. Suppose further that we have an object O that is at 15°C at t_1. In the next subinterval, the temperature of O is either 15°C or some temperature other than 15°C. If it is some temperature other than 15°C, then there is a discontinuous variation in the temperature from one interval to the next unless the temperature $15 \pm \varepsilon$°C of the object in that next interval is such that there is no temperature between 15°C and 15 ± ε°C that it is possible for the object O to possess. (The intuitive idea here is, roughly, that a process is continuous only if it is passes through all of the possible values that could lie on the trajectory between the starting point of the process and the endpoint of the process. If there are possible values that have been skipped, then the process is discontinuous, with discontinuities at the skipped values.)

If this is right, then the assumption that there are only finitely many mereological atoms has significant consequences for the possibility of continuous processes in the world. Suppose that we have two qualitatively identical objects and that we apply different amounts of heat to them in a period of one minute, so that the temperature of O_1 rises from 15°C to 16°C during the course of our minute, while the temperature of O_2 rises from 15°C to 17°C during the course of our minute. Given that any temperature that O_2 possesses is a temperature that O_1 could possess, and that any temperature that O_1 possesses is a temperature that O_2 could possess, it follows that it cannot be that the heating of both O_1 and O_2 are continuous processes: Either O_2 skips over temperatures as it passes from one interval to the next or O_1 fails to change temperature in some cases in which it passes from one interval to the next – and in neither of these cases is it true that there is continuous change of temperature in both objects.

The case that we considered above involved only two objects. When we move to consider more objects, we get more stringent constraints on continuity in situations in which there are only finitely many mereological atoms. The counterintuitive nature of these constraints provides a strong *pro tanto* reason for thinking that it is not the case that there are only finitely many mereological atoms. Of course, this *pro tanto* reason could be defeated by other considerations; nonetheless, at the very least, one should not be too hasty in supposing that one can accept the claim that there are only finitely many mereological atoms.

(I think that a similar conclusion can be drawn from the *tile argument* in the case of discrete space. If we suppose that space is composed of very small square tiles, then it seems to follow that the length of the hypotenuse of a right-angled isosceles triangle is equal to the length of each of the other two sides, since there are just as many square tiles along the hypotenuse as there are along each of the other two sides. Moreover, if we suppose that space is composed of very small tiles of some other shape, then it seems that we can show that the Pythagorean theorem fails to hold for some directions privileged relative to the grid of tiles. Either way, it seems that we are wrong to suppose that space is a grid of tiles. Even if the tile argument is not the immediate *reductio* that it appears to be, it surely suffices to show that we should be very wary about supposing that we can easily make sense of the suggestion that space is composed of a discrete set of points.)

The argument that I have given in this section relies on the assumption that a process is continuous only if it is passes through all of the possible values that could lie on the trajectory between the starting point of the process and the endpoint of the process. This is a very weak constraint. Some may think that a process is continuous only if the points along its trajectory can be indexed using a segment of the real numbers: There is no sense in which counting the natural numbers in their standard order involves some kind of continuity. But, of course, to insist on this account of continuity without further argument would be to beg the question against those who suppose that there are only finitely many mereological atoms. If I am right, we needn't beg any questions in order to cast doubt on the claim that there are only finitely many mereological atoms.

7.8 OUR UNIVERSE

It is sometimes suggested that there is no such thing as *our universe*, even though there are such things as the familiar material objects with which we are in daily contact. Since one of the reasons that is given for this suggestion turns on scepticism about unrestricted mereological composition, there is some justification for concluding the present chapter with an examination of this view.

Van Fraassen (1995) offers three kinds of reasons that we might have for supposing that there is no such thing as *our universe*.

A first kind of reason is this: We know from set theory that there are limits on the size of things and that assumptions about the existence of 'total' entities – for example, the set of all non-self-membered sets – are apt to lead to paradox. Since the universe would be a 'total' entity, we have reason to be cautious about postulating its existence.

A second kind of reason is this: If the world exists, then it is a mereological sum: the sum of all the things that exist. To believe in the existence of such a thing, we need to accept the principles of mereology, and, in particular, the principle of unrestricted composition. But we should not accept the principles of mereology – in particular, we should not accept the principle of unrestricted mereological composition – and so we have no reason to believe that the world exists.

A third kind of reason is this: The expression 'the world' is only superficially a noun; in fact, it is a context-dependent term that indicates the domain of discourse of the sentence in which it occurs, on the occasion of utterance. It plays this role sometimes by denoting the domain and sometimes by purporting to denote an entity of which the members of the domain are parts. However, in the latter case, we need not take the purported denotation seriously; rather, it is to be construed as metaphor, colourful language, rhetorical extravagance, or the like. In all cases, then, the important semantic function is merely the contextually constrained indication of the domain of discourse. Consequently, there is never good reason to suppose that 'the world' really refers to an entity.

None of these arguments strikes me as very impressive.

First, while it is true that some kinds of assumptions about the existence of 'total entities' lead to contradictions, it is hard to see what relevance this has to the existence of worlds. Suppose, for example, that one thinks of worlds in the way that Lewis (1986) does, that is, as maximal collections of suitably externally related objects (the model for the external relations being classical spatiotemporal relations). Whatever problems one thinks there are with Lewis's story, one should not think that there are cardinality problems that arise just given the worlds. Even if one took the worlds to be sets of objects, it isn't clear that troubles would arise – it's not as if we must be supposing that there are proper class many objects in each world, or that there are proper class many worlds;[1] and, in any case, it would just be a mistake to think that the worlds are sets of objects. On the contrary, the objects are *parts* of the worlds – and the mereological relation that this involves is not a relation that generates infinite collections from finitely many ur-elements.

[1] Lewis(1986) certainly does not allow that there are proper class many worlds, or that there are worlds that have proper class many parts. For a contrasting view – and for an explanation of some of the benefits that might accrue – see Nolan(1996).

Second, while it is true that belief in the principle of unrestricted mereological composition might play a role in arguments for the existence of the world, one is not obliged to believe that principle in order to accept the conclusion that the world exists (and, in any case, there are reasons for thinking that there is nothing wrong with the principle of unrestricted mereological composition). One might think, for example, that whenever one has some things, there is a thing of which all those things are parts, while denying that, whenever one has some things, there is a thing that is exactly the mereological sum of those things. In other words, perhaps the principle of unrestricted mereological composition is false, and yet it is impossible for there to be two things that are not both parts of the same thing. (By 'part', I mean 'proper or improper part', of course.) Consequently, it is just a mistake to think that commitment to the existence of the world requires commitment to the principle of unrestricted mereological composition (or, indeed, to any other objectionable mereological principles).

Third, it isn't plausible to suggest that 'the world' is – or could always be – understood 'distributively' in ordinary language (and that when thus understood, there must always be some contextually supplied restriction on the 'distributed' collection). Clearly, we do ordinarily make claims in which 'the world' must be understood 'collectively': 'The world is an awesome place', 'God's world is perfect', and so on. No argument from ordinary language or ordinary practice can show that these claims are unintelligible. Moreover, it is a commonplace amongst cosmologists – both prescientific and scientific – that the world exists. One could not understand what they say unless there is some sense in which one understands the collective, unrestricted, use of the expression 'the world'. No doubt, it is perfectly correct to claim that 'the world' often functions as a restricted 'distributive' quantifier; but there is no argument from this data to the conclusion that 'the world' never functions properly as an unrestricted 'collective' quantifier.[2]

[2] It's curious that van Fraassen just ignores that part of the OED definition of 'world' that doesn't fit his case, viz.,'the universe, or a region of it'. Perhaps uses in this sense are all metaphorical, colourful, or rhetorically extravagant – but if so, this needs to be argued from metaphysics, i.e., it is not a conclusion that is strongly supported by merely linguistic data.

Another kind of reason that some people have thought to give for denying that there is any such thing as *the* world turns on an alleged ambiguity, or discourse relativity, in the interpretation of the existential quantifier. On this Carnapian view, there are different kinds of discourses, and for each discourse, the *internal* question of whether the kinds that the discourse quantifies over exist is trivial (analytic); the *external* question of whether the kinds that the discourse quantifies over is purely pragmatic (is it useful to continue using this discourse?); and there is no other intelligible question about existence to be asked. So, in particular, there is no way of asking, in the one breath, whether objects that belong to different discourses (or frameworks, or theories) exist – and hence there is no sense to be given to the question of whether there is one world or many.

Even if this Carnapian position could be vindicated – and I must confess that my money is on the Quinian alternative that denies the Carnapian distinction between different senses of the existential quantifier – there is no reason to think that it is relevant to our present concerns. After all, we can take it that our question is one about the *physical* universe – that is, the subject of investigation of physical cosmology. The assumption that there is a single physical world – which is all that the present kind of objection is putting in doubt – is not one that the Carnapian thesis tells against.

Perhaps there is some other reason why we should not suppose that there is any such thing as the world. However, I can't imagine what those reasons could be. Moreover – putting into practice the motto that the best form of defence is attack – there are positive reasons why we should think that there is such a thing as the world. In particular, it is hard to imagine what alternative is supposed to be put in place of this assumption. There are things that stand in physical relations. What could it possibly be like for there to fail to be a total of things that stand in these kinds of relations? Compare: There are some people under the roof. What could it possibly be like for there to fail to be a total of people under the roof? True enough, there might be cases for semantic decision: borderline cases of people, borderline cases of being under the roof, and the like. But we can precisify, and then get determinate answers. In this case, we might end up with bounds, rather than a definite answer. But nothing like that could happen in the case of the physical universe – so what problems could there be left to face?

Furthermore, it is – and has been for at least seventy years – standard practice for scientific cosmologists to suppose that there is a unique physical world, which their theories seek to model and describe. If you spend a bit of time reading popularisations of scientific cosmology and informal expositions of theories in scientific papers, you will find that it is virtually impossible to resist the conclusion that almost all scientists naturally suppose that there is a unique world. In these circumstances, it seems natural to me to think that some very powerful argument is required before this assumption should be given up.

8

Some Philosophical Considerations

To this point, the discussion of various different subject areas – space-time, physics, probability, decision, mereology – has taken classical mathematics more or less for granted. But there are various more fundamental considerations that need to be taken into account in assessing the material that we have already examined.

We begin with an account of some basic distinctions that are frequently adverted to in discussions of the infinite: the distinction between actual and merely potential infinities, the distinction between completed and incomplete infinities, the distinction between additive and accretive infinities, and the distinction between abstract and concrete infinities.

Next, we turn our attention to pure mathematics and to the range of views that it is possible to take about the infinite in pure mathematics. We propose some very general constraints that it is plausible that any acceptable philosophy of pure mathematics must accept, and set out a rough taxonomy. In the light of that taxonomy, we then consider various ways in which one might try to justify the claim that it is reasonable to accept the axioms and methods of classical mathematics.

After a brief survey of some of the outstanding problems that are raised by classical set theory, we turn to the question of the range of views that it is possible to take about the infinite in applied mathematics, connecting the discussion in the previous parts of this chapter to the discussion in earlier chapters of this book. Finally, to round out the chapter, we provide some remarks on two topics that we have not yet mentioned but that cannot be passed over in a comprehensive discussion of the infinite: Skolem's paradox and the debate about the usefulness of infinitesimals in natural scientific theorising.

8.1 DISTINCTIONS

There are various philosophical distinctions that require attention in any extended discussion of the infinite. In particular, there is the distinction – or family of distinctions – between *actual infinities* and merely *potential infinities.* The main aim of this section is to try to arrive at a clear understanding of the range of views that can be distinguished using these kinds of labels.

(a) Actual versus Potential

Let's suppose, for now, that we can help ourselves to quantification over the natural numbers: For example, we can make sense of the claim that, for each natural number n, there is a point in space that is more than n metres in distance from the centre of the Earth. If we suppose that we can make sense of quantification over the natural numbers, then there are various different grades of involvement with the infinite that we can distinguish.

Consider the following two claims:

1. For each natural number n, there is a point in space p, such that p is more than n metres from the centre of the Earth.
2. There is a point in space p, such that, for each natural number n, p is more than n metres from the centre of the Earth.

Clearly, (2) is stronger than (1); indeed, (2) entails (1). Each is plausibly construed to be a claim to the effect that there is an actual infinity of some kind. However, only the second claim requires that there are points that are infinitely distant from the centre of the Earth. For the first claim to be true, all that is required is that there are infinitely many points, each of which is at some particular finite distance from the Earth. While enemies of infinity will suppose that there are no true claims of either form, it is not necessary for friends of infinity to suppose that there are true claims of both forms. I have already indicated that I think that it is at least somewhat controversial to suppose that there are true $\exists\forall$-claims but that it is much less controversial to suppose that there are true $\forall\exists$-claims. In much of the following discussion, I shall suppose that the claims in which we are primarily interested have the $\forall\exists$-structure.

In our initial examples, we have helped ourselves to quantification over the natural numbers. So, the most general form of the kind of example that we are presently considering is this: $(\forall n \in N)(\exists X)(f(X) > n)$.[1] Instances of this claim are not modal; they tell us only about what is true at the actual world. But we are also interested in claims about what could be true; and the introduction of the modal operators $\Diamond$ – 'it is possible that' – and $\Box$ – 'it is necessary that' – make it possible to consider a variety of new claims. At the very least, we need to distinguish between:

3. $(\forall n \in N)\Diamond(\exists X)(f(X) > n)$
4. $\Diamond(\forall n \in N)(\exists X)(f(X) > n)$
5. $\Diamond(\exists X)(\forall n \in N)(f(X) > n)$

If we think about these claims in terms of possible worlds, then 3 says that, for each n, there is a possible world in which a function on some things takes a value greater than n; 4 says that there is a possible world in which, for each n, there is a function on some things that takes a value greater than n; and 5 says that there is a possible world in which there is a function on some things that takes a value that is greater than n for all $n \in N$. Among these claims, again, 3 is weaker than 4, and 4 is weaker than 5 (and, indeed, 5 entails 4, and 4 entails 3). Each of these claims is plausibly a claim about 'the potential infinite': None of them entails anything at all about what is actually the case – at least, setting aside considerations about the existence of the natural numbers themselves. While I think that it is at least somewhat controversial to suppose that there are true claims of the $\Diamond\exists\forall$-form, I also think that it is less controversial to suppose that there are true claims of the $\Diamond\forall\exists$-form, and much less controversial to suppose that there are true claims of the $\forall\Diamond\exists$-form. Here, we can distinguish *three* different

[1] Here, the variable X is a variable of plural quantification: $(\exists X)f(X) > n$ says that there are some things such that a function defined on these things takes a value greater than n. Ordinary objectual quantification is the special case in which we consider just one thing at a time.

views amongst those who allow that there are potential infinities but deny that there are actual infinities: There are those who allow that there are true claims of the $\Diamond\exists\forall$-form; there are those who allow that there are true claims of the $\Diamond\forall\exists$-form but that there are no true claims of the $\Diamond\exists\forall$-form; and there are those who allow only that there are true claims of the $\forall\Diamond\exists$-form.

Perhaps it will help to illustrate the distinctions here by means of an example. Consider the case of distances between objects. Among those who reject the claim that, for any *n*, there are objects that are more than *n* metres apart, there are those who allow that there are possible worlds in which there are objects that are more than *n* metres apart for all *n*; there are those who allow that there are possible worlds in which, for any *n*, there are objects that are more than *n* metres apart; and there are those who allow only that, for any *n*, there is a possible world in which there are objects that are more than *n* metres apart. All of these positions can be described as views according to which distance is merely potentially infinite – but they give different senses to the idea that distances could increase, or could be increased, without limit.

Apart from the extreme views that we have considered so far, there are more nuanced views that discriminate among different domains of objects and among different classes of propositions. One can imagine someone who holds that it is possible that there is a domain of objects in which, for each *n*, there are more than *n* objects – $\Diamond (\exists X) (\forall n \in N) (f(X) > n)$ – but who also insists that, while it is necessary that, for any pair of objects, there is an *n* such that those objects are no more than *n* metres apart, there is a possible world in which, for any *n*, there are objects that are more than *n* metres apart – $\Diamond (\forall n \in N) (\exists X) (f(X) > n)$. On this view, while there are potential infinities of objects in the $\Diamond\exists\forall$-sense, distances between objects are potentially infinite only in the $\Diamond\forall\exists$-sense. In turn, this view might be extended with the additional claim that, while, for any *n*, there is a possible world in which there are objects that travel at more than *n* metres per second in some inertial frame of reference, there is no world in which, for any *n*, there are objects that travel at more than *n* metres per second in some inertial frame of reference. That is, it might be said that the velocities of objects – in inertial frames of reference – are potentially infinite only in the $\forall\Diamond\exists$-sense.

As we have already noted, there are many different domains – and many different classes of predicates – for which questions about the infinite arise. One need not take the same kind of view about objects in general, the part/whole relation, the extent of space, the divisibility of space, the extent of time, the divisibility of time, temperature, utility streams, inverse probabilities, and so forth – or, at any rate, if one holds that one is rationally required to take the same kind of view in all of these cases, then it seems that one needs to give extensive justification for that contention.

There are some cases that require further discussion at this point. In particular, it should be noted that we can make further distinctions if we allow ourselves to take account of temporal discriminations and make some controversial assumptions about the overall structure of the world. To keep things simple, let's restrict our attention to worlds in which a global time function can be defined, so that we have an unambiguous meaning for the expressions 'the state of the world at time *t*' and 'the world as it is at time *t*'. Moreover, let's suppose that the actual world is one of these worlds.

Start with the current, actual global state of the world, G – the world as it is now. Suppose that there are many possible worlds that share the history of our world to the present but whose histories diverge thereafter; and suppose that there are worlds that share the current state of the world – or, at any rate, have a state of the world that is qualitatively indistinguishable from G – but in which the history of the world prior to G is different. (Of course, both of these claims are controversial. If we suppose that the actual world is deterministic, then there will be no worlds of the first kind that have the same laws as the actual world; and if we further suppose that the laws in the actual world are all time-symmetric, then there will be no worlds of the second kind that have the same laws as the actual world.) We shall call worlds that share the history of our world to G G-worlds, worlds that share the current state of our world but not its history G*-worlds, and worlds that are either G-worlds or G*-worlds G#-worlds.

Here are some claims that one might make about the *past* in G-worlds and G*-worlds:

$(1)_p$ $(\exists n)$: There are no more than *n* days prior to G.
$(2)_p$ $(\forall n)$: There are more than *n* days prior to G.

$(3)_p$ $(\exists n)$ ($\forall$G-worlds): There are no more than n days prior to G.
$(4)_p$ ($\forall$G-worlds) $(\forall n)$: There are more than n days prior to G.
$(5)_p$ ($\forall$G*-worlds) $(\exists n)$: There are no more than n days prior to G.
$(6)_p$ ($\exists$G*-worlds) $(\forall n)$: There are more than n days prior to G.
$(7)_p$ $(\forall n)$ ($\exists$G*-worlds): There are more than n days prior to G.

And here are some claims that one might make about the future in G#-worlds:

$(1)_f$ $(\exists n)$: There are no more than n days subsequent to G.
$(2)_f$ $(\forall n)$: There are more than n days subsequent to G.
$(3)_f$ ($\forall$G#-worlds) $(\exists n)$: There are no more than n days subsequent to G.
$(4)_f$ ($\exists$G#-worlds) $(\forall n)$: There are more than n days subsequent to G.
$(5)_f$ $(\forall n)$ ($\exists$G#-worlds): There are more than n days subsequent to G.

If one claims that the past must be finite but that the future is potentially infinite, then I take it that one is committed to $(3)_p$ and $(5)_p$, and either to $(5)_f$ or to both $(4)_f$ and $(5)_f$. Of course, one might prefer to couch these claims in terms of sentential operators for tense and modality, rather than in terms of quantification over worlds and times – but the translation is straightforward and left as an exercise for those who care. Moreover, while there is an ambiguity in the claim that the future is merely potentially infinite, it remains to be seen whether the ambiguity matters in the context of real philosophical debates.

(b) Completed versus Potential

There are occasions on which potential infinities are contrasted with *completed* infinities. I shall take it that completed infinities are a subcase of actual infinities in which the members of the actually infinite collection have a special kind of linear ordering. I shall call the kind of ordering in question a C-ordering. Candidates to be C-orderings include certain kinds of generative and ancestral relations: x is the cause of y, x is the father of y, x is the day before y, and so forth. We shall come back at the end of our discussion to the question of whether we can give a more complete specification of C-orderings.

To keep things simple, let's just focus on cases in which a collection has a complete linear order, so that it is isomorphic – under the ordering – to a (perhaps improper) segment of the integers.

If we consider a collection of this kind that has a first element (under the relevant ordering), then, if the collection is a completed infinity, there is no subsequent element of the collection *at which* the collection can be said to be completed or *by which* the collection can be said to be completed. If, for example, we are considering a possible world in which there is a first day, then there is no day in that world at which the collection of days form a completed infinity. Nonetheless, it may be that, from a standpoint external to the possible world, we can say of its days that they form a completed infinity, for it contains infinitely many days that are ordered by the "is the next day after" relation.

If we consider an arbitrary element in a collection of the kind under consideration, then there are two directions in which we might look to seek a subcollection that constitutes a completed infinity: one that follows the sense of the relevant ordering, and hence that has the element in question as its first element; and one that opposes the sense of the relevant ordering, and hence that has the element in question as its last element. Suppose, for example, we are considering a possible world in which there is an infinite series of generations. Then, on the one hand, we can consider whether a particular man X_1 is the first member of a C-series[2] whose members are related by the "x begets y" relation: X_1 begets X_2; X_2 begets X_3; . . . , and, hence, we can also consider whether that man is the last member of a C-series whose members are related by the "x is begotten by y" relation: . . . ; X_3 is begotten by X_2; X_2 is begotten by X_1. And, on the other hand, we can consider whether that man is the last member of a C-series whose members are related by the "x begets y" relation: . . . X_{-1} begets X_0; X_0 begets X_1; and, hence, we can also consider whether that man is the first member of a C-series whose members are related by the "x is begotten by y" relation: X_1 is begotten by X_0; X_0 is begotten by X_{-1}; . . . .

It might be claimed that it is a constraint on the notion of C-orderings that it cannot be that both a relation and its converse are C-orderings. Plainly enough, if we suppose that there are cases in which the converse of a C-ordering is not a C-ordering, then there are cases

[2] A C-series is a series whose members are ordered by a C-ordering.

in which an infinite collection can be completed only in one direction. If, for example, we suppose that the "*x* is the day after *y*" relation is a C-ordering, whereas the "*x* is the day before *y*" relation is not a C-ordering, then we shall suppose that there cannot be a completed infinity of days in which there is a last member under the "*x* is the day after *y*" relation. If we suppose further that there are no standpoints suitably external to the "*x* is the day after *y*" relation, then we can say that there cannot be a completed infinity of days under this C-ordering.

Of course, in actual cases, the main points of contention will be: (1) whether there are standpoints suitably external to an ordering that is a candidate to be a C-ordering; and (2) whether the candidate to be a C-ordering is, indeed, a C-ordering. I take it that, if we ask whether the "*x* is the day after *y*" relation is a C-ordering, the only way that we have of answering this question is to ask whether the number of past days could be infinite: This relation is a C-ordering iff the number of past days cannot be infinite. No further content has been given to the notion of a C-ordering than this. Consequently, while I think that we can take it to be an analytic truth that no C-ordering generates a completed infinity – "no completed infinity can be formed by successive addition" – it would be plainly misguided to suppose that the following argument is compelling.

1. No infinite collection can be complete under a C-ordering.
2. If the past were infinite, then the past would be complete under the C-ordering "*x* is the day after *y*."
3. Therefore, the past cannot be infinite.

If the past can be infinite, then it is not true that the relation "*x* is the day after *y*" is a C-ordering: In order to have warrant to accept the second premise of this argument, one must already have warrant to accept its conclusion.

(c) Addition versus Accretion

At the beginning of our discussion of the distinction between actual infinities and merely potential infinities, we helped ourselves to the assumption that we could quantify over the natural numbers. Given the cases that we wish to consider, that assumption is insufficient; we also need to consider cases that arise under the assumption that we can quantify over other collections of numbers such as the rational numbers and, in particular, the real numbers.

If we have a collection that is ordered by the natural numbers, then the collection forms a series. Under the ordering, there is a first member of the series, second member of the series, third member of the series, and so on. In general, each member of the series but the first member – if there is one – is preceded by another member of the series; and each member of the series but the last member – if there is one – is succeeded by another member of the series. Thus, in the case of collections of this kind, it *can* make sense to say that the members of the series are related each to the next by a relation of "successive addition". For example, one might say that the series of days is constituted by a relation of "successive addition": Each day is "added" to the day that came immediately before it.

However, matters are different if we have a collection that is ordered by the rational numbers or the real numbers. If we have a collection that is ordered by the rational numbers, then, under that ordering, that collection does not form a series. Since the ordering in question is *dense*, between any two distinct elements of the collection there is a third element distinct from each, under the ordering. So, in the case of a collection of this kind, it makes no sense to say that the members of the series are related each to the next by a relation of "successive addition": Given any member of the collection, there is no next member for it to be related to in this way. Of course – as we learned from Cantor – it may be that there is some other relation under which the elements of our collection are ordered by the natural numbers, and so it may be that the elements of our collection stand in a relation of "successive addition" under that different ordering. But, equally, it may be that there is no plausible way in which the elements of our collection may be supposed to stand in a relation of "successive addition".

If we have a collection that is ordered by the real numbers, then matters are different again. In this case – again as we learned from Cantor – there is no way of ordering the collection so as to make them form a series. If we have a collection that is ordered by the real numbers, then there is no way of reordering the collection under which it makes sense to say that the elements of the collection stand in a relation of "successive addition". So, for example, if the collection of instants of time is ordered by the real numbers, then it makes no sense to say that instants of time are related by "successive addition", even if it is true that seconds, days, hours, and years are so related. Moreover, If time is composed of instants, then it doesn't make any sense to say that time itself is ordered by a relation of "successive addition", despite the fact that there are temporal entities – weeks, months, decades – that are so ordered.

Since there is a terminological hole that has arisen, I propose that we use the term "progressive accretion" to describe the case in which a collection has a dense ordering: If time is composed of instants, and if the ordering of those instants is dense, then the instants of time stand in a relation of "progressive accretion". Given this terminological decision, it follows that, if one wants to deny that instants of time stand in a relation of "progressive accretion" – that is, if one wants to insist that the mereological atoms of time stand in a relation of "successive addition" – then one is obliged to maintain that the mereological atoms of time are discrete: There are only finitely many mereological atoms of time in any day, year, century, millennium, and so on.

(d) Abstract versus Concrete

The last distinction to which I wish to draw attention is one that we mentioned at the beginning of the first chapter of this book. When we worry about whether there can be infinite collections of entities, there are certain kinds of entities for which this question seems far more pressing than it does for other kinds of entities. If, for example, we suppose that there are natural numbers, then it seems that one might suppose that it is relatively unproblematic to suppose that there are infinitely many natural numbers, while nonetheless supposing that there is something deeply troubling about the thought that there is a one-one correspondence between the natural numbers and objects that occupy more than 1 cm^3 of space, or days that elapse in the course of history, or shortest distances in metres to points to which one might travel by spaceship. Of course, one might think that it is problematic to suppose that there are infinitely many numbers even if one supposes that there are numbers – more about this in the next section – but the point to be registered here is that it is not obviously unreasonable to suppose that one might wish to distinguish between the numbers and such things as physical objects, days elapsed, and shortest traversable integral distances in the way indicated.

If we suppose that numbers exist, then we should not suppose that an infinity of numbers would be a nonactual infinity – that is, we cannot suppose that we can use the distinction between actual and merely potential infinities in order to divide the cases currently under consideration.

Perhaps we might think that, if numbers exist, then an infinity of numbers would be a not merely actual infinity; that is, we might suppose that what is crucial here is the existence of contingent – as opposed to necessary – infinite collections. However, it is not obvious that all of the entities that belong on the "numbers" side of our divide are necessary existents. Consider, for example, propositions. If one supposes that there are singular propositions and that a singular proposition exists at a world only if the constituents of that proposition exist at that world, then one will suppose that there are contingently existent propositions. Nonetheless, it seems that the existence of infinitely many propositions – and, indeed, the existence of infinitely many singular propositions – would be no more worrying than is the existence of infinitely many numbers. (Another example that might be considered here is sets. If we suppose that there are impure sets,[3] then, given the resources of standard set theory, there are plenty of infinite collections of contingently existing sets. For instance, consider the infinite series of sets that is generated by starting with a contingently existing object o, and forming singletons: {o}, {{o}}, {{{o}}}, etc.)

A more plausible suggestion is that the distinction we seek discriminates between infinite collections of abstract entities and infinite collections of nonabstract – concrete – entities. If there are abstract entities of a certain kind – sets, functions, propositions, properties, possible worlds, and so forth – then it seems that the existence of an infinite collection of entities of that kind is no more worrying than the existence of an infinite collection of numbers. Of course, this proposal immediately raises various questions: In particular, one would like to know more about how to draw the distinction between abstract entities

[3] Impure sets are sets of which it is not true that they, and their members, and the members of their members, and so forth, are all free of ur-elements or individuals.

and nonabstract entities. I offer no more than a tentative sufficient condition: If an object is neither an embedder of nor embedded in a network of causal relations, then that object is abstract. (I suppose that the physical universe is not an abstract object, even though – plausibly – it is not embedded in a network of causal relations. Hence, it would count as abstract unless we made the provision that something that embeds a network of causal relations need not be abstract.) While this formulation is obviously too crude and in need of refinement, it seems to divide most cases in a way that accords with intuition: If they exist, then numbers, sets, propositions, properties, and functions are all plausibly abstract according to this formulation.

If possible worlds are given a Lewisian realist construal, then they are not abstract; else, I think, possible worlds are abstract. That, too, seems right: Opinion varies about whether possible worlds are abstract objects. However, an infinity of Lewisian possible worlds may still seem to be less problematic than an infinity of physical objects, days elapsed, or shortest traversable integral distances. In that case, one might suppose that the requisite distinction is not really between the abstract and the concrete, but rather between that which embeds or is embedded in the causal network to which we belong and that which neither embeds nor is embedded in the causal network to which we belong.

As I have already mentioned, it is contentious whether we should suppose that there are numbers, sets, propositions, properties, and so forth. However, we don't really need to explore this issue here. On the one hand, if there are numbers, sets, propositions, properties, and so forth, then it is fair to ask whether there can be infinite collections of these things; on the other hand, if there are no numbers, sets, properties, propositions, or whatever, we can still ask questions about the infinitary nature of talk that appears to refer to things of these kinds. If there are natural numbers, then it is fair question of whether there are infinitely many natural numbers; if there are no natural numbers, it is still a fair question of whether we can understand theories that appear to assert that there are infinitely many natural numbers.

8.2 PHILOSOPHIES OF PURE MATHEMATICS

Given the fundamental role that mathematical concepts play in our understanding of the infinite, it is reasonable to think that the most telling criticisms of theories that claim that there are actually infinite and/or potentially infinite domains of objects would be criticisms of the use of these concepts in mathematics. If we suppose that we can arrive at a coherent mathematical conception of infinite collections, then we ought to be able to construct a philosophy of mathematics that explains how we are able to do this. In the next few sections of this chapter, I review various considerations that are relevant to the question of whether we can construct a philosophy of mathematics that explains how we are able to arrive at a coherent mathematical conception of infinite collections. Since the best discussion that I know of these matters is contained in Lavine (1994), I shall draw fairly extensively on Lavine's work.

(a) General Desiderata

The first question to be addressed is what we want from a philosophy of mathematics in this area. I suppose that the answer is something like this. If we suppose that there is a certain domain of objects – or, if, more generally, we suppose that a certain kind of theory is true – then it seems reasonable to insist that we ought to be able to give some rough account of how it can be that it is *reasonable* for us to *believe* that there are those objects and that the theory in question is true. Some people might think that, if we suppose that there is a certain domain of objects – or if, more generally, we suppose that a certain kind of theory is true – then it is also reasonable to insist that we ought to be able to give some rough account of how it could be that we could *know* that there are those objects and that the theory in question is true. In order to prescind from an investigation into the connections between knowledge and certainty – and, more generally, in order to prescind from an investigation of the vexed topic of the analysis of knowledge – I shall suppose that it is enough to have a good enough account of how one can come by reasonable belief in the area in question; I don't think that anything of importance to the current project will turn on this assumption.

If we suppose that we can come by reasonable belief about a certain domain of objects – or if, more generally, we suppose that we can come by reasonable belief that a particular theory is true – then it is reasonable to insist that we ought to be able to give some rough account of how that reasonable belief is related to *experiences* that play a role in warranting our belief that there are those objects and that the theory in question is true. Again, there may be people who want to insist on a stronger constraint at this point. Perhaps, for example, one might think that one can have a reasonable belief that there is a mathematical object that possesses a certain kind of property only if one has an experience associated with the possession of an appropriate property by an appropriate object that makes it reasonable for you to believe that the mathematical object has the property in question. Since this stronger constraint seems defensible, we shall not suppose from the outset that it must be set aside; however, we shall see soon enough that there are many *prima facie* plausible philosophies of mathematics that do not meet this stronger constraint.

(b) A Rough Taxonomy

Against the background of our theoretical desiderata, we can distinguish a number of broadly different approaches to the philosophy of mathematics. Since a philosophy of mathematics is required to coordinate a theory about experience, a theory about what it is reasonable to believe, and a theory about what there is (and what is true of what there is), there are distinctions that can be applied in each of these areas. In this taxonomy, when I talk about putative numbers, I'm talking about numbers that are postulated in classical mathematics: entities that would exist if all of classical mathematics were true and the quantifiers used in classical mathematics were ontologically committing.

1. *Strict Finitism*: A strict finitist in the realm of experience is someone who is sceptical that we can make sense of the idea of experiencing particular, sufficiently large numbers. A strict finitist in the realm of reasonable belief is someone who doubts that we can reasonably believe that certain putative large numbers really are numbers. A strict finitist in the realm of ontology is someone who believes that certain putative large numbers are not numbers. While the three types of strict finitism are independent, we can certainly imagine a theorist who endorses all three; perhaps we can also imagine theorists who endorse, say, strict finitism in the realm of experience, but who do not endorse strict finitism in the other realms. There are instances of

theorists who have been strict finitists – or, at any rate, who have seriously countenanced a strict finitism – of one or another of these kinds. For example, van Dantzig (1955) asks whether $10^{10^{10}}$ is a finite number; and Isles (1992) asks whether there is any evidence that 2^{65536} is a natural number. (Lavine uses $10^{10^{10^{10}}}$ as his example of a putative number that might be sufficiently large to serve the purposes of a strict finitist.)

2. *Liberal Finitism*: A liberal finitist in the realm of experience is someone who thinks that we cannot make sense of the idea of experiencing sufficiently large numbers but who refrains from nominating any particular sufficiently large numbers of this kind. A liberal finitist in the realm of reasonable belief is someone who thinks that there are putative sufficiently large numbers that cannot reasonably be believed to be numbers but who refrains from nominating any particular putative sufficiently large numbers as a case in point. A liberal finitist in the realm of ontology is someone who thinks that there are putative sufficiently large numbers that are not numbers but who refrains from nominating any particular putative sufficiently large numbers as a case in point. As in the previous case, while the three types of liberal finitism are independent, we can certainly imagine a theorist who endorses all three; moreover, we may also be able to imagine a theorist who endorses, say, liberal finitism in the realm of experience, while rejecting liberal finitism in the other realms.

3. *Potential Infinitism*: A potential infinitist in the realm of experience is someone who thinks that, while we can make sense of the idea of experiencing *any* number, no matter how large, we cannot make sense of the idea of experiencing *all* of the numbers: To any point in time, there are only finitely many experiences of numbers, but there is no upper bound to the experiences of numbers that there might be in the future. A potential infinitist in the realm of reasonable belief is someone who thinks that, while we can reasonably believe of any putative number, no matter how large, that it is a number, we cannot reasonably believe of all putative numbers, no matter how large, that they are numbers: To any point in time, there are only finitely many putative numbers that can reasonably be believed to be numbers, but there is no upper bound to the putative numbers that might reasonably be believed to be numbers in the future. A potential infinitist in the realm of ontology is someone who thinks that, while *any*

putative number is a number, it is not the case that *all* putative numbers are numbers: To any point in time, there are only finitely many putative numbers that are numbers, but there is no upper bound to the putative numbers that are numbers in the future. Once again, while the three types of potential infinitism are independent, we can certainly imagine theorists who endorse all three; and we can also imagine theorists who endorse only one or two of these types of potential infinitism, while rejecting the third. Two examples that involve potential infinitism of one or more of these kinds are *intuitionism* and *constructivism*. Both of these views require the adoption of nonclassical logic and yield a version of mathematics that is very different from classical mathematics. While intuitionistic mathematics and classical mathematics are incomparable – neither is included in the other – there are versions of constructive mathematics that are properly contained in classical mathematics. Moreover, while an intuitionist is a potential infinitist in the realm of ontology, a constructivist can take almost any position in the realm of ontology, including that of an actual infinitist: Constructivism is a view about experience and reasonable belief, not a view about ontology.

4. *Actual Infinitism*: An actual infinitist in the realm of experience is someone who thinks that we can make sense of the idea of experiencing all of the numbers. An actual infinitist in the realm of reasonable belief is someone who thinks that we can reasonably believe of all putative numbers that they are numbers. An actual infinitist in the realm of ontology is someone who thinks that all putative numbers are numbers. Those who accept classical mathematics – that is, those who hold that all of the (uncontroversial) theorems of classical mathematics are true – are plausibly taken to be actual infinitists in at least the latter two of these three senses.

As Lavine emphasises – and as we have, in effect, already noted – it should not be supposed that strict finitism, liberal finitism, potential infinitism, and actual infinitism in the realm of ontology are a linearly ordered series of views. While strict finitism, liberal finitism and actual infinitism are all developed with classical logic, potential infinitism is developed within a nonclassical logic. In consequence, it is not true that each of these views delivers a successively larger part of classical mathematics: Potential infinitism merely overlaps classical mathematics; it is not properly contained within it.

8.3 KNOWING THE INFINITE

If we suppose that we can tell a story according to which it is reasonable to believe all of classical mathematics, then, plausibly, we need to be able to tell a story about how we can make sense of the idea of experiencing all of the numbers. More generally, we need to be able to tell a story about how it is that our mathematical experience is adequate for the classical mathematical theory that we have developed. There have been various theories that have been developed to try to explain how it is that we can have reasonable beliefs about infinite mathematical objects on the basis of our – undeniably – finite experiences. In this section, we shall briefly survey some of the theories of this kind.

1. *Via Negativa*: One might take the view that all reasonable beliefs about the properties of the infinite are based on reasonable beliefs about the general properties of the finite and infinite and the further, evidently reasonable, claim that the infinite is that which is not finite. As Lavine (1994: 181) encapsulates it: You understand 'finite'. You understand 'not'. So you understand 'Not finite'. So you understand 'Infinite'. What's the problem? Well, the difficulty is that there are axioms in classical set theory that cannot be obtained in this way. In particular, neither the Axiom of Choice nor the Axiom of Replacement can be justified by the *via negativa*. Since we want a theory that will justify all of classical mathematics, we cannot rest content with this one.

2. *Formalism*: There are various different formalist approaches to the philosophy of mathematics. The core idea is that what we might mistakenly take to be reasonable belief about the properties of the infinite is actually reasonable belief about (finite) descriptions of the infinite. We shall briefly mention a few of the varieties of formalism, and then indicate some of the general weaknesses of this kind of approach to philosophy of mathematics.

According to *game formalism*, mathematics is just a series of manipulations of objects – numerals, sentences of a formal language, and so on – according to arbitrary stipulated rules. According to *meta-game formalism*, mathematics is the theory of formal games (in the game formalism sense). According to *deductivism*, mathematics is the deduction of consequences from axioms.

One obvious difficulty with all of these formalist views is that they are plainly unable to explain the ways in which mathematicians select axioms (and, more generally, subject matters). In set theory, for example, there are various questionable assumptions – Choice, Replacement, Power Set – that have been selected by mathematicians and that have been argued for by mathematicians. But if any of the formalist theories is correct, then it seems quite mysterious how we could make sense of this selection and justification of axioms.

Another obvious difficulty with all of these formalist views is that they lack the resources to explain the application of mathematics to nonmathematical domains. There are many mathematical results that have numerous different practical applications. Lavine's example is group theory: The same theorems from group theory find application to the solution of polynomial equations, the characterisation of the interactions of elementary physical particles, the devising and cracking of codes, the manipulation of Rubik's cube and related games, and so forth. But, of course, the same point can be made about almost any branch of pure mathematics. Yet if any of the formalist theories is correct, it seems quite mysterious how mathematical theories could have application to anything outside mathematics: Games are not the right category of thing to have applications.

A third difficulty that faces formalist views is that they lack the resources to explain why we suppose that some mathematical theories are more fundamental than others, and why we are confident that our most fundamental theories – for example, set theory – are consistent. Any satisfactory philosophy of mathematics needs to be able to account for the fact that we treat mathematics as a single corpus: The results from one mathematical theory can be freely applied in other mathematical domains. Furthermore, any satisfactory philosophy of mathematics needs to be able to make sense of the suggestion that set theory is a foundational mathematical theory and to explain how it is that mathematicians have come to believe that set theory and arithmetic are consistent theories. At the very least, it is highly doubtful that there is any formalist theory that can do all of these things.

While the discussion to this point is hardly conclusive, I am inclined to think that there is not much prospect that a formalist philosophy of mathematics can be developed that will meet these difficulties (and others that have not been mentioned here). If we are interested in explaining and justifying the practice of classical mathematicians, then we shall need to look elsewhere.

3. *Hilbert's Finitism*: While the details of Hilbert's finitism are subject to dispute, the broad outline of Hilbert's program is relatively clear. There are two parts to the program. In the first part, we construct a finitary mathematics that is incontestable in every respect; in the second, we build the rest of classical mathematics on top of the incontestable finitary base, using methods that are themselves incontestable. The details of the construction of finitary mathematics need not concern us here; however, we need to say a little more about the way in which Hilbert proposed to found all of the classical mathematics on a finitary mathematical base. The basic idea is simple: A piece of classical (infinitary) mathematics is justified in Hilbert's eyes if it has an axiomatization that can be proven to be consistent using a finitary proof, that is, a proof that is sanctioned by finitary mathematics and finitary logic.

It is almost universally accepted that Hilbert's program cannot be carried through. The stumbling block is Gödel's second incompleteness result: No theory that meets certain mild conditions can prove its own consistency. If Hilbert's program were successfully carried out, then set theory – a theory that meets the mild conditions of Gödel's second incompleteness result – would have proven its own consistency. (As Detlefsen (1986) argues, there is enough wiggle room to ensure that there is not here a *proof* of the impossibility of the carrying out of Hilbert's program. However, the kinds of considerations to which Detlefsen appeals do not provide good reasons for supposing that Hilbert's program is *feasible* after all.)

It should not be supposed that this is the only major problem that faces Hilbert's proposal. Even if it were possible to show, using finitary means, that all of classical mathematics is consistent relative to finitary mathematics, it is not clear that that provides enough justification for classical mathematics. As we noted in connection with formalism, classical mathematics requires the selection and justification of certain axioms; but there is nothing in the carrying out of Hilbert's program that can explain or justify the selection of axioms. If we want to meet the general desiderata set out above for a philosophy of mathematics, then it seems that Hilbert's program will not give us what we want.

In sum, our examination of attempts to explain how we can have reasonable beliefs about infinite mathematical objects on the basis of our finite experiences has so far ended in disappointment: The kinds of philosophies of mathematics that were prominent in the early part of the twentieth century are not adequate to the task. While we shall return to this quest, we first make a detour to consider approaches to the problem of the justification of acceptance of infinitary mathematics that have a very different rationale.

8.4 PUTTING CLASSICAL MATHEMATICS FIRST

If we think of the theories mentioned in the previous section as attempts to figure out what we can reasonably believe in mathematics on the basis of uncontroversial doxastic assumptions – for example, the assumption that we can perform finite series of operations with finite strings of symbols – then we can think of the theories to be mentioned in the current section as attempts to justify the claim that we can reasonably believe all of classical mathematics on the basis of rather more tendentious doxastic assumptions. We shall consider three ways in which one might try to argue that our doxastic capacities unproblematically equip us for reasonable belief in all of the fundamental axioms and rules of classical mathematics.

1. *Gödelian Intuition*: It is a remarkable fact that the vast majority of working mathematicians, in all cultures, and from diverse backgrounds, find themselves in agreement about the naturalness – and, indeed, the self-evident correctness – of accepting certain mathematical axioms. As Gödel put it, "the axioms force themselves upon us as being true". Now, of course, there are various ways in which one might try to deflate the apparent importance of this observation – for example, by appealing to sociological theories about the way in which mathematical intuition is collusive, or the product of accidental social and historical forces, and so forth. Nonetheless, there is at least some reason to suppose that the way in which the axioms of classical mathematics "force themselves upon us" is evidence that we do have a kind of intuitive grasp of the objects of classical mathematics.

The most obvious difficulty with approaches of this kind is that it is remarkably difficult to give any intelligible account of the link or connection between the domain of objects in which the alleged reasonable belief is held, and the cognitive faculties and abilities that we can confidently suppose human mathematicians to possess. Certainly, Gödel himself gave no more than the scantest hints about how it is that he supposed classical mathematicians secure reliable access to the objects of classical mathematics.

It might also be objected that there has always been an at least sizable minority of mathematicians who have rejected the claim that the axioms and procedures of classical mathematics are self-evidently correct. There have been many mathematicians who have been happy to allow that the axioms and methods of classical mathematics have proven to be fruitful, while nonetheless insisting that there is no good reason to suppose that the axioms are true and the methods conducive to the attainment of truth. Moreover, if it turns out – as it may – that most mathematicians can be trained to judge in advance whether results are classically acceptable or whether they are acceptable only on finitist, intuitionist, or constructivist principles, then it might be said that what we really have firm intuitions about is what follows from what according to selected rules and principles.

Finally, it must be noted that there is less agreement at the 'frontiers' of mathematics. In particular, there are many places where the infinite seems to be a locus of disagreement – for example, in disputes about the axiom of choice.

2. *Indispensability*: We might suppose that there is no way in which our mathematical beliefs can be neatly partitioned from our beliefs in other areas, and, in particular, from our beliefs in the natural sciences. Given that so many of our beliefs – in, say, all of the various areas of physics and chemistry – require classical mathematics both for their very formulation and for their justification, we can then insist that acceptance of classical mathematics is justified in the very same way that acceptance of the natural sciences is justified in general – however that might be. There is no special mathematical intuition that must be invented in order to justify acceptance of the axioms and procedures of classical mathematics; rather, acceptance of the axioms and procedures of classical mathematics is justified because we are justified in accepting the results and claims of natural science, and those results and claims require classical mathematics for their formulation and justification.

There are at least two kinds of difficulties with this kind of suggestion. First – and perhaps most important – it seems that there is no way that the Quine-Putnam indispensability arguments can licence acceptance of the parts of set theory in which we are most interested. Quine himself admitted that his indispensability argument provided no reason for accepting the Axiom of Replacement. It is not very controversial that there are various axioms of set theory – Choice, Replacement, Power Set – whose ready acceptance by mathematicians is not well explained by the role that these principles play in mathematics that is required for – or that is a natural extension of mathematics that is required for – natural science.

Second, one might suspect that the amount of mathematics that is ineliminably required for physics and chemistry is actually much less than many have supposed: A case can be made that almost all of the mathematics that is required for physics and chemistry can be found in Peano arithmetic (and, indeed, in a tiny fragment thereof). It is not just that physics and chemistry have no use for the inaccessible cardinals – and neither is it just that hypotheses about inaccessible cardinals cannot be justified as the natural extensions of principles that are foundational for familiar physics and chemistry; rather, the worry here is that there is really only a small fragment of classical mathematics that is genuinely required for the purposes of the natural sciences.[4]

3. *Structuralism and Second-Order Theories*: We might suppose that the difficulties that we encounter when we ask about the justification of the acceptance of classical mathematics stems from the misguided thought that we should interpret classical mathematical theories as first-order theories, that is, as theories that can be formulated in a first-order language in which one quantifies only over objects but not over predicates. If this assumption is set aside, then there are various alternative views that arise for consideration. We might suppose, for example, that mathematics is actually concerned with the investigation of *structures* – domains of properties and relations – rather than with the investigation of domains of objects. Relatedly, we might suppose that, contrary to what was long received opinion, classical mathematical practice is actually founded in classical second-order logic – or, at least, some restricted version of classical second-order logic – and not in classical first-order logic.

One difficulty with any approach of this kind is that the doxastic credentials of second-order logic are hardly any more secure than

[4] For a forceful statement of a worry of this kind, see Feferman (1989).

the doxastic credentials of classical mathematics. While there may be something appealing in the suggestion that the foundations of mathematics are just more mathematics – second-order logic is not, after all, free of controversial mathematical commitments – it is hard to see how any approach of this kind could lend support to the conclusion that our doxastic capacities unproblematically equip us for reasonable belief in all of the fundamental axioms and rules of classical mathematics. It may well be true that we do better to suppose that some kind of second-order theory – for example, the schematic second-order set theory that is described in Lavine (1994: 226ff.) – provides foundations for classical mathematics; but it is not at all clear what kind of contribution this supposition can make to the task of understanding how it can be reasonable to accept the axioms and procedures of classical mathematics.

In sum, our examination of ways in which one might try to argue that our doxastic capacities unproblematically equip us for reasonable belief in all of the fundamental axioms and rules of classical mathematics appears to end in disappointment. While it seems to me that there is something right in each of the approaches that I have mentioned, it also seems to me that none of them provides a compelling argument for the conclusion that our doxastic capacities unproblematically equip us for reasonable belief in all of the fundamental axioms and rules of classical mathematics. Of course, a more extensive discussion might overturn this tentative conclusion – there is, after all, much more to be said about each of the kinds of views that has been mentioned here; nonetheless, I think that there is good enough reason to turn our attention elsewhere.

8.5 EXTRAPOLATION FROM FINITE MATHEMATICS

The question that we have been considering – the question of how it is that our doxastic capacities equip us for reasonable belief in the axioms and rules of classical mathematics – is one of the main topics of investigation in Lavine (1994). After canvassing the various options that we have mentioned in the previous two sections of this chapter, Lavine presents an alternative proposal: He claims that the concept of the infinite in classical mathematics arises as an extrapolation from experience of the indefinitely large.

As Lavine notes, the idea of an indefinitely large collection – a collection that is too large to count using specified resources in specified ways, a collection of a *zillion* things – is not problematic in the same way as the idea of an infinitely large collection. We certainly understand the idea of a collection that is indefinitely large, relative to certain kinds of interests and purposes: It is easy to specify contexts in which we are happy to allow that we simply cannot count the number of stars in the sky, the number of refugees who would like political asylum in our country, the number of books that we wish that we had time to read, the number of grains of sand on a beach, the number of hours that we have wasted watching reality television, or the like. Of course, when we say that we "cannot" count these things, our claim relies on an implicit qualification: Setting aside whatever worries about vagueness might arise, we could commit resources to the task of, say, accurately recording hours spent watching television sufficient to allow us to say with considerable confidence how many hours have been spent watching reality television. Moreover, in each of these cases, we can easily estimate upper bounds that we can be quite sure the cardinalities of the collections in question do not exceed: The number of stars visible to any one of us on a given cloudless night at a particular time of that night is not particularly large – not more than a few thousand – even though the practical difficulties that confront a naked-eye count are considerable.

Given that we do understand the idea of a collection whose cardinality cannot be determined using the techniques and methods that are readily available to us – the idea of a collection that is too large for us to count given our current abilities, interests, and so forth – it seems that we can also understand the idea of a collection that is simply too large to count, *tout court* – the idea of a collection that is too large for anyone to count, regardless of his or her abilities, interests, and so forth. But according to Lavine, that just is the idea of an infinite collection: We arrive at the idea of the infinite by extrapolation from the idea of the indefinitely large, abstracting away from contextual dependence on abilities, interests, and the like.

Of course, even if this is plausible as an account of the content of the idea of the infinite, there are various questions that must be addressed before we have even the beginnings of a satisfactory account of how it can be reasonable to accept the axioms and rules of classical mathematics. First, we need to be convinced that there is a process of extrapolation from a theory that it is reasonable for us to accept to, say, classical set theory. Second, we need to be convinced that something like this process of extrapolation actually played a role in the development and widespread acceptance of classical set theory. Third, we need to be convinced that the theory from which we extrapolate in order to get to classical set theory is, indeed, a codification of reasonable beliefs about indefinitely large collections.

Lavine claims that Mycielski's finite mathematics provides a codification of reasonable beliefs about indefinitely large collections that can satisfy at least the first and the third of the above demands. We have already seen – in chapter 2 above – that finite mathematics is a natural theory for indefinitely large collections and that any theory T can be obtained from $\mathrm{Fin}(T)$ by a process of "decontextualisation". Of course, in practice, we mostly go in the other direction: We already have the axiomatization for T, and then construct the axiomatization for $\mathrm{Fin}(T)$. However, the relationship between the axiomatization for $\mathrm{Fin}(T)$ and the axiomatization for T is as described: If we remove the restrictions to indefinitely large collections on the quantifiers in $\mathrm{Fin}(T)$, we obtain the theory T.

Given this much, it seems that we have the materials to understand all of the axioms and methods of classical mathematics. There is nothing in talk about infinite collections that cannot be understood as a decontextualising generalisation from talk about indefinitely large collections. So, if we wish to insist that there is some serious conceptual difficulty involved in the understanding of classical mathematics, then we need to insist that there is some serious conceptual difficulty involved in the decontextualising generalisation of talk about indefinitely large collections.

Of course, even if we accept that the above considerations establish that we are able to understand classical mathematics, it can hardly be supposed that they establish that it is reasonable to believe that classical mathematics is all acceptable. Since every theory has an equivalent in finite mathematics, one might suppose that what Mycielskian considerations establish is that there is no reason to accept any parts of classical mathematics that are not also parts of finite mathematics. Far from vindicating the infinite in mathematics, Mycielskian considerations lead to the final overthrow of the infinite in mathematics!

As Lavine notes, it is clear that this is a possible response to the results presented at the end of chapter 2. However, other responses are possible. In particular, considerations about the absence of principles in finite theory that do not extrapolate to infinite set theory, when combined with observations about the vastly greater complexity of Fin(ZFC) when compared with ZFC, can surely be taken to provide one kind of reason for preferring classical mathematics to finite mathematics. Moreover, if we are inclined to attribute some kind of objectivity – some independence of epistemic limitation – to the theorems of mathematics, then it seems that we should prefer classical mathematical theories to their finite mathematical counterparts on the grounds that the latter embed a kind of epistemic restriction – "relative to current projects, interests, abilities, and so forth" – that is removed in the counterpart classical theories. Those with realist and/or objectivist tendencies are unlikely to feel at home in Mycielskian finite mathematics.

Perhaps even more than in other parts of this book, it must be emphasised here that the above discussion barely begins to disclose the richness and complexity of recent discussions of the infinite in pure mathematics. Liberal finitism, potential infinitism, and actual infinitism all have very distinguished contemporary defenders. Gödelian intuition, Quine-Putnam indispensability, structuralism, and second-order strategies have all been given serious and demanding defences by proponents of actual infinitism. We are very far from achieving any kind of consensus about infinity in the philosophy of mathematics. Nonetheless, the above summary may have some value as an indication of where major controversies lie.

8.6 SOME NOTES ABOUT SET THEORY

Before we move on to a discussion of philosophies of applied mathematics, it is worth taking a brief detour to consider how matters currently stand with classical set theory. There are three matters that I wish to discuss. The first concerns the way in which the notion of "collection" is understood in set theory; the second concerns some issues that are not particularly well understood; and the third concerns those axioms that introduce the actual infinite into set theory.

1. *Logical versus combinatorial conceptions of sets*: One of the major themes of Lavine (1994) is the contrast between two different conceptions of sets. On the one hand, there is the *logical* conception of set, according to which sets obey a principle of comprehension: Each set is associated with a definition or rule that characterises the members of the set. On the other hand, there is the *combinatorial* conception of set, according to which sets are arbitrary collections that need only be defined by the enumeration of their terms. On the combinatorial conception of set, some sets are associated with definitions or rules that characterise the members of the set, but these are special cases: It is left open by the combinatorial conception of set that there are collections whose members cannot be characterised by any definition or rule (in anything that we would recognise as a language).

It is well known that early logical conceptions of set – for example, in the work of Frege – gave rise to paradoxes. Moreover, it is also well known that attempts to avoid these paradoxes while holding on to principles of comprehension gave rise to baroque complexities – for example, in Russell's ramified theory of types. On the other hand, it is also well known that the combinatorial conception of set faces no similar difficulty: If the combinatorial conception of set leads to paradox, then so too does basic arithmetic. It is plausible to suppose that, from Cantor onwards, working mathematicians have almost all adopted a combinatorial conception of sets; it has largely been philosophers interested in the philosophical foundations of mathematics who have been tempted to adopt a logical conception of sets. Consequently – as Lavine emphasises – it is plausible to claim that there has never really been a "crisis" in the foundations of mathematics generated by the so-called set-theoretical paradoxes: There has never been occasion for working mathematicians to feel threatened by the existence of the paradoxes that are generated by naïve comprehension principles.

2. *Open Questions*: There are problems that arise in obtaining a satisfactory collection of axioms for set theory on either of the approaches mentioned in the previous subsection.

On the one hand, as Lavine emphasises, it is very hard to see how Choice, Replacement, and Infinity are to be justified on logical approaches to set theory. For instance, why should we suppose that, just because there is a definition or rule that characterises each of the sets $S_1, \ldots, S_k, \ldots$, there is a definition or rule that characterises any choice set that is formed by taking one of the members from each of the S_i? Of course, it is clear that Choice is not similarly problematic for the combinatorial conception of sets: Given the sets $S_1, \ldots, S_k, \ldots$, the combinatorial conception demands that there be choice sets that are formed by taking one of the members from each of the S_i.

On the other hand, it is rather hard to see how the Power Set axiom is to be integrated into the combinatorial conception of sets. While Choice, Infinity, and Replacement are obvious principles to govern combinatorial collections, it is not at all clear why we should think that, for any combinatorial collection *a*, there is another collection whose members are all of the subcollections of *a*. Indeed, many have followed von Neumann in supposing that there are classes – collections that are "too big" to be sets – that obey an axiom of *limitation of size*. Moreover, it is worth noting that Power Set is not similarly problematic for the logical conception of sets: Given that there is a definition or rule that characterises the set *a*, there is a definition or rule that characterises the power set of *a*.

In the face of these – and other – difficulties, Lavine (1994: 153) is moved to observe that our understanding of the foundations of set theory is hardly better than was d'Alembert's understanding of the foundations of analysis in the second half of the eighteenth century. Is set theory first-order or second-order? Does set theory have one intended domain or many? Are all collections sets? Can limitation of size – and limitation of comprehensiveness and the iterative conception of set – be accommodated within a coherent conception of sets? Where does Power Set fit into a combinatorial conception of sets? However, against this emphasis that we are nearly as confused about the foundations of set theory as analysts were confused about the foundations of analysis prior to Weierstrass, Lavine (1994: 162) also notes that, just as analysts prior to Weierstrass knew a lot about analysis despite their ignorance about some foundational questions, so, too, we know quite a lot about set theory and about the mathematically infinite. The fact that set theory is not a finished theory should not mislead us into supposing that we don't, in fact, know a very great deal about infinite sets.

3. *Infinite Power.* The last point to be noted in this section is short and simple. When, in chapter 2, we looked at the principles that are used in set theory in the generation of infinite sets, we found a role for Infinity – in moving from the finite to the countably infinite – and Power Set – in moving from the countably infinite through the accessible cardinals. Of course, we also find a role for Choice and Replacement in generating new sets of any given cardinality, once we have sets of those cardinalities. But, quite apart from this latter consideration, we see that we don't yet have a conception of set on which both of the fundamental principles that are used to generate infinite sets in the lower reaches of infinite set theory are unproblematic: Infinity is not an obviously natural component of the logical conception, and Power Set is not an obviously natural component of the combinatorial conception. So there may be some reason to withhold assent from the claim that we do, in fact, know a very great deal about infinite sets: It may not have been all that comfortable to have been an analyst in the latter half of the eighteenth century.

8.7 PHILOSOPHIES OF APPLIED MATHEMATICS

Corresponding to the range of available philosophies of pure mathematics, there is a similar range of available philosophies of applied mathematics, that is, of views about domains to which mathematical theories can be properly applied. On the plausible assumption that mathematics can be used to accurately describe contingent processes and/or structures – and, in particular, on the plausible assumption that mathematics can be used to accurately describe *physical* processes and/or structures – there is a range of views that one can take about the kinds of mathematical theories that can have this kind of application. In this section, we consider the range of views that are available and provide some general desiderata that any philosophy of applied mathematics ought to meet.

(a) General Desiderata

We begin, then, with the question of what we want from a philosophical theory of the application of pure mathematics to contingent physical processes and/or structures. I suppose that the answer to this question is something like this. If we suppose that there is a true theory of some domain of objects according to which those objects have properties that are accurately characterised by the application of a particular piece of pure mathematics, then it seems reasonable to insist that we ought to be able to give some rough account of how it can be that it is *reasonable* for us to *believe* that those objects – processes, structures – have the properties that are attributed to them by the mathematical theory in question. As before, there may be people who think that it is not sufficient to talk of reasonable belief here and that we should instead insist on a constraint that is formulated in terms of knowledge; but, as before, I claim that nothing of any importance for the current project turns on the decision to focus on the case of reasonable belief.

Moreover, if we suppose that we can come by reasonable belief about a certain domain of objects – or if, more generally, we suppose that we can come by reasonable belief that a particular theory is true – then it is reasonable to insist that we ought to be able to give some rough account of how that reasonable belief is related to *experiences* that play a role in warranting our belief that there are those objects and that the theory in question is true. Again, there may be people who want to insist on a stronger constraint at this point: Perhaps, for example, one might think that it is reasonable to insist that one can have a reasonable belief that there are objects that possesses a certain kind of property only if one has an experience associated with the possession of an appropriate property by an appropriate object that makes it reasonable for one to believe that the objects have the property in question. However, I shall not assume that we need to impose any stronger constraint of this kind.

(b) A Rough Taxonomy

Against the background of our theoretical desiderata, we can distinguish a number of broadly different philosophical approaches that it is possible to take towards the question of contingently instantiated infinities. Since a comprehensive theory in any domain can be expected to coordinate a theory about experience, a theory about what it is reasonable to believe, and a theory about what there is (and what is true of what there is), there are distinctions that can be applied to each of these kinds of subtheories. The taxonomy that we produce will be written in a language that assumes actual infinitism in the domain of pure mathematics: We allow ourselves to quantify unrestrictedly over all of the natural numbers. However, this fact is merely the product of expedience: We could formulate the distinctions in terms that are acceptable to any of the views under discussion (using fictionalist operators and the like).

1. *Finitism*: A finitist in the realm of experience is someone who is sceptical that we can make sense of the idea of encountering in experience domains, processes, and structures that are properly characterised by sufficiently large or by sufficiently small yet nonzero numbers. Roughly, the finitist in the realm of experience supposes that there is – and must be – a finite upper limit to the number of objects that can be presented to a subject in experience and that there is – and must be – a finite upper limit and a finite nonzero lower limit to magnitudes that can be presented to a subject in experience. Finitism in the realm of experience is not a particularly contentious doctrine: There are many people who are prepared to suppose that there is – and can be – no way in which either the potentially infinite or the actually infinite is presented to a subject in either a single experience or a finite course of experiences.

A finitist in the realm of reasonable belief is someone who doubts that we can reasonably believe that there is no finite upper limit to the number of objects in some particular domain; who doubts that we can reasonably believe that there is no finite upper limit to the magnitudes of properties and relations that are true of objects in some domain; and who doubts that we can reasonably believe that there is no finite nonzero lower limit to magnitudes of properties and relations that are true of objects in some domain. Roughly, the finitist in the realm of reasonable belief doubts that it can ever be reasonable to hold a belief of the $\forall\exists$-form or a belief of the $\forall\Diamond\exists$-form. Clearly, there is a range of attitudes that might be mentioned here: Instead of doubting that one can hold reasonable beliefs of the kind in question, one might hold that it is simply unreasonable ever to hold one of these beliefs. I shall not fuss about the range of attitudes in what follows.

A finitist in the realm of ontology is someone who believes that there is, and must be, a finite upper limit to the number of objects in any particular domain; who believes that there is, and must be, a finite upper limit to the magnitudes of properties and relations true of objects in any domain; and who believes that there is, and must be, a finite nonzero lower limit to the magnitudes of properties and relations true of objects in any domain. Roughly speaking, according to the finitist in the realm of ontology, the contingently existing world is – and must be – everywhere finite. Strictly speaking, there are several different components to the view of the finitist in the realm of ontology that ought to be distinguished. First, this finitist holds the actual world is finite in the ways specified. Second, this finitist holds that every possible world is finite in the ways specified. Third, this finitist holds that there are only finitely many possible worlds. A similar point can be made to clarify the view that I have attributed to finitists in the realm of reasonable belief: The view is that one cannot reasonably believe that there are nonfinite possible worlds, and neither can one reasonably believe that there are infinitely many possible worlds.

It is perhaps worth noting that the distinction between strict finitism and liberal finitism in the philosophy of pure mathematics is not echoed in our taxonomy of views that can be adopted in the philosophy of applied mathematics. The point of that distinction in the philosophy of pure mathematics is to discriminate between those who are prepared to use extramathematical grounds to give examples of putative numbers that are not numbers and those who are prepared to endorse only the existentially generalised claim that there are putative numbers that are not numbers. Consequently, there is no reason to expect to find this distinction echoed in a philosophy of applied mathematics, since there can be no interesting dispute over whether it is appropriate to use extramathematical grounds to make estimations of extramathematical quantities.

It is perhaps also worth noting that a finitist in the realm of ontology has a thoroughly digital conception of reality: There are minimum and maximum possible amounts of absolutely everything, and there are only finitely many distinct possible components that can be recombined in the constitution of a possible world. While finitism in the realm of experience is relatively uncontroversial, finitism in the realm of ontology is far more controversial – though perhaps defensible if one is a finitist in the realm of pure mathematics.

Actual Infinitism: An actual infinitist in the realm of experience is someone who thinks that at least one infinite domain of objects is given in experience, who thinks that at least one infinite magnitude is given in experience, or who thinks that at least one infinitesimal magnitude is given in experience. Amongst actual infinitists in the realm of experience, there will be those who suppose that there are encounters of the infinite in experience of the ∃∀-form and those who suppose that there are encounters of the infinite in experience of the ∀∃ - form but that there are no encounters of the infinite in experience of the ∃∀-form.

An actual infinitist in the realm of reasonable belief is someone who thinks that one can reasonably believe that there is an infinite domain of objects, that there is an infinite magnitude, or that there is an infinitesimal magnitude. Thus, an actual infinitist in the realm of reasonable belief will allow either that one can reasonably hold beliefs of the ∃∀-form or that one can hold reasonable beliefs of the ∀∃-form. Amongst actual infinitists in the realm of reasonable belief, we thus distinguish between those who allow that one can also hold reasonable beliefs of the ∃∀-form and those who deny that one can hold any reasonable beliefs of the ∃∀-form.

An actual infinitist in the realm of ontology is someone who holds that there is an infinite domain of objects, that there is an infinite magnitude, or that there is an infinitesimal magnitude. Thus, roughly, an actual infinitist in the realm of ontology holds either that there are true claims of the ∃∀-form or that there are true claims of the ∀∃-form. Amongst actual infinitists in the realm of ontology, we can distinguish between those who hold that there are true claims of the ∃∀-form and those who deny that there are any true claims of the ∃∀-form.

Potential Infinitism: A potential infinitist in the realm of experience is someone who is neither a strict finitist nor an actual infinitist in the realm of experience. There are several different kinds of potential infinitists in the realm of experience. Some potential infinitists in the realm of experience hold that the strongest claims that can be given in experience have the ∀◇∃-form: It can be given in experience that, for any natural number *n*, it is possible that there be a function on some things that takes a value greater than *n*. Other potential infinitists in the realm of experience hold that the strongest claims that can be given in experience have the ◇∀∃-form: It can be given in experience that it is possible that, for any natural number *n*, there be a function on some things that takes a value greater than *n*. Yet other potential infinitists in the realm of experience hold that the strongest claims that can be given in experience have the ◇∃∀-form: It can be given in experience that it is possible that there are some things that are such that, for any *n*, a function on those things takes a value greater than *n*.

A potential infinitist in the realm of reasonable belief is someone who is neither a strict finitist nor an actual infinitist in the realm of reasonable belief. There are several different kinds of potential infinitists in the realm of reasonable belief. Some potential infinitists in the realm of reasonable belief hold that the strongest view that one can have about any domain has the ∀◇∃-form: One can reasonably believe that, for any natural number *n*, it is possible that there be a function on some things that takes a value greater than *n*. Other potential infinitists in the realm of reasonable belief hold that the strongest view that one can have about any domain has the ◇∀∃-form: One can reasonably believe that it is possible that, for any natural number *n*, there be a function on some things that takes a value greater than *n*. Yet other potential infinitists in the realm of reasonable belief hold that the strongest view that one can have about any domain has the ◇∃∀-form: One can reasonably believe that it is possible that there are some things which are such that, for any *n*, a function on those things takes a value greater than *n*.

A potential infinitist in the realm of ontology is someone who holds that, while there are true claims of the ∀◇∃-form, there are no true claims of the ◇∀∃-form. It is important to remember that we are talking only about domains of contingently existing objects and contingently instantiated magnitudes at this point – for, otherwise, there is some danger that our characterisation of potential infinitism will lapse into incoherence. On the assumption that possible worlds are, themselves, necessary existents, there is no difficulty in allowing the potential infinitist to hold that there are at least as many possible worlds as there are natural numbers; if, on the other hand, what is possible depends on what is actual, then there is at least some reason to suppose that the potential infinitist in the realm of ontology will need to accept at least one claim of the ∀∃-form.

It is worth noting that the way that we have chosen to use the labels "actual infinitism" and "potential infinitism" in our characterisation of approaches to the philosophies of applied mathematics may not fit neatly with *all* of the uses of these terms in the literature. While I think that the application of these terms in the domain of philosophy of pure mathematics is relatively unproblematic – at least for purposes of taxonomy – there may be genuine difficulties involved in the extension of this vocabulary to other domains. At least part of the uncertainty here lies in the fact that one of the major topics of debate concerns "the possibility of actual infinities" or – perhaps better – "the possibility of contingently instantiated infinities". Given that standard uses of the expression "potential infinity" are bound up with modal considerations, and in particular, with modalised conceptions of the future, there is typically considerable scope for clarification of the claim that the future is only "potentially infinite".

(c) An Example Reconsidered

In Chapter 4, we considered various questions that arise when one thinks about spacetime in the context of the distinction between the finite and the infinite. Given the distinctions that we have just drawn between different philosophies of applied mathematics, we can add a little more precision to that earlier discussion.

An ontological finitist about the compositional structure of spacetime supposes that there are natural numbers n and m such that there can be no more than n mereological temporal atoms and there can be no more than m mereological spatial atoms.

An ontological actual infinitist about the compositional structure of spacetime either supposes that, in the actual world, for all n, there are more than n mereological temporal atoms and/or there are more than n mereological spatial atoms or supposes that, in the actual world, there are no mereological temporal atoms and/or mereological spatial atoms.

An ontological potential infinitist about the compositional structure of spacetime is neither an ontological finitist about the compositional structure of spacetime nor an ontological actual infinitist about the compositional structure of spacetime. Thus, an ontological potential infinitist about the compositional structure of spacetime supposes that, for all n, there are possible worlds in which there are more than n mereological temporal atoms and n mereological spatial atoms – and some ontological potential infinitists about the compositional structure of spacetime also suppose that there are possible worlds in which, for all n, there are more than n mereological temporal atoms and n mereological spatial atoms – while denying both of the claims that are characteristically endorsed by ontological actual infinitists about the compositional structure of spacetime.

Of course, it is easy enough to apply these distinctions – and the other distinctions that have been drawn in this chapter – to any of the other subject matters that have been discussed in this book. Since this is straightforward, it can be left as an exercise for the reader. We turn our attention, instead, to two important philosophical questions about the infinite that have not yet been addressed in our discussion.

8.8 SKOLEM'S PARADOX

As we noted in chapter 2, section 5 (a), it is one of the fundamental results of modern logic – the downward Löwenheim-Skolem theorem – that, if a set of sentences in first-order predicate calculus has a model, with a domain of any infinite cardinality, then it has a model with a denumerable domain. This result is sometimes thought to cast doubt on the idea that we could have good reason to suppose that there are nondenumerable infinities and, more generally, to create a "paradox" in the foundations of logic and set theory.

Roughly, the "Skolem paradox" runs as follows. Suppose that we construct a theory of the natural numbers that includes a sentence that is naturally interpreted to say that there are nondenumerably many sets of natural numbers. Then, by the downward Löwenheim-Skolem theorem, there will be a model for our theory with a countable domain, that is, there will be an interpretation of the theory in a domain that consists of only denumerably many sets of natural numbers in which our sentence comes out true. But how can a sentence that says that there are nondenumerably many sets of natural numbers be true in a domain in which there are only denumerably many sets of natural numbers? Doesn't this result show that we can't so much as succeed in making the claim that there are nondenumerably many sets of natural numbers?

Before we discuss Skolem's paradox, it will help to have a more precise statement of the impressionistic argument that we just gave. We shall follow Boolos and Jeffrey (1980: 153) in the construction of this more precise statement.

Say that one ordered pair $\langle x, y\rangle$ of natural numbers *precedes* another ordered pair $\langle i, j\rangle$ of natural numbers *in the order O* iff either $x+y<i+j$ or $x+y=i+j$ and $x<$ i. Define the pairing function $J(x, y) = z$ iff $\langle x, y\rangle$ is the $z+1$th pair in the order O. Note that $J(x, y)$ is a one-one function from pairs of natural numbers to natural numbers. A set w of natural numbers is an *enumerator* of a set E of sets of natural numbers iff ($\forall z$: z is a set of natural numbers)$\{z$ is in $E \rightarrow$ ($\exists x$: x is a natural number) ($\forall y$: y is a natural number) [y is in $z \leftrightarrow J(x, y)$ is in w]$\}$. Note that a set E of sets of natural numbers is denumerable iff E has an enumerator.

Consider a language that contains the names **0**, **1**, **2**, . . . , the two-place function symbol **J**, the one-place predicate letters **N** and **S**, and the two-place predicate letter $\in$. We shall consider interpretations in which the elements of the domain are nothing other than natural numbers and sets of natural numbers, in which **J** is assigned the pairing function (extended to take the value 17 if either x or y is a set), **N** is true of any number, **S** is true of any set (of numbers), and $\in$ is true of y, z iff the number y is in the set z. On the standard interpretation, the domain contains all of the sets of natural numbers; on nonstandard interpretations, this need not be so.

In every interpretation, the sentence $\sim(\exists w{:}Sw)(\forall z{:}Sz)(\exists x{:}Nx)(\forall y{:}Ny)\{y \in z \leftrightarrow J(x,y)\in w)$ is true iff there is no enumerator of the set of all sets of numbers in the domain of the interpretation that is itself in the domain of the interpretation. In particular, then, this sentence is true in the standard interpretation, since – as we learned from Cantor – there is no enumerator of the set of all sets of natural numbers. However, by the downward Löwenheim-Skolem theorem, there is an elementarily equivalent subinterpretation of the standard interpretation that contains only denumerably many elements, and hence in which the sentence $\sim(\exists w{:}Sw)(\forall z{:}Sz)(\exists x{:}Nx)(\forall y{:}Ny)\{y \in z \leftrightarrow J(x, y) \in w)$ is true, even though what it seems to say is that there is no enumerator of the sets in that denumerable domain.

What to say? Well, the most important point to make is surely that what a sentence can be understood to mean or to say depends on the domain over which it is interpreted. There is no difficulty in supposing that the sentence in questions *says* that there are nondenumerably many sets when its quantifiers are taken to range over all of the natural numbers and all of the sets of natural numbers. However, if we interpret the sentence in a restricted domain so that the quantifiers range over only some of the natural numbers and/or some of the sets of natural numbers, then that sentence need not say that there are nondenumerably many sets; rather, what it will say is that the domain of the interpretation contains no enumerator of the set of sets of numbers in the interpretation – and, of course, *that* is true in any elementarily equivalent subinterpretation of the standard interpretation.

While this may seem to be a satisfactory resolution of "Skolem's paradox", it can hardly be supposed that these considerations bring discussion to an end. As Wright (1985) argues, there is a question of whether the notion of 'intended interpretation' can bear the weight that it is required to carry in this response. On the one hand, there is a whole battery of sceptical arguments – to be found in the writings of Quine, Putnam, Kripke, and others – that seem to undermine the very idea of determinacy of meaning and interpretation. If those arguments can be sustained, then we should be wary of any claims about determinate intended interpretations. On the other hand, there are worries that are specific to the question of the existence of nondenumerable infinities. Wright claims that, unless we are prepared to suppose that the Cantorian diagonalisation proofs are unrestrictedly applicable pieces of informal mathematical reasoning, then we are not justified in supposing that the intended interpretation of arithmetic commits us to the existence of nondenumerably many sets of natural numbers. If there is some independent reason for supposing that we do not really understand talk about noneffectively enumerable denumerably infinite sets of natural numbers, then there is independent reason for supposing that the Cantorian diagonalisation proofs are not unrestrictedly applicable pieces of informal mathematical reasoning.

Setting aside the sceptical arguments about determinacy of meaning – which we do not have the resources to explore here – it seems plausible to suggest that the worry that Wright gives voice to is a version of the main worry that arises in the case of Lavine's explanation of how it is that we really do understand the infinite: Can we make sense of the idea that we can extrapolate from our idea of collections that are indefinitely large (relative to given contexts, purposes, and interests) to the idea of collections that are infinitely large *tout court*, that is, regardless of contexts, purposes, and interests? It seems to me that Skolem's paradox can be taken to pose a genuine challenge to our understanding of the infinite iff there are grounds for supposing that there is something wrong with extrapolation from our idea of collections that are indefinitely large (relative to given contexts, purposes, and interests) to the idea of collections that are infinitely large *tout court*, that is, regardless of contexts, purposes, and interests. This takes in Wright's concern as a special case: Skolem's paradox can be taken to pose a genuine challenge to our understanding of the infinite if there is independent reason for supposing that the Cantorian diagonalisation proofs are not unrestrictedly applicable pieces of informal mathematical reasoning, but rather proofs that are applicable only in certain contexts for certain purposes.

Wright allows that there are just two ways in which the Cantorian might meet the challenge of explaining talk about noneffectively enumerable denumerably infinite sets of natural numbers. On the one hand, if one espouses a logical conception of sets, then one has to sever the bond between *property* and *possible predication*: One has to allow that there are properties that cannot even possibly be claimed to be exemplified by particular objects, and one has to allow that there are uncountably many possible languages that are pairwise only partially intertranslatable. On the other hand, if one espouses a combinatorial conception of sets, then one has to be able to understand what it would be actually to complete an infinite but arbitrary selection from the set of natural numbers; but the literature on supertasks surely suggests that we do not actually have this understanding.

As Wright himself allows, neither of these considerations amounts to a knockdown argument: If we do suppose that we have an understanding of the infinite, then there is nothing in what he says that should undermine our confidence that our supposition is correct. On the one hand, even if one espouses a linguistic conception of properties, it is not clear why one should not suppose that there are properties of which no human agent – nor any substantially idealised human agent – is ever able to form a clear conception; and if one adopts a more metaphysical conception of properties – for example, as universals or tropes – then it is hard to see why one should suppose that there is even *prima facie* difficulty in the suggestion that there are properties of which we cannot possibly form any conception. Moreover, even if we allow that the logical conception of sets really does force the Cantorian in the direction of accepting that there are uncountably many possible languages that are pairwise only partially intertranslatable, it is not at all clear why the Cantorian cannot just outsmart his interlocutor at this point: Why shouldn't we suppose that there are many more possibilities than Wright is prepared to countenance? On the other hand – as the discussion in chapter 3 above suggests – the literature on supertasks hardly has the dialectical teeth that Wright is willing to attribute to it: There is no obvious reason why the literature on supertasks should cause Cantorians to review their occupation of paradise. However, if we happen to share Wright's understanding of these matters, then it seems to me that we might reasonably suppose that Skolem's paradox provides additional confirmation of our suspicion that understanding of the infinite eludes our grasp. While the practice of classical mathematicians – that is, the practice of the vast majority of working mathematicians – strongly suggests widespread confidence that we have a secure understanding of the infinite, it cannot be denied that there are some mathematicians and philosophers who are prepared to dissent from this tacit majority view.

8.9 INFINITESIMALS

There are scattered remarks about infinitesimals throughout the preceding pages, but there are various questions from the recent literature on infinitesimals that have not yet been addressed. The purpose of this section is to develop a slightly more concentrated discussion of infinitesimal magnitudes.

There are various areas in mathematics in which an intuitive conception of infinitesimal magnitudes played an important historical role: in particular, and most famously, in the development of the differential and integral calculi. Both Newton and Leibniz worked with infinitesimal quantities in their introductions of the differential and integral calculi; both were vulnerable to the criticism – deployed by Berkeley, among others – that they inconsistently required that infinitesimal quantities are both zero and nonzero.[5] There is a question whether Leibniz thought of infinitesimals as anything more than convenient fictions; however, as Earman (1975) argues, it seems plausible to suppose that Leibniz thought that magnitudes that are incomparably small with

[5] For further discussion, see, e.g., Priest (1987; 1995).

respect to ordinary magnitudes are indispensable for the differential and integral calculi, even if there is a rigorous metaphysical sense in which magnitudes that are incomparably small with respect to ordinary magnitudes are not real.

With the development of classical analysis, infinitesimals fell into disrepute. It was eventually acknowledged on all hands that the conception of infinitesimal that had figured in the early development of the differential and integral calculi is inconsistent,[6] and subsequent developments of more rigorous foundations for these calculi had no need of magnitudes that are incomparably small with respect to ordinary magnitudes. Moreover, while one might have thought that the notions of the infinite and the infinitesimal ought to stand or fall together – since, intuitively, an infinitesimal magnitude is merely the multiplicative inverse of an infinite magnitude – the development of the Cantorian theory of the transfinite did nothing to rehabilitate the standing of infinitesimals.[7] On the contrary, Cantor was a vocal opponent of infinitesimal and provided various arguments against the existence of infinitesimals.

The return of a notion of the infinitesimal to something like respectability did not occur until the development of nonstandard analysis by Robinson in the early 1960s. As we noted in chapter 2, it is possible to use techniques from mathematical logic that were developed in the first half of the twentieth century to show that there are nonstandard models of the natural numbers – containing infinite elements, that is, elements that are larger than all standard natural numbers – and nonstandard models of the real numbers – containing not only infinite elements but also infinitesimal elements, that is, elements that are nonzero, positive, and yet smaller than all standard positive real numbers. This work – and the subsequent development of internal set theory – certainly shows that one can have a consistent theory

[6] See Cleve (1971) and Cutland et al. (1988) for an interesting discussion of Cauchy's conception of infinitesimals.

[7] From the standpoint of Conway's theory, we might observe that the Cantorian infinite cardinals do not have multiplicative inverses, since they correspond to what Conway calls "gaps" in his number field. I take it that this fact helps to explain why development of the Cantorian theory of the transfinite did nothing to rehabilitate the standing of infinitesimals, even though it is true that, in many cases, infinitesimal magnitudes are just the multiplicative inverses of infinite magnitudes.

in which there are infinitesimal elements: One can, indeed, construct models in which there are magnitudes that are incomparably small with respect to ordinary magnitudes. Moreover, as we also noted in chapter 2, this work shows that it is possible to develop the differential and integral calculi in a context in which one makes use of nonstandard models for familiar theories of numbers.

Despite this "rehabilitation" of the infinitesimal, there are questions that one can ask about the significance that can be attributed to the existence of infinitesimals in nonstandard models of the real numbers. Perhaps the most significant questions arise as a result of the fact that there are no canonical systems of nonstandard numbers: Whereas, up to isomorphism, there is a canonical system of natural numbers and a canonical system of real numbers, there is not, even up to isomorphism, a canonical system of nonstandard natural numbers or nonstandard real numbers. For any standard number system, there are many enlargements to correlative nonstandard systems, but none of those enlargements has any distinctive features that might plausibly be taken as grounds for claiming that it is canonical.

There are various morals that might be drawn from these observations. For example, Machover (1993) argues that, while nonstandard analysis is a powerful tool that can be used to supplement familiar classical techniques, it would be a mistake to suppose that students could be trained exclusively in the techniques of nonstandard analysis, without any mention of the corresponding classical theories. Secure pedagogical foundations require canonical theories, and these are not to be found in the work of Robinson and Nelson. For another example, Earman (1975) argues that it is a mistake to suppose that modern nonstandard analysis somehow vindicates Leibniz's views about infinitesimals: The motives and procedures that Leibniz had for the introduction of infinitesimals are not supported in the absence of canonical theories. More generally – as prefigured in some of the discussion in chapter 3 – there is a worry about the application of noncanonical theories to real-world problems, if one wishes to treat one's models with full ontological seriousness: There is nothing left of the idea that there is a fact of the matter as to which is the right model (at least up to isomorphism) if the theories with which one is dealing are not canonical.

Despite this kind of worry, there are people who have claimed that recent developments in the theory of infinitesimals allow us to make progress on long-standing philosophical problems. So, for example, McLaughlin and Miller (1992) argue that one obtains a more satisfactory analysis of Zeno's paradoxes if one makes use of the resources of internal set theory than if one appeals simply to the resources of classical mathematics. I think that McLaughlin and Miller are wrong about the particular case – their arguments rely on a confusion of epistemological considerations with ontological considerations – and wrong in general: Given both the conservative nature of nonstandard analysis and the absence of canonical nonstandard models, it is very hard to believe that this kind of theory of infinitesimals has any significance for fundamental metaphysics. While we can agree with Segel (1991) that it may often be advantageous to use the techniques of nonstandard analysis in solving real world problems, this is always merely a matter of computational tractability: The use of nonstandard analysis may yield numerical answers, but it does not yield insight into philosophical problems such as those that are raised by Zeno's paradoxes.[8]

There is at least one respect in which the above discussion may require further refinement. Parallel to the rehabilitation of *arithmetic* infinitesimals – via the work of Robinson and Nelson – there has also been a rehabilitation of *geometric* infinitesimals in the category-theoretic work of Lawvere, Kock, and others. As observed by Bell (1988), it seems that rigorous "seventeenth century" style proofs of the basic principles of the differential and integral calculi can be developed within topoi, that is, within one of the general types of categories. In this part of category theory, we can make rigorous sense of the idea that a curve is composed of infinitesimal straight lines – *linear infinitesimals* – and of the idea that a volume is composed of infinitesimal lines or planes – *indivisibles*. Moreover, and more generally, in this part of category theory, we can formulate differential geometry more or less in its entirety without resorting to classical analytical methods. However, there is at least one catch: The 'internal logic' of topoi is intuitionistic rather than classical; linear infinitesimals are infinitesimals in a strongly nonconservative sense. (To note just two points: Algebraic

[8] For a contrary opinion, see Fenstad (1985).

systems that contain linear infinitesimals cannot form a field; and if there are linear infinitesimals, then it is not true that every pair of distinct points determines a unique line.)[9]

In conclusion, it is perhaps worth remarking that the worries about the noncanonical nature of nonstandard number systems applies no less to nonstandard infinite numbers than it does to nonstandard infinitesimals. Given recent developments in mathematics – for example, Conway's description of **No** – it is very hard to believe that infinitesimals are not in all respects on equal footing with infinite numbers. Consequently, we should have similar misgivings about claims – such as the one advanced by Ehrlich that was discussed in chapter 4, section 3 – that there are contingent magnitudes or domains that are properly characterised using nonstandard numbers. Perhaps, though, these misgivings can be assuaged by the thought that the difficulties here are principally epistemological, so that arbitrary selection of nonstandard models can be justified, at least in some cases.

8.10 CONCLUDING REMARKS

As with much of the preceding discussion, the remarks in this chapter have covered a vast terrain in a mostly superficial way.

While I shall not add any more to the direct discussion of the infinite, there is one final topic – or family of topics – about which we need to make some general remarks This topic is, roughly speaking, connections between the ideas of infinite regress and sufficient reason.

[9] Given the nonconservative nature of the theory, it is not so obviously wrong to claim – as Bell (1988: 290) does – that we obtain a more satisfactory response to Zeno's puzzles if we adopt a conception of motion that makes use of the notion of geometric infinitesimals. Nonetheless, Bell's proposal seems to involve a suspicious equivocation on the question of whether motion is, or is merely represented by, a smoothly varying infinitesimal velocity vector.

9

Infinite Regress and Sufficient Reason

The main topic of this chapter is infinite regress. There are many types of things – arguments, explanations, theories, beliefs, and so forth – that some say are vitiated by infinite regress in particular cases. I would like to have some clarity about what the charge of infinite regress amounts to, and what can be said for and against it, in these various different domains. However, before we turn to our investigation of infinite regress, there are some questions about principles of sufficient reason that it will be useful to examine: For, at least *prima facie*, there is good reason to think that allegations about the malign consequences of infinite regresses are typically tied to claims about the violation of nonnegotiable principles of sufficient reason.

9.1 STRONG PRINCIPLES OF SUFFICIENT REASON

One sometimes hears or reads about "*the* principle of sufficient reason". The definite article here is a mistake: There are many different principles of sufficient reason, and there is good reason to think about which of these principles most deserves attention. At any rate, that's my main excuse for starting this discussion with the following template for constructing *strong* principles of sufficient reason:

1. **O** (for every **FG** there is a **DE** why that **GF**s rather than **Q** possible alternatives).

   O is an operator, or a string of operators, for example: it is necessarily the case that . . . , it is knowable *a priori* that . . . , it is a requirement of right reason to believe that . . . , it is a claim that should not be given up without an overwhelmingly good argument that . . . , and the like.

G is an ontological category: proposition, state of affairs, fact, feature of the world, and the like.

F is a restriction, or string of restrictions, on the ontological category: true, obtaining, contingent, empirical, and the like.

E is an ontological kind: reason, explanation, and the like.

D is a qualification of the ontological kind: sufficient, complete, necessary, full, or the like.

Q is a quantifier: any, every, each, and the like.

The following is an example of a principle that fits the template.

2. Necessarily for each contingent feature of the world there is a complete explanation why the world has that contingent feature rather than each other alternative contingent feature that it might have had.

This is a particularly interesting instance: If complete explanation is cashed out in terms of necessitation or entailment, then it is very tempting to suppose that (2) entails that there are no contingent features of the world. There may well be other instances of our schema that are trivially true because there are no **FGs** – and for this reason, one might be tempted to amend the template to read as follows.

3. If there are **FGs**, then **O** (for every **FG**, there is a **DE** why that **GFs** rather than **Q** possible alternatives).

However, I doubt that there are any interesting cases in which this amendment is required. Moreover, of course, there is no point in amending (2) in this way; the problem for it – at least given the further assumptions about explanation – is not that there are no contingent features of the world, but rather that it appears to entail that there are none.

Despite the evident flexibility of my formulation, one might still have reasons for thinking that the template is insufficiently general. In particular, there is one familiar class of principles of sufficient reason that fails evidently to fit the template. Using the same vocabulary as before, there are claims of the following form.

(1*) **O** (for every **FG** there is a (distinct) **F′G′** that is a **DE** why that **GF**s rather than **Q** possible alternatives).

These claims clearly ought to count as principles of sufficient reason. To accommodate this – and similar – cases, I propose to count (1) as the basic template and to count (1*) as a natural extension of the basic template.

Even if it turns out that there are *other* reasons why my template is insufficiently general, it is plain that there are many different strong principles of sufficient reason that might be constructed according to it. Moreover, it seems to me that there are many interesting general features of strong principles of sufficient reason that can be discussed without filling in more details.

9.2 SELF-EXPLANATION AND SUFFICIENT REASON

In the template (1*), I have used parentheses to hedge on the question of whether something can explain itself. I don't believe that any hedge is needed here; however, no doubt there are other philosophers who are prepared to contest the need for the qualification 'distinct'.

It seems to me to be plainly true that no true proposition, fact, obtaining state of affairs, or feature of the world can be explained in terms of itself. If one asks "Why S?", one can never be satisfied with the alleged explanation "Because S!", though I think one might be perfectly well satisfied with the claim that S has no explanation (or that no explanation is known, or the like). It is true that in colloquial language it is common for people to say that something or other is "self-explanatory"; but what they mean when they say this is usually that the thing in question is *obvious,* not that it literally provides its own explanation. (If I say that certain instructions are "self-explanatory", what I mean is that you will need no further assistance in order to be able to follow them; I do not mean, for example that there could not be a competent speaker of the language who is unable to follow them without some further assistance.[1])

Although this point seems plain to me, I recognise that it is not plain to others. Indeed, there are apparently many philosophers who hold that there are some true propositions, obtaining states of affairs, facts, or features of the world that, quite literally, explain themselves. In particular, there are many philosophers who appear to hold that there is something about God's existence that is self-explanatory. However, it seems to me that any insistence on God's *aseity* – that is, on the radical independence of God and God's attributes – is bound to lead, instead, to the conclusion that those aspects of God's existence have no explanation. As intimated above, 'A because A' is always an explanatory solecism; hence 'A explains A' can never be true.

9.3 NECESSITATION AND SUFFICIENT REASON

In constructing the template, I was tempted to hedge on the question of whether principles of sufficient reason must be formulated in terms of 'full' explanation, or the like. Again, I don't believe that any hedge is needed here; however, it is possible that there may be some philosophers who question the need for – or perhaps the intelligibility of – qualifications such as 'full' when applied to explanations and reasons.

It seems to me to be fairly uncontroversial to claim that the single most important feature of strong principles of sufficient reason is that, whatever else it requires, the relation of 'being a full explanation for' – or 'being a sufficient reason for', or the like – imposes a strong modal demand on its terms. If A is a full explanation for B, then A *necessitates* B; if A is a sufficient reason for B, then A *necessitates* B; and so forth. If it is possible to have A and not B, then A alone can be neither a full explanation for nor a sufficient reason for B. If one asks "Why B?", then one will not suppose that "Because A" is a satisfactory response,

[1] See Champlin (1988: 187–9) for a more detailed discussion of this kind of approach to the understanding of self-explanation. Champlin denies that the claim that something is 'self-explanatory' amounts to the claim that it is 'obvious'. While this sounds right in the case of, say, written instructions – which, as Champlin claims, can be 'self-explanatory' only if they have a certain kind of complexity that is arguably incompatible with being 'obvious' – it is not so clear that it is right in other cases.

if one is seeking a sufficient reason for B, and yet there is nothing that rules out having A and not B.

Of course, the above considerations are not intended to conflict with the evident truth that answers to why-questions very often are not intended to provide sufficient reasons in this sense. It is a well-attested part of the pragmatics of explanation that very often it is acceptable to respond to a why-question by adverting to a contextually salient part of a sufficient reason: The lighting of a match may be sufficient to burn down a forest, given the laws and background conditions that obtain, but one is not required to enumerate those laws and background conditions when one explains why the forest burned down.

Furthermore, the above considerations are not intended to conflict with the evident truth that there may be cases in which we are in no position to give any informative answer to why-questions. Why did the fair dice that I rolled come up six? If there is a sufficient reason why the dice came up six, then there is some detailed story about the laws of nature, the motion that I imparted to the dice, and other physical background conditions at the time that I rolled the dice that jointly entail the dice's coming up six – but there may be no interesting or salient detail in this story to which we can advert in explaining why the dice came up six. Our strong principles of sufficient reason are ontological principles that are fully consistent with the acknowledgment that sufficient reasons may be forever beyond our ken.

Finally, there is but one alternative to the acceptance of strong principles of sufficient reason. If there is nothing else that necessitates B, and if – as we have already suggested – it cannot be that B provides a sufficient reason for itself – then the only remaining possibility is that B is brutely contingent, perhaps as the result of objective chance: There is no sufficient reason for B. This is not to say that there cannot be probabilistic explanations of B – perhaps B was very likely indeed given A – and neither is it to say that there cannot be causal explanations of B, provided that causal explanations can be probabilistic. However, it is to insist that there is no possibility of holding that there are explanations that provide sufficient reasons and yet do not necessitate. In particular, it is to insist that one cannot suppose that personal explanations – explanations couched in terms of agent causation – provide sufficient reasons for actions unless the factors appealed to in those explanations necessitate the actions.

If, for example, agents are supposed to have libertarian freedom, and to exercise this freedom when they decide what to do, then – since libertarian freedom is, by definition, inconsistent with necessitation – it follows that the free actions of free agents are objectively chancy or brutely contingent, and hence lack sufficient reasons for their occurrence.

9.4 PROBLEMS FOR STRONG PRINCIPLES OF SUFFICIENT REASON

We have already noted one of the most important objections to strong principles of sufficient reason, in the special case of the principle that, necessarily, for each contingent feature of the world there is a complete explanation of why it is that way rather than each other way that it might have been. If this *prima facie* plausible objection can be substantiated, then it seems plausible to suppose that it will generalise: All of the strong principles of sufficient reason are vulnerable to the suspicion that they are susceptible of trivialisation.

Let's start with our special case. If we suppose that there are contingent features of the world, then it seems very reasonable to suppose that there is a maximal contingent feature of the world: the way that the entire world – the world in sum – contingently is. But if there is a way that the entire sum of contingency contingently is, and if complete explanation rules out self-explanation, then the only way that our principle can be satisfied is if there are no contingent features of the world. If there are contingent features of the world, then there can be no complete explanation of why the sum of all of the contingent features of the world is the way that it is: If there are contingent features of the world, then there must be brutely contingent features of the world.

Consider a different case. Suppose we hold that it is knowable *a priori* that, for every true proposition that p, there is a distinct true proposition that q that fully explains why p is true. If we suppose that there are propositions that are contingently true, then it seems reasonable to suppose that there is a maximal contingently true proposition: that contingently true proposition that is the conjunction of all of the contingently true propositions. If there is a true proposition that provides a complete explanation for the truth of p, then it cannot be a contingently true proposition, since no proposition can (completely) explain its own truth. But no necessary proposition can completely explain the truth of a contingently true proposition: Propositions entailed by a necessarily true proposition are themselves necessarily true. So, on the assumption that there is a maximal contingently true proposition, it follows that there are contingently true propositions whose truth has no explanation: There are contingently true propositions that are brutely true.

The general structure of the argument here is clear. If we can suppose that there is a maximal FG, then – under plausible assumptions – we cannot also suppose that, for each FG, there is a distinct FG – F′G′, say – that provides a complete explanation for FG. Consequently, unless the plausible assumptions can be denied, those who wish to defend strong principles of sufficient reason are required to maintain that there are no maximal entities of the kinds that are quantified over – or schematically represented – in those principles. That is, proponents of strong principles of sufficient reason are required to maintain that there is no maximal contingently true proposition, no maximal contingent feature or property, no maximal contingent fact or state of affairs, and so forth.

Of course, there are many other kinds of reasons that one might have for refusing to accept strong principles of sufficient reason. Those who claim that there is no maximal contingently true proposition, no maximal contingent feature or property, no maximal contingent fact or state of affairs, and so forth, may nonetheless claim that there are brutely contingently true propositions, brutely contingent features or properties, brutely contingent facts or states of affairs, and so on. If, for example, quantum mechanics provides us with reasons for supposing that there are objectively chancy events, then we have reasons to reject strong principles of sufficient reason quite apart from the general difficulty that we have been examining here. But, quite apart from these further considerations, the general difficulty that we have considered is already sufficient to prompt us to consider whether there are ways that we can weaken principles of sufficient reason to arrive at more acceptable claims.

9.5 WEAKER PRINCIPLES OF SUFFICIENT REASON

There are many ways in which one might try to weaken the schema with which we began. One suggestion – advocated, for example, by Gale and

Preuss (1999) – is to replace the demand for full explanation with a demand for the possibility of full explanation:

4. **O** (for every **FG**, it is possible that there is a **DE** why that **GFs** rather than **Q** possible alternatives).

However – as Fitch (1955) argues – it is a perhaps surprising truth that (4) is logically equivalent to (1): We do not actually obtain a weaker principle under this proposal, and hence the same objections that we lodged against (1) can be lodged with equal efficacy against (4) (see Oppy (2000b) for further details).

Another suggestion – advocated, for example, by Koons (1997) – is to replace the demand for full explanation with the demand to seek full explanation except when one has reason to suppose that there is no full explanation to be had.

5. **O** (for every **FG**, one should suppose that there is a **DE** why that **GFs** rather than **Q** possible alternatives, unless one has good reason to suppose that there is no such explanation to be had).

While one might quibble about the details of the formulation of this principle – perhaps, for example, one should seek full explanation only in circumstances in which one has good reason to suppose that there is full explanation to be had, rather than in circumstances in which one lacks good reason to suppose that there is no full explanation to be had – it seems that some methodological principles of this kind are unexceptionable. However – despite Koons's claims to the contrary – I think that it is hard to believe that a principle of this kind has any metaphysical bite: It is consistent with this methodological principle that the world is replete with objective chance and brute contingency.

A third suggestion – perhaps implicitly suggested by Craig (1979a) and many others – is to restrict the domain or subject matter in which it is appropriate to impose the demand for full explanation. So, for example, rather than suppose that every contingently true proposition has a complete explanation for its truth, we might suppose, instead, that every contingently true proposition *of some particular kind* has a complete explanation for its truth. In general:

6. **O** (for every **FG** of kind K, there is a **DE** why that **GFs** rather than **Q** possible alternatives).

Of course, if we were to suppose that

7. **O** (for every **FG** of kind K, there is a (distinct) **FG** of kind K that (fully) explains why that **GF**s rather than **Q** possible alternatives)

then we would be vulnerable to the same general objection that we mentioned in the previous section: If there is a maximal FG of kind K, then there must be FGs of kind K that do not have a complete explanation of the required type. But in (6), there is no assumption that the complete explanation of why GFs, when an FG is of kind K, adverts to a distinct FG of that same kind K. So, for example, if we suppose that the coming into existence of any object requires a complete explanation, (6) does not require us also to suppose that the coming into existence of any object requires a complete explanation in terms of the coming into existence of some other object.

While it seems plausible to suppose that (6) avoids difficulties that might be raised by maximal FGs of the relevant kinds K, there are other worries that one might have about endorsing particular instantiations of (6). In particular, depending on the range of possible alternatives that is under consideration, the demand for full explanation may still force us into the position of requiring that it is a necessary truth that GFs. If, for example, we want a full explanation for the coming into existence of a given object, and if that full explanation is required to rule out all possible alternatives to the existence of that object, then it must be the case that the coming into existence of the given object is necessary: If there are possible alternatives that are not ruled out by the offered explanation, then we do not have a *complete* explanation of the coming into existence of the given object, since we do not have an explanation of why this happened rather than one of the alternatives that has not been ruled out.

In view of these difficulties, it might be suggested that we move to a fourth proposal – perhaps even more plausibly supposed to be implicit in Craig (1979a) and others – which gives up the insistence on full or complete explanation.

8. **O** (for every **FG** of kind K, there is an **F′G′** that *partly* explains why that **GF**s rather than **Q** possible alternatives).

Of course, the notion of partial explanation at work here might be provided with further clarification; however, let us suppose that we have a good enough grasp of the idea of explanations that are consistent with the contingency of that which is explained (as, plausibly, for example, in the case of probabilistic causal explanations). Moreover, let's ignore the worry that, in moving to (8), we have given up on the search for a plausible principle of *sufficient* reason: In the light of our earlier discussion in section 9.3, at best, (8) yields various principles of *partially sufficient* reason.

Given the assumption that we do have a good enough grasp of the notion of a partially sufficient reason, we might also revisit some of the stronger principles that were considered previously and discarded. Consider, for example, the following.

9. **O** (for every **FG** there is a (distinct) **FG** that partly explains why that **GF**s rather than **Q** possible alternatives).

Can we suppose, for instance, that, necessarily, for each contingent feature of the world there is a partial explanation of why it is that way rather than each other way that it might have been? No; here we have the same difficulty as before: If there is a maximal contingent feature, then there is nothing that is available to explain why it is as it is except for whatever noncontingent features there may be. But how could noncontingent features figure in any kind of explanation of what contingent features of the world are as they are (rather than any other way that they might have been)?

In view of these considerations, it seems that remaining plausible candidate principles of sufficient reason can be no stronger than (8), that is, roughly, no stronger than the claim that there is a partial explanation for everything that belongs to some privileged domains, but that there are also domains in which there is not even a partial explanation for some of the members of those domains. If that's right, then there is clearly a demand that proponents of (8) need to meet before they are entitled to rely on instances of (8): They must have some reason for supposing that the instances of (8) that they accept are true. Since they tacitly accept that there are brute contingencies of one kind or another – that is, contingencies that do not have even a partial explanation – they need to have reasons for endorsing those instances of (8) that they happen to endorse, and reasons for rejecting those instances of (8) that they happen to reject.

Consider, again, the claim that the coming into existence of any object requires an explanation of why that object comes into existence rather than not coming into existence. In the present context, we are directed to consider the claim that the coming into existence of any object requires a partial explanation of why that object comes into existence rather than not coming into existence. If we suppose that there is an initial state of the universe, then, while the objects that exist in that initial state may be contingently existent, there is no obvious sense in which they come into existence: There is no previous time at which they did not exist. So there is nothing in our claim that requires us to suppose that the existence of objects in the initial state requires even partial explanation. On the other hand, if we suppose that there is no initial state of the universe, then, for each object that comes into existence, there is a partial explanation of its coming into existence in terms of the earlier coming into existence of objects – and so our principle is satisfied, even if there is not even a partial explanation of the existence of the infinite chains of objects, each of which is such that its existence is partially explained by the existence of prior objects in that chain.

While it is very plausible to suppose that there are acceptable instances of (8), it is not at all clear that there are acceptable instances of (8) that can be used to rule out some of the scenarios that were discussed in chapter 3, and of which it was suggested that they might be in violation of plausible principles of sufficient reason. (See, e.g., the conclusions of the discussions of Tristram Shandy and Counting to Infinity.) More generally, the constraints that we have found it necessary to place on (8) make it seem rather implausible that (8) will have important consequences for the kinds of metaphysical questions that we are most concerned to pursue.

9.6 INFINITE REGRESSES

I think that the preceding discussion makes it plausible to suppose that it is not going to be easy to object to infinite regresses on the grounds that they violate plausible principles of sufficient reason. True enough, in particular cases, one may be able to find an instance of (8) that plausibly conflicts with the claim that there is an infinite regress of a given kind – but, at the very least, it is hard to suppose that the fact that there are acceptable instances of (8) gives us some reason to suppose that there cannot be infinite regresses. However, in order to make the nature of this claim clear, we need to say more about exactly what infinite regresses are supposed to be. Once we have done this, we shall be in a better position to examine the question of why they might be supposed to be a bad thing.

We start with the idea of a linearly ordered infinite sequence, and, for simplicity, we focus on the case in which the linear order is complete (so that for any elements x and y, either $x < y$, or $x = y$, or $x > y$ under this order). It is not the case that every linearly ordered infinite sequence constitutes an infinite regress: There is a further constraint that needs to be satisfied before a linearly ordered infinite sequence is an infinite regress.

In section 8.1 (b), I introduced the idea of a C-ordering, that is, of a linear ordering under which it is impossible for there to be an infinite sequence that instantiates that linear ordering and in which there is no first element under that linear ordering. That idea seems to come close to capturing the formal structure of an infinite regress: At least roughly, an infinite regress is a C-ordering in which there is no first element under that C-ordering.[2] This way of thinking about infinite regresses entails that infinite regresses are, *ipso facto*, objectionable: As a matter of definition, there cannot be a C-ordering in which there is no first element under that C-ordering. Hence, if this proposal is right, then, *ipso facto*, there cannot be an infinite regress. But, of course, the mere fact that there cannot be an infinite regress does not entail that there is no use for the definition that has just been made:

[2] Clark (1988) provides an interesting – and apparently distinct – account of infinite regress arguments. On this account, an infinite regress *argument* is an indirect derivation with the following structure. First, it is noted that it is uncontroversial – unconditionally and categorically true – that a predicate 'F' is instantiated. Second, a target thesis TF – to be reduced to absurdity – is introduced. It is then shown that TF entails that nothing instantiates the predicate 'F' unless there is an infinite succession of elements, which stand in an upward F-preserving relation RF and yet which are downward dependent on the R-heredity of the relation RF. Finally, it is concluded that the existence of an infinite succession of elements, which stand in an upward F-preserving relation RF and yet which are downward dependent on the R-heredity of the relation RF, is inconsistent with the claim that any of these elements is unconditionally and categorically F. If Clark is right about this, then perhaps we can take his account to spell out in more detail what it is for an ordering to be a C-ordering.

For example, any theory, explanation, definition, or argument that entails that there is an infinite regress is thereby reduced to absurdity, if, as a matter of definition, it is impossible for there to be an infinite regress.

Of course, this terminological decision is unimportant: We could equally well say that an infinite regress is any linear ordering that lacks a first element under that ordering, and then insist that infinite regresses are acceptable iff they are not C-orderings. But whether or not we choose this route, we are left with the substantive task of determining which orderings are C-orderings. And, as I argued in section 8.1 (b), it is hard to see that we have any way of determining whether a given ordering is a C-ordering other than by asking whether it is possible for there to be an infinite sequence under that ordering that has no first element under that ordering.

There are many cases – of many different kinds – in which philosophers have alleged that there is an infinite regress. Moreover, there are many cases in which philosophers have alleged that we have evidence that a particular case does involve an infinite regress because it is a case in which there is a violation of a plausible principle of sufficient reason. However, as we have just noted, it is actually hard to discover any uncontroversial principle of sufficient reason – or partial sufficient reason – that can play the role of identifying cases in which one has an infinite regress.

Perhaps we might try proposing something like the following.

10. **O** (for every **FG** that belongs to a C-ordering **C**, either there is a distinct **FG** that belongs to **C** that partly explains why that **GF**s rather than **Q** possible alternatives, or else **FG** is the first member of the C-ordering and there is an **F′G′** that does not belong to **C** that partly explains why that **GF**s rather than **Q** possible alternatives).

However, it is not obvious why we should suppose that every C-ordering must be such that the first element under the C-ordering has even a partial explanation. After all, we have already noted that – under plausible assumptions – partial explanation cannot be universal. So we ought to restrict (10) to C*-orderings, that is, to C-orderings for which partial explanation does extend to the first element of the C-ordering.

11. **O** (for every **FG** that belongs to a C*-ordering **C**, either there is a distinct **FG** that belongs to **C** that partly explains why that **GF**s rather than **Q** possible alternatives or **FG** is the first member of the C*-ordering and there is an **F′G′** that does not belong to **C** that partly explains why that **GF**s rather than **Q** possible alternatives).

I take it that this principle is not controversial: Given the way that we have defined the notion of a C*-ordering, we can be sure that (11) is true. But, of course, in actual cases, almost all of the important philosophical work will remain to be done: For what will be controversial in any given case is whether a particular ordering is, indeed, a C*-ordering. While we can connect together the notions of *completed infinity*, *infinite regress*, and *partial sufficient reason*, the establishment of those connections provides us with no assistance when we ask how we are to break into the circle of connections to sort particular cases. If, for example, we suppose that events are related by a causal relation – a kind of partial sufficient reason – then the question of whether (11) applies to that causal relation cannot be answered in independence from the question of whether that causal relation is a C*-ordering on events. Those who suppose either that there are no initial events or that there are initial events whose occurring lacks partial sufficient reason will suppose that the causal relation is not a C*-ordering on events, and hence will reject the relevant version of (11).

As we noted at the beginning of this chapter, there are various different areas in which allegations of infinite regress may be imputed. In the example that we just considered, the charge is that a theory or system of belief allows that there is an ordering relation that is instantiated in the world under which there are infinitely many entities related by the ordering, but in which there is no first (or last) element under that ordering. So, for example, theories or systems of belief that allow that there is an infinite past – that is, an infinite series of past times and/or past events, such that each time of event is preceded by earlier times and/or events – are alleged to involve an infinite regress. And, of course – given our earlier terminological stipulation – in this case, whether or not an infinite series of past times and/or past events does involve an infinite regress depends on whether or not these series form C*-orderings under the relevant ordering relations. (As we noted, we might have made an alternative stipulation according to which these series automatically do involve infinite regress, but under which it is a substantive question of whether *these* infinite regresses are problematic.)

Another area where allegations of infinite regress may be imputed is in the domain of explanation. If I undertake to answer a question of a certain kind, and if the answer that I give prompts another question of exactly the same kind, then there is some temptation to allege that my initial answer involves an infinite regress. So, for example, if you assert that time flows, and, in response to my question about what it is with respect to which time flows, you respond that there is a hypertime with respect to which time flows, then there is a clear sense in which you question invites the charge that it involves an infinite regress: For the same questions – about whether hypertime flows, and, if so, what it flows with respect to – will just arise again in the case of hypertime. In this case, it seems to me that the right way to understand this exchange is as follows. The proponent of hypertime is committed to the claim that there is an infinite hierarchy of times, each of which flows with respect to the next order of time in the hierarchy. The allegation of the opponent is that this hierarchy of hypertimes constitutes a C*-ordering. It is quite unclear how we are to decide whether an infinite hierarchy of hypertimes does constitute a C*-ordering (though perhaps, in this case, we can suppose that the metaphysical extravagance involved in this supposition is sufficient to render it inferior to alternative hypotheses).

I am inclined to think that this example generalises. Often enough, the initial point of an allegation of infinite regress against a purported explanation is to draw attention to the fact that there is an infinite series of some kind that is at least implicitly required by the explanation; but whether or not this allegation has any genuine force turns on the further question of whether the infinite series in question constitutes a C*-ordering. Sometimes, it may be that an allegation of infinite regress against a purported explanation is intended to draw attention to the fact that an explanation fails to provide a *complete* sufficient reason; however, in these cases, our earlier discussion suggests that the allegation should be treated with considerable suspicion. If – as I have claimed – there are no acceptable strong principles of sufficient reason, then it is never a good objection to a purported explanation that it fails to provide a complete sufficient reason (of the kind that is required by strong principles of sufficient reason): Since an acceptable explanation must leave some things unexplained, it is never a good objection to a purported explanation that it is 'regressive' in this sense. Of course, there are many ways in which explanations can be inadequate, including ways in which explanations can be objectionably incomplete – but the mere fact that an explanation leaves *something* unexplained is not a serious difficulty for that explanation.

9.7 CONCLUDING REMARKS

I have argued that one ought not to accept principles of sufficient reason that are stronger than instances of the following.

8. **O** (for every **FG** of kind K, there is an **F′G′** that *partly* explains why that **GF**s rather than **Q** possible alternatives).

Moreover, I have noted that there are quite fundamental disputes about instances of:

11. **O** (for every **FG** that belongs to a C*-ordering **C**, either there is a distinct **FG** that belongs to **C** that partly explains why that **GF**s rather than **Q** possible alternatives or **FG** is the first member of the C*-ordering and there is an **F′G′** that does not belong to **C** that partly explains why that **GF**s rather than **Q** possible alternatives).

For future purposes, the main point that I want to insist on here is that we should not forget that we cannot suppose that the instances of (8) and/or (11) that we wish to accept – if, indeed, there are instances of (8) and/or (11) that we wish to accept – are supported by stronger principles of a similar kind *unless* we are prepared to commit ourselves to principles that seem utterly implausibly strong. If we suppose that there is contingency in the world – as we must, for example, if we suppose that there is libertarian freedom of action and libertarian freedom of choice – then we cannot consistently suppose that the instances of (8) and/or (11) that we accept are supported by instances of similar principles that are stronger than (8) and (11).

Conclusion

Since the primary purpose of this book has been to achieve a view of the range of positions that might be taken concerning the concept of the infinite, it is appropriate to conclude with a reasonably full account of the positions that we have identified. If the following taxonomy is adequate, then any view about the concept of the infinite will fall into one of these categories.

First, there is a **strict finitism** that maintains that we have no proper use of the concept of the infinite: The kind of extrapolation from the finite to the infinite that one might suppose furnishes us with an understanding of the infinite is simply not up to the task, and there is no plausible substitute. On this approach, classical mathematics is rejected; the only mathematics that is countenanced is finite mathematics. Moreover, the only theories in other domains that are acceptable are those that posit none but finite domains and finite magnitudes. There are only finitely many possible worlds, each with a finite "frame", and composed of finitely many mereological atoms.

Second, there is a range of **weak potential infinitisms**, each of which supposes, roughly, that we have proper use for some claims of the $\forall\Diamond\exists$-form, but no proper use for claims of the $\Diamond\forall\exists$-form: While we can understand the idea that, for each (putative) natural number, it is possible that some things are characterised by that (putative) number, we cannot understand the idea that it is possible that, for each (putative) number, there are some things that are characterised by that (putative) number. On this approach, classical mathematics is rejected, and some kind of intuitionism or constructivism is embraced. Moreover, on this approach, all actual and possible domains and magnitudes are taken to be finite: There is no sense to be made of the suggestion that there are – or could be – infinite totalities of any kind. However, this kind of view does allow that the domain of possibilities itself constitutes an infinite totality: There are infinitely many ways that things could be. Typically, this kind of view is wedded to a modal account of time and the future: While the past constitutes a kind of "realised" totality, the future does not.

Third, there is a range of **moderate potential infinitisms**, each of which supposes, roughly, that we have proper use for some claims of the ◇∀∃-form, but no use for claims of the ◇∃∀-form: While we understand the idea that it is possible that, for each number, there are some things that are characterised by that number, we cannot understand the idea that it is possible that there are functions on some things whose magnitude along some dimension exceeds every number. I take it that this kind of view accepts classical mathematics in general but rejects the suggestion that we need the infinite branches of classical mathematics in order to provide an accurate description of any of the features of any possible world. On this view, while there are infinite magnitudes, these magnitudes are all abstract in nature: There are not – and cannot be – infinite magnitudes of concrete entities.

Fourth, there is a range of **strong potential infinitisms**, each of which supposes, roughly, that we have proper use for some claims of the ◇∃∀-form, but no proper use for claims of the ∀∃-form. On these views, we understand perfectly well the claim that it is possible that there are functions on some things whose magnitude along some dimension exceeds every number, but we deny that there are any things for which it is true that there is no upper bound to the magnitude of some function on those things. On these views, we accept classical mathematics, and we allow that we need the infinite branches of classical mathematics in order to provide an accurate description of the features of some possible worlds – but we deny that there are any features of the actual world that require this kind of description.

Fifth, there is a range of **weak actual infinitisms**, each of which supposes, roughly, that we have a proper use for some claims of the ∀∃-form, but no proper use for claims of the ∃∀-form. Plainly, any view of this kind is committed to classical mathematics and to the claim that we need the infinite branches of classical mathematics in order to provide an accurate description of some features of the actual world.

Sixth, there is a range of **strong actual infinitisms**, each of which supposes, roughly, that we have a proper use for some claims of the ∃∀-form. For example, a view that maintains that, for each *n*, there are objects that are more than *n* metres apart but that also insists there are no objects that, for each *n*, are more than *n* metres apart, is a strong actual infinitism: Under the given assumptions, there is a domain of objects that is such that, for each *n*, there are more than *n* objects in that domain. This example shows that weak actual infinitisms may be rather odd views: For, given the second-order nature of the ∃-quantifier in our characteristic claims, one may need to work hard to avoid commitment to a claim of the ∃∀-form when one accepts a claim of the ∀∃-form. Of course, if this point is correct, then it also shows that moderate potential infinitisms are odd views, for more or less the same reason.

Given the point noted at the end of the previous paragraph, it seems reasonable to claim that there are four contending views about the concept of the infinite that have not yet been ruled out: strict finitism, weak potential infinitism, strong potential infinitism, and strong actual infinitism. If we suppose that we understand classical mathematics, then either we shall be strong potential infinitists or we shall be strong actual infinitists: Either way, plausibly, we shall suppose that it is a contingent matter whether classical conceptions of infinity find application to the actual world. To reject the suggestion that it is a contingent matter whether classical conceptions of infinity find application to the extramathematical world, either we shall be intuitionists or constructivists – hence rejecting classical mathematics and, very likely, classical logic – or we shall be strict finitists.

If we suppose that the kinds of arguments that were presented in chapter 1 and discussed in chapter 3 are cogent, then it seems that we are required to be either weak potential infinitists or strict finitists: We can only suppose that there is some serious *general* conceptual problem involved in the application of classical mathematics to the extramathematical world if we suppose that there is some serious conceptual problem with classical mathematics itself.

As we noted in our earlier discussion, the general classification of views is largely silent on the positions that can be taken on individual questions. Consider, for example, the question about the magnitude of the future. There is no obvious reason why a strong actual infinitist – for example, someone who holds that there are, now, infinitely many objects in the universe – cannot hold that the future is finite and, indeed, that the future is necessarily finite. If, for example, you hold that every possible universe is a big bang universe and that every possible big bang universe is closed, then, *a fortiori*, you hold that the future is necessarily finite. While this combination of views is not widespread, it is not obvious that it is immediately dismissible out of hand. The general point to be made here is that, within each of the general views – except for strict finitism – there are decisions to be made about particular subject matters that can be settled only by considerations that pertain to that particular subject matter. What a strong actual infinitist believes about the status of the future is not determined by features of strong actual infinitism; rather, it depends on particular beliefs about the nature of the future.

Perhaps there is one important exception to the observation that has just been made. Given the way in which the modal conception of time enters into the justification of intuitionistic and constructivist accounts of mathematics, it is plausible to claim that weak potential infinitists cannot be finitists about time: This is an area in which they are required to be weak potential infinitists. However, for strong potential infinitists, questions about the infinite aspects of time are not to be settled other than by considerations about the nature of time distinct from the kinds of considerations that are supposed to provide the foundations for intuitionism and constructivism.

Before closing, it is perhaps worth emphasising once more that there seem to be evident costs to every stance that one might take on questions about the infinite.

On the one hand, a blanket ban on the infinite seems to bring crippling difficulties. Infinity is everywhere in classical mathematics. In particular, real analysis provides foundations for everything from the calculus to the mathematical theory of probability. Moreover, infinity is found everywhere in the foundations of science and our ordinary thought about the world: Consider, for example, familiar conceptions of the divisibility of space and time. Because the infinite lurks everywhere both in our ordinary thought about the world and in science, it is very hard to see how we could live without it.

On the other hand, involvement with the infinite brings with it a huge range of difficulties. In particular, there are the many puzzles and paradoxes that have been outlined in the pages of this book. Moreover, there are the many quite fundamental problems that arise for such apparently simple notions as counting, adding, maximising, and so forth. Because we are so firmly wedded to limit notions – "best", "first", "greatest", "maximum", and so forth – that do not sit easily with the infinite, it is very hard to see how we can make our peace with the infinite.

References

Abian, A. 1978. "Passages between Finite and Infinite." *Notre Dame Journal of Formal Logic* 19:452–6.

Allis, V., and T. Koetsier. 1991. "On Some Paradoxes of the Infinite." *British Journal for Philosophy of Science* 42:187–94.

Allis, V., and T. Koetsier. 1995. "On Some Paradoxes of the Infinite II." *British Journal for Philosophy of Science* 46:235–47.

Almog, J. 1999. "Nothing, Something, Infinity." *Journal of Philosophy* 96:462–78.

Alper, J., and M. Bridger. 1997. "Mathematics, Model and Zeno's Paradoxes." *Synthese* 110:143–66.

Angel, L. 2002. "Zeno's Arrow, Newton's Mechanics, and Bell's Inequalities." *British Journal for the Philosophy of Science* 53:161–82.

Arntzenius, F., and D. McCarthy. 1997. "The Two Envelope Paradox and Infinite Expectations." *Analysis* 57:42–50.

Arsenijivic, M. 1989. "How Many Physically Distinguished Parts Can a Limited Body Contain?" *Analysis* 49:36–42.

Baker, G., and P. Hacker. 1984. *Language, Sense and Nonsense.* Oxford: Blackwell.

Bell, J. 1979. "The Infinite Past Regained: A Reply to Whitrow." *British Journal for the Philosophy of Science* 30:161–5.

Bell, J. 1988. "Infinitesimals." *Synthese* 75:285–315.

Belot, G. 2001. "The Principle of Sufficient Reason." *Journal of Philosophy* 98:55–74.

Benacerraf, P. 1962. "Tasks, Supertasks, and the Modern Eleatics." *Journal of Philosophy* 59:765–84.

Benacerraf, P. 1965. "What Numbers Could Not Be." *Philosophical Review* 74:47–73.

Benacerraf, P. 1985. "Skolem and the Sceptic." *Proceedings of the Aristotelian Society,* supp. vol. 59:85–115.

Benardete, J. 1964. *Infinity: An Essay in Metaphysics.* Oxford: Clarendon.

Bennett, J. 1971. "The Age and Size of the World." *Synthese* 23:127–46.

Berresford, G. 1981. "A Note on Thomson's Lamp 'Paradox.'" *Analysis* 41: 1–3.

Black, M. 1951. "Achilles and the Tortoise." *Analysis* 11:91–101.

Blake, R. 1926. "The Paradox of Temporal Process." *Journal of Philosophy* 23:645–54.

Blum, R., and J. Rosenblatt. 1972. *Probability and Statistics*. Philadelphia: W. B. Saunders.

Boolos, G., and R. Jeffrey. 1980. *Computability and Logic*, 2nd ed. Cambridge: Cambridge University Press.

Bostock, D. 1972/3. "Aristotle, Zeno, and the Potential Infinite." *Proceedings of the Aristotelian Society* 73:37–5.

Brook, P. 1965. "White at the Shooting Gallery." *Mind* 74:256.

Broome, J. 1995. "The Two-Envelope Paradox." *Analysis* 55:6–11.

Brown, P. 1965. "A Medieval Analysis of Infinity." *Journal for the History of Philosophy* 3:242–3.

Cain, J. 1995. "Infinite Utility." *Australasian Journal of Philosophy* 73:401–4.

Cajori, F. 1915. "The History of Zeno's Arguments on Motion." *American Mathematical Monthly* 22:1–7, 39–47, 77–83, 109–15, 143–9, 179–86, 215–21, 253–8, 292–7.

Cargile, J. 1992. "On a Problem about Probability and Decision." *Analysis* 52:211–16.

Carnap, R. 1956. "Empiricism, Semantics, and Ontology." In *Meaning and Necessity: A Study in Semantics and Modal Logic*, (2nd ed., enlarged.) Chicago: Chicago University Press.

Castell, P., and D. Batens. 1994. "The Two Envelope Paradox: The Infinite Case." *Analysis* 54:46–9.

Chad, A. 1997. "The Principle of Sufficient Reason and the Uncaused Beginning of the Universe." *Dialogue* 36:555–62.

Chalmers, D. 2002. "The St. Petersburg Two Envelope Paradox." *Analysis* 62:155–7.

Champlin, T. 1988. *Reflexive Paradoxes*. London: Routledge.

Chase, J. 2002. "The Non-Probabilistic Two Envelope Paradox." Analysis 62:157–60.

Chihara, C. 1965. "On the Possibility of Completing an Infinite Process." *Philosophical Review* 74:74–87.

Christensen, R., and J. Utts. 1992. "Bayesian Resolution of the 'Exchange Paradox.' " *American Statistician* 46:274–6.

Clark, M., and N. Schackel. 2000. "The Two Envelope Paradox." *Mind* 109:415–42.

Clark, P., and S. Read. 1984. "Hypertasks." *Synthese* 61:387–90.

Clark, R. 1988. "Vicious Infinite Regress Arguments." In J. Tomberlin (ed.), *Philosophical Perspectives*, vol. 2: *Epistemology*. Atascadero, Calif.: Ridgeview, 369–80.

Clayton, P. 1996. "The Theistic Argument from Infinity in Early Modern Philosophy." *International Philosophical Quarterly* 36:5–17.

Cleve, J. 1971. "Cauchy, Convergence and Continuity." *British Journal for Philosophy of Science* 22:27–37.

Cohen, R., and L. Lauden, eds. 1983. *Physics, Philosophy and Psychoanalysis.* Dordrecht: Reidel.

Conway, D. 1974. "Possibility and Infinite Time: A Logical Paradox in St. Thomas' Third Way." *International Philosophical Quarterly* 14:201–8.

Conway, D. 1983. "Concerning Infinite Chains, Infinite Trains, and Borrowing a Typewriter." *International Journal for Philosophy of Religion* 14:71–86.

Conway, D. 1984. "'It Would Have Happened Already': On One Argument for a First Cause." *Analysis* 44:159–66.

Conway, J. 1976. *On Numbers and Games.* London: Academic.

Corbett, S. 1988. "Zeno's Achilles: A Reply to John McKie." *Philosophy and Phenomenological Research* 49:325–31.

Cornman, J., and K. Lehrer. 1968. *Philosophical Problems and Arguments: An Introduction.* Indianapolis: Hackett.

Cowen, T., and J. High. 1988. "Time, Bounded Utility, and the St. Petersburg Paradox." *Theory and Decision* 25:219–23.

Craig, W. 1979a. *The Kalām Cosmological Argument.* London: Macmillan.

Craig, W. 1979b. "Whitrow, Popper, and the Impossibility of an Infinite Past." *British Journal for the Philosophy of Science* 30:166–70.

Craig, W. 1985. "Professor Mackie and the *Kalām* Cosmological Argument." *Religious Studies* 20:367–75.

Craig, W. 1988. "Quentin Smith on Infinity and the Past." *Philosophy of Science* 55:453–5.

Craig, W. 1991a. "Time and Infinity." *International Philosophical Quarterly* 31:387–401.

Craig, W. 1991b. "Theism and Big Bang Cosmology." *Australasian Journal of Philosophy* 69:492–503.

Craig, W. 1993. "Graham Oppy on the Kalām Cosmological Argument." *Sophia* 32:1–11.

Craig, W., and Q. Smith. 1993. *Theism, Atheism and Big Bang Cosmology.* Oxford: Clarendon.

Cutland, N. et al. 1988. "On Cauchy's Notion of Infinitesimal." *British Journal for Philosophy of Science* 39:375–8.

Dauben, J. 1977. "Georg Cantor and Pope Leo XIII: Mathematics, Theology, and the Infinite." *Journal of the History of Ideas* 38:85–108.

Dauben, J. 1990. *Georg Cantor: His Mathematics and Philosophy of the Infinite.* Princeton: Princeton University Press.

Davis, M. 1977. *Applied Non-Standard Analysis.* New York: John Wiley.

Day, T. 1987a. "Aquinas on Infinite Regress." *International Journal for Philosophy of Religion* 22:151–64.

Day, T. 1987b. "Infinite Regress Arguments." *Philosophical Papers* 16:155–64.

Detlefsen, M. 1986. *Hilbert's Program: An Essay on Mathematical Instrumentalism.* Dordrecht: Reidel.

Devlin, K. 1991. *The Joy of Sets.* Berlin: Springer-Verlag.

Diamond, P. 1965. "The Evaluation of Infinite Utility Streams." *Econometrica* 33:170–7.

Diamond, R. 1964. "Resolution of the Paradox of Tristram Shandy." *Philosophy of Science* 31:55–8.

Drake, F. 1974. *Set Theory: An Introduction to Large Cardinals*. Amsterdam: North-Holland.

Dreier, J. 2003. "Boundless Good." Unpublished ms.

Dretske, F. 1965. "Counting to Infinity." *Analysis* 25:99–101.

Earman, J. 1975. "Infinities, Infinitesimals, and Indivisibles: The Leibnizian Labyrinth." *Studia Logica* 7:236–51.

Earman, J. 1995. *Bangs, Crunches, Whimpers and Shrieks*. Oxford: Oxford University Press.

Earman, J., and J. Norton. 1993. "Forever Is a Day: Supertasks in Pitowsky and Malament-Hogarth Spacetimes." *Philosophy of Science* 60:22–42.

Earman, J., and J. Norton. 1996. "Infinite Pains: The Trouble with Supertasks." In A. Morton and S. Stich (eds.), *Benacerraf and His Critics*. Oxford: Blackwell.

Eells, E. 1988. "Quentin Smith on Infinity and the Past." *Philosophy of Science* 55:453–5.

Ehrlich, P. 1982. "Negative, Infinite and Hotter Than Infinite Temperatures." *Synthese*. 50:233–77.

Ehrlich, P. 1994. *Real Numbers, Generalisations of the Real, and Theories of Continua*. Dordrecht: Kluwer.

Ehrlich, P. 1997. "From Completeness to Archimedean Completeness." *Synthese* 110:57–76.

Evans, G. 1978. "Can There Be Vague Objects?" *Analysis* 38:208.

Faris, J. 1996. *The Paradoxes of Zeno*. Gateshead: Athenaeum.

Feferman, S. 1989. "Infinity in Mathematics: Is Cantor Necessary?" *Philosophical Topics* 17:23–45.

Fenstad, J. 1985. "Is Non-Standard Analysis Relevant for the Philosophy of Mathematics?" *Synthese* 62:289–301.

Fetzer, J. (ed.) 1984. *Principles of Philosophical Reasoning*. Totowa, N.J.: Rowman and Allanheld.

Fishburn, P. 1972. *Mathematics of Decision Theory*. Paris: Mouton.

Fitch, F. 1955. "A Logical Analysis of Some Value Concepts." *Journal of Symbolic Logic* 28:135–42.

Forrest, P. 1996. "How Innocent Is Mereology?" *Analysis* 56:127–31.

Fraenkel, A., Y. Bar-Hillel, and A. Levy. 1973. *Foundations of Set Theory*. Amsterdam: North-Holland.

Gale, R., and A. Pruss. 1999. "A New Cosmological Argument." *Religious Studies* 35:461–76.

Gamow, G. 1946. *1, 2, 3, . . . Infinity*. London: Macmillan.

Gellman, J. 1994. "Experiencing God's Infinity." *American Philosophical Quarterly* 31:53–61.

George, A. 1991. "Goldbach's Conjecture Can Be Decided in One Minute: On an Alleged Problem for Intuitionism." *Proceedings of the Aristotelian Society* 91:187–9.

Godfrey, R. 1993. "Paradoxes and Infinite Numbers." *Philosophy* 68:541–5.

Gonshor, H. 1986. *An Introduction to the Theory of Surreal Numbers.* Cambridge: Cambridge University Press.

Goodman, L. 1971. "Ghazālī's Argument from Creation." *International Journal of Middle Eastern Studies* 2:67–85, 168–88.

Grier, M. 1998. "Transcendental Illusion and Transcendental Realism in Kant's Second Antinomy." *British Journal for the History of Philosophy* 98:47–70.

Gruender, C. 1966. "The Achilles Paradox and Transfinite Numbers." *British Journal for Philosophy of Science* 17:219–31.

Grünbaum, A. 1950. "Relativity and the Atomicity of Becoming." *Review of Metaphysics* 4:143–86.

Grünbaum, A. 1952a. "A Consistent Conception of the Extended Linear Continuum as an Aggregate of Unextended Elements." *Philosophy of Science* 19:288–306.

Grünbaum, A. 1952b. "Messrs. Black and Taylor on Temporal Paradoxes." *Analysis* 12:144–8.

Grünbaum, A. 1953. "Whitehead's Method of Extensive Abstraction." *British Journal for Philosophy of Science* 4:215–26.

Grünbaum, A. 1955. "Modern Science and Refutation of the Paradoxes of Zeno." *Scientific Monthly* 81:234–9. Reprinted in Salmon (1970), 164–75.

Grünbaum, A. 1967. *Modern Science and Zeno's Paradoxes.* Middleton, Conn.: Wesleyan University Press; especially "Zeno's Metrical Paradox of Extension," 115–35. Reprinted in Salmon (1970), 176–99.

Grünbaum, A. 1968. "Are 'Infinity Machines' Paradoxical?" *Science* 159:396–406.

Grünbaum, A. 1973a. "Can an Infinitude of Operations Be Performed in a Finite Time?" In Grünbaum (1973b).

Grünbaum, A. 1973b. *Philosophical Problems of Space and Time.* Dordrecht: Reidel.

Hájek, A. 2003. "Waging War on Pascal's Wager." *Philosophical Review* 112:27–56.

Haldane, J. 1983. "A Benign Regress." *Analysis* 43:115–16.

Harrison, C. 1996. "The Three Arrows of Zeno." *Synthese* 107:271–92.

Harrison, E. 1987. *Darkness at Night: A Riddle of the Universe.* Cambridge: Harvard University Press.

Hart, W. 1975/6. "The Potential Infinite." *Proceedings of the Aristotelian Society* 76:247–64.

Hazen, A. 1976. "Expressive Completeness in Modal Language." *Journal of Philosophical Logic* 5:25–46.

Hazen, A. 1993. "Slicing It Thin." *Analysis* 53:189–92.

Hazewinkel, M., ed. 1989. *Encyclopedia of Mathematics,* vol. 3. Dordrecht: Kluwer.

Hinton, J., and C. Martin. 1953/4. "Achilles and the Tortoise." *Analysis* 14:56–68.

Holgate, P. 1994. "Mathematical Notes on Ross' Paradox." *British Journal for Philosophy of Science* 45:302–4.

Horgan, T. 2000. "The Two-Envelope Paradox, Non-Standard Expected Utility, and the Intensionality of Probability." *Nous* 34:578–602.

Huby, P. 1971. "Kant or Cantor: That the Universe, If Real, Must Be Finite in Both Space and Time." *Philosophy* 46:121–32.

Huby, P. 1973. "Cosmology and Infinity." *Philosophy* 48:186–7.

Huggett, N. 1999. "Atomic Metaphysics." *Journal of Philosophy* 96:5–24.

Hughes, P., and G. Brecht. 1975. *Vicious Circles and Infinity.* New York: Doubleday.

Humphrey, T. 1974. "How Descartes Avoids the Hidden Faculties Trap." *Journal of the History of Philosophy* 12:371–7.

Isles, D. 1992. "What Evidence Is There That 2^{65536} Is a Natural Number?" *Notre Dame Journal of Formal Logic* 33:465–80.

Jackson, F., P. Menzies, and G. Oppy. 1994. "The Two Envelope Paradox." *Analysis* 54:43–5.

Jacquette, D. 1993. "Kant's Second Antinomy and Hume's Theory of Extensionless Indivisibles." *Kant-Studien* 84:38–50.

Jaki, S. 1969. *The Paradox of Olber's Paradox.* New York: Herder and Herder.

Jeffrey, R. 1983. *The Logic of Decision*, 2nd ed. Chicago: University of Chicago Press.

Johnson, P. 1993. "Wholes, Parts, and Infinite Collections." *Philosophy* 67:367–79.

Johnson, P. 1994. "More about Infinite Numbers." *Philosophy* 69:369–70.

Jones, P. 1946. "Achilles and the Tortoise." *Mind* 55:341–5.

Jordan, J., ed. 1994. *Gambling on God.* Lanham, Md.: Rowman and Littlefield.

Jourdain, P. 1910. "The Flying Arrow: An Anachronism." *Mind* 19:42–55.

Jozsa, R. 1986. "An Approach to the Modelling of the Physical Continuum." *British Journal for the Philosophy of Science* 37:395–404.

Kanomori, A. 1991. *The Higher Infinite.* Berlin: Springer-Verlag.

Katětor, M., and P. Simon. 1997. "Origins of Dimension Theory." In C. Aull and R. Lower (eds.), *Handbook of the History of General Topology*, vol. 1. Dordrecht: Kluwer, 113–34.

King, H. 1949. "Aristotle and the Paradoxes of Zeno." *Journal of Philosophy* 46:657–70.

Klein, P. 2003. "When Infinite Regresses Are Not Vicious." *Philosophy and Phenomenological Research* 66:718–29.

Knorr, 1982. "Infinity and Continuity: The Interaction of Mathematics and Philosophy in Antiquity." In Kretzmann (1982).

Knuth, D. 1974. *Surreal Numbers.* London: Addison-Wesley.

Koetsier, T., and V. Allis. 1997. "Assaying Supertasks." *Logique et Analyse* 159:291–313.

Kolmogorov, A. 1933/56. *Foundations of the Theory of Probability*, translated by N. Morrison. New York: Chelsea.

Koons, R. 1997. "A New Look at a Cosmological Argument." *American Philosophical Quarterly* 34:193–211.

Kragh, H. 1996. *Cosmology and Controversy.* Princeton: Princeton University Press.

Krausser, P. 1988. "On the Antinomies and the Appendix to Kant's Dialectic in Kant's Critique and Philosophy of Science." *Synthese* 77:375–401.

Kretzmann, N., ed. 1982. *Infinity and Continuity in Ancient and Medieval Thought.* Ithaca, N.Y.: Cornell University Press.

Kusraer, A., and S. Kutateladze. 1990. *Non-Standard Methods of Analysis.* Dordrecht: Kluwer.

Lauwers, L. 1997. "Infinite Utility: Insisting on Strong Monotonicity." *Australasian Journal of Philosophy* 75:222–33.

Lavine, S. 1991. "Is Quantum Mechanics an Atomistic Theory?" *Synthese* 89:253–71.

Lavine, S. 1994. *Understanding the Infinite.* Cambridge: Harvard University Press.

Lavine, S. 1995. "Finite Mathematics." *Synthese* 103:389–420.

Lawrence, N. 1950. "Whitehead's Method of Extensive Abstraction." *Philosophy of Science* 17:142–63.

Lear, J. 1981. "A Note on Zeno's Arrow." *Phronesis* 26:91–104.

Lee, H. 1965. "Are Zeno's Paradoxes Based on a Mistake?" *Mind* 74:563–70.

Levi, I. 1980. *The Enterprise of Knowledge.* Cambridge: MIT Press.

Lewis, D. 1986. *On the Plurality of Worlds.* Oxford: Blackwell.

Lewis, D. 1991. *Parts of Classes.* Oxford: Blackwell.

Littlewood, J. 1953. *A Mathematician's Miscellany.* London: Methuen.

Loparic, Z. 1990. "The Logical Structure of the First Antinomy." *Kant-Studien* 81:280–303.

Machover, M. 1993. "The Place of Non-Standard Analysis in Mathematics and Mathematics Teaching." *British Journal for Philosophy of Science* 44:205–12.

Mackie, J. 1982. *The Miracle of Theism.* Oxford: Clarendon.

Maor, E. 1987. *To Infinity and Beyond.* Boston: Birkhaüser.

Marmura, M. 1957. "The Logical Role of the Argument from Time in the Tahāfut's Second Proof for the World's Pre-Eternity." *Muslim World* 47:306–14.

McClennan, E. 1994. "Finite Decision Theory." In Jordan (1994).

McGrew, T., D. Shier, and H. Silverstein. 1997. "The Two Envelope Paradox Resolved." *Analysis* 57:28–33.

McLaughlin, W. 1994. "Resolving Zeno's Paradoxes." *Scientific American* (November): 66–71.

McLaughlin, W. 1998. "Thomson's Lamp Is Dysfunctional." *Synthese* 116:281–301.

McLaughlin, W., and S. Miller. 1992. "An Epistemological Use of Non-Standard Analysis to Answer Zeno's Objections against Motion." *Synthese* 92:371–84.

McClennen, E. 1994. "Pascal's Wager and Finite Decision Theory." In Jordan (1994).

Monk, N. 1997. "Conceptions of Space-Time: Problems and Possible Solutions." *Studies in the History and Philosophy of Modern Physics* 28, no. 1:1–34.

Moore, A. 1988. "Aspects of the Infinite in Kant." *Mind* 97:205–23.

Moore, A. 1989. "A Problem for Intuitionism: The Apparent Possibility of Performing Infinitely Many Tasks in a Finite Time." *Proceedings of the Aristotelian Society* 89:17–34.

Moore, A. 1990. *The Infinite.* London: Routledge.

Moore, A. 1992. "A Note on Kant's First Antinomy." *Philosophical Quarterly* 42:480–5.

Moore, A., ed. 1993. *Infinity.* Dartmouth: Aldershot.

Moore, M. 2002. A Cantorian Argument against Infinitesimals." *Synthese* 133:305–30.

Morriston, W. 1999. "Must the Past Have a Beginning?" *Philo* 2:5–19.

Morriston, W. 2002c. "Craig on the Actual Infinite." *Religious Studies* 38:147–66.

Mundy, B. 1987. "Faithful Representation, Physical Extensive Measurement Theory and Archimedean Axioms." *Synthese* 70:373–400.

Mycielski, J. 1981. "Analysis without Actual Infinity." *Journal of Symbolic Logic* 46:625–33.

Mycielski, J. 1986. "Locally Finite Theories." *Journal of Symbolic Logic* 51:59–62.

Nalebuff, B. 1989. "The Other Person's Envelope Is Always Greener." *Journal of Economic Perspectives* 3:171–81.

Nelson, E. 1977. "Internal Set Theory: A New Approach to Non-Standard Analysis." *Bulletin of the American Mathematical Society* 83, no. 6:1165–98.

Nelson, E. 1987. *Radically Elementary Probability Theory.* Princeton: Princeton University Press.

Nelson, M. 1991. "Utilitarian Eschatology." *American Philosophical Quarterly* 28:339–47.

Ng, Y. 1995. "Infinite Utility and van Liedekerke's Impossibility: A Solution." *Australasian Journal of Philosophy* 73:408–12.

Nolan, D. 1996. "Recombination Unbound." *Philosophical Studies* 84:239–62.

Nolan, D. 2001. "What Wrong with Infinite Regresses?" *Metaphilosophy* 32:523–38.

Nolan, D. 2002. *Topics in the Philosophy of Possible Worlds.* London: Routledge.

North, J. 1983. "Finite and Otherwise: Aristotle and Some Seventeenth Century Views." In Shea (1983):113–48.

Oakes, R. 1997. "The Divine Infinity: Can Traditional Theists Justifiably Reject Pantheism." *Monist* 80:251–65.

O'Briant, W. 1979. "Is Descartes' Evil Spirit Finite or Infinite?" *Sophia* 18:28–32.

Oderberg, D. 2002a. "Traversal of the Infinite, the 'Big Bang,' and the *Kalam* Cosmological Argument." *Philosophia Christi* 4, no. 2: 303–34.

Oderberg, D. 2002b. "The Tristram Shandy Paradox: A Reply to Graham Oppy." *Philosophia Christi* 4, no. 2: 351–60.

O'Leary-Hawthorne, J., and A. Cortens. 1995. "Towards Ontological Nihilism." *Philosphical Studies* 79, no. 2:143–65.

Oppy, G. 1990. "On Rescher on Pascal's Wager." *International Journal for Philosophy of Religion* 30:159–68.

Oppy, G. 1991. "Craig, Mackie and the *Kalām* Cosmological Argument." *Religious Studies* 27:189–97.

Oppy, G. 1995a. "Inverse Operations with Transfinite Numbers and the *Kalām* Cosmological Argument." *International Philosophical Quarterly* 35, no. 2:219–21.

Oppy, G. 1995b. "*Kalām* Cosmological Arguments: Reply to Professor Craig." *Sophia* 34:15–29.

Oppy, G. 1995c. *Ontological Arguments and Belief in God.* New York: Cambridge University Press.

Oppy, G. 1995d. "Professor William Craig's Criticisms of Critiques of *Kalām* Cosmological Arguments by Paul Davies, Stephen Hawking, and Adolf Grünbaum." *Faith and Philosophy* 12:237–50.

Oppy, G. 1996a. "Pascal's Wager Is a Possible Bet (but Not a Very Good One): Reply to Harmon Holcomb III." *International Journal for Philosophy of Religion* 40:101–16.

Oppy, G. 1996b. "Review of W. Craig and Q. Smith, *Theism, Atheism and Big Bang Cosmology.*" *Faith and Philosophy* 13:125–33.

Oppy, G. 1997a. "Countable Fusion Not Yet Proven Guilty: It May Be the Whiteheadian Account of Space Whatdunnit." *Analysis* 57, no. 4:249–53.

Oppy, G. 1997b. "Pantheism, Quantification, and Mereology." *Monist* 80, no. 2:320–36.

Oppy, G. 2000a. "*Humean* Supervenience?" *Philosophical Studies* 101, no. 1:75–105.

Oppy, G. 2000b. "On 'A New Cosmological Argument.'" *Religious Studies* 36:345–53.

Oppy, G. 2001. "Time, Successive Addition, and the *Kalām* Cosmological Argument." *Philosophia Christi* 3:181–91.

Oppy, G. 2002a. "Arguing about the *Kalām* Cosmological Argument." *Philo* 5, no 1:34–61.

Oppy, G. 2002b. "More Than a Flesh Wound: Reply to Oderberg." *Ars Disputandi* 2:1–11. [Http://www.ArsDisputandi.org].

Oppy, G. 2002c. "The Tristram Shandy Paradox: A Response to David S. Oderberg." *Philosophia Christi* 4, no. 2:335–49.

Oppy, G. 2003. "From the Tristram Shandy Paradox to the Christmas Shandy Paradox: Reply to Oderberg." *Ars Disputandi* 3:1–24. [Http://www.ArsDisputandi.org].

Oppy, G. 2004. "Faulty Reasoning about Default Principles in Cosmological Arguments." *Faith and Philosophy* 21:242–9.

Owen, G. 1958. "Zeno and the Mathematicians." *Proceedings of the Aristotelian Society* 58:199–222.

Pasyakov, B. 1989. "Dimension." In Hazewinkel (1989), pp. 188–90.

Peers, A. 1975. *Dimension Theory of General Spaces.* Cambridge: Cambridge University Press.

Perez-Laraudogoitia, J. 1997. "Classical Particle Dynamics, Indeterminism, and a Supertask." *British Journal for the Philosophy of Science* 48:49–54.

Perez-Laraudogoitia, J. 1998. "Infinity Machines and Creation *Ex Nihilo.*" *Synthese* 115:259–65.

Perez-Laraudogoitia, J. 2000. "Priest on the Paradox of the Gods." *Analysis* 60:152–5.

Perez-Laraudogoitia, J. 2002a. "On the Dynamics of Alper and Bridger." *Synthese* 131:157–71.

Perez-Laraudogoitia, J. 2002b. "Just as Beautiful but Not (Necessarily) a Supertask." *Mind* 111:281–7.

Perez-Laraudogoitia, J. 2002c. "Two Ways of Looking at a Newtonian Supertask." *Synthese* 131:173–89.

Perez-Laraudogoitia, J. 2003. "A Variant of Benardette's Paradox." *Analysis* 63:124–31.

Pomerlau, W. 1985. "Does Reason Demand That God Be Infinite?" *Sophia* 24:18–27.

Potter, M. 1996. "Taming the Infinite." *British Journal for the Philosophy of Science* 47:609–19.

Price, H. 1992. "Metaphysical Pluralism." *Journal of Philosophy* 89:387–409.

Priest, G. 1987. *In Contradiction.* Dordrecht: Kluwer.

Priest, G. 1991. "The Limits of Thought – and Beyond." *Mind* 100:361–70

Priest, G. 1995. *Beyond the Limits of Thought.* Cambridge: Cambridge University Press.

Priest, G. 1999. "On a Version of One of Zeno's Paradoxes." *Analysis* 59:1–2.

qFiasco, F. 1980. "Another Look at Some of Zeno's Paradoxes." *Canadian Journal of Philosophy* 10:119–30.

Quine, W. 1953. "On What There Is." In *From a Logical Point of View.* Cambridge: Harvard University Press, 1–19.

Radner, M. 1998. "Unlocking the Second Antinomy: Kant and Wulff." *Journal for the History of Philosophy* 36:413–41.

Rapaport, A. 1998. *Decision Theory and Decision Behaviour.* London: Macmillan.

Robinson, A. 1961. "Non Standard Analysis." *Indagationes Mathematicae* 23: 432–40.

Robinson, A. 1966. *Non-Standard Analysis.* Amsterdam: North-Holland.

Robinson, A. 1973. "Metamathematical Problems." *Journal of Symbolic Logic* 38:500–16.

Ross, S. 1988. *A First Course in Probability*, 3rd ed. London: Macmillan.

Rucker, R. 1982. *Infinity and the Mind.* Sussex: Harvester.

Russell, B. 1903. *The Principles of Mathematics.* London: Allen & Unwin.

Russell, B. 1929. *Our Knowledge of the External World.* New York: Norton, 182–98. Reprinted in Salmon (1970), 45–58.

Sainsbury, M. 1995. *Paradoxes.* New York: Cambridge.

Salmon, W., ed. 1970. *Zeno's Paradoxes.* Indianapolis: Bobbs-Merrill.

Samuelson, P. 1977. "St. Petersburg Paradoxes: Defanged, Dissected and Historically Described." *Journal of Economic Literature* 15:24–55.

Sanford, D. 1969. "Time May Have a Stop." *Analysis* 29:206

Sanford, D. 1975. "Infinity and Vagueness." *Philosophical Review* 87:520–35.

Sanford, D. 2003. "Fusion Confusion." *Analysis* 63:1–4.

Schlesinger, G. 1994. "A Central Theistic Argument." In Jordan (1994).

Schock, R. 1982. "Dividing by Zero." *Logique et Analyse* 25:213–15.

Schoen, E. 1990. "The Sensory Presentation of Divine Infinity." *Faith and Philosophy* 7:3–18.

Scott, A., and D. Scott. 1997. "What Is in the Two Envelope Paradox?" *Analysis* 57:34–41.

Segel, L. 1991. "The Infinite and Infinitesimal in Models for Natural Phenomena." *Reviews of Modern Physics* 63:225–38.

Segerberg, K. 1976. "A Neglected Family of Aggregation Problems in Ethics." *Nous* 10:221–47.

Shannon, G. 1997. "Some Definitions of 'The Smallest Infinity.'" *Logique et Analyse* 160:345–56.

Shearman, J. 1908. "Infinite Divisibility." *Mind* 17:394–6.

Sherry, D. 1988. "Zeno's Metrical Paradox Revisited." *Philosophy of Science* 55:58–73.

Sierpinski, W. 1965. *Cardinal and Ordinal Numbers.* Warsaw: PWN-Polish Scientific.

Simons, P. 1987. *Parts: A Study in Ontology.* Oxford: Clarendon.

Skyrms, B. 1966. *Choice and Chance.* Belmont: Dickenson.

Skyrms, B. 1983. "Zeno's Paradox of Measure." In Cohen and Lauden (1983):223–54.

Skyrms, B. 1993. "A Uniform Positive Probability on Natural Numbers." Unpublished ms.

Skyrms, B., and W. Harper, eds. 1988. *Causation, Chance and Credence,* vol. 1. Dordrecht: Kluwer.

Small, R. 1986. "Tristram Shandy's Last Page." *British Journal for the Philosophy of Science* 37:213–16.

Smith, Q. 1985. "Kant and the Beginning of the World." *New Scholasticism* 59:339–48.

Smith, Q. 1987. "Infinity and the Past." *Philosophy of Science* 54:63–75.

Smith, Q. 1988. "The Uncaused Beginning of the Universe." *Philosophy of Science* 55:39–57.

Smith, Q. 1991. "Atheism, Theism and Big Bang Cosmology." *Australasian Journal of Philosophy* 69:48–65.

Smith, Q. 1993. "Reply to Craig: The Possible Infinitude of the Past." *International Philosophical Quarterly* 33:109–15.

Smith, Q. 1995a. "A Defence of a Principle of Sufficient Reason." *Metaphilosophy* 26:97–106.

Smith, Q. 1995b. "Internal and External Causal Explanation of the Universe." *Philosophical Studies* 79:283–310.

Smith, Q. 1997. "Simplicity and Why the Universe Exists." *Philosophy* 72:125–32.

Smith, Q. 1999. "The Reason the Universe Exists Is That It Caused Itself to Exist." *Philosophy* 74:579–86.

Smith, Q. 2000. "Problem's with John Earman's Attempt to Reconcile Theism with General Relativity." *Erkenntnis* 52:1–27.

Sorabji, R. 1983. *Time, Creation and the Continuum.* London: Duckworth.

Sorenson, R. 1994. "Infinite Decision Theory." In Jordan (1994).

Stroyon, K., and W. Luxemburg. 1976. *Introduction to the Theory of Infinitesimals*. London: Academic.

Stump, E. 1997. "Simplicity." In P. Quinn and C. Taliaferro (eds.), *A Companion to Philosophy of Religion*. Oxford: Blackwell.

Sweeney, E. 1993. "Thomas Aquinas' Double Metaphysics of Simplicity and Infinity." *International Philosophical Quarterly* 33:297–317.

Swinburne, R. 1966. "The Beginning of the Universe." *Proceedings of the Aristotelian Society* 40:125–38.

Swinburne, R. 1968. *Space and Time*. London: Macmillan.

Taylor, R. 1951. "Mr. Black on Temporal Paradoxes." *Analysis* 12:38–44.

Taylor, R. 1952. "Mr. Wisdom on Temporal Paradoxes." *Analysis* 13:15–17.

Taylor, R. 1963. *Metaphysics*. Englewood Cliffs: Prentice-Hall.

Teller, P. 1989. "Infinite Renormalisation." *Philosophy of Science* 56:238–57.

Thomason, S. 1982. "Euclidean Infinitesimals." *Pacific Philosophical Quarterly* 63:168–85.

Thomson, J. 1954. "Tasks and Supertasks." *Analysis* 15:1–13.

Thomson, J. 1970. "Comments on Professor Benacerraf's Paper." In Salmon (1970), 130–8.

Tomberlin, J., ed. 1988. *Philosophical Perspectives*, vol. 2. Atascadero, Calif.: Ridgeview.

Ushenko, A. 1946. "Zeno's Paradoxes." *Mind* 55:151–65.

Vallentyne, P. 1993. "Utilitarianism and Infinite Utility." *Australasian Journal of Philosophy* 71:212–17.

Vallentyne, P. 1995. "Infinite Utility: Anonymity and Person-Centredness." *Australasian Journal of Philosophy* 73:413–20.

Vallentyne, P., and S. Kagan. 1997. "Infinite Utility and Finitely Additive Value Theory." *Journal of Philosophy* 94:5–26.

Van Bendegem, J. 1987. "Zeno's Paradoxes and the Tile Argument." *Philosophy of Science* 54:295–302.

Van Bendegem, J. 1994. "Ross' Paradox Is an Impossible Super-task." *British Journal for Philosophy of Science* 45:743–8.

Van Cleve, J. 1981. "Reflections on Kant's Second Antimony." *Synthese* 47:481–94.

Van Dantzig, D. 1955. "Is $_{10}10^{10}$ a Finite Number?" *Dialectica* 9:273–7.

Van Fraassen, B. 1995. "'World' Is Not a Count Noun." *Nous* 29:139–57.

Van Liederkerke, L. 1995. "Should Utilitarians Be Cautious about an Infinite Future?" *Australasian Journal of Philosophy* 73:405–7.

Vaught, R. 1995. *Set Theory: An Introduction*, 2nd ed. Boston: Birkhaüser.

Vilenkin, N. 1995. *In Search of Infinity*. Boston: Birkhaüser.

Vlastos, G. 1966a. "A Note on Zeno's Arrow." *Phronesis* 11:3–18.

Vlastos, G. 1966b. "Zeno's Race Course." *Journal of History of Philosophy* 4:95–108.

Wagner, C. 1999. "Misadventures in Conditional Expectation: The Two Envelope Paradox." *Erkenntnis* 51:233–41.

Walker, R. 1997. "Sufficient Reason." *Proceedings of the Aristotelian Society* 97:109–23.

Watling, J. 1952. "The Sum of an Infinite Series." *Analysis* 13:39–46.
Weingard, R. 1979. "General Relativity and the Length of the Past." *British Journal for the Philosophy of Science* 30:170–2.
Weirich, P. 1984. "The St. Petersburg Gamble and Risk." *Theory and Decision* 17:193–202.
Weyl, H. 1946. *Philosophy of Mathematics and Natural Science.* Princeton: Princeton University Press.
White, A. 1965. "Achilles at the Shooting Gallery." *Mind* 74:141–2.
White, M. 1987. "The Spatial Arrow Paradox." *Pacific Philosophical Quarterly* 68:71–7.
Whitrow, G. 1978. "On the Impossibility of an Infinite Past." *British Journal for Philosophy of Science* 29:39–45.
Wiggins, D. 1996. "Sufficient Reason: A Principle in Diverse Guises, Both Ancient and Modern." *Acta Philosophica Fennica* 61:117–32.
Williams, J. 1981. "Justified Belief and the Infinite Regress Argument." *American Philosophical Quarterly* 18:85–8.
Wilson, P. 1991. "What Is the Explanandum of the Anthropic Principle?" *American Philosophical Quarterly* 28:167–73.
Wisdom, J. 1941. "Why Achilles Does Not Fail to Catch the Tortoise." *Mind* 50:58–73.
Wisdom, J. 1952. "Achilles on a Physical Racecourse." *Analysis* 12:67–72.
Wittgenstein, L. 1975. *Remarks on the Foundations of Mathematics.* Oxford: Blackwell.
Wolfson, H. 1966. "Patristic Arguments against the Eternity of the World." *Harvard Theological Review* 59:354–67.
Wolfson, H. 1976. *The Philosophy of the Kalām.* Cambridge: Harvard University Press.
Wright, C. 1985. "Skolem and the Sceptic." *Proceedings of the Aristotelian Society* supp. vol.: 116–37.
Yablo, S. 2000. "A Reply to New Zeno." *Analysis* 60:148–51.
Zabell, S. 1988. "Symmetry and Its Discontents." In Skyrms and Harper (1988), 155–90.
Zangari, M. 1994. "Zeno, Zero, and Indeterminate Forms: Instants in the Logic of Motion." *Australasian Journal of Philosophy* 72:187–204.
Zuckero, M. 2001. "A Dissolution of Zeno's Paradoxes of the Dichotomy and the Flight of the Arrow." *Dialogue* 43:46–51.

Index